CAXTON
DICTIONARY

CAXTON EDITIONS

First published in Great Britain by
CAXTON EDITIONS
an imprint of
the Caxton Book Company Ltd
16 Connaught Street
Marble Arch
London W2 2AF

This edition copyright
© 1999 CAXTON EDITIONS

Prepared and designed
for Caxton Editions by
Superlaunch Limited
PO Box 207
Abingdon
Oxfordshire OX13 6TA

Consultant editor Bruce Howard

ISBN 1 84067 071 1

A copy of the CIP data for this book is available from
the British Library upon request

Printed and bound in India

Abbreviations

abbr	abbreviation
adj	adjective
adv	adverb
art	article
aux	auxiliary
cap	capital
comp	comparative
conj	conjunction
def	definite
dem	demonstrative
etc	et cetera
esp	especially
f	feminine
fam	familiar
fig	figurative
fpl	feminine plural
gr	grammar
indef	indefinite
interj	interjection
inv	invariable
m	masculine
mpl	masculine plural
n	noun
npl	noun, plural
num	number
pej	pejorative
pl	plural
poss	possessive
pp	past participle
prep	preposition
pron	pronoun
sl	slang
superl	superlative
t	tense
usu	usually
vi	intransitive verb
vr	reflexive verb
vt	transitive verb
vulg	vulgar

A

a the indefinite article, used before a consonant *see* an.

aback *adv* backwards; by surprise.

abacus *n* a square tablet on the top of a column; a counting frame.

abandon *vt* to forsake entirely; to desert; careless freedom of action.

abandoned *adj* deserted; depraved.

abase *vt* to bring low; disgrace.

abash *vt* to make ashamed.

abate *vt* to lessen.

abattoir *n* a slaughterhouse.

abbey *n* (*pl* abbeys) a monastery or convent.

abbot, abbess *n* the head of an abbey, nunnery or monastery.

abbreviate *vt* to shorten.

abdicate *vt* to resign; to relinquish.

abdomen *n* the lower belly.

abduct *vt* to kidnap; to lead away by force.

aberration *n* a wandering from the right way; a mental lapse.

abet *vt* to aid or to encourage (in crime etc).

abeyance *n* (in ~) suspense.

abhor *vt* to shrink from in horror; to detest.

abhorrent *adj* repugnant.

abide *vi* to stay in a place; to dwell; * *vt* to wait for; to endure.

ability *n* the power to do a thing; skill; (*pl* abilities) the powers of the mind.

abject *adj* mean; base.

abjure *vt* to renounce on oath.

ablaze *adv* on fire; in a blaze.

able *adj* capable; skilful.

ablution *n* the act of washing.

ably *adv* with ability.

abnormal *adj* not normal; irregular.

aboard *adv*, *prep* on board; in a ship.

abode *n* residence.

abolish *vt* to put an end to.

abominable *adj* hateful.

abomination *n* hatred; the object of hatred.

aborigine *n* the original inhabitant of a country.

abortion *n* the termination of a pregnancy.

abound *vi* to be in great plenty.

about *prep* around; near to; concerning; * *adv* around; nearly.

above *prep* to be in a higher place than; more than; * *adv* in a higher place.

abreast *adv* side by side.

abridge *vt* to shorten; to condense.

abroad *adv* at large; in a foreign country.

abrupt *adj* broken off; sudden; curt in manner or speech.

abscess *n* a gathering of pus in some part of the body.

abscond *vi* to fly from justice.

absence *n* the state of not being present.

absent *adj* not present.

absentee *n* one who is absent.

absolute *adj* total, complete.

absolutely *adv* unconditionally.

absolution *n* a freeing from guilt or punishment.

absolve *vt* to free from, as from guilt or punishment; pardon.

absorb *vt* to soak up; to engross.

absorbent *adj* able to soak up moisture.

abstain *vi* to refrain.

abstinence *n* a refraining from anything, *esp* from strong drink.

abstract *vt* to draw from; to separate and consider by itself; to summarise.

abstract *adj* existing in the mind only; not concrete; * *n* a summary.

abstracted *adj* lost in thought.

absurd *adj* contrary to reason; ridiculous.

abundance *n* great plenty.

abuse *vt* to misuse; to insult

abusive *adj* insulting.

abyss *n* a bottomless gulf.

academic *adj* of an academy or university; theoretical; * *n* a member of staff in a university.

academy *n* a school of arts or sciences.

accede *vi* to assent to.

accelerate *vt* to increase the speed of.

accent *n* a stress or modulation of the voice; a manner of speaking.

accentuate *vt* to emphasise.

accept *vt* to receive; to admit.

acceptance *n* reception; approval.

access *n* approach; admission.

accessible *adj* within reach; affable.

accession *n* the act of acceding; addition; succession to a throne.

accessory *adj* additional; * *n* an accomplice.

accident *n* a mishap.

acclaim *n* praise; enthusiastic approval; * *vt* to applaud.

acclamation *n* a shout of joy or approval.

acclimatise *vt* to accustom to a new climate; to become used to.

accolade *n* a high honour; praise.

accommodate *vt* to make suitable; to adapt; to provide lodging for.

accommodation *n* lodgings; a loan.

accompaniment *n* the music played to accompany a singer or other performer.

accompany *vt* to go with; to perform music along with.

accomplice *n* a partner in crime.

accomplish *vt* to achieve.

accord *n* harmony; agreement.

accordingly *adv* consequently.

accost *vt* to speak to without invitation; to solicit.

account *n* a reckoning; a bill; narration; * *vt* to reckon; * *vi* to give reasons; to explain (*with* for).

accountable *adj* responsible.

accountant *n* a professional keeper or inspector of accounts.

accoutrements *npl* military kit other than dress and arms.

accredited *adj* officially recognised; generally accepted.

accrue *vi* to come from growth.

accumulate *vt* to heap up; * *vi* to increase.

accumulation *n* a heap; a collection.

accuracy *n* precision.

accurate *adj* exact; precise.

accursed *adj* lying under a curse.

accusation *n* a charge brought against someone.

accusative *adj*, *n* the case of nouns, pronouns and adjectives being the object of an action.

accuse *vt* to charge with a crime; to blame.

accustom *vt* make used to.

ace *n* a single spot on cards or dice; an expert.

acerbity *n* sourness; bitterness.

acetic *adj* sour; like vinegar.

ache *vi* to be in pain; * *n* a gnawing pain.

achieve *vt* to accomplish.

achievement *n* an accomplishment through effort.

acid *adj* sharp or sour to the taste; * *n* a substance which releases hydrogen ions in water.

acidity *n* sourness.

acknowledge *vt* to recognise; to admit the truth of.

acorn *n* the fruit of the oak.

acoustics *n* the science of sound; the sound properties of a room or hall.

acquaint *vt*, *vr* to make familiar with.

acquiesce *vi* to agree tacitly.

acquire *vt* to obtain; to gain.

acquisition *n* that which is acquired.

acquisitive *adj* eager to possess things.

acquit *vt* to declare not guilty.

acquittal *n* the process of being acquitted; performance of some duty.

acre *n* an area of 4840 square yards (0.4047 hectares).

acrid *adj* sharp to the taste or smell.

acrimonious *adj* (of a situation) full of bitterness.

acrobat *n* a performer of gymnastic feats.

acronym *n* a word made up of initial letters of words.

across *prep*, *adv* on the other side of; spanning, crosswise.

act *vi* to conduct oneself; * *vt* to do; to perform; to play on the stage; to pretend; * *n* a deed; a part of a play; law, as an act of parliament; pretence.

acting *n* performance of a role.

action *n* the fact or process of acting; a lawsuit; a battle.

actionable *adj* furnishing grounds for a legal action.

active *adj* busy; lively.

activity *n* an occupation a person is engaged in.

actor, actress *n* one who acts.

actual *adj* existing in fact.

actuary *n* a specialist in statistics

especially regarding insurance.

actuate *vt* to put into action.

acumen *n* sharpness of perception.

acute *adj* sharp; keen; intense.

adage *n* a proverb; a maxim.

adagio *adj, adv* in music, slow; * *n* a slow movement.

adamant *adj* stubbornly resolute.

adapt *vt* to adjust or change to suit a purpose.

add *vt* join; to find sum of.

addendum *n* (*pl* **addenda**) something added.

addict *vt* (*usu* passive *with* to) to be dependent on; * *n* one addicted to something, *esp* narcotics.

addition *n* act of adding; the thing added; * ~al *adj* added on.

address *vt* to direct ones attention to; to speak to; * *n* a discourse; the location of a house.

adept *n, adj* well skilled (person).

adequate *adj* sufficient; passable.

adhere *vi* to stick; to cling.

adherent *adj* sticking to.

adhesion *n* the act or state of sticking to; adherence.

adhesive *adj* sticking; sticky.

adipose *adj* fatty.

adjacent *adj* lying near or adjoining.

adjective *n* a word which qualifies a noun.

adjoining *adj* being next to and joined to.

adjourn *vt* to postpone; * *vi* to leave off for a time.

adjudicate *vt* to act as a judge; to give a ruling on.

adjunct *n* a subordinate or incidental thing, an assistant a word used to modify the meaning of another word in a sentence.

adjust *vt* to set right; to fit.

adjustable *adj* able to be adjusted.

administer *vt* to manage; to dispense.

administration *n* management; the executive part of a government.

admiral *n* the commander of a fleet or navy.

Admiralty *n* the department administering British naval affairs.

admiration *n* respect, warm approval; the object of this.

admire *vt* to regard with respect.

admissible *adj* allowable.

admission *n* admittance; an acknowledgement of fault etc; one admitted to hospital.

admit *vt* to allow to enter; to grant.

admittance *n* the right or process of admission.

admonish *vt* to warn; to reprove.

adolescence *n* the time between adulthood and childhood; puberty.

adopt *vt* to take and raise as one's own (child); to accept responsibility for.

adorable *adj* deserving of adoration; lovable.

adoration *n* worship paid to a deity; profound reverence; deep affection.

adore *vt* to worship; to love intensely.

adorn *vt* to deck with ornaments; to beautify.

adrenaline *n* a hormone released by the adrenal glands which acts as a stimulant.

adrift *adv* at the mercy of circumstance; floating at random.

adroit *adj* skilful; dextrous.

adulation *n* servile flattery.

adult *adj* fully grown; of or exclusively suitable for adults.

adulterate *vt* to debase by mixture.

adultery *n* voluntary sexual relations between a married person and someone other than their spouse.

advance *vt* to move or put forward; to pay beforehand; * *vi* to go forward; * *n* a going forward.

advanced *adj* far in progress; ahead of the times.

advancement *n* promotion of a person, cause or plan.

advantage *n* a favourable state; gain; a term in tennis.

advent *n* arrival; the four weeks before Christmas.

adventure *n* a hazardous enterprise; an exciting experience; * *vt, vi* to risk or hazard.

adverb *n* a word which modifies a verb, adjective or another adverb.

adversary *n* an enemy; an antagonist.

adverse *adj* hostile; contrary.

adversity *n* misfortune.

advertise *vt* draw attention to in order to sell, hire etc.

advertisement *n* a public notice proclaiming something.

advice *n* an opinion offered; counsel.

advise *vt* to counsel; to warn; to inform; * *vi* to deliberate or consider.

advocate *n* one who pleads for another; * *vt* to plead in favour of; to defend, *esp* in a law court.

aegis *n* protection; an impregnable defence.

aerate *vt* charge a liquid with a gas to produce effervescence.

aerial *adj* of the air; * *n* a device, antenna to receive and transmit radio waves.

eyrie *n* the nest of a bird of prey.

aeroplane *n* an aircraft with fixed wings.

aesthetics the philosophy of the beautiful, *esp* in art.

afar *adv* at, to or from a distance.

affable *adj* friendly; good natured.

affair *n* a business matter; an event; a love affair.

affect *vt* to act upon; to move the feelings of; to pretend.

affection *n* fondness; love.

affidavit *n* a written declaration upon oath.

affiliate *vt* to attach to a society or other body.

affinity *n* relation by marriage; liking; similarity; chemical attraction.

affirm *vt* to assert; to declare.

affix *vt* fasten; * *n* a syllable or letter added to a word.

afflict *vt* to cause pain or sorrow.

affliction *n* distress; pain; the cause of this.

affluence *n* abundance; wealth.

afford *vt* to yield; to supply; to have sufficient for a given purpose.

affray *n* a fight; a disturbance.

affront *vt* to insult openly; * *n* such an insult.

afloat *adv*, *adj* floating; at sea.

afoot *adv* in motion; happening.

afraid *adj* struck with fear; feeling regret.

afresh *adv* anew.

aft *adj*, *adv* astern.

after *adj* later; * *prep* later in time than; behind; * *adv* later in time.

aftermath *n* the result or after effects *usu* of something unpleasant.

afternoon *n* the time from noon to evening.

afterthought *n* a thing added or thought of subsequently.

afterwards *adv* subsequently.

again *adv* once more.

against *prep* in opposition to; in expectation of.

age *n* a period of time; an epoch; the length of a person's life; * *vi*, *vt* to grow or make old.

agency *n* means; a specialised or specific business; the business of an agent.

agenda *npl* business to be transacted at a meeting.

agent *n* one who acts; a deputy; a spy.

agglomeration *n* a heap.

aggrandise *vt* to magnify.

aggravate *vt* to intensify; to exasperate.

aggregate *vt* to collect; * *adj* total; * *n* the sum of parts.

aggression *n* the first act of hostility.

aggrieved *adj* having a grievance

aghast *adj*, *adv* horrified.

agile *adj* nimble.

agitate *vt* to excite; to stir up.

agitator *n* one who excites discontent or revolt.

agnostic *n* one who disclaims any knowledge of God.

agog *adv* in eager excitement.

agonise (*also* ~ize) *vi* to suffer mental anguish, to suffer agony.

agony *n* extreme pain of body or mind; anguish.

agrarian *adj* relating to land and agriculture.

agree *vi* to be in concord; to suit.

agreeable *adj* suitable to; pleasing; grateful.

agreement *n* harmony; the holding of the same opinion; an arrangement between parties.

agriculture *n* the science of cultivation.

aground *adv* stranded; on the shore.

ahead *adv* further forward; in the lead; further advanced; in one's path; directly forward.

aid *vt* to help; * *n* help.

AIDS (Acquired Immune Deficiency Syndrome) *n* a fatal condition caused by the HIV virus, transmitted in bodily fluids.

ail *vi* to be ill.

ailment *n* an illness.

aim *vi* to point a remark, weapon etc; to intend; * *vt* to level or direct as a firearm; * *n* intention; purpose.

air *n* the atmosphere; a light breeze; a tune; bearing (*npl*) affected manner; * *vt* to expose to the air; to dry.

aircraft *n* any machine that flies.

airing *n* exposure to fresh air *esp* for an excursion; exposure of laundry etc to warm air; expression of ones opinions.

airline *n* a company or organisation running aeroplanes for transportation.

airplane *see* aeroplane.

airport *n* a place where aircraft land, take off and undergo repairs.

air raid *n* an attack by aircraft.

airtight *adj* not allowing air in or out.

airy *adj* open to the air; fresh; casual; light-hearted.

aisle *n* a part of a church; a passage in a church; a passage in a supermarket.

ajar *adv* partly open.

akin *adj* related to by blood; similar.

alabaster *n* a translucent form of gypsum.

alacrity *n* eagerness; briskness.

alarm *n* sudden surprise; fright; * *vt* to give notice of danger.

alarming *adj* disturbing.

albino *n* a person with abnormally white skin and hair and pink eyes.

album *n* a book for autographs, sketches, etc; a long-playing record containing several tracks.

albumen *n* white of egg.

alchemy *n* the medieval forerunner of chemistry, aimed at changing base metals into gold, etc.

alcohol *n* a colourless, volatile substance forming the active ingredient in beer, wine, spirits etc, chemical name ethanol; drink containing this; a class of organic substances containing hydroxyl groups.

alcove *n* a recess.

ale *n* a fermented malt liquor; beer.

alert *adj* vigilant; * *vt* to warn.

algebra *n* the branch of maths concerned with the symbolic manipulation of equations.

alias *adv* otherwise; * *n* (*pl* aliases) an assumed name.

alibi *n* the claim that one was elsewhere when a crime was committed.

alien *adj* foreign; unfamiliar; hostile; extraterrestrial; * *n* a foreigner.

alienate *vt* to transfer property; to estrange; to cause hostility towards.

alight *vi* to get down; to settle on; * *adj*, *adv* on fire.

alike *adj* like; similar; * *adv* in the same manner.

alimony *n* an allowance paid by one party to another during or after the termination of a marriage.

alive *adj* living; lively.

alkali *n* a substance, as potash and soda, which neutralises acids.

all *adj* every one; * *n* everything; * *adv* wholly; entirely.

allay *vt* to ease; to assuage.

allege *vt* to assert, often without proof.

allegiance *n* loyalty.

allegorical *adj* figurative.

allegory *n* a narrative in which meaning is represented symbolically.

allegro (music) in a brisk tempo.

alleviate *vt* to reduce pain, suffering etc.

alley *n* a narrow walk or passage.

alliance *n* state of being allied; league; the countries forming this.

allied *adj* united by treaty.

alligator *n* a large reptile of the order *Crocodilia* native to America and China with a broader and shorter head than that of the crocodile.

alliteration *n* the repetition of a letter at the beginning of two or more words in close succession.

allocate *vt* assign to.

allot *vt* to apportion.

allow *vt* to let; to admit the truth or the possibility of; to grant.

allowance *n* a sum allotted.

alloy *vt* to mix with baser metals; * *n* a mixture of metals.

allude *vi* to refer to indirectly.

allure *vt* to entice; to decoy.

alluring *adj* attractive.

allusion *n* an indirect reference.

alluvial *adj* deposited by water.

ally *vt* to unite by friendship, marriage, or treaty; * *n* an associate.

almanac *n* an annual table containing a calendar and other information.

almighty *adj* omnipotent; * *n* God.

almond *n* the nut of the almond tree, *Prunus dulcis*.

almost *adv* nearly.

aloft *adv* in the sky; on high.

alone *adj* solitary; * *adv* separately.

along *adv* lengthways; * *prep* by the side of.

aloof *adv* apart; distant; unsympathetic.

aloud *adv* audibly.

alphabet *n* the letters of a language.

alpine *adj* pertaining to high mountains; of the Alps; * *n* a small plant growing on mountainsides.

already *adv* before the time in question.

also *adv* likewise; too.

altar *n* an elevated stone on which sacrifices were offered; the communion table.

alter *vt, vi* to change.

alteration *n* partial change.

altercation *n* an angry dispute.

alternate *adj* by turns; * *vt* to follow by turns.

alternative *n* a thing available instead of another.

although *conj* though.

altitude *n* height.

alto (music) *adj* high; * *n* contralto.

altogether *adv* wholly.

altruism *n* devotion to others.

aluminium *n* a soft, white, light metal.

always *adv* at all times.

amalgam *n* a mixture or blend; a mixture of mercury with another metal, *usu* silver.

amalgamate *vt, vi* to unite; to combine; * *vi* to alloy a metal with mercury.

amass *vt* to form into a mass; to heap up; to accumulate.

amateur *n* a non-professional participant; one who engages in a sport purely for pleasure.

amaze *vt* to astonish.

amazement *n* in a state of great surprise.

ambassador *n* a diplomatic representative of a country abroad.

amber *n* a yellow-brown fossil resin used for jewellery.

ambidextrous *adj* able to both hands alike.

ambiguity *n* doubtfulness of meaning.

ambiguous *adj* doubtful; obscure.

ambit *n* compass; scope.

ambition *n* desire to succeed.

amble *vi* to walk at an easy pace.

ambulance *n* a vehicle for transporting the sick or wounded.

ambush *n* the place or act of lying in wait in order to surprise.

amen *adv* so be it.

amenable *adj* easily led; co-operative; accountable.

amend *vt* to correct; to improve.

amendment *n* a minor improvement in a document.

amends *npl* compensation.

amenity *n* pleasantness; (~ies *pl*) pleasant or useful features.

amethyst *n* a violet or purple precious variety of quartz.

amiable *adj* loveable; pleasant; friendly.

amicable *adj* friendly; kind.

amid, amidst *prep* in the middle of.

amiss *adj* in error; improper; * *adv* improperly.

ammonia *n* a pungent colourless gas forming a strong alkali when dissolved in water; that solution.

ammunition *n* military stores generally; things used for charging fire-arms; explosive military devices; any helpful data to be used in an argument.

amnesty *n* a general pardon.

amok *n*, *adv* to run ~ to attack all and sundry.

amoeba *n* (*pl* amoebae) any aquatic protozoan of the genus *Amoeba*, *esp A proteus*.

among, amongst *prep* amidst.

amorous *adj* inclined to or showing love.

amorphous *adj* shapeless.

amount *vi* to result in; * *n* the sum total.

ampere *n* the Standard International unit of electrical current.

amphibian *n* (*pl* amphibia) animals able to live both on land or in water.

amphibious *adj* able to live in water and on land; (of a vehicle) built to operate on land and water.

amphitheatre *n* a circular, *usu* unroofed, building containing tiers of seats about a clear central space.

ample *adj* abundant; sufficient.

amplification *n* enlargement.

amplifier *n* a device which amplifies electrical signals.

amplify *vt*, *vi* to enlarge; to make louder; to fill out.

amply *adv* fully; copiously.

amputate *vt* to remove surgically.

amulet *n* a charm.

amuse *vt* to entertain; to cause laughter.

amusement *n* entertainment.

amusing *adj* droll; diverting.

an *adj* the indefinite article, used before words beginning with a vowel sound.

anachronism *n* the assignment of an event or circumstance out of its era.

anaemia *n* a deficiency of red blood cells or haemoglobin leading to pallor and weariness.

anaesthetic *adj* producing insensibility; * *n* a substance which produces insensibility.

anagram *n* a word formed by permuting the order of the letters of another.

analogous *adj* corresponding.

analogy *n* similarity.

analyse *vt* examine in detail; to show essence, meaning or structure of.

analysis *n* (*pl* analyses) the process of analysing.

analyst *n* one who analyses.

anarchic *adj* without rule or government; disordered.

anarchist *n* one who opposes all forms of government.

anathema *n* an object of detestation.

anatomy *n* the science dealing with physical structure of animals and plants; the art of dissection,

ancestor *n* a forebear.

ancestry *n* lineage; descent.

anchor *n* a metal device that grips the sea bed used for mooring a ship; * *vt* to hold fast by an anchor.

anchorage *n* a place where a ship can anchor.

ancient *adj* old; antique.

ancillary *adj* subservient or subordinate.

and *conj* a word joining words or phrases; also; in addition, consequently.

andante *adj* (music) slow.

anecdote *n* a short, often amusing, story.

anemometer *n* an instrument for measuring the force of the wind.

anger *n* wrath; * *vt* to enrage.

angle *n* the inclination of two lines; to one another; a viewpoint.

angle *vi* to fish with hook and line.

angler *n* one who fishes with hook and line.

Anglican *adj* pertaining to the Church of England.

angry *adj* full of anger; wrathful.

anguish *n* severe mental or physical pain.

angular *adj* sharp-cornered; (of a person) thin and bony.

animal *n* an organism having sensation and voluntary motion.

animate *vt* to give life to; enliven; to produce the appearance of movement by animation.

animated *adj* lively; living; (film,

etc) made by animation.

animation *n* life; vigour; the art of drawing objects and filming them to create moving images on film or tape.

animosity *n* a feeling of strong hostility.

ankle *n* the joint which connects the foot with the leg.

annals *npl* a yearly record of events.

annex *vt* to subjoin; to take possession of.

annexe *n* an extension to a building, separate or not.

annihilate *vt* completely destroy.

anniversary *n* a day on which some event is annually celebrated.

annotate *vt* to write notes upon.

announce *vt* to make known.

annoy *vt* to cause slight anger or mental distress to.

annual *adj* yearly; lasting a year; * *n* a book published yearly.

annul *vt* to make of no effect; to repeal.

anoint *vt* to apply oil to a person; *esp* as a religious ceremony.

anomaly *n* irregularity.

anonymous *adj* nameless; unsigned.

another *adj* an additional; one more of a similar type; someone or thing else.

answer *vt* to reply to; to solve; * *n* a reply; a solution.

answerable *adj* accountable.

antagonism *n* opposition; hostility.

antagonist *n* an opponent.

Antarctic *n* the continent at the South Pole.

antecedent *adj* going before; * *n* that which goes before; a person's history.

antechamber *n* ante-room.

antedate *vt* exist at an earlier date; to assign (*esp* incorrectly) an earlier date to.

antelope *n* a kind of deer.

antemeridian *adj* before midday; a.m.

antenna *n* (*pl* antennae) one of the feelers of an insect; an aerial.

anterior *adj* nearer the front; prior.

ante-room *n* a room leading to another.

anthem *n* a piece of Scripture set to music; a hymn of praise *esp* = national anthem.

anthology *n* a collection of poems or prose.

anthracite *n* a kind of coal which burns almost without flame.

antics *npl* buffoonery and posturing.

anticipate *vt* to be aware of a thing in advance; to forestall.

anticlimax *n* a tame ending to a striking beginning.

anticlockwise *n* rotational motion in the opposite sense to the normal motion of the hands of a clock.

anticyclone *n* a system of winds rotating outwards from a region of high pressure.

antidote *n* a remedy for poison or any evil.

antipathy *n* aversion; dislike.

antipodes *npl* points at opposite sides of the world.

antiquarian *adj* of or dealing in antiques or rare books.

antiquated *adj* old-fashioned; out of date.

antique *adj* old; * *n* an ancient relic, object of value or work of art.

antiquity *n* ancient times; great age; (*pl* antiquities) remains of ancient times.

anti-racism *n* the policy and practise of opposing racism.

antiseptic *adj* counteracting sepsis; sterile.

antithesis *n* (*pl* antitheses) the direct opposite, contrast.

antler *n* each of the branched horns of a stag.

anvil *n* an iron block on which metals are worked in forging; (*anatomy*) a bone in the middle ear.

anxiety *n* concern; worry.

anxious *adj* troubled; worried; eager.

any *adj* one, no matter which, of several; some, no matter how much.

aorta *n* the artery leading from the heart.

apace *adv* fast.

apart *adj*, *adv* separate; aside; in pieces.

apartment *n* a room; a flat.

apathetic *adj* indifferent.

apathy *n* want of feeling; indifference.

ape *n* any primate of the family *pongidae* characterised by having no tail *eg* gorillas, chimpanzees, humans; * *vt* to mimic.

aperture *n* an opening.

apex *n* (*pl* apices) the summit.

apiary *n* a place where bees are kept.

apiece *adv* for each one.

aplomb *n* self-possession.

apocalypse *n* any disastrous event resembling the events described in the Revelations of St John of Patmos.

apocryphal *adj* of doubtful authenticity; mythical.

apologise *vi* to make an apology.

apology *n* that which is said in defence or as an expression of regret.

apoplexy *n* a rush of extreme emotion, *esp* anger; (medical) stroke.

apostate *n* one who renounces his religion or his party.

apostrophe *n* a punctuation mark used to indicate the removal of letters or numbers or the possessive case.

appal *vt* to dismay or horrify.

appalling *adj* shocking; unpleasant.

apparatus *n* (*pl* apparatus) the equipment needed for a specific purpose or function, *esp* scientific; a political or other complex organisation.

apparel *n* clothing; * *vt* to dress.

apparent *adv* evident; seeming.

apparition *n* a ghost or phantom.

appeal *vi*, *vt* to plead; to carry to a higher court; * *n* entreaty; the state of being attractive or desirable.

appear *vi* to become visible; to seem; to present oneself formally or publicly *esp* on stage or as a party or as council in a law court.

appearance *n* act of coming into sight; semblance.

appease *vt* to pacify; to calm.

appellant *n* one who appeals.

appellation *n* a name; a title.

append *vt* to add; to attach.

appendage *n* something added; an external organ, *eg* a tail.

appendicitis *n* inflammation of the appendix.

appendix *n* an adjunct; a supplement; a prolongation; (in full vermiform appendix) a small outgrowth of tissue forming a tube-like sac attached to the lower end of the small intestine.

appertain *vi* relate to; to belong as a possession or right; be appropriate.

appetite *n* a desire to satisfy bodily needs, *esp* for food or sexual satisfaction.

appetise *vt* to whet the appetite.

applaud *vt* to praise *esp* by clapping the hands.

apple *n* the fruit of a tree of the genus *mallus*.

appliance *n* the act of applying; the thing applied; a device or machine *usu* for domestic use.

applicable *adj* that which may be applied; suitable.

applicant *n* one who applies, *esp* for work.

application *n* the act of applying; a formal request for a position, membership etc; the use to which something is put; diligence.

apply *vt* to fasten or attach; * *vi* to suit; to make a formal request for something.

appoint *vt* assign an office or post to; to fix; to nominate.

appointment *n* a post or office available for applicants; an arrangement to meet at a specified time and place.

apposite *adj* apt; well expressed.

appraise *vt* to fix or set a price or value on; to evaluate the performance of formally.

appreciable *adj* large enough to be noticed; significant; considerable.

appreciate *vt* to value; to be grateful to or thankful for; * *vi* to rise in value.

apprehend *vt* to seize; to arrest; to anticipate with fear; to understand.

apprehension *n* seizure; dread; understanding.

apprehensive *adj* fearful.

apprentice *n* one who is learning a trade or occupation by being employed in it at lower than usual wages for a specified period; * *vt* to bind as an apprentice.

apprise *vt* to inform.

approach *vt, vi* to come near; * *n* the act of drawing near; an avenue.

approbation *n* approval.

appropriate *vt* to take possession of *usu* unlawfully; * *adj* suitable.

appropriateness *n* the state of being suitable.

approval *n* a favourable opinion.

approve *vt* to consider good; to sanction.

approximate *adj* near to; almost right or close to ; * *vt* to bring near; * *vi* to come near.

apricot *n* the fruit of and the tree *Prunus arencia*, the colour of the ripe fruit (orange-yellow).

April *n* the fourth month of the year.

apron *n* a garment covering and protecting the front of a person's clothes, *esp* a cook's apron.

apt *adj* suitable; having a tendency.

aptitude *n* natural facility.

aquarium *n* (*pl* aquaria) a vessel or tank or building for aquatic plants and animals.

aquatic *adj* living or growing in water; (*pl*) water sports.

aqueduct *n* a conduit made for conveying water.

aqueous *adj* of, containing or like water.

arable *adj* fit for ploughing and crop production; * *n* arable land or crops.

arbiter *n* an arbitrator in a dispute; a judge; an authority; one who has complete control of something.

arbitrary *adj* based on or derived from uninformed or random choice; despotic; capricious.

arc *n* a part of a circle or curve.

arcade *n* a covered passage, *esp* containing shops.

arcane *adj* understood only with special knowledge; esoteric; secret; mysterious.

arch *n* a curved structure as an opening or supporting a bridge or roof.

arch~ *prefix* chief; superior; pre-eminent. *eg* archbishop *n* a chief bishop.

archaeology *n* the study of human history through the excavation of sites and the study of physical remains.

archaic *adj* antiquated; obsolete.

archdeacon *n* a church dignitary, next in rank to a bishop.

archer *n* a person who shoots with a bow and arrow.

archipelago *n* a group of islands; a sea abounding in islands.

architect *n* one who designs and supervises the construction of buildings, ships etc.

architecture *n* the science of designing buildings etc; the style of a building as regards design and construction; buildings and other structures collectively; the structure and internal organisation of a computer.

archive *n* (*usu* in *pl*) a collection of, *esp* public, records; the place where they are kept.

Arctic *adj* pertaining to the regions about the North Pole.

ardent *adj* fervent; eager.

ardour *n* warmth; eagerness; passion.

arduous *adj* difficult.

area *n* the extent or measure of a surface; any enclosed or specified ground; any enclosed or sunken space.

arena *n* an open space of ground for contests or games.

argue *vt, vi* to discuss; to dispute.

argument *n* a reason offered; a plea; a controversy.

argumentative *adj* prone to argument.

arid *adj* dry; parched.

arise *vi* to rise up; to come about.

aristocracy *n* government by the nobility; the nobility.

aristocrat *n* a noble.

arithmetic *n* the science of numbers; computation.

arm *n* the limb from the shoulder to the hand; a weapon; armour; (in *pl*) heraldic devices; * *vt* to furnish with arms; * *vi* to take up arms.

armada *n* a fleet of warships.

armament *n* war equipment of an army, ship or vehicle.

armistice *n* a truce.

armour *n* defensive dress; protective cladding, *usu* metal; armoured vehicles.

armoury *n* a place for keeping arms.

armpit *n* the hollow under the shoulder.

army *n* an organised force armed for fighting on land.

aroma *n* perfume.

aromatic *adj* fragrant; (chemistry) containing unsaturated rings, *esp* containing benzene rings.

around *prep* about; encircling; * *adv* on every side.

arouse *vt* to stir up.

arraign *vt* to indict; to accuse.

arrange *vt* to put in order; to prepare for; to plan; to adjust a musical work for different instruments.

array *n* order; (maths) a matrix; * *vt* to draw up in order; to adorn.

arrear *n* (generally *pl*) that which remains unpaid.

arrest *vt* to stop; to apprehend; * *n* a seizure by warrant.

arrival *n* the act of coming to a place.

arrive *vi* to come; to reach; to succeed.

arrogance *n* haughtiness; insolent bearing.

arrogant *adj* haughty; overbearing; self-important.

arrow *n* a barbed shaft shot from a bow.

arsenal *n* a public establishment for making or storing weapons of war.

arsenic *n* the element arsenic; (in full **arsenic trioxide**, As) a highly toxic white powder.

arson *n* the malicious setting on fire of property.

art *n* practical skill; cunning; creative activity concerned with the production of works of

imaginative designs, as in the fine arts.

arterial *adj* pertaining to arteries; (*esp* of a road) main, important, connecting large cities.

artery *n* a muscle lined tube which conveys blood under pressure, on which one can feel a pulse; a main road, etc.

artful *adj* skilful; crafty.

article *n* a separate item; composition (in a newspaper, magazine, journal etc); a part of speech, a, the etc; * *vi* to stipulate.

articulate *adj* distinct; clear and intelligible; having joints; * *vi* to utter distinct sounds.

artifice *n* an artful device or deception.

artificial *adj* made by human art or effort rather than occurring naturally; not real (*eg* plastic flowers).

artillery *n* cannon and heavy guns in general; the troops who manage them.

artist *n* one skilled in some art, especially the fine arts.

artistic *adj* characteristic of art; aesthetic.

artless *adj* unaffected.

as *adv*, *conj*, *prep* like; because; in the same way; playing the part of.

asbestos *n* an incombustible, fibrous silicate mineral.

ascend *vi* to rise; * *vt* to climb.

ascendancy, ascendency *n* controlling power; sway.

ascent *n* rise; upward slope.

ascertain *vt* to make certain; to find out.

ascetic *adj* unduly rigid in self-denial and self-discipline.

ascribe *vt* to attribute.

asepsis *n* the absence of disease causing agents.

aseptic *adj* free from contamination from disease causing agents (bacteria, viruses etc); surgically sterile.

ash *n* (often in *pl*) the powdery residue left from burning any substance; (in *pl*) the remains of a human body after cremation or decomposition; * *n* any forest tree of the genus *Fraxinus* with silvery grey bark; its wood.

ashamed *adj* affected by shame or guilt.

ashen *adj* of or resembling ash; pale.

ashore *adv, adj* on or to the shore.

aside *adv* on one side; apart; * *n* words spoken by an actor to an audience only; an incidental remark.

asinine *adj* belonging to or resembling the ass; stupid.

ask *vt* to request; * *vi* to make inquiry.

askance, askant *adv* sideways; squinting.

askew *adv, adj* obliquely; awry.

asleep *adj, adv* sleeping.

asp *n* a small viper, *Vipera aspis*, found in southern Europe; the Egyptian cobra, *Naja haje*.

aspect *n* a particular issue in a matter; appearance; outlook.

asperity *n* roughness; harshness.

aspersion *n* calumny, lie; (*esp pl*) slander; defamation.

asphalt *n* a kind of pitch used for paving.

aspiration *n* ardent desire; ambition.

aspire *vi* to aim at high things.

ass *n* either of two kinds of mammal of the horse genus: *Equus africanus* of Africa and *Equus hemionus* of Asia; (in general use) a donkey; a fool.

assail *vt* to attack.

assassin *n* a (*usu* paid) killer, especially of political targets.

assassinate *vt* to kill for political motives.

assault *n* an attack; * *vt* to assail.

assay *n* proof; analysis of ores; * *vt* to try.

assemblage *n* a collection of persons or things.

assemble *vt* to bring together; * *vi* to come together.

assembly *n* a gathering of people to consult together; a putting together of many parts to make a whole.

assent *n* consent; * *vi* to agree.

assert *vt* to state clearly; vindicate a claim to; * *vr* to insist on ones

right to; demand recognition.

assertive *adj* asserting oneself confidently.

assess *vt* to rate; to value or estimate amount, worth, etc.

asset *n* a useful or valuable thing; property regarded as having value.

assiduous *adj* constantly diligent.

assign *vt* to designate; to allot; to make over to another.

assignable *adj* that may be assigned.

assignation *n* an appointment to meet; a making over by transfer of title.

assignment *n* an allotment or legal transfer; a task assigned to someone.

assimilate *vt* to make similar to; to absorb; to digest.

assist *vt* to help; * *vi* to lend help.

assistant *n* one who assists.

assize *n* (historically also in *pl*) a court sitting periodically in each county in England and Wales for the administration of both civil and criminal law.

associate *vt* to join in company with; * *vi* to keep company with; * *n* a companion; a business colleague or partner.

association *n* act of associating; union.

assort *vt* to arrange; * *vi* to suit.

assortment *n* a varied collection.

assuage *vt* to allay; to calm.

assume *vt* to take for granted; to usurp; * *vi* to claim more than is due.

assurance *n* a positive declaration that something is true; a guarantee; self-confidence; impudence; insurance.

assure *vt* to confirm; to make certain; to insure.

assuredly *adv* certainly.

asterisk *n* a star-shaped mark used in printing (*) to indicate an omission, cross-reference, footnote, etc.

astern *adv* (marine) behind; to the rear; backwards.

asteroid *n* a small rocky body orbiting the sun.

asthma *n* a disease marked by shortness of breath.

astigmatism *n* a defect on the cornea of the eyes causing incorrect focusing.

astonish *vt* to amaze.

astound *vt* to astonish; to stun.

astral *adj* relating to the stars.

astray *adv* away from the correct path.

astride *adv* with the legs apart or on either side of something.

astringent *n* a medicine that contracts the tissues; * *adj* binding; constricting; harsh; sharp; bracing.

astrology *n* the study of the motion of the stars as having some effect on human affairs.

astronomical *adj* pertaining to astronomy; very large.

astronomy *n* the scientific study of celestial objects, space and the universe as a whole.

astute *adj* shrewd; crafty.

asunder *adv* apart; into parts.

asylum *n* sanctuary; protection *esp* for those pursued by the law.

at *prep* expressing location, time, a state of activity, or rate.

atheism *n* the disbelief in the existence of God.

athlete *n* one skilled in exercises, *esp* track and field events.

athletic *adj* pertaining to an athlete; strong; active.

atlas *n* a collection of maps.

atmosphere *n* the air surrounding the earth; pervading influence.

atmospheric *adj* pertaining to the atmosphere.

atoll *n* a ring-shaped coral reef enclosing a lagoon.

atom *n* the smallest particle that can take part in purely chemical (as distinct from nuclear) reactions, consisting of a small massive nucleus surrounded by a cloud of electrons; anything extremely small.

atomic *adj* pertaining to or consisting of atoms; pertaining to atomic energy or weapons.

atone *vi* to make up for; to expiate.

atrocious *adj* abominable; very wicked.

atrocity *n* horrible wickedness.

atrophy *n* a wasting away.

attach *vt* to join; to affix; * *vi* to adhere.

attaché *n* one attached to the suite of an ambassador or a diplomatic mission.

attack *vt* to assault; * *n* an assault; seizure by a disease.

attain *vi* to arrive at; * *vt* to reach; to gain.

attainment *n* accomplishment.

attempt *vt* to try to do; * *n* an essay; effort.

attend *vt* to wait on; to be present at; * *vi* to pay regard.

attendant *adj* accompanying; * *n* one who waits on or accompanies.

attention *n* heed; courtesy.

attentive *adj* heedful; courteous; diligent.

attenuate *vt* to make slender; to reduce in force, value or virulence; to reduce the amplitude of an electrical signal.

attest *vt* to bear witness to.

attestation *n* testimony.

attic *n* a garret; a room or storing space under the roof of a house.

attire *vt* to dress; * *n* dress

attitude *n* posture; a position or viewpoint taken on some matter.

attorney *n* a person, *esp* a lawyer, empowered to act for another in business or legal matters.

attract *vt* to draw to; to entice.

attractive *adj* having the power of attracting; enticing; pretty.

attribute *vt* to ascribe, to impute; * *n* a quality; an attributive adjective or noun.

attributive *adj* a grammatical term referring to an adjective or noun which precedes the word it modifies and expresses an attribute *eg* blue in: the blue car.

attrition *n* the act of wearing down by rubbing.

attune *vt* to put in tune; to adjust to or acclimatise.

auburn *adj* reddish brown colour.

auction *n* a sale, *usu* held in public, in which successively higher offers are made for the item on sale, the article going to the highest bidder; the sequence of bids in the card game bridge.

audacious *adj* daring; impudent.

audacity *n* daring; impudence.

audible *adj* sufficiently loud to be heard.

audience *n* an assembly of spectators or listeners; reception.

audit *n* an official examination of accounts; a systematic review (*eg* a safety audit).

auditor *n* one who examines accounts.

auditory *adj* pertaining to the sense of hearing; * *n* an audience.

auger *n* a tool, resembling a corkscrew, for boring holes.

augment *vt* to make larger; to increase; * *n* increase.

augmentation *n* increase.

augur *vt* suggest a specified outcome; portend, bode.

august *adj* regal; imposing.

August *n* the eighth month of the year.

aunt *n* the sister of one's father or mother.

auricle *n* the external ear; either of the two ear-like cavities of the heart.

aurora australis *n* the southern lights.

aurora borealis *n* the northern lights.

auspices *npl* patronage; omens.

auspicious *adj* fortunate; favourable.

austere *adj* stern; severe.

austerity *n* sternness; severity; living without luxuries.

authentic *adj* genuine.

authenticate *vt* to attest; to confirm.

authenticity *n* genuineness.

author, authoress *n* the original writer of a book, article etc.

authoritative *adj* official; decisive; recognised as true.

authority *n* legal power or right; a person or organisation exercising this power.

authorise *vt* to sanction.

autocracy *n* absolute government by one person.

autocrat *n* an absolute ruler.

autograph *n* a signature.

automatic *adj* self-acting; carried out without conscious thought.

automaton *n* (*pl* automata) a self-moving machine, or a person acting like one.

autonomy *n* self-government.

autopsy *n* the examination of a dead body to discover the cause of death.

autumn *n* the third season of the year.

auxiliary *adj* helping; * *n* a person or thing that helps.

avail *vt, vi* to profit; * *vi* to be of use; * *n* advantage; use.

available *adj* attainable.

avalanche *n* a vast snow slide.

avarice *n* greed of gain.

avenge *vt* to take satisfaction for; to harm in retaliation.

avenue *n* an approach to; a broad street.

average *n* medium; * *adj* medial; moderate; not outstanding in ability; * *vi* to form a mean.

averse *adj* disinclined.

aversion *n* dislike.

avert *vt* to turn aside or away from.

aviary *n* a place for keeping birds.

aviation *n* the art of flying.

aviator *n* one who flies aeroplanes.

avoid *vt* to shun.

avoirdupois *n, adj* a system of weight, in which a pound contains sixteen ounces.

avow *vt* to declare with confidence; to confess frankly.

await *vt* to wait for; to expect

awake *vt* to rouse from sleep; * *vi* to cease from sleep; * *adj* not sleeping.

awaken *vt, vi* to awake.

award *vt* to adjudge; * *vi* to make an award; * *n* a judgment; a reward or prize.

aware *adj* informed; cognisant.

away *adv* absent; at a distance.

awe *n* fear; fear mingled with reverence; * *vt* to strike with fear.

awful *adj* very bad; terrible.

awhile *adv* for some time.

awkward *adj* inexpert; inelegant; deliberately unhelpful; difficult.

awry *adj, adv* twisted; distorted; gone wrong.

axe *n* an instrument *usu* of iron

with a sharp blade and wooden handle for chopping.

axiom *n* a self-evident truth.

axiomatic *adj* self-evident.

axis *n* (*pl* axes) the line about which a body revolves; a reference line along which co-ordinates are measured.

axle *n* the pole on which a wheel turns.

azure *adj* sky-blue.

B

babble *vi* to talk idly; to talk incoherently or inarticulately; * *n* idle talk; murmur, as of a brook.

baboon *n* any of various large types of monkey of the genera *Papio* and *Mandrillis*.

baby *n* a child just born; a young animal.

bachelor *n* an unmarried man; a graduate of a university or college.

bacillus *n* (*pl* bacilli) any rod-shaped bacterium; any pathogenic bacterium.

back *n* the rear or (in beasts) the upper part of the body; * *vt* to support; to cause to recede; * *adv* to the rear.

backbite *vt* to speak evil of secretly.

backbone *n* the spine; strength.

background *n* the ground behind; the setting of a picture or photograph; that which has taken place beforehand causing and leading up to an event, etc; social status.

backslide *vi* to degenerate; to relapse.

backward *adj* lagging behind; dull.

backwoods *npl* outlying forest districts.

bacon *n* cured meat from the back or sides of a pig.

bacteriology *n* the study of bacteria.

bacterium *n* (*pl* bacteria) any of a large group of micro-organisms lacking organelles and a central nucleus.

bad *adj* wicked; immoral.

badge *n* a distinguishing mark or emblem.

badger *n* a burrowing quadruped; * *vt* to worry; to pester.

badminton *n* a game like lawn tennis played with shuttlecocks.

baffle *vt* to frustrate; to defeat.

bag *n* a sack; a pouch; a purse.

baggage *n* luggage.

bagpipe *n* a wind instrument.

bail *vt* to liberate from custody on security for reappearance; to free (a boat) from water; to bale; * *n* security given for release; the small bar placed on the stumps in cricket.

bailiff *n* a sheriff's officer who executes writs and processes and carries out arrests; a landowner's or landlord's steward or agent.

bait *n* food to trap or lure animals or fish; an enticement; * *vt* to furnish with a lure; to harass, especially by verbal teasing.

bake *vt* to dry and harden by fire; to cook in an oven.

balance *n* a pair of scales; equilibrium; difference of two sums; the sum due on an account; * *vt* to bring to an equilibrium; to settle; * *vi* to hesitate.

balance sheet *n* a statement of assets and liabilities.

balcony *n* a railed or walled platform projecting from a window; an upper tier of seats in a theatre or cinema.

bald *adj* (of a person) with the scalp wholly or partly lacking hair; bare; paltry.

bale *n* a bundle or package of goods or hay; * *vt* to free a boat from water; (*with* out) to escape from aircraft by parachute; to bail.

baleful *adj* gloomy; menacing; harmful; malignant; destructive.

ball *n* a round body; a dance.

ballad *n* a narrative poem; a popular sentimental song.

ballast *n* heavy matter carried in a ship or the car of a hot air balloon to keep it steady.

ballet *n* a theatrical dance.

balloon *n* a large bag filled with a

gas which makes it float in the air.

ballot n a system of voting; * vi to vote by ballot.

balmy adj (of weather) pleasantly mild and calm.

balsam n soothing ointment.

bamboo n a giant woody grass of the mainly tropical subfamily *Bambusidae*.

bamboozle vt to hoax; to confuse.

ban n a prohibition; an edict; * vt to curse; to forbid.

banal adj commonplace; vulgar.

banana n a curved yellow fruit; the tree (*Musa sapientium*) which bears it.

band n that which binds; a company of people acting together, *eg* a group of musicians; * vt to unite in a troop.

bandage n a cloth for a wound, etc; * vt to bind with a bandage.

bandit n a robber.

bandoleer n a shoulder strap for carrying cartridges.

bandy vt to exchange, especially words in anger; to pass to and fro.

bandy-legged adj having crooked legs.

baneful adj pernicious; poisonous.

bang vt to thump; * n a heavy blow.

bangle n a bracelet or anklet.

banish vt to drive away; to exile.

banister n the supports for the uprights of a staircase.

banjo n a six-stringed musical instrument.

bank n ground rising from the side of a river, lake, etc; a financial establishment which invests money deposited by customers, makes loans, exchanges currency etc; * vt to deposit in a bank.

banking n the business of a banker.

bankrupt n one who cannot pay his debts; * adj unable to pay debts; insolvent.

banner n a standard.

banns npl the proclamation of marriage.

banquet n a feast.

banter vt to tease good-humouredly; * n good-humoured teasing.

baptise vt to christen.

baptism n an immersion in or sprinkling with water as part of the ceremony of joining the Christian church.

bar n a bolt; obstacle; a long piece of wood or metal; a tribunal; barristers collectively; anything that prohibits or obstructs; a counter where liquors are served; a unit of pressure roughly equal to atmospheric pressure; * vt to prohibit.

barb n the notched tip of a fishing hook or arrow.

barbarian adj savage; uncivilised; * n a savage.

barbarity n the state or qualities of a barbarian; ferociousness.

barbarous adj cruel; inhuman.

barbed adj jagged with hooks or points.

barber n a hairdresser.

bare adj uncovered; empty; worn; * vt to make naked; to reveal.

barefaced adj shameless.

bargain n a gainful transaction; a cheap purchase; * vi to make a bargain.

barge n a flat-bottomed boat for freight used on canals and rivers; * vi to push in bodily.

bark n the outer covering of a tree; a barque; the noise made by a dog; * vt to strip bark off; to treat with bark; to make the cry of dogs.

barley n a species of grain used for food, and the making of malt liquors and spirits.

barmaid / barman n a woman / man who serves at a public house bar.

barn n a building for storing grain, etc.

barometer n an instrument for measuring the pressure of the atmosphere.

baron n a peer of the lowest rank.

baroness n a baron's wife; a female baron.

baronet n the lowest order of hereditary titles.

barrack n (usu pl) buildings for housing soldiers; * vt to jeer loudly at.

barrage *n* a bar or dam constructed across a river; the firing of heavy artillery; a continuous onslaught as of words or blows.

barrel *n* a cylindrical container, bulging slightly in the middle, used for storing ale or beer (= 36 gallons); a cylindrical tube forming part of a gun.

barren *adj* unfruitful; sterile.

barricade *n* a temporary fortification; a barrier; * *vt* to bar.

barrier *n* a fence; a bar.

barrister *n* a lawyer called to the bar and entitled to plead at the higher courts.

barrow *n* a small handcart; a burial mound.

barter *vi* to traffic by exchange; * *vt* to exchange in commerce; * *n* traffic by exchange.

baritone *n* a male voice between tenor and bass.

basalt *n* a dark volcanic rock, often found in columnar form.

base *adj* low; worthless; * *n* foundation; support; a substance which reacts with acids to form salts and water.

baseless *adj* groundless.

basement *n* the ground floor.

bashful *adj* modest; shy.

basic *adj* relating to a base; fundamental.

basil *n* an aromatic herb of the genus *Ocimum, esp O basilicum*.

basilica *n* a hall or church with double colonnades.

basin *n* a broad shallow dish; a reservoir; a dock; the land drained by a river.

basis *n* (*pl* **bases**) a base; groundwork.

bask *vi* to lie in the sun.

basket *n* a wicker container.

bass *n* the lowest part in musical harmony; the lowest male voice.

bassoon *n* a musical wind instrument.

bastard *adj* (*pej*) illegitimate; * *n* a person whose parents are unmarried; (*vulg*) a despicable person.

baste *vt* to beat with a stick; to drip fat on meat while roasting; to sew with temporary stitches.

bastion *n* a fortification standing out from a rampart; a natural rock formation resembling this; something regarded as protective.

bat *n* a flying mammal like a mouse of the order *Chiroptera*; a club used to strike the ball, as in cricket; * *vi* to play with a bat.

batch *n* a number of things forming a group or dealt with together; an instalment; the quantity of bread baked at one time; a quantity.

bath *n* a place to bathe in; immersion in water.

bathe *vt* to immerse in water; * *vi* to take a bath.

baton *n* a staff, a truncheon; a thin stick used by a conductor of music.

battalion *n* a military body three or more companies strong.

batten *n* a strip of wood used to hold something in place; * *vt* to fasten with battens.

batter *vt* to beat repeatedly; * *n* a cooking mixture of flour, eggs and milk.

battery *n* a fully equipped artillery unit; a device which chemically stores electrical charge; (law) an act, including touching, inflicting unlawful physical violence against a person.

battle *n* encounter of two armies; a combat.

battlement *n* a parapet with fortifications.

battleship *n* a large warship furnished with heavy artillery.

bauble *n* a showy trinket or toy of little value.

bawl *vi* to shout; to weep loudly.

bay *adj* reddish-brown; * *n* an inlet on the shore of the sea or a lake; the laurel tree, *Laurus nobilis*; the bark of a dog; * *vt* to bark at.

bayonet *n* a dagger-like weapon attachable to a rifle.

be *vi* to exist; to remain.

beach *n* the shore of the sea; * *vt* to run (a vessel) on a beach.

beached *adj* driven on a beach; stranded.

beacon *n* a flare; a signal of

danger; * vt to light up.

bead n a little ball strung on a thread; a small drop of liquid.

beak n the bill of a bird.

beaker n a large drinking cup; a glass vessel.

beam n a main timber in a building; part of a balance which sustains the scales; a ray of light; * vi to shine; to smile broadly.

bean n a name of several kinds of pulse or peas.

bear vt to carry; to suffer; to bring forth; to permit; * vi to suffer; to produce.

bear n any large mammal of the family Ursidae; * vt to carry, bring or take; to show or be marked or distinguished by; to produce; to give birth; to sustain; to endure; to veer in a specific direction.

beard n the hair on the face.

bearer n a carrier.

bearing n manner, appearance and general demeanour.

beast n an animal; a brutal man.

beat vt to strike; to overcome; * vi to throb; to sail against the wind; * n a stroke; rhythmic stroke of the heart; musical rhythm.

beauteous adj beautiful.

beautiful adj full of beauty.

beauty n a collection of aesthetic attributes pleasing to the senses, esp sight; loveliness; elegance; a property of elementary particles.

becalm vt to make calm.

because conj by cause of; on this account; since.

beckon vi to nod or make a summoning sign.

become vi to come to be; * vt to suit.

becoming adj fitting; graceful.

bed n a piece of furniture used to sleep on; the channel of a river; a layer; a stratum; * vt to lay in a bed; to sow; * vi to go to bed.

bedding n the coverings (sheets, pillows etc) of a bed.

bedeck vt to adorn.

bedraggle vt to soil by trailing along the wet ground.

bedraggled adj untidy; dishevelled.

bedroom n a sleeping room.

bedsit n one room with cooking and sleeping facilities.

bedstead n a frame for supporting a bed.

bee n (in full honey bee) a stinging insect of the family Apis which collects pollen and honey and produces honey and wax and lives in large communities, esp the domesticated Apis mellifera.

beef n the flesh of an ox, bull or esp cow.

beeline n a direct line or way.

beer n an alcoholic drink made from fermented malt, flavoured with hops.

beeswax n the wax secreted by bees for their combs.

beet n any vegetable of the genus Beta with edible roots.

beetle n any insect of the order Coleoptera, with front wings modified to form hard protective cases; a wooden mallet; * vi to jut; to hang over threateningly.

befall vt to happen to.

befit vt to suit.

before prep, adv in front of; earlier than; rather than; onward.

beforehand adv in advance.

befriend vt to act as a friend to.

beg vt to ask in charity; to ask earnestly; to avoid answering a question; to take for granted.

beget vt to procreate; to produce.

beggar n one who begs; * vt to reduce to poverty; to be beyond, especially description.

begin vi to commence; * vt to enter on.

beginner n one who begins; a novice.

beginning n the first stage; start.

begrudge vt to envy the possession of.

beguile vt to dupe; to divert from pleasantly; to charm.

behalf n in the interests of; support.

behave vt to conduct (oneself); * vi to act.

behaviour n conduct.

behead vt to cut off the head.

behind prep in the rear of; * adv backwards.

behold vt to look upon; to regard with attention.

beholden *adj* obliged.

being *n* existence; a creature.

belay *vt* to fasten a rope by winding round something; (marine) (*sl*) desist.

belch *vt* to utter violently; to expel wind from the stomach through the mouth.

beleaguer *vt* to besiege; to vex; to harass.

belfry *n* a bell tower.

belie *vt* to represent falsely; to fail to be equal to.

belief *n* faith; trust; opinion.

believe *vt* to accept as true.

belittle *vt* to make smaller; to disparage.

bell *n* a metallic vessel for making ringing sounds when struck; anything in the form of a bell; * *vt* to put a bell on.

bellicose *adj* pugnacious.

belligerent *adj* waging war; quarrelsome; * *n* a person or nation engaged in a conflict.

bellow *vi* to roar like a bull; * *n* a roar.

bellows *npl* an instrument for supplying wind to blow up fires, or sound an organ.

belly *n* that part of the body which contains the stomach and bowels; the abdomen; * *vt, vi* to swell; to bulge.

belong *vi* to be the property of; to appertain to; to be a member.

belongings *npl* personal possessions.

beloved *adj* greatly loved.

below *prep* under; beneath; * *adv* in a lower place.

belt *n* a girdle; a band; a stripe; area, *eg* of trees.

bemoan *vt* to lament.

bemused *adj* muddled.

bench *n* a long seat which accommodates several people; a long work table; a judge's seat in court; judges collectively.

bend *vt* to curve; to direct to a certain point; to adjust for one's own purpose; * *n* a curve.

beneath *prep*, *adv* below; under.

benefactor *n* a person who confers a benefit.

benefit *n* an act of kindness; a favour; something that brings improvement; a payment made under social security, welfare, insurance etc; * *vt* to do a service to.

benevolence *n* kindness; charity.

benign *adj* gentle; kind; fortunate; beneficial; (medical) not malignant.

bent *n* bias of mind; aptitude; a wiry grass of the genus *Agrostis*.

benzene *n* a colourless, volatile liquid with a ring-like molecular structure, used as a solvent.

bequeath *vt* to leave by will.

bequest *n* a legacy.

bereave *vt* to deprive of someone dear by death.

berry *n* a pulpy fruit containing seeds.

berserk *adj* frenzied.

berth *n* a place in which a moored ship lies; a place for sleeping in a train, ship, etc; * *vt* to moor.

beseech *vt* to entreat.

beset *vt* to surround; to attack from every direction.

besetting *adj* habitual.

beside, besides *prep* by the side of; near; * *adv* moreover.

besiege *vt* to lay siege to.

besotted *adj* infatuated.

best *adj* the superlative of good; * *adv* the superlative of well; * *vt* to defeat; to beat.

bestial *adj* brutish; sexually depraved; of or like an animal.

bestiality *n* bestial conduct; sexual intercourse between a human and an animal.

bestow *vt* to gift; to present with.

bestride *vt* to stride over or across; to span.

bet *n* a wager; * *vt* to wager.

betide *vi* to befall; to happen.

betoken *vt* to imply; to foreshadow.

betray *vt* to prove false to; to give away a confidence, secret etc.

betrothal *n* mutual promise to marry.

better *adj* comparative of good; * *adv* comparative of well; * *vt* to advance; to outdo.

between *prep* in the middle.

bevel *n* an instrument for setting angles.

beverage *n* a drink.

bevvy *n* (*pl* ~ies) *sl* an alcoholic drink.

bevy *n* a flock of birds; a collection of people (formerly women).

bewail *vt* to lament.

beware *vt, vi* (only in infinitive or imperative) be cautious.

bewilder *vt* to perplex.

bewitch *vt* to enchant.

beyond *prep* on the farther side of; post; not within reach; * *adv* at a distance; further on.

bias *n* weight on one side; a bent; a prejudice; * *vt* to incline to one side.

bib *n* a cloth or plastic cover tied round the neck (of a child) to protect clothing from food spillage.

Bible *n* the Holy Scriptures of the Christian faith.

biblical *adj* pertaining to the Bible.

bibliography *n* an account, description or reference list of books on a subject.

bibliomania *n* a passion for possessing books.

bibliophile *n* a lover of books.

biceps *npl* the muscles on the front of the upper arm.

bicker *vi* to quarrel.

bicycle *n* a two-wheeled vehicle propelled by pedals.

bid *vt* to ask; to order; to offer; * *n* an offer, as at an auction.

biddable *adj* obedient.

bidding *n* an invitation; a command.

biennial *adj* lasting for two years; taking place once in two years.

bifurcate(d) *adj* forked or divided into two.

big *adj* great; large.

bigamy *n* having two wives or husbands at once.

bigot *n* a person obstinately wedded to particular, *esp* intolerant, ideas.

bilateral *adj* two-sided.

bile *n* the bitter secretion of the liver; ill-nature.

bilge *n* the bulging part of a cask; the breadth of a ship's bottom.

bilingual *adj* in two languages; able to speak in two languages.

bilious *adj* affected by bile.

bill *n* the beak of a bird; an instrument for pruning; an account of money due; draft of a new law as presented to parliament; a poster or leaflet.

billabong *n* (Australian) a branch of a river forming a pool of stagnant water.

billet *n* a small note in writing; lodgings; a situation; * *vt* to quarter, as soldiers.

billet-doux *n* (*pl* billets-doux) a love letter.

billiards *npl* a game played on a table with balls and cues.

billion *n* one thousand million; (less frequent, British) a million million.

billow *n* a wave; a soft upward flow.

bin *n* a receptacle for rubbish.

binary *adj* twofold; the number system using two as a base.

bind *vt* to tie; to oblige; to cover (a book); to make firm; to bandage; * *vi* to cohere; to be obligatory.

binding *n* the cover and sewing of a book; * *adj* obligatory.

binocular *adj* adapted for both eyes; * *npl* field or opera glasses.

binomial *adj, n* an algebraic expression with two terms.

biochemistry *n* the study of the chemistry of living organisms.

biogenesis *n* the doctrine that living matter springs only from living matter.

biography *n* written life of a person; auto~ when written by themselves.

biology *n* the study of the science of living organisms.

bipartite *adj* having two parts.

biped *n* an animal with two feet.

bird *n* a feathered, egg-laying vertebrate with wings of the class *Aves*.

birth *n* the emergence of an infant from its mothers womb; origin; ancestry.

birthright *n* a right of possession on is entitled to by birth.

biscuit *n* a hard, flat, sweet or plain cake.

bisect *vt* to cut in half.

bishop *n* the head of a diocese.

bishopric *n* the office of a bishop;

a diocese.

bit *n* a small part of something; the metal part of a bridle; a boring tool used with a brace.

bitch *n* a female dog or wolf; (*pej*) a malicious or spiteful woman.

bite *vt* to crush or sever with the teeth; to cause to smart; * *n* a wound made by biting; a mouthful.

biting *adj* sharp; piercingly cold; sarcastic.

bitter *adj* sharp to the taste; severe; painful.

bitumen *n* a pitch-like substance used for road surfacing.

bivalve *n* any of a group of aquatic molluscs of the class *Bivalvia*, with their bodies contained within shells.

bivouac *n* a temporary encampment of soldiers for the night in the open air.

bizarre *adj* fantastic; odd; strange

black *adj* having no light; dark; gloomy; sullen; atrocious; wicked; * *n* the darkest colour; * *vt* to make black.

blackboard *n* a board for writing on with chalk.

blacken *vt* to make black; * *vi* to grow black or dark; to speak ill of.

blackguard *n* a scoundrel; * *vt* to revile.

blackleg *n* one who works during a strike.

blackmail *n* money extorted by threats, *esp* of disclosure of harmful information; * *vt* to commit the crime of blackmail.

black market *n* illegal buying and selling when restrictions are in force.

blackout *n* total darkness when lighting has failed or been switched off, a loss of consciousness temporarily.

blacksmith *n* a smith who works in iron.

bladder *n* a membrane in animals containing the urine; a container made of flexible material resembling this; a blister.

blade *n* a leaf, the cutting part of a sword, knife etc; the flat part of an oar.

blame *vt* to censure; * *n* censure; fault.

blameless *adj* free from blame.

blanch *vt* to make white; * *vi* to grow white.

blancmange *n* a dessert made from flavoured cornflour and milk.

bland *adj* mild; gentle; uninteresting; insipid.

blandish *vt* to soothe; to flatter.

blandishment *n* flattery.

blank *adj* white; empty; * *n* a void space.

blanket *n* a woollen covering.

blank verse *n* verse without rhyme.

blare *vi* to give forth a loud, harsh sound.

blarney *n* flattery; insincere talk.

blasé *adj* satiated; used up; bored.

blast *n* a gust of wind; the sound of a wind instrument; a violent explosion; harsh criticism; * *vt* to blight.

blatant *adj* noisy and loud; glaringly obvious.

blaze *n* a flame; a fire; brilliance; * *vi* to flame; * *vt* to noise abroad.

bleach *vt* to make white.

bleak *adj* dreary; exposed.

bleat *vi* to cry as a sheep; * *n* the cry of a sheep.

bleed *vi* to emit or lose blood; to emit some fluid; * *vt* to take blood from; to remove a fluid from (*eg* bleeding a radiator).

bleeding *n* a flow of blood; the operation of letting blood; the drawing of sap from a tree.

blemish *vt* to mar; to tarnish; it a stain; dishonour.

blend *vt* to mix together; * *n* a mixture.

bless *vt* to make happy; to invoke a blessing.

blessed *adj* happy; holy.

blessing *n* a benediction; a prayer of thanks; good wishes.

blight *n* that which withers up or destroys wholesale; mildew; * *vt* to wither up; to blast; to cause failure.

blind *adj* without the sense of sight; unable to appreciate something; having no outlet; * *n* a screen; a pretext; * *vt* to make blind.

blindfold *adj* having the eyes covered.

blindly *adv* heedlessly.

blink *vi* to wink; to twinkle; * *vt* to shut the eyes upon.

blinker *n* a flap to prevent a horse from seeing sideways.

bliss *n* perfect happiness.

blister *n* a watery bubble on the skin; a similar swelling on any surface; * *vt* to raise a blister; to castigate vigorously.

blithe *adj* joyful.

blizzard *n* a violent snowstorm.

bloated *adj* inflated.

blob *n* a small roundish lump of matter; a drop of liquid; a spot of colour.

block *n* a heavy piece of wood; a lump of solid matter; a piece of wood in which a pulley is placed; buildings in a group; an obstacle; * *vt* to shut up; to obstruct.

blockade *n* a close siege by troops or ships; * *vt* to besiege closely.

blond, **blonde** *adj* having fair hair; of a fair complexion.

blood *n* the oxygenating fluid, *usu* red, which circulates in the body of animals; kindred; * *adj* pertaining to blood.

bloodshot *adj* inflamed.

bloodthirsty *adj* eager for bloodshed.

blood vessel *n* an artery or a vein.

bloody *adj* stained with blood; cruel.

bloom *n* a blossom; a flower; state of healthy youthfulness; * *vi* to blossom.

blossom *n* the flower of a plant; * *vi* to bloom.

blot *vt* to spot; to stain; to dry; * *n* a spot or stain; a disgrace.

blotch *n* a spot or discoloured patch.

blotting paper *n* absorbent paper to dry up ink.

blouse *n* a woman's loose, *usu* lightweight, upper garment, resembling a shirt; the upper garment worn of part of a soldier or airperson's battledress.

blow *vi* to make a current of air; to pant; to cause to fly apart or be removed by an explosion; * *vt* to impel by wind; (*with* up) to inflate; to explode; * *n* a blast; a heavy punch; a stroke; a misfortune.

blowpipe *n* a tube for heating flame by blowing air through it; a tube for blowing poison darts; the tube used in glass blowing.

blubber *n* the fat of whales;(*sl*) excessive fat; * *vi* to weep noisily.

bludgeon *n* a short club.

blue *n* the colour of the sky; one of the seven primary colours; a university athletic distinction; * *adj* of a blue colour; sky-coloured; depressed; * *vt* to dye a blue colour.

blueprint *n* a photographic print, blue upon white; a plan used as a basis of future work.

bluff *adj* hearty; blunt; * *n* a steep projecting bank; * *vt*, *vi* to persuade or deceive by a show of boldness or strength.

blunder *vi* to err stupidly; * *n* a mistake; an error.

blunt *adj* not sharp; unceremonious; rude; straightforward; * *vt* to make blunt or dull.

blur *n* a stain; a blot; a hazy impression; * *vt* to stain; to obscure.

blurt *vt* to utter suddenly or unadvisedly.

blush *vi* to redden in the face; * *n* a red colour in the face caused by shame, embarrassment, etc

bluster *vi* to roar like wind; to swagger; to boast and bully; * *n* swaggering.

boa *n* a constrictor snake of the family *Boidae*; a feathery or fur scarf.

boar *n* an uncastrated male pig; (in full wild boar) the wild pig *Sus scrofa* from which domesticated pigs were bred.

board *n* a strip of timber, *usu* long and narrow; a table; a thin slab of wood or similar *usu* with covering used for some purpose, *eg* a chessboard; food supplied regularly for payment; persons seated round a table; a council; a group of people in charge of a company; the deck of a ship; * *vt* to cover with boards; to supply with food; to enter a train, bus etc.

boarder *n* one who receives food and lodging at a stated charge.

boarding house *n* a house where board and lodging are provided for payment.

boast *vi* to brag; * *vt* to magnify; * *n* a bragging utterance.

boat *n* a small vessel, propelled by oars, sail or an engine; (in general use) a ship of any size; a boat shaped jug (as sauce boat).

boatswain, bo'sun, bosun, bo's'n *n* a petty or warrant officer on board ship.

bob *n* something that hangs or plays loosely; a short jerking motion; a woman's short haircut; * *vt* to move with a short jerking motion; * *vi* to play to and fro or up and down; to curtsey.

bobbin *n* a winding pin; a reel.

bode *vt* to portend.

bodice *n* the upper part of a dress; an inner vest; a corset.

body *n* the whole frame of a person or animal; the trunk or main part of an animal or human being or a thing; a material object; a person; a dead body; a group of people; size of type.

bodyguard *n* one appointed to guard the safety of another.

bog *n* a marsh, (*sl*) a toilet.

bogus *adj* sham.

boil *vi* (of a liquid) to bubble from the action of heat; to seethe; * *vt* to heat to a boiling state; * *n* a sore pus-filled swelling caused by the infection of a hair follicle.

boisterous *adj* stormy; noisy; loud and high-spirited.

bold *adj* daring; * ~ness *n* courage.

bolster *n* a long thick pillow; * *vt* to hold up; to give support to a person.

bolt *n* an arrow; a thunderbolt; a sliding bar and socket used to fasten a door; * *vi* to leave suddenly; * *vt* to fasten; to swallow hastily.

bomb *n* an explosive shell.

bombard *vt* to attack with continual fire and bombs; to attack with words and questions.

bombast *n* high-sounding words.

bombastic *adj* inflated; turgid; pompous.

bona fide *adv, adj* in good faith; genuine.

bond *n* that which binds; obligation; a legal deed; (*pl*) chains; a place where dutiable goods are stored; * *vt* to grant a bond in security for money; to store till duty is paid.

bondage *n* slavery.

bonded *adj* liable to pay duty.

bone *n* the hard part of the skeleton; * *vt* to take out bones from.

bonfire *n* a large open-air fire.

bonk *vt* hit resoundingly; * *vi* bang; * *vt, vi* (*vulg*) to have sexual intercourse; * *n* an instance or act of bonking.

bonnet *n* a headdress.

bonny *adj* beautiful.

bonus *n* a premium; extra gift to shareholders; an addition to a salary.

book *n* a written or printed work consisting of sheets of paper bound together; * *vt* to reserve beforehand; to note a person's particulars for a minor offence.

booking office *n* an office where people buy tickets in advance.

book-keeper *n* one who keeps accounts.

bookmaker *n* a person who takes bets on events and pays out winnings.

bookworm *n* one who pores over books.

boom *n* a long pole to extend the bottom of a sail; a chain barrier across a river or harbour; a hollow roar; a period of prosperity in commerce; in film studies, a long pole with a microphone at the end; * *vi* to roar; to make a loud, deep noise; to boost; to prosper.

boomerang *n* an Australian Aboriginal missile which when thrown returns to the thrower; * *vi* to return in such a fashion; (of a plan) to backfire.

boon *n* a favour; something helpful.

boor *n* a rustic; a rude, unhelpful person.

boot *n* a covering for the foot.

booth *n* a temporary shed; a stall; a cubicle for voting or for a telephone.

booty *n* spoil; plunder.

border *n* the outer edge of anything; the boundary line between two countries; * *vi* to approach near; * *vt* to surround with a border.

bore *vt* to make a hole in; to pester; to weary by being dull, uninteresting or repetitious; past case of bear; * *n* the hole made by boring; the diameter of a tube; a tiresome person; a great tidal wave.

born *pp* of bear to bring forth.

borne *pp* of bear to carry.

borrow *vt* to ask or receive as a loan.

bosom *n* the breast; the seat of the affections; * *adj* beloved.

boss *n* a knob; a master; a manager; * *vt* to be domineering; to be or act as a boss.

botany *n* the study of the science of plants.

botch *vt* to perform clumsily.

both *adj*, *pron* the two; * *conj* as well.

bother *vi* to annoy; * *vi* to trouble oneself; * *n* a trouble.

bothersome *adj* causing trouble.

bottle *n* a narrow-mouthed vessel of glass or plastic; the contents of a bottle.

bottom *n* the lowest part; the ground under water; foundation; the buttocks; * *vt* to found or build upon.

bough *n* a branch of a tree, *esp* a main one.

boulder *n* a large, generally smooth, rock.

bounce *vi* to spring or rush out suddenly; to rebound; to boast; * *n* springiness; a boast.

bound *n* a boundary; a leap; * *vt* to limit; * *vi* to leap; * *adj* obliged; sure; ready; destined.

boundary *n* a bounding line; a border.

bounden *adj* obligatory.

boundless *adj* unlimited.

bounteous *adj* generous; liberal.

bountiful *adj* bounteous; ample.

bounty *n* liberality; a premium to encourage trade; a reward.

bouquet *n* a bunch of flowers; a perfume from wine.

bourgeois *n* a middle-class citizen; * *adj* humdrum; selfishly materialistic; upholding the interests of the capitalist class.

bourgeoisie *n* the capitalist class; the middle class.

bout *n* a contest; a spell.

bovine *adj* of or relating to cattle; dull, stupid.

bovine spongiform encephalopathy *n* (BSE) a brain disease of cattle characterised by the progressive degeneration of brain tissue, leaving holes so that the result resembles a sponge, the disease agent thought to be a corrupted protein.

bow *vt* to bend; * *vi* to make a reverence; * *n* a bending of the head or body as an act of respect or greeting; the curved forepart of a ship; * *n* a weapon to shoot arrows; a rainbow; a stick for playing on violin strings; a slipknot.

bowed *adj* bent like a bow.

bowels *npl* the lower intestines; in the depths.

bowl *n* a ball of wood, or hard rubber; (*pl*) the game played with such bowls; a large roundish dish; * *vi* to play with bowls; to deliver a ball at cricket.

bowler *n* one who plays bowls; to deliver a ball at cricket; a stiff felt hat.

box *n* a case or receptacle for holding anything; a seat in a theatre; a blow; a tree or shrub; * *vt* to put in a box; to strike; * *vi* to fight with the fists.

boxer *n* a pugilist, a breed of dog.

boy *n* a male child.

boycott *vt* to refuse dealings with.

brace *n* a support; a bandage; a couple; a boring tool; (*pl*) suspenders; * *vt* to tighten; to straighten up; to strengthen.

bracelet *n* an ornament for the wrist.

bracing *adj* invigorating.

bracken *n* a species of fern.

bracket *n* a support for something fixed to a wall; a mark [] or () in writing or printing to enclose words; * *vt* to place within or connect by brackets; to group.

brackish *adj* salt; saltish.

brag *vi* to talk big; * *n* a boast.

braggart *adj* boastful; * *n* a boaster.

braid *vt* to weave together strands of hair, thread, etc; * *n* a plaited band.

brain *n* the centre of thought and sensation; the soft matter within the skull.

braise *vt* to cook in a covered pan.

brake *n* a device on a wheel to reduce speed or to stop motion; a type of wagon.

bran *n* the husks of ground corn.

branch *n* the offshoot of a tree; the offshoot of anything, as of a river, family; * *vi* to spread in branches; (*with* out) to broaden or increase one's activities.

brand *n* a burning piece of wood; a mark made with a hot iron; a trademark; a particular make (of goods); * *vt* to mark with a hot iron; to denounce.

brandish *vt* to shake; wave.

brandy *n* a spirit distilled from wine or fermented fruit juice.

brass *n* a yellow alloy of copper and zinc; brass section of an orchestra or band; impudence.

brassière *n* a woman's undergarment supporting the breasts; *abbrev* bra.

brat *n* an ill-behaved child.

bravado *n* bluster.

brave *adj* daring; valiant; * *vt* to defy.

brawl *vi* to quarrel noisily; * *n* uproar.

brawn *n* the flesh of a boar; muscle; strength.

bray *vi* to make a loud harsh sound, as an ass; * *n* the cry of an ass.

brazen *adj* made of brass; impudent.

brazier *n* a worker in brass; a portable fire.

breach *n* the act of breaking; quarrel; * *vt* to make a gap in.

bread *n* baked dough made from flour, *usu* leavened with yeast and moistened; (also daily ~) income; (*sl*) money; * *vt* cover with breadcrumbs for cooking.

breadth *n* width.

break *vt* to sever by fracture; to rend; to tame; to interrupt; to dissolve any union; to tell with discretion; * *vi* to come to pieces; to burst forth; * *n* an opening; a breach; a pause.

breakdown *n* a failure or stoppage due to mechanical malfunction; a nervous or mental collapse; an analysing and classifying of an entity into its separate parts.

breaker *n* a large, crested wave.

breakfast *n* the first meal in the day.

breakwater *n* a mole or bar to break the force of the waves.

breast *n* either of the mammary glands on a woman's chest; the corresponding part of a man's body; the chest; (*fig*) the affections; * *vt* to face.

breastbone *n* the bone of the breast.

breath *n* the air drawn into and expelled from the lungs; life; pause; a gentle breeze.

breathe *vt, vi* to take breath; to live; to utter.

breathing *n* respiration.

breathless *adj* out of breath.

bred *pp* of breed.

breech *n* the hinder part (*esp* of a gun); (*pl* breeches) garment for men worn on the lower parts of the body.

breed *vt, vi* to bring forth; to educate; to rear; * *n* offspring; kind.

breeding *n* the raising of a breed; good manners.

breeze *n* a light wind.

brethren *npl* of brother.

breve *n* a note in music.

brevity *n* shortness.

brew *vt* to prepare from malt; to concoct; to scheme; * *vi* to make beer; to infuse tea; * *n* the mixture formed by brewing.

brewery *n* the place where beer is brewed.

bribe *n* a to act *esp* illegally or dishonestly by making some payment or granting some favour in order to gain advantage; * *vt* to gain over by bribes.

bric-à-brac *n* old curios.

brick *n* a rectangular block of

baked clay or other material used in building.

bricklayer *n* one who builds with bricks.

bride *n* a woman about to be or newly married.

bridegroom *n* a man about to be or newly married.

bridesmaid *n* a woman who attends on a bride during a wedding.

bridge *n* a roadway across a river; a structure to carry people, vehicles, railways across; something that serves to fill a gap or helps communication; a platform on a ship from which the captain issues commands; a card game like whist; * *vt* to build a bridge over.

bridle *n* the headgear used to control a horse; a restraint.

brief *adj* short; concise; * *n* a document instructing a barrister to appear as an advocate in court; instructions for completing some task; (*pl*) underpants without legs; * *vt* to instruct a barrister; instructions for the completion of a task.

brigade *n* a British infantry unit containing several brigades and forming part of a division; an organised or uniformed band of workers *eg* fire brigade

brigadier *n* the officer who commands a brigade, more senior than a colonel and immediately subordinate to a major general; a staff officer of the same rank.

bright *adj* emitting or reflecting much light; lively; clever.

brilliant *adj* sparkling; * *n* a diamond.

brim *n* the rim of anything.

brine *n* salt water.

bring *vt* to lead; to fetch; to produce; to cause to happen.

brink *n* the edge; the margin; the moment before a happening, often a disaster.

brisk *adj* lively.

brisket *n* the breast of an animal.

bristle *n* a stiff hair; * *vt, vi* to stand on end; to show anger.

brittle *adj* apt to break.

broach *n* a roasting spit; * *vt* to pierce, as with a spit; to tap; to open up.

broad *adj* wide.

broaden *vi* to grow broad; * *vt* to make broad.

broadside *n* a discharge of all the guns on one side of a ship; a verbal onslaught.

brocade *n* a silk stuff with raised pattern.

brochure *n* a pamphlet.

brogue *n* a strong shoe formerly of raw hide; a marked accent, *esp* Irish.

broken *adj* crushed; ruined.

broker *n* an agent who buys and sells for others.

bromide *n* an compound of bromine and another group; potassium bromide used as a sedative.

bronchus *n* (*pl* **bronchi**) either of the tubes branching from the windpipe; **bronchia** *npl* any of their ramifications, the air passages of the lungs.

bronchitis *n* inflammation of the mucous membrane in the bronchial tubes.

bronze *n* an alloy of copper and tin; its colour.

brooch *n* an ornament to pin on a dress.

brood *vi* (of birds) to sit on eggs; to ponder anxiously; * *n* offspring.

brook *n* a small stream; * *vt* to bear.

broom *n* a shrub with yellow flowers; a brush.

broth *n* a thin soup of meat or fish stock.

brother *n* a fellow son of the same parents; a male fellow member of a trade union; a working or lay member of a male religious order.

brotherhood *n* the relationship of a brother; an association.

brow *n* the ridge over the eye; the forehead; the edge of a cliff.

browbeat *vt* to bully.

brown *adj* dusky; tanned; * *n* a colour resulting from the mixture of red, black, and yellow.

brownie *n* a junior Guide.

browse *vt* to feed upon; to read through casually.

bruise *vt* to crush; to injure and cause discolouration of the skin without drawing blood; * *n* a skin discolouration from a blow.

brunette *n* a woman with a dark complexion and dark hair; * *adj* having such hair.

brunt *n* the chief impact, burden or effect of one entity, event or force upon another.

brush *n* an implement with bristles for cleaning by rubbing or sweeping or for painting; a skirmish; a thicket; the tail of a fox; * *vt, vi* to sweep; to touch lightly.

brushwood *n* small trees and shrubs growing together.

brusque *adj* abrupt; rude.

brutal *adj* cruel.

brute *adj* purely physical; sheer, as in brute force; * *n* a beast; a brutal person.

bubble *n* a fluid film enclosing air; an air filled cavity in a solidified liquid such as amber; a transparent domed cavity; * *vi* to rise in bubbles.

buccaneer *n* a pirate.

buck *n* the male of various animals *esp* deer, hares and rabbits; * *vi* to jump violently.

bucket *n* a pail.

buckle *n* a strap or belt fastener; * *vt* to fasten; to bend.

buckshot *n* coarse lead shot.

bud *n* a young shoot or flower; * *vi* to put forth buds.

budding *n* a method of grafting buds; * *adj* promising.

budge *vt* to move; to stir.

budget *n* a financial statement; an estimate for expenditure; * *vt, vi* to put on a budget; to plan; to make a budget.

buff *n* a yellow colour; the bare skin; * *adj* light yellow; * *vt* to clean or shine by rubbing.

buffer *n* anything for deadening the shock of collisions.

buffet *n* a sideboard; a refreshment bar; a meal where people serve themselves; a blow; a slap; * *vt* to box; to contend against.

buffoon *n* a clown; one who plays the fool to amuse; a fool.

bugle *n* a hunting horn; a kind of trumpet.

build *vt* to construct; to establish; * *vi* to form a structure; * *n* make; form.

building *n* an edifice; the construction of such structures.

building society *n* a financial organisation, owned by its members, where deposits of money are paid interest and loans are made especially for house buying and mortgages.

bulb *n* a round root; a light bulb; any similarly-shaped object.

bulbous *adj* swelling out.

bulge *n* a swelling; a rounded projection; * *vt* to swell out.

bulk *n* size; the main mass; cargo.

bulky *adj* large and awkwardly shaped.

bull *n* the male of cattle, elephant and whale; an edict of the pope; an expression containing ludicrous inconsistency.

bullet *n* a metal missile shot from firearm.

bulletin *n* an official news report; a regular list of information published by an organisation.

bullion *n* precious metal such as gold, refined into ingots.

bully *n* one who uses strength or power to coerce by fear; * *vt* to insult and threaten.

bulwark *n* a rampart; a person or thing acting as a strong buffer.

bump *n* a heavy blow, or the noise of it; a lump produced by a blow; * *vt* to crash or knock against.

bumper *n* a brimful glass; a protective metal bar fixed at the front and rear of a vehicle to absorb shock.

bumptious *adj* self-assertive.

bun *n* a small cake; a round coil of hair worn at the nape of the neck.

bunch *n* a cluster.

bundle *n* a package; * *vt, vi* to tie in a bundle; to hurry off.

bungalow *n* a one-storeyed house.

bungle *vi* to botch; * *n* a clumsy performance.

bunion *n* a lump on the foot *esp* on the side at the base of the big toe.

bunk *n* a sleeping berth; a narrow bed.

bunker *n* a large container for storing fuel; a sandpit hazard on a golf course; an underground shelter.

bunting *n* stuff of which flags are made; flags.

buoy *n* a floating navigation mark; * *vt* to keep afloat; (*with* up) to give support or encouragement to.

buoyancy *n* capacity for floating; cheerfulness; resilience.

buoyant *adj* floating; light; cheerful.

bur, burr *n* a prickly clinging fruit, seed case or flower head.

burden *n* a load; something hard or wearisome to bear; a chorus; * *vt* to load; to oppress.

bureau *n* (*pl* bureaux) a writing table; a chest of drawers; a government office.

bureaucracy *n* centralised administration of government; the officials in such an administration, *esp* regarded as oppressive, petty and inflexible; unnecessary officialdom.

burgeon *vt*, *vi* to flourish; to grow rapidly and profusely.

burglar *n* one who commits burglary.

burglary *n* the act of entering a house with the intention of committing robbery, rape, actual or grievous bodily harm, or damage.

burial *n* the act of burying; internment.

burlesque *adj* comic; * *n* a caricature; a satirical play caricaturing some subject.

burly *adj* stout; portly; of a strong build.

burn *vt*, *vi* to consume with fire; to be on fire; to rage fiercely; * *n* a hurt caused by fire; a rivulet.

burnish *vt* to polish; * *n* polish.

burrow *n* a hole in the earth made by rabbits, etc; * *vi* to excavate.

bursar *n* a treasurer; a student who holds a bursary.

bursary *n* a scholarship.

burst *vi* to fly or break open; to rush forth; * *vt* to break by force.

bury *vt* to put into a grave; to cover; to conceal.

bus *n* (*pl* buses) a large passenger vehicle, *esp* one for carrying the public on a fixed route; a defined set of conductors for carrying data and control signals within a computer.

bush *n* a shrub; a thicket.

business *n* occupation; concern.

busk *vi* to entertain (*esp* music) for voluntary payment on the street.

bust *n* the bosom; the figure from head to chest in sculpture.

bustle *vi* to hustle; * *n* hurry.

busy *adj* occupied; * *vt* to employ.

busybody *n* a meddler.

but *conj*, *prep*, *adv* yet, except, only.

butcher *n* one who kills or sells animals for food; * *vt* to slaughter.

butler *n* the principle servant of a household in charge of a wine cellar, pantry etc.

butt *n* the end of a thing; a mark to be shot at; an object of ridicule; a cask of wine; * *vt* to strike with the head.

butter *n* the substance obtained from cream by churning; * *vt* to spread with butter; to flatter grossly.

buttercup *n* a wild yellow cup-shaped flower of the genus *Ranunculus*.

butterfly *n* (*pl* ~flies) any winged insect of the order *Lepidoptera*, often brightly coloured; a showy, insubstantial person; a swimming stroke.

button *n* a knob or disc for fastening; a badge; * *vt* to fasten with buttons.

buttress *n* a construction to support and strengthen a wall; a prop; * *vt* to support by a prop.

buxom *adj* jolly; large and shapely; busty.

buy *vt* to purchase.

buzz *vi* to hum; * *n* a humming noise.

by *prep*, *adv* used to denote the instrument, agent, or manner; at the rate of; not later than.

bye *interj* shortening of goodbye;

* *n* in certain games, reaching the second round without playing an opponent in the first; a ball scoring a run in cricket without being hit by a batsman.

bylaw *n* a local law.

bypass *n* a road that skirts a town; a rerouting, especially of blood flow into the heart; * *vt* to go round so as to avoid.

bystander *n* a spectator.

byway *n* a side road.

byword *n* a common saying; a proverb.

C

cabbage *n* any of several varieties of *Brassica oleracea* with green leaves forming a round head.

cabin *n* a hut; a room in a ship; * *vt* to confine.

cabinet *n* a closet; a showcase; the ministers of state.

cable *n* a thick rope of wire or hemp; a thick conducting wire; * *vt* to send by cable.

cadence *n* a fall of the voice at the end of a sentence.

cadet *n* a younger brother; a military pupil.

cadge *vt*, *vi* to go about begging.

cadmium *n* a bluish white toxic metal.

café *n* a small restaurant; a coffee bar.

cage *n* a wire frame, forming an enclosure *esp* to confine birds or beasts.

cairn *n* a heap of stones as landmark or memorial.

cajole *vt* to wheedle; to persuade by smooth words.

cake *n* baked dough in various forms; fancy bread; a flat compact mass.

calamity *n* misfortune; disaster.

calculate *vt* to count; to think out; to estimate; to scheme.

calculus *n* (maths) a particular calculational technique; the branch of mathematics concerned with rates of change (differential calculus) and the calculation of the area enclosed by curves (integral calculus).

calendar *n* a system of classifying dates into months, days and seasons; an almanac; a list of coming events.

calf *n* the young of the cow; the fleshy lower part of the leg.

calibre *n* the diameter of the bore of a gun; quality.

call *vt* to name; to summon; * *vi* to utter a loud sound; to make a short visit; * *n* a summons; a short visit; a bird's note; a need.

calligraphy *n* the art of writing.

calling *n* a vocation.

callipers *n*, *npl* compasses for measuring the diameter of convex bodies, or for internal dimensions; a metal support strapped to the leg for support.

callous *adj* hardened; unfeeling.

calm *adj* still; quiet; windless; * *n* tranquillity; * *vt* to soothe; to pacify.

calorie *n* a unit of heat, the heat required to raise one gram of water by on degree Kelvin; a unit measuring the energy of food (in full **kilocalorie**).

calve *vi* to give birth to a calf.

calypso *n* a West Indian story in song to a syncopated rhythm.

camber *n* the slight curve upward towards the centre of a road surface from the edges.

camera *n* an apparatus for taking photographs or cinema and television pictures; (law, **in ~**) in a judge's private room, hence in secret; closed.

camp *n* the ground on which tents are pitched; a (collection of) tent(s); those who support a cause or party.

campaign *n* an organised course of action for some purpose, *esp* to arouse public interest *eg* an election campaign; the operations of an army in war.

campus *n* the grounds (and buildings) of a university.

can *n* a metal vessel; a tin; * *vi* (*past* **could**) to be able.

canal *n* an artificial watercourse

for boats; a duct or channel in the body.

canary *n* any of various small finches of the genus *Serinus*, *esp* *S canaria*; a songbird with yellow plumage, native to the Canary islands.

cancel *vt* to strike out; to delete; to annul; to undo or call off.

cancer *n* a malignant tumour; an evil influence spreading uncontrollably.

candid *adj* frank; outspoken; fair and unprejudiced.

candidate *n* an applicant for a post or office; someone worthy to he chosen; someone taking an examination.

candle *n* a stick of wax with a wick for lighting.

candour *n* frankness.

cane *n* a walking stick; a thin stick for supporting plants; * *vt* to beat with a cane.

canine *adj* pertaining to dogs.

canine tooth *n* the pointed tooth between the incisors and the premolars.

canister *n* a small box; an explosive shell.

cannabis *n* a hemp plant of the genus *Cannabis*, *esp* Indian hemp; the narcotic found in the leaves and pollen of cannabis plants.

cannibal *n* an individual which eats members of its own species; * *adj* relating to cannibalism.

cannon *n* a large gun mounted on a carriage; an impact and rebound; * *vt* to collide with.

canoe *n* a skiff driven by paddles.

canon *n* a decree; a law; a rule or criterion; a list of an author's works accepted as genuine; a cathedral cleric.

canonise *vt* (in the Christian church) formally to recognise that a person belongs to the canon (list) of saints.

canopy *n* a covering above an object such as a throne.

cantankerous *adj* cross.

cantata *n* a short oratorio.

canteen *n* a restaurant within or attached to a place of work,

school etc; the box holding a set of cutlery; a water flask.

canter *n* a moderate gallop; * *vi* to move at a moderate gallop.

cantilever *n* a large supporting bracket; a principle applied in bridge making.

canto *n* a division of a poem.

canvas *n* a coarse cloth; sails of ships; a painting.

canvass *vt* to solicit the votes of in elections.

canyon, **cañon** *n* a long, narrow mountain gorge.

cap *n* a covering for the head; a top piece; * *vt* to put a cap on; to excel.

capable *adj* efficient; able.

capacity *n* volume; ability.

capacitor *n* an electrical component used to store charge.

cape *n* a headland; a sleeveless coat.

caper *vi* to skip; * *n* a leap; a prank.

capillary *adj* of or like a hair; (of a tube) of hairlike internal dimension; * *n* (*pl* **capillaries**) a small blood vessel.

capital *adj* chief; (of a crime) punishable by death; * *n* the top of a column; the chief city; money and assets; accumulated wealth *esp* for reinvestment.

capitalist *n* one who invests capital; an advocate of capitalism.

capitalise *vt* to convert into capital.

capitulate *vi* to surrender, *esp* on stated conditions.

capricious *adj* fickle; unreliable.

capsize *vt* to upset.

capsule *n* a gelatin case containing a drug to be swallowed; a covering; a detachable compartment of a spacecraft.

captain *n* a commander, a leader; the commander of a ship; the commander of a company; the pilot of a civil aircraft.

caption *n* a the explanatory text under an illustration; a subtitle.

captivate *vt* to fascinate.

captive *n* a prisoner.

capture *n* arrest; * *vt* to seize.

car *n* a motor vehicle; a railway carriage of a specified type.

carafe *n* a glass water bottle.

carat *n* a unit of weight for

precious stones equal to 200 milligrams; a measure of purity for gold, the purest being designated 24-carat in the UK.

caravan *n* a company travelling together; a house on wheels.

carbohydrate *n* any of a large number of energy producing compounds of carbon, hydrogen and oxygen *eg* sugar, starch.

carbolic *n* (in full carbolic acid) phenol *esp* when used as a disinfectant.

carbon *n* a non-metallic element occurring naturally as diamond, graphite and charcoal, and in all organic compounds.

carburettor *n* the device in an internal combustion engine making and controlling the mixture of air and fuel.

carcass *adj* the body of a dead animal.

card *n* a piece of pasteboard for various purposes; * *vt* to comb wool or other fibres before spinning.

cardamom *n* an aromatic SE Asian plant *Elettaria cardamomum*; its seed pods used as a spice.

cardboard *n* a thick card.

cardiac *adj* pertaining to the heart.

cardigan *n* a knitted garment with front fastenings.

cardinal *adj* chief; * *n* a Roman Catholic dignitary.

care *n* solicitude; attention; * *vi* to be anxious; to have regard; to look after; to provide for.

career *n* a race; a profession; * *vi* to proceed rapidly and without control.

careful *adj* anxious; cautious.

careless *adj* heedless; thoughtless.

caress *vt* to fondle; * *n* an embrace.

cargo *n* freight.

caricature *n* a ludicrous portrait; * *vt* to burlesque; to parody.

caries *n* decay and crumbling of a tooth or bone.

carnage *n* slaughter.

carnal *adj* sensual; sexual; of the body or flesh; profane rather than spiritual.

carnation *n* a rose-pink colour; a cultivated variety of clove pink with variously coloured flowers; the flowers.

carnival *n* a gala day; public merry-making; a travelling funfair.

carnivorous *adj* feeding on flesh.

carol *n* a song of joy, especially one sung at Christmas.

carouse *vi* to drink freely.

carp *vi* to find fault; * *n* any freshwater fish of the family *Cyprinidae*, *esp Cyprinus carpio*.

carpenter *n* one who works wood.

carpet *n* a woven cover for floors.

carriage *n* a vehicle; the price of carrying; behaviour; bearing.

carrion *n* putrid flesh.

carrot *n* a reddish vegetable, *Daucus Carota*, with a tapering root; (*sl*) something offered as a reward.

carry *vt* to bear; to convey; to gain; to behave.

cart *n* a vehicle with two wheels for carrying goods.

carte blanche *n* (*pl* cartes blanches) a blank paper; unconditional terms.

cartel *n* an informal, unlawful, association of producers conspiring to maintain prices or control production.

cartilage *n* gristle.

cartography *n* science of making maps.

carton *n* a cardboard box.

cartoon *n* a humorous or satirical topical sketch; a comic strip often animated.

cartridge *n* a case containing the charge in a bullet.

carve *vt* to cut; to engrave.

cascade *n* a waterfall.

case *n* a box; a covering; an event; a suit in court; an ailment or disease being medically treated; the patient undergoing treatment; (grammar) form in the inflection of nouns; * *vt* to put in a case.

cash *n* money; * *vt* to turn into money.

cashier *n* one who has charge of money; * *vt* to dismiss.

cashmere *n* fabric woven from the hair of Kashmir goats.

casino *n* a gaming hall.

cask *n* a barrel.

casket *n* a small often decorated case for precious objects; a small case for holding cremated ashes.

casserole *n* a covered dish for cooking; the food stewed in a casserole.

cassock *n* a garment worn by clerics and choristers.

cast *vt* to throw; to throw off, to let fall; to condemn; to model; * *n* a throw; a squint; a mould; a company of actors.

castaway *n* a shipwrecked person; thrown away.

castigate *vt* to reprimand severely; to chastise.

casting *n* that which is cast in a mould; the allotting of actors to their roles.

castle *n* a fortress; an imposing mansion.

castling *n* the move in chess of the king by two squares along its rank, with the nearer rook placed on the square over which the king passed.

castor *n* a small cruet; a small wheel.

castor oil *n* a medicinal oil used as a purgative.

castrate *vt* to geld.

casual *adj* accidental; occasional; informal; careless.

casualty *n* an accident; a person injured or killed in an accident or a war.

cat *n* a domesticated animal *Felis catus.*

cataclysm *n* a deluge; an upheaval.

catacomb *n* an underground vault.

catalogue *n* a list; a register.

catapult *n* a sling.

cataract *n* a waterfall; a disease of the eye.

catarrh *n* inflammation of the mucus membrane in the nose; the resultant discharge.

catastrophe *n* disaster; the denouement of a drama.

catch *vt* to lay hold on; to grasp; to entangle; to receive by contagion; to get; * *n* a grasping; a type of fastening; a hidden obstacle.

catechism *n* a manual of instruction by questions and answers, especially of religious tenets.

categorical *adj* unconditional; absolute.

category *n* a class, order, division or type.

cater *vi* to provide provisions, etc.

cathedral *n* the principal church in a diocese.

cathode *n* the negatively-charged terminal of an electrical device (*opp* anode).

catholic *adj* universal; general; * *n* a member of the universal Christian Church.

cation *n* a positively charged ion (*opp* anion).

cattle *npl* bovine livestock.

caucus *n* a party organisation or clique.

causal *adj* implying cause.

cause *n* that which produces an effect; origin; an enterprise; * *vt* to bring about.

causeway *n* a paved way.

caustic *adj* burning; biting; sarcastic.

cauterise *vt* to sear or burn, especially in treating a wound.

caution *n* care; pledge; * *vt* to warn.

cautious *adj* wary; careful.

cavalcade *n* a procession of persons on horseback; a company of horsemen.

cavalier *adj* careless; haughty.

cavalry *n* originally mounted troops, now referring to tank regiments.

cave *n* an underground hollow; * *vt, vi* (*with* in) to collapse; to yield.

caveat *n* a warning.

cavern *n* a large cave.

cavity *n* a hollow within a solid body; a hole in a tooth.

cease *vi* to leave off; to stop; * *vt* to put a stop to.

ceaseless *adj* incessant.

cede *vt* to give up.

ceiling *n* the upper inside surface of a room.

celebrate *vt* to commemorate; to accord high praise to.

celebrity *n* fame; a famous person.

celestial *adj* heavenly.

celibacy *n* commitment to

abstention from sexual relations and marriage.

cell *n* a small room; a cave; the microscopic unit of an organism consisting of cytoplasm and a membrane; a vessel containing electrodes and an electrolyte for current generation of electrolysis.

cellar *n* an underground room used for storage *esp* of wine and coal.

cellophane *n* a thin transparent wrapping material made of viscose.

cellular *adj* consisting of cells.

cement *n* mortar; a bond of union; * *vt* to unite closely.

cemetery *n* a burial place.

censor *n* one supporting the removal of objectionable matter from publicly-disseminated media such as broadcasting, books, films; a critic.

censure *n* blame; reproof; * *vt* to judge; to blame.

census *n* an official count of a population, often with various other statistics noted.

centenarian *n* one a hundred years old.

centenary *n* the hundredth anniversary or its commemoration.

centigrade *adj* having a scale of a hundred degrees; (= Celcius).

centimetre *n* a distance of one hundredth of a metre.

central *adj* at the centre; most important; principal.

centralise *vt* to move to the centre; to cause to be under a central jurisdiction.

centre *n* the middle point; a nucleus; * *vt* to collect to a point.

centrifugal *adj* tending to fly from a centre.

centrifugal force *n* the outward force on a body in a rotating frame of reference.

centripetal force *n* the force which causes the inward acceleration of a body moving in an orbit.

century *n* a hundred years.

ceramic *adj* pertaining to pottery.

cereal *adj* pertaining to corn; * *n* a grain plant; a breakfast food from the grains of such a plant.

cerebral *adj* of the brain; intellectual rather than emotional.

ceremony *n* outward rite; pomp; observance.

certain *adj* sure; particular.

certainty *n* definite truth; undoubted fact.

certificate *n* a written testimony.

certify *vt* to declare; to attest.

cessation *n* stoppage.

chafe *vt* to warm by rubbing; to irritate (skin) by rubbing; * *n* rage.

chaff *n* the husk of corn; banter; * *vt* to banter; to make fun of laughingly.

chagrin *n* vexation.

chain *n* a series of links; a measure of length; (*pl*) bondage; * *vt* to confine with chains.

chair *n* a separate seat for one person; an official seat; a professorship.

chalet *n* a Swiss cottage; a ski lodge or (holiday) house modeled on this.

chalice *n* a goblet; a communion cup.

chalk *n* a soft limestone; * *vt* to mark with chalk.

challenge *n* a summons to engage in a contest, fight, sporting challenge etc; a summons to justify or prove something; * *vt* to defy; to call into question.

challenged *adj* (euphemism or jocular) descriptive of some disability, or the absence of some attribute: — vertically ~ of smaller than average stature.

chamber *n* an apartment; a public body.

champ *vt* to chew; to bite.

champion *n* a defender of a cause; a victor; * *vt* to uphold.

championship *n* state of being a champion; a contest held to find a champion.

chance *n* accident; opportunity; luck; * *vi* to happen; * *adj* casual.

chancellor *n* the head of a university or court.

chancery *n* a division of the High Court.

chandelier *n* a branching lamp with many lights that hangs from a ceiling.

change *vt* to alter; to exchange; * *n* variety; small coins.

channel *n* a watercourse; a narrow sea; a communications medium; a band of frequencies used in radio and television transmission, *esp* those used by a particular station; * *vt* to groove; to convey; to guide.

chant *vt*, *vi* to sing; to intone; * *n* a song.

chaos *n* disorder; total confusion.

chapel *n* a place for private worship with its own altar and dedication; a place of worship connected to an otherwise secular organisation.

chaplain *n* an clergyman attached to a chapel.

chapter *n* a division of a book.

char *vt* to burn; * *n* any small trout-like fish of the genus *Salvelinus*.

character *n* a letter or figure; the distinguishing attributes of a person or thing; nature; quality; a part in a play.

characteristic *adj* distinctive.

charcoal *n* charred wood.

charge *vt* to load; to fill; to price; to entrust; to accuse; to command; to attack; * *n* care; cost; attack; order; accusation.

chargeable *adj* imputable.

charger *n* a device for charging a battery; a cavalry horse.

charitable *adj* benevolent; generous in giving; lenient.

charity *n* benevolence; a money-raising fund or institution.

charlatan *n* a quack.

charm *n* a spell; * *vt* to delight.

charming *adj* enchanting.

chart *n* a map; a table of information.

charter *n* a written granting of rights from a legislature; * *vt* to hire.

chase *vt* to pursue *n* pursuit; hunt.

chasm *n* a deep cleft.

chassis *n* the frame of a motor vehicle.

chaste *adj* pure.

chastise *vt* to punish.

chat *vi* to gossip; * *n* talk.

chatter *vi* to talk idly; to jabber; * *n* talk.

chauffeur *n* one employed to drive a car.

chauvinism *n* jingoism; excessive support for a cause, or group etc.

cheap *adj* of a low price; common; inferior.

cheapen *vt* reduce in price; to belittle.

cheapskate *n* a miser.

cheat *vt* to deceive; to swindle; * *n* a trick; a swindler.

check *vt*, *vi* to stop; to curb; to chide; to control; * *n* position in chess; a control.

checkmate *n* the winning move in chess.

cheek *n* the side of the face; impudence.

cheer *n* happiness; good spirits; a shout of joy; * *vt* to brighten; to applaud.

cheese *n* a food made by draining and pressing the curd of milk.

chef *n* a head cook.

chemical *n* a substance obtained from or used in a chemical process.

chemise *n* an undergarment worn by females.

chemist *n* one trained in chemistry; a pharmacy.

chemistry *n* the science of the properties and nature of substances.

chemotherapy *n* medical treat-ment, *esp* of cancer, by the use of chemicals.

cheque *n* an order, to one's bank, for money to be paid to the payee.

chequer *n* a square pattern; (*pl*) draughts.

cherish *vt* to treasure.

cheroot *n* a kind of cigar.

cherry *n* any of several trees of the genus *Prunus* bearing small red fruit; that fruit; a bright red colour.

chess *n* the king of board games.

chest *n* a large box; the breast.

chestnut *n* the tree *Castinus sativa* (also called **sweet chestnut**); its edible nut; its wood; any other tree of the genus *Castanea*; (in full **horse chestnut**) any large ornamental tree of the genus *Aesculus*; its inedible nut; a stale joke; * *adj* reddish-brown.

chew *vt* to masticate.

chic *n* style; * *adj* stylish.

chicanery *n* trickery.

chick *n* the young of birds.

chicken *n* a domestic fowl, *esp* young; the fowl prepared as food; its flesh.

chickenpox *n* an infectious disease with a rash of small blisters.

chicory *n* a plant, *Cichorium intybus*, the root of which when roasted and ground is used as a substitute or with coffee.

chide *vt, vi* to reprove; to scold.

chief *adj* first; leading; * *n* a leader.

child *n* an infant; offspring.

childhood *n* the stage between birth and adolescence.

childlike *adj* innocent.

chill *n* a cold fit; * *adj* cold; * *vt* to discourage.

chime *n* a harmony of bells; (*pl*) a set of bells; * *vi* to accord.

chimney *n* a smoke escape.

chimpanzee *n* either of two apes of central and West Africa *Pan troglodytes* or (in full pygmy chimpanzee) *Pan paniscus*.

chin *n* the front of the lower jaw.

china *n* porcelain.

chink *n* an opening; a crack; * *vt, vi* to jingle as of coins.

chintz *n* calico, patterned and coloured.

chip *n* a fragment; * *vt* to cut into chips.

chiropody *n* the treatment of the feet and their ailments.

chirp *vi* to cheep.

chisel *n* a cutting tool; * *vt* to cut or engrave.

chivalry *n* knighthood; gallantry.

chloride *n* any compound of chlorine.

chlorine *n* a gaseous element used in bleach and disinfectants.

chloroform *n* a volatile liquid anaesthetic.

chlorophyll *n* the green pigment of plants, responsible for light absorbtion in photosynthesis.

chocolate *n* a beverage and sweet from cacao; its colour.

choice *n* option; selection; preference; * *adj* select; precious.

choir *n* a band of singers; the place especially in church where they sit.

choke *vt* to suffocate; * *vi* to be blocked up.

cholera *n* an infectious and deadly disease caused by water contaminated with the bacterium *Vibrio cholerae*.

choose *vt* to prefer; to select.

chop *vt* to cut to pieces.

chopsticks *n* two wooden, ivory or plastic sticks used to eat, originating from Indo-China.

choral *adj* belonging to, sung by or written for a choir.

chord *n* three or more musical notes played together.

chorus *n* a company of singers; musical refrain.

chosen *adj* select.

Christ *n* Jesus of Nazareth, the Christian Messiah.

christen *vt* to baptise; to name.

Christian *n* a professed follower of Christ.

Christmas *n* the festival of Christ's nativity, 25 December.

chrome, chromium *n* a hard metal used in steel alloys and electroplating.

chronic *adj* permanent.

chronicle *n* a diary of events; history; * *vt* to record.

chronology *n* the order and time of *esp* historical events.

chrysalis *n* the grub stage of certain insects.

chubby *adj* plump.

chuck *vt* to tap under the chin; to toss; to pitch; to give up; to throw away.

chuckle *vi* to laugh in the throat; to exult; * *n* a half-suppressed laugh.

chum *n* a close friend.

chunk *n* a short thick piece.

church *n* a building consecrated to the worship of God; a christian group.

churlish *adj* surly; sullen.

churn *n* a vessel in which milk is agitated to make butter; a milk container.

chute *n* a sloping channel or slide for water, rubbish, logs etc

cider *n* fermented apple juice.

cigar *n* a roll of tobacco leaf for smoking.

cigarette *n* a paper cylinder of shredded tobacco.

cinder *n* the residue of coal or wood which is no longer burning.

cinema *n* a building where films are shown.

cinnamon *n* any tree of the genus *Cinnamomum*, *esp C zeylanicum*, yielding an aromatic spice; that spice; a yellow-brown colour.

cipher, cypher *n* the figure 0; any numeral; a person or thing of no importance; a secret writing; the key to this.

circle *n* a round figure; a group; its bounding line; a ring; a class; * *vt, vi* to move round; to enclose.

circuit *n* area; extent; journey of judges to hold courts; a detour; the path of an electric current.

circuitous *adj* roundabout.

circular *adj* round; * *n* a notice.

circulate *vi* to move in a circle; to pass from person to person or place to place; * *vt* to spread.

circulation *n* circulating; the area centred and the number sold, of a newspaper etc; the flow of blood through the arteries and the veins; currency.

circumcise *vt* to cut off the foreskin.

circumference *n* the bounding line of a circle; the distance round.

circumflex *n* an accent (^) on vowels marking contraction, etc.

circumlocution *n* a roundabout mode of speaking.

circumnavigate *vt* to sail round.

circumscribe *vt* to enclose; to limit.

circumspect *adj* wary.

circumstantial *adj* indirect; incidental.

circumvent *vt* to avoid by going round; to evade; to outwit.

circus *n* (*pl* **circuses**) an enclosed circular area or place for performances; a travelling show of entertainers and animals.

cirro- *prefix* denoting cloud types formed at high altitudes (6,100m / 20,000ft).

cirrocumulus *n* cloud forming a broken layer of thin fleecy clouds at high altitude.

cirrostratus *n* cloud forming a thin fairly uniform layer at high altitude.

cirrus *n* (*pl* **cirri**) a thin, trailing high-altitude cloud.

cistern *n* a water tank.

citation *n* quotation; summons.

cite *vt* to summon; to quote.

citizen *n* a member of a state, either native or naturalised; an inhabitant of a city.

citrus *n* any tree of the genus *citrus*, *eg* orange, lemon, etc; the fruit.

city *n* a large town, strictly one containing either a cathedral or university.

civet *n* (in full **civet cat**) a slender catlike animal of the family *Viveridae*, *esp V civetta* of central Africa; the perfume obtained from the secretions of its anal gland.

civic *adj* of a city; municipal.

civil *adj* pertaining to citizens; non-military; polite; (law) civil, as distinct from criminal law.

civilian *n* one engaged in civil, not military pursuits.

civilisation *n* an advanced system of social development; places having one.

clad *pp* of clothe.

claim *vt* to demand as due; to state one's ownership of; * *n* a formal demand; the thing claimed.

clairvoyance *n* extra-sensory perception, *esp* of the future.

clamber *vi* to scramble over.

clamour *n* shouting; uproar; * *vi* to demand with shouts.

clamp *n* a gripping appliance; * *vi* to fasten or grip.

clan *n* a family; a tribe.

clandestine *adj* secret; underhand.

clap *vt* to strike together noisily, *esp* the hands; * *n* explosive sound as of thunder.

clapper *n* the tongue of a bell.

claret *n* the red wine of Bordeaux; * *adj* claret-coloured.

clarify *vt, vi* to make clear; to make transparent; to purify.

clarinet *n* a reed instrument.

clash *vi* to make a noise by collision; to be antagonistic to or incompatible; * *n* noisy collision; jarring.

clasp *n* an embrace; a hook; * *vt* to fasten; to embrace.

class *n* a rank; a group, *esp* a social one; a body of students learning together; a standard or grade of worth; * *vt* to arrange in classes.

classic *adj* of the first rank; * *n* a work, or thing, of the first rank.

classical *adj* of the art, literature or culture of the ancient world, *esp* Greece and Rome; (music) following traditional principles and intended to be of permanent rather than ephemeral value; of the period from *c* 1750–1800.

classify *vt* to arrange; to categorise; designate as officially secret.

clatter *vi* to make rattling noises; to talk noisily; * *n* a rattling noise.

clause *n* a part of a sentence; a single item in a greater document.

claustrophobia *n* a morbid fear of confined spaces or being shut in.

clavicle *n* the collarbone.

claw *n* a hooked nail; a crab's pincer; * *vt* to gouge with claws or nails.

clay *n* heavy soil.

claymore *n* a large two-edged sword; a basket-hilted sword.

clean *adj* free from dirt; pure; * *vt* to purify; to cleanse.

clear *adj* bright; shining; limpid; fair; plain; shrill; * *adv* manifestly; * *vt* to make clear; to free from suspicion.

clearing *n* the act of making clear; a settling up; land cleared of trees.

cleavage *n* a splitting or tendency to split.

cleave *vt* to split; to sever.

cleaver *n* a butcher's axe or knife.

clef *n* a mark to show the key in music.

cleft *n* a crevice; a fissure.

clemency *n* mercy.

clementine *n* a citrus fruit, thought to be a hybrid between a tangerine and a sweet orange.

clench *vt* to hold tight; to close muscles tightly.

clergy *npl* the ministers of the Christian religion.

cleric *n* a clergyman.

clerical *n* originally pertaining to the clergy, more recently to office work.

clerk *n* an office employee; an official who looks after records.

clever *adj* adroit; talented.

click *vi* to clink; to make a faint sharp sound, as of clockwork.

client *n* a customer.

clientèle *n* clients collectively.

cliff *n* a steep rock face.

climate *n* the prevailing weather conditions of an area; the prevailing public mood or opinion.

climax *n* the highest point; an ascending scale; orgasm.

climb *vi*, *vt* to ascend; to mount.

clinch *vt* to settle finally (a deal, an argument); to fasten; to grasp; * *n* a grip hindering the use of the arms; a tight embrace.

cling *vi* to adhere.

clinic *n* a place for the care of outpatients; a private hospital; doctors practising in a group.

clinker *n* a mass of slag or lava; the hard residue of burnt coal.

clip *vt* to shear; to trim with scissors; to cut off words when speaking; to fasten with a clip; * *n* a clasp to fasten together; an extract from a film.

clique *n* a party; a set; an exclusive group.

cloak *n* a loose outer garment; a pretext; * *vt* to hide; to veil.

clock *n* a timepiece.

clockwork *n* the machinery of a clock; unfailing regularity.

clod *n* a lump of earth; a stupid fellow.

clog *n* a shoe with a wooden sole.

cloister *n* a monastery or convent; a covered walk there or in a college.

close *vt* to shut; to finish; * *vi* to end; * *adj* shut fast; tight; dense; near; stingy; secretive; * *n* the end; an enclosed place; a courtyard or its entrance; the precincts of a cathedral.

closet *n* a small room or recess; * *vt* to shut up.

closure *n* a stoppage; a closing.

clot *n* a curdled or coagulated mass (*esp* of blood); * *vi* to become thick.

cloth *n* a woven fabric.

clothe *vt* to attire.

clothes *n* dress; coverings.

cloud *n* a condensed mass of water vapour floating high in the atmosphere; a mass of smoke or dust; * *vt* to darken; to obscure; to hide.

clove *n* the dried flower bud of the tropical plant *Eugenina aromatica* used as a spice; this plant; one segment of a bulb of garlic.

clover *n* any leguminous plant of the genus *Trifolium*.

clown *n* a jester; a circus entertainer.

cloy *vt* to glut; to surfeit with sweetness.

club *n* a cudgel; a golf stick; a society of people; their meeting place; (*pl*) a suit at cards; * *vt* to beat with a club; * *vi* to join together.

clue *n* a guide or help to solve a puzzle or crime.

clump *n* a thick cluster; the sound made by heavy or clumsy footsteps.

clumsy *adj* awkward; graceless; tactless.

cluster *n* a bunch; * *vi* to keep close together.

clutch *vt* to seize; to grasp; * *n* the lever that puts an engine in or out of action; a collection of eggs hatched at one time; a brood of chickens.

coach *n* a four-wheeled close vehicle; a long-distance bus; a sports trainer.

coagulate *vt*, *vi* to curdle; to clot; of liquid, to thicken to a semi-solid state.

coal *n* a black mineral used as fuel.

coalesce *vi* to unite; to fuse; to merge.

coalition *n* a party union; an alliance.

coarse *adj* rude; gross; crude.

coast *n* the seashore; * *vi* to sail along a shore; to travel without mechanical power, *esp* downhill.

coaster *n* a vessel which trades along the coast; a protective mat to place under a glass or bottle.

coastguard *n* an organisation keeping watch on the coast and shipping to mount rescues and prevent smuggling.

coat *n* an outer garment; a covering; a layer; * *vt* to cover.

coax *vt* to wheedle; to persuade by gentleness or flattery.

cobble *vt* to mend coarsely; * *npl* stones dressed to a cuboid form; * ~d *adj* (a road) surfaced with such stones.

cobbler *n* a mender of shoes.

cobweb *n* a spider's web.

cocaine *n* an alkaloid derived from coca, or synthesised; used as an anaesthetic or as a recreational stimulant.

cochineal *n* a scarlet dye used *esp* for colouring food; the dried bodies of the female of the Mexican insect *Dactylopius coccus* yielding this.

cock *n* a male bird; a tap; the hammer of a gun; * *vt* to set erect.

cockney *n* a native of the east end of London; * *adj* pertaining to a cockney.

cockpit *n* a pilot's compartment in an aeroplane.

cocktail *n* a drink composed of a mixture of spirits and other ingredients.

cocoa *n* cacao seeds; the beverage made from them.

coconut *n* the fruit of the coconut palm, *Cocos nucifera*; the palm.

cocoon *n* the case spun by several species of insect larvae; any protective covering resembling this.

cod *n* (*pl* **cod**) any large fish of the family *Gadidae*, *esp Gadus morrhua*.

coddle *vt* to be over-protective; to cook (an egg) in water below boiling point.

code *n* a collection of laws, rules, or signals; a system of pre-arranged signals to transmit secret messages; a piece of text in a computer program.

codicil *n* a supplement to a will.

codify *vt* to systematise laws, rules etc

coefficient *adj* co-operating; * *n* a factor in an expression.

coerce *vt* to force; to compel.

coercion *n* the act of compulsion; government by force.

coexist *vi* to live together, especially peacefully; to exist at the same time.

coffee *n* a drink made from the roasted and ground beans of a tropical shrub of the genus *Coffea*; a cup of this; the shrub; the seeds.

coffer *n* a chest for holding valuables.

coffin *n* the coffer or chest to contain a corpse for burial.

cog *n* the tooth of a wheel.

cogent *adj* (of arguments) convincing; compelling.

cogitate *vi* to ponder.

cognition *n* perception.

cohabit *vi* to dwell together.

cohere *vi* to stick together.

coherent *adj* connected; (of speech) intelligible; logical and consistent; (physics, of waves) having a constant phase relationship.

cohesion *n* the act of or tendency to stick together; (physics) the sticking together of molecules of the same substance.

coil *vt* to wind into a ring; * *n* a ring or rings into which a rope, etc, is wound, or a spiral of a thing wound, especially a wire for electric current.

coin *n* a piece of money; * *vt* to mint; to invent a new word or phrase.

coincide *vi* to correspond in space or time; to agree exactly.

colander *n* a strainer for food.

cold *adj* not hot; chilly; indifferent; * *n* absence of heat; an illness resulting from cold.

colic *n* a griping abdominal pain.

collaborate *vi* to work jointly, *esp* in a literary or scientific undertaking; to co-operate treasonably with an occupying force.

collage *n* a picture or piece of artwork composed of scraps of paper and materials pasted on a surface.

collapse *n* a breakdown; a fall; a failure; * *vi* to fall; to break down.

collar *n* a band worn round the neck; the neckband of a garment.

collate *vt* to examine and compare, as books, etc.

collateral *adj* side by side; indirect.

colleague *n* a fellow worker.

collect *vt*, *vi* to bring together; to infer; to accumulate things as a hobby; * *n* a short prayer.

collected *adj* self-possessed.

collection *n* act of collecting; that which is collected; an accumulation of things of value or interest; money gathered for a purpose.

collective *adj* taken as a whole.

college *n* an institution of scholars; a centre of higher learning.

collide *vi* to strike against each other.

collider *n* (physics) an accelerator in which two beams of elementary particles are caused to collide.

collier *n* a coal miner; a coal ship.

colliery *n* a coal mine.

collision *n* act of striking together; conflict.

colloquial *adj* conversational; informal and non-literary of talk.

collude *vi* to connive.

colon *n* a mark of punctuation, thus (:); the large intestine.

colonel *n* the commander of a regiment.

colonial *adj* pertaining to a colony; * *n* a person belonging to a colony.

colony *n* a settlement in a new country.

colossal *adj* huge.

colour *n* the hue or appearance of a body to the eye; a pigment; complexion; pretence; (*pl*) a flag; * *vt* to tinge; to varnish; to embellish; * *vi* to blush.

colt *n* a young, ungelded, male horse, *usu* less than four years old.

column *n* a pillar; a body of troops; a section of a page; a line of figures.

coma *n* a stupor; a lengthy period of unconsciousness.

comatose *adj* torpid; death-like.

comb *n* a toothed appliance for dressing hair; * *vt* to arrange hair with a comb; to search for thoroughly.

combat *vi* to fight; * *vt* to oppose; * *n* a fight; a contest.

combination *n* a union; an alliance of persons; a collection of numbers or other objects chosen from a larger set, without regard to order; a, *usu* forced, sequence of moves in chess to achieve some aim.

combine *vt* to join; to possess disparate qualities; * *vi* to league together.

combustible *adj* inflammable.

combustion *n* a burning.

come *vi* to move forward; to draw near; to arrive; to happen.

comedian *n* an actor of comic roles; one who entertains by telling jokes.

comedy *n* drama written to amuse.

comely *adj* good-looking.

comet *n* a body of ice and dust in an eccentric orbit around the sun, visible in the night sky by its tail of gas and dust.

comfort *vt* to console; to gladden; * *n* consolation.

comic *adj* relating to comedy; amusing.

comma *n* a mark of punctuation, thus (,).

command *vt* to order; to govern; to have at one's disposal.

commandant it the military officer in charge of men or an establishment.

commandeer *vt* to appropriate.

commander *n* one who commands.

commanding *adj* dominating; authoritative.

commemorate *vt* to celebrate the memory of someone or something.

commence *vi, vt* to take the first step; to begin.

commend *vt* to praise; to recommend.

commendation *n* praise, an award.

commensurate *adj* proportional.

comment *vi* to make remarks or criticisms; * *vt* to annotate; * *n* an explanatory note.

commentary *n* a book of comments or notes; a spoken explanation of events as they take place.

commentator *n* one who reports and explains events.

commerce *n* exchange of goods, trade.

commiserate *vt* to pity; to condole with.

commission *n* trust; warrant; a percentage; a body of commissioners; the appointment of a soldier to officer's rank; a business or task given or entrusted to someone; * *vt* to require the services of.

commissionaire *n* a porter or messenger.

commit *vt* to entrust; to consign especially to custody; to perpetrate.

committal *n* the act of committing.

committee *n* a body appointed to manage any matter on behalf of a larger body.

commodious *adj* spacious and suitable.

commodity *n* any article of commerce.

commodore *n* the commander of a squadron.

common *adj* general; usual; of no rank; of little value; * *n* an open public ground.

common sense *n* sound practical sense, *esp* in mundane matters; the day to day ideology of the bourgeoisie.

commonwealth *n* the public good; the state; a republic; a federation of states.

commotion *n* tumult; disorder.

communal *adj* belonging to a community or commune; shared; common to.

commune *vi* to confer with privately or spiritually; * *n* a group of people living together and sharing everything.

communication *n* news; a message; (*pl*) the exchange of information and ideas by any means.

communion *n* intercourse; celebration of the Lord's Supper.

communism *n* the doctrine of common ownership of capital, *esp* Marxism.

communist *n* an advocate of communism.

community *n* the body of the people; a body of people living in the same locality.

commutable *adj* exchangeable.

commute *vt, vi* to travel a distance daily between home and work; to exchange; to lessen; to reduce the length of a prison sentence.

compact *adj* solid; dense; * *vt* to consolidate; * *n* an agreement.

compact disc *n* a storage medium for information which is electronically 'read' by a laser.

companion *n* a comrade; a friend.

company *n* a body of guests, of traders, or of soldiers; a business; a ship's crew.

comparable *adj* similar.

comparative *adj* relative.

compare *vt* to examine side by side; simultaneously to liken and contrast.

comparison *n* relation; simile; illustration; (grammar) inflection in an adjective.

compartment *n* a separate space divided off; one such division of a railway carriage for passengers; something separate; a category.

compass *n* a circuit; limit; range; an instrument with a magnetic needle pointing to the north; (*usu* in *pl*) an instrument for describing circles.

compassion *n* sympathy.

compatible *adj* consistent; able to live with agreeably; of like mind.

compatriot *n* one of the same country.

compel *vt* to drive; to urge; to force.

compendium *n* a summary.

compensate *vt* to make amends for; to requite; * *vi* to atone.

compete *vi* to strive (as rival); to contend.

competent *adj* well qualified; able.

competition *n* rivalry; a contest; a match.

competitor *n* a rival.

compile *vt* to collect and structure information.

complacent *adj* pleased with oneself; smug.

complain *vi* to grumble at; to be dissatisfied with; to lament; to make a charge; to feel unwell.

complainant *n* a plaintiff.

complaint *n* a grumble; an accusation; an ailment.

complaisant *adj* politely deferential; willing to please; acquiescent.

complement *n* the full quota, allowance or number.

complementary *adj* completing.

complete *adj* finished; * *vt* to finish; to fulfil.

complex *adj* involved; difficult; * *n* a whole composed of many parts *eg* buildings or units.

complexion *n* the colour of the face; aspect.

complexity *n* intricacy.

compliant *adj* yielding; docile.

complicate *vt* to make complex or difficult.

complication *n* something that worsens or adds to a difficulty; a medical condition following on and arising from the original malady.

complicity *n* state of being an accomplice.

compliment *n* an expression of praise or admiration; * *vi* to praise; to congratulate.

comply *vi* to acquiesce.

component *adj* constituent; * *n* a constituent part.

compose *vt* to write, especially music; to calm.

composed *adj* calm; serene.

composer *n* a writer of music.

composition *n* a putting together; the thing composed, as a piece of music or literature; the makeup of something.

compost *n* vegetable matter rotted down as manure.

composure *n* calmness.

compound *vt, vi* to put together; to mix; to adjust; * *adj* composed of two or more parts; * *n* (chemistry) a substance composed of two or more elements; an enclosure.

comprehend *vt* to understand.

comprehensive *adj* inclusive; of wide scope; * *n* a secondary school accepting pupils of all abilities.

compress *vt* to press together; * *n* a soft pad to apply to a wound.

compression *n* the compressing; the reduction in volume of the fuel air mixture in a cylinder of a internal combustion engine before ignition.

comprise *vt* to contain; to consist of.

compromise *n* a settlement by agreement; * *vt* to settle by mutual concessions; to endanger; to embarrass.

compulsion *n* force; an overpowering urge.

compulsory *adj* obligatory.

compunction *n* remorse.

computation *n* reckoning.

compute *vt* to count; estimate.

computer *n* an electronic device that processes data according to instructions fed into it.

comrade *n* a workmate or companion; a fellow soldier; a fellow socialist.

concave *adj* curving inwards.

conceal *vt* to hide.

concede *vt* to yield; to grant.

conceit *n* vanity; an exaggerated opinion of oneself.

conceive *vti* to comprehend; to think; to become pregnant.

concentrate *vt* to collect to one point; to direct the mind solely to one aim or object; to condense in order to increase the strength of something.

concentric *adj* having a common centre.

concept *n* a general idea; an abstract idea.

concern *vt* to interest oneself in; to apply to; to cause anxiety to; * *n* anxiety.

concert *n* agreement; harmony; a musical performance.

concerted *adj* planned; combined.

concertina *n* a musical instrument.

concerto *n* a musical opus for a solo instrument and orchestra.

concession *n* a grant; the act of yielding.

conch *n* a thick heavy spiral shell of various gastropod molluscs of the family *Strombidae*; any of these gastropods.

concise *adj* brief, pointed.

conclave *n* the assembly of cardinals for the election of a pope; a close assembly.

conclude *vt, vi* to end; to deduce.

concoct *vt* to devise; to plot; to produce from a mixture of ingredients; to fabricate.

concomitant *adj* accompanying; * *n* a connected circumstance.

concord *n* union; harmony.

concordance *n* agreement; a complete index.

concourse *n* a gathering; a crowd; a large area where crowds can gather.

concrete *adj* solid; real, not abstract; * *n* a mass of stones and mortar.

concur *vi* to unite; to agree.

concurrent *adj* happening at the same time; agreeing; attendant.

concussion *n* a violent shock, especially of an explosion or heavy blow; unconsciousness due to a heavy blow to the head.

condemn *vt* to censure; to sentence.

condensation *n* state of being condensed; an abridgement.

condense *vt* to compress; to liquefy; to reduce by cutting, especially of text or recorded speech.

condenser *n* a chamber in which steam is condensed; a capacitor.

condescend *vi* to stoop; to deign; to be patronising.

condiment *n* seasoning or spice.

condition *n* state; case; stipulation; illness; * *vt* to train to produce a consistent response.

conditioned *adj* depending; relative.

condole *vi* to sympathise.

condone *vt* to pardon.

conducive *adj* leading to; contributing to.

conduct *n* behaviour; management: escort; * *vt* to lead; to manage; to behave; to direct an orchestra; to transmit *eg* heat or electricity.

conduction *n* property by which bodies transmit heat or electricity.

conductor *n* a leader; a director of an orchestra; one who is in charge of a train; a thing which conducts electricity or, less often, heat.

conduit *n* a channel; a subway for pipes.

cone *n* a pointed figure with a

circular base; the fruit of firs.

confection *n* a mixture; a sweet.

confederacy *n* a league.

confederate *adj* allied; * *n* an ally; a fellow conspirator; * *vt*, *vi* to unite.

confer *vi* to consult together; * *vt* to give or bestow.

conference *n* a meeting for consultation.

confess *vt* to own; to admit; * *vi* to make a confession.

confidant(e) *n*, *m(f)* trusted friend.

confide *vi*, *vt* to trust wholly; to entrust.

confidence *n* trust; assurance.

confidential *adj* private; privy to secrets.

configuration *n* the arrangement of parts or elements in a thing; (physics) the state of a system as the position and momenta, or in quantum systems the wave functions, of the constituent particles.

confine *n* a boundary; * *vt* to restrain; to shut up.

confinement *n* imprisonment; childbirth.

confirm *vt* to ratify; to corroborate; to admit to communion in church.

confirmation *n* proof; verification of some fact by an independent authority; the ceremony of full admittance of a person into the Christian church.

confiscate *vt* to seize as forfeit

conflagration *n* a great fire.

conflict *n* a struggle; a fight; strife; an emotional upset; * *vi* to be at variance.

conflicting *adj* contradictory.

confluence *n* a flowing together; the meeting of streams.

conform *vt*, *vi* to adapt; to comply.

confound *vt* to confuse; to astound; to overthrow.

confront *vt* to face; to oppose; to challenge face to face.

confuse *vt* to mix together; to derange; to perplex.

congeal *vt* to coagulate; to thicken.

congenial *adj* kindred; having like natures or tastes; compatible.

congenital *adj* hereditary.

congested *adj* overcrowded; clogged with blood etc; blocked.

conglomeration *n* forming a rounded mass.

congratulate *vt* to compliment; to felicitate.

congregate *vt*, *vi* to meet together.

congress *n* an assembly; the legislature of the United States; sexual intercourse.

congruent *adj* suitable; agreeing; corresponding.

congruous *adj* accordant; corresponding; appropriate.

conic(al) *adj* cone-like; cone-shaped.

conifer *n* an evergreen tree of the order *Coniferales*, typically bearing cones and needle like leaves.

conjecture *n* supposition; * *vt* to surmise.

conjoin *vt* to unite.

conjugal *adj* pertaining to marriage.

conjugate *vt* to inflect (a verb); * *adj* joined in pairs.

conjunction *n* connection; a connecting word.

conjuncture *n* a combination of events; a state of affairs.

conjure *vt* to summon up by magic; * *vi* to juggle.

connect *vt* to join; to associate; to link by telephone; to transfer from one vehicle to another to continue a journey.

connive *vi* to concur in a wrong.

connoisseur *n* an expert; a judge of fine arts.

connotation *n* the implied meaning; the resultant meaning.

conquer *vt* to gain by force; to vanquish; * *vi* to overcome.

conqueror *n* a victor.

conscience *n* the sense of right and wrong.

conscientious *adj* high principled; regulated by conscience; thorough; diligent.

conscious *adj* aware; sensible of.

conscript *n* one compulsorily enrolled to serve in the army or navy.

consecrate *vt* to set apart for sacred use; to dedicate.

consecutive *adj* following in order.

consent *n* concurrence; agreement; permission; * *vi* to assent; to acquiesce; to permit.

consequence n result; inference; importance.

consequent adj following; resulting.

consequential adj pompous.

conservation n preservation, especially of the environment and natural resources.

conservative adj averse to change; * n one opposed to political changes; (when capitalised) a Tory.

conservatory n a greenhouse.

conserve vt to keep in a sound state; to keep safe; to preserve or pickle food.

consider vt, vi to think on; to ponder; to weigh up; to examine.

consign vt to hand over to another.

consignment n goods consigned.

consist vi to be composed of.

consistency n the degree of firmness; harmony; being true to one's previous ideas.

consistent adj fixed; compatible; reliably unchanging in deed or thought.

consolation n solace; a comfort.

console vt to comfort.

consolidate vt to make solid; to strengthen.

consonant adj accordant; consistent; * n a letter or sound that is not a vowel.

consort n a partner; a wife or husband; a companion; * vi to associate with unsuitable people; to agree; to accord.

consortium n a combining for a special purpose.

conspicuous adj outstanding; noticeable.

conspire vi to plot together.

constable n a policeman or woman; a peace-officer.

constant adj steadfast; faithful; * n a fixed quantity.

constellation n a group of stars.

consternation n dismay.

constipation n difficulty in moving the bowels.

constituency n the political subdivision of a borough, consisting of several wards, which returns a parliamentary candidate; the voters in this.

constituent adj component; being a part of a whole; * n a member of a constituency; one essential part of a whole.

constitute vt to set up; to compose; to appoint.

constitution n the condition of the body; the underlying, or fundamental, framework of laws according to which a state is governed.

constitutional adj of, pertaining to a constitution; * n a walk taken for one's health.

constrain vt to force; to necessitate; to restrain; to imprison.

constrict vi to contract; to compress; to limit free movement.

constrictor n any snake (esp a boa) which kills its prey by coiling round it and compressing it; (medical) a muscle which compresses or contracts an organ in the body.

construct vt to build; to devise.

construe vt to interpret; to analyse the syntax of a sentence.

consul n a state agent in foreign towns.

consulate n the office or residence of a consul.

consult vi, vt to take counsel; to consider; to seek advice.

consultant n a consulting physician.

consume vt, vi to eat or drink; to destroy; to use up; to squander.

consumer n one who buys goods and uses services.

consummate vt to finish, to perfect; completion of a marriage by sexual intercourse; * adj complete; perfect.

consumption n expenditure.

contact n a touching together; a business acquaintance; one who has been close to a person with a contagious disease; * vt to get in touch with.

contagious adj infectious, spread by touch.

contain vt to hold; to restrain.

contaminate vt to corrupt; to pollute.

contemplate vt to meditate on; to consider.

contemporary adj belonging to

the same time; * n one who lives at the same time; a person of the same age.

contempt n scorn; disregard.

contend vi to strive; to vie; to dispute.

content adj satisfied; * vt to please; to satisfy; * n satisfaction; capacity; (pl) the thing, or things, held by a container.

contentious adj quarrelsome; descriptive of that which is disagreed about.

contest vt, vi to call in question; to strive; to contend; to emulate; * n a competition.

context n the circumstances relevant to an event or speech.

continent adj chaste; moderate; able to control urination and defecation; * n a large mass of land; the mainland of Europe.

contingency n a possible event; accident.

contingent adj incidental; conditional; that may happen; * n a quota; a detachment of troops; a possible happening.

continual adj incessant.

continue vi to remain; to persevere; * vt to prolong; to extend.

continuity n unbroken sequence; the detailed work to maintain the self-consistency of a film or drama, esp with regard to dress, weather and properties.

continuous adj uninterrupted.

contort vt to twist; to pull out of shape.

contour n outline; form; a line on a map joining all points at the same height above sea level.

contraband n smuggled goods.

contract vt to reduce; to incur; to shorten (a word); to be affected by a disease; * vi to shrink; to make a mutual agreement; * n an agreement; a bond.

contraction n shrinking; a shortening; tensing of a muscle.

contractor n a person undertaking a contract, esp one to provide manpower, services etc.

contradict vt to deny; to say the contrary.

contralto n the lowest singing voice of a woman.

contraption n a devise; a gadget; an improvised or complicated contrivance.

contrary adj opposite; adverse; opposed; perverse; * n the opposite.

contrast vt to set in opposition; to show up the differences in; * vi to stand in contrast to; * n opposition; difference.

contravene vt to oppose; to transgress.

contribute vt to give; to write magazine articles; to make suggestions.

contrite adj penitent.

contrive vt to invent; to devise; to achieve, often by unusual means.

control n restraint; authority; a standard to compare with and check against, esp in scientific experiment; * vt to regulate; to be in command.

controversy n a disagreement or dispute over some matter, generally in public.

contusion n a severe bruise.

conundrum n a riddle.

convalesce vi to recover health.

convection n (physics) the circulation of heat by the motion of a hotter mass of fluid through a colder one.

convene vi to assemble; to call a meeting; * vt to convoke.

convenience n ease; comfort; something useful and labour saving; a public lavatory.

convenient adj suitable.

convent n a nunnery.

convention n an assembly; an accepted social custom.

conventional adj customary; following accepted rules.

converge vi to tend to the same point.

convergent adj approaching; meeting; arriving at the same point or result.

conversant adj familiar with; versed in.

conversation n the informal exchange of ideas, information, trivia etc by talking.

converse *vi* to talk familiarly; * *n* the very opposite; conversation.

convert *vt*, *vi* to transform; to change; * *n* one who has changed his opinion, practice, or religion.

convertible *adj* transformable; * *n* a car with a folding or detachable roof.

convex *adj* curved outwards.

convey *vt* to transport; to carry; to transfer especially the title of a property; to make known.

convict *vt* to prove to be guilty; * *n* a criminal undergoing sentence.

convince *vt* to persuade; to satisfy.

convivial *adj* festive; jovial; sociable.

convolute(d) *adj* rolled, coiled on itself; involved; difficult to follow.

convoy *vt* to escort; * *n* a group of ships all sailing together.

convulse *vt* to agitate violently; * *vi* to cause spasms of helpless laughter.

cook *vt* to prepare food; to concoct; * *n* one who prepares food.

cool *adj* moderately cold; self-possessed; * *vt* to make cool.

coop *n* a cage or pen for poultry.

cooper *n* one who makes barrels.

co-operate *vi* to act, work together with another.

co-operative *adj* operating jointly; helpful; * *n* (an organisation) owned and run by its members with profits shared equally.

co-opt *vt* to elect into a body, by vote of its members.

co-ordination *n* act of co-ordinating; harmonious movement of parts of the body.

cope *vt* to cover; to grapple (with); to manage something successfully.

copier *n* a transcriber; a machine that makes copies; an imitator.

copious *adj* abundant.

copper *n* a reddish metal.

copperplate *n* an engraver's plate; the print from it; style of handwriting.

copse *n* a thicket.

copulate *vi* to have sexual intercourse.

copy *n* an imitation; matter to be set up in type; * *vt* to imitate; to transcribe.

copyright *n* the sole right to publish.

coquetry *n* flirtation.

coral *n* a sea rock built up from the skeletons of minute organisms.

cord *n* a thin rope; a band.

cordial *adj* hearty; * *n* a refreshing drink.

cordon *n* a line or chain of police or soldiers barring entry to an area.

corduroy *n* a thick cotton stuff corded or ribbed.

core *n* the heart; the essence; the seed-bearing centre of fruit; the centre of the earth below the mantle.

co-respondent *n* a joint respondent in divorce proceedings.

coriander *n* an umbelliferous plant, *Coriandrum sativum*; the small round aromatic fruit is used for flavouring when dried, as are the leaves, dried or not.

cork *n* a tree or its bark; a stopper; * *vt* to stop with a cork.

corn *n* grain such as wheat or oats; a horny growth on the foot.

cornea *n* the transparent membrane over the eye.

corner *n* the point where two lines or several planes meet; a difficult or dangerous situation; a free kick from the corner of the pitch in football.

cornerstone *n* the indispensable stone, part, or basis.

cornet *n* a brass instrument resembling trumpet; a cone-shaped wafer for ice cream.

cornice *n* the upper moulding of a column; a plaster moulding round a ceiling.

corolla *n* the inner envelope; the petals of a flower.

corollary *n* an additional inference from approved proposition.

corona *n* the atmosphere of the sun, seen as a halo in total eclipses.

coronation *n* the ceremony of investiture of a monarch.

coroner *n* an officer who holds an inquest in a case of sudden death.

corporal *n* the lowest rank of non-commissioned officer; * *adj* pertaining to the body; physical; material.

corporate *adj* formed into a legal body; united; joint.

corporation *n* a body corporate, empowered to act as an individual.

corporeal *adj* material; not spiritual.

corpse *n* the dead body of a human being.

corpulent *adj* portly; fat.

corpuscle *n* a red or white blood cell.

correct *adj* right; * *vi* to make right; to chastise.

correlate *vi* to be reciprocally related; * *vt* to determine the relations between.

correspond *vi* to be like or similar; to agree; to write to.

corridor *n* a passage in a building or train linking rooms or compartments.

corroborate *vt* to strengthen; to confirm.

corrode *vt* to eat or wear away by degrees; to rust.

corrosion *n* wearing away through chemical action.

corrugate *vt* to wrinkle; to fold into parallel ridges.

corrupt *vt* to taint morally; to infect; to bribe; * *vi* to become debased or vitiated; * *adj* tainted; depraved.

corset *n* a close-fitting undergarment supporting the lower body.

cortège *n* a train of attendants; a funeral procession.

cortex *n* the outer membrane of an organ, *esp* the cerebral ~ of the brain and the renal ~ of the kidneys; tree bark.

corundum *n* an extremely hard form of alumina, used *esp* as an abrasive (emery), and varieties of which are used as gemstones (*eg* ruby and sapphire).

coruscate *vi* to flash; to glitter.

corvette *n* a small naval escort vessel.

cosy *adj* snug; * *n* a teapot cover.

cosmetic *n* a skin beautifier; a superficial improvement, *usu* leaving some underlying fault; * *adj* correcting; improving.

cosmic *adj* relating to the universe.

cosmology *n* the science of the universe as a whole.

cosmonaut *n* a Russian astronaut.

cosmopolitan *n* a citizen of the world; a much travelled person; someone without national prejudices; * *adj* unprejudiced.

cosmos *n* the universe.

cost *vt* to be bought for; to set a price on; to cause; * *n* charge; price; trouble.

costal *adj* pertaining to the ribs.

costume *n* an established mode of dress; garb; attire; clothing worn by actors.

cot *n* a small house; a small bed.

coterie *n* a small social group of people with like interests; a clique.

cottage *n* a small house.

cotton *n* a soft substance in the pods of several plants; cloth made of cotton.

cotton wool *n* cotton in the raw state bleached and sterilised.

couch *vt* to express in specific language or mode of speech; * *n* a bed; a sofa.

cough *n* a noisy explosion of air from the lungs; * *vt*, *vi* to make a violent effort to expel the air from the lungs.

could past tense of can, to be able; was able.

coulomb *n* the S.I. unit of electrical charge equal to the amount of charge transferred by a current of one ampere in one second.

council *n* an assembly; a governing or advisory body elected or appointed.

counsel *n* deliberation; advice; design; a barrister; * *vt* to advise; to recommend.

count *vt* to number; * *vi* to reckon; to rely on; to matter or be of importance; * *n* reckoning.

countenance *n* the face; air; aspect; favour; * *vt* to favour.

counter *n* a shop table; (*pl*) tokens for card games; * *vt* to parry; * *adj* rival; opposite.

counteract *vt* to act in opposition to; to hinder; to check; to neutralise.

counterbalance *vt* to weigh against with an equal weight or power.

counterfeit *vt*, *vi* to forge; to copy; * *adj* fraudulent; * *n* a forgery.

counterfoil *n* a part of a form showing the essential information of the greater part, kept for reference after the latter has been distributed.

countermand *vt* to annul a former command; * *n* a contrary order.

counterpane *n* a bed cover.

counterpart *n* a corresponding part or person; a duplicate.

counterpoint *n* the art of musical composition; the sounding or playing of two or several melodies or parts at the same time.

countersign *vt* to sign with an additional signature; * *n* a password.

countess *n* a noble woman of equal rank to, or the wife of, an earl.

countless *adj* innumerable.

country *n* a large tract of land; a region; a kingdom or state; the public; rural parts; * *adj* rural.

county *n* a shire or division of a country.

coup *n* a stroke or blow; a masterstroke.

coupé *n* a closed car with two doors and a sloped back, accommodating four people.

couple *n* a pair; a man and his wife; * *vt, vi* to unite; to copulate.

couplet *n* two lines that rhyme.

coupling *n* the links connecting railway carriages or machine parts.

coupon *n* a ticket entitling holder to some money, service, or privilege.

courage *n* bravery.

courier *n* an express messenger.

course *n* a route; line of conduct; a track; a series of lectures; range of subjects; a layer of stones in masonry; a stage in a meal, *eg* dessert.

court *n* an enclosed area; the retinue of a sovereign; judges in session; flattery; * *vt* to woo; to flatter; to seek.

courtesy *n* politeness.

courtier *n* an attendant at a royal court.

courtly *adj* dignified.

court martial *n* (*pl* **courts martial**) a court to try military or naval offences.

courtship *n* wooing.

cousin *n* **first cousin** the child of one's uncle or aunt; (**second, third cousin**) subsequent generations of offspring of first cousins.

cove *n* a small inlet.

covenant *n* a contract; a compact; * *vi, vt* to enter into a formal agreement.

cover *vt* to cloak; to shelter; to defend; to wrap up; to include; to understudy; to write a newspaper report; * *n* a cloak; disguise; shelter; insurance against.

covert *adj* secret; private; * *n* a shelter.

covet *vt* to desire eagerly; to envy.

cow *n* a female of domestic cattle, whale, elephant etc; * *vt* to terrorise; to intimidate.

coward *n* one who exhibits a marked lack of bravery.

cower *vi* to crouch; to waver or tremble through fear.

cowl *n* a monk's hood; a covering over a chimney to aid ventilation.

coxswain *n* the person who steers a boat or has charge of a ship's boat.

coy *adj* shy; reserved.

crab *n* any of numerous ten-footed crustaceans having the front pair of legs modified to form pincers; the flesh of a crab, *esp Cancer pagurus*, as food.

crack *n* a chink; a sudden sharp sound; * *vt, vi* to split; to break; to break a code; to break open (as safe); to make a joke; to give in under pressure.

cracker *n* a small firework; a hard biscuit.

crackle *vi* to make small sharp noises.

cradle *n* an infant's bed on rockers; a framework under a ship for launching or supporting it; a frame for a broken limb; * *vt* to lay or rock in a cradle.

craft *n* ability; guile; manual art; trade; a ship or aircraft.

craftsman *n* a skilled worker.

crafty *adj* cunning.

crag *n* a steep rugged rock.

cram *vt, vi* to stuff; to coach for an examination.

cramp *n* a spasmodic contraction of a muscle; * *vt* to affect with spasms; to restrain; to hamper.

cramped *adj* restrained; restricted; of handwriting, small and hard to read.

crane *n* a long-legged, long-necked bird of the family *Gruidae*, *esp* the grey *Grus grus* of Europe; a machine for raising heavy weights; * *vi* to stretch out one's neck.

cranium *n* the skull.

crank *n* the bent part of an axle which converts reciprocal motion into rotation and vice versa; a bend or turn; * *adj* loose; * *vt* to wind.

crash *vi* to fall with a clatter; to collide with or fall violently; * *n* a noise of breakage; a collapse especially financial; a failure; a violent impact or descent.

crass *adj* gross; dense; stupid.

crate *n* a wooden packing case.

crater *n* the bowl-shaped mouth of a volcano; a hole or depression caused by an explosion or meteor impact.

cravat *n* a neckcloth.

crave *vt* to ask earnestly; to have an intensely strong desire for.

craven *n* a coward; * *adj* cowardly.

craving *n* a morbid desire.

craw *n* the crop of fowls.

crawl *vi* to creep on hands and knees; to be servile towards; * *n* a crawling motion; slow motion; a swimming stroke.

crayon *n* a pencil of coloured chalk; a coloured drawing.

craze *vt* to shatter; to derange; * *vi* to become crazy; * *n* an inordinate desire or enthusiasm; a passing fashion.

crazy *adj* mentally deranged.

creak *vi* to make a grating sound; * *n* a sharp, grating sound.

cream *n* the oily part of milk from which butter is made; the best of anything; * *vt* to take off cream from.

crease *n* a mark made by folding; the lines marking the batsman's stance (in cricket); * *vt* to make creases in.

create *vt* to make out of nothing; to cause to be; to shape; to invent; to appoint.

creation *n* the universe; an original work of any kind.

creative *adj* original; imaginative.

creator *n* the Supreme Being; a producer.

creature *n* a human being; a mere tool.

crèche *n* a public nursery for children.

credence *n* credit; trust.

credential *n* warrant; voucher (*pl*) testimonials.

credible *adj* worthy of belief.

credit *n* belief, reputed integrity; transfer of goods on trust; side of an account in which payment is entered; money possessed or at one's disposal; distinction given to an examinee for good marks; * *vt* to trust; to believe; to sell or lend in trust.

creditor *n* one to whom a debt is owed.

credulity *n* simplicity; over-trustfulness.

creed *n* a set of principles or opinions, *esp* as a philosophy of life.

creek *n* a small natural bay.

creep *vi* to crawl; to move stealthily; to be servile; to shiver.

creeper *n* a creeping plant.

cremate *vt* to consume by burning.

creosote *n* an oily liquid, antiseptic and wood preservative.

crescent *n* a figure shaped like the new moon; * *adj* increasing.

crest *n* a tuft on the head of certain birds; the plume of feathers on a helmet; a device or symbol of a family or office; the top of a hill.

crestfallen *adj* dejected.

cretaceous *adj* chalky.

crevice *n* a cleft; a fissure.

crew *n* a company; a gang; the personnel of a ship or aircraft.

crib *n* a child's bed; a small habitation; a rack; a stall for cattle; a literal translation or list of answers often used illicitly by students in examinations; * *vt* to confine; to pilfer; to copy illicitly.

crick n a cramp in the neck.

cricket n any grasshopper-like insect of the order *Orthoptera*, and *esp* of the family *Gryllidae*, making a characteristic chirping noise; a game, between teams of eleven players taking turns to bowl at a wicket defended by a batting player from the other team.

crime n a serious offence punishable under the law; an evil act.

criminal adj guilty; wicked; * n one who has broken the criminal law.

crimp vt to curl; to seize; to pinch or fold together.

crimson n a deep red colour; * adj of a deep red.

cringe vi to fawn; to crouch.

crinkle vi to wrinkle; * vt to be corrugated or crimped; * n a wrinkle.

cripple n a lame person; * vt to lame; to disable.

crisis n (pl **crises**) a turning point; a critical moment; an emergency.

crisp adj brittle; friable; fresh and bracing; * n a thin potato chip.

criterion n (pl **criteria**) a standard; a rule regarded as a measure of judgment.

critic n one who judges the merits of literary, artistic or musical works; a reviewer; a censor.

critical adj censorious; crucial; exacting; (physics, of a substance, model) undergoing a phase transition.

critique n a review.

croak vi to make a hoarse noise in the throat; * n the cry of raven or frog.

crochet n a type of knitting, some with a hooked needle.

crockery n china dishes; earthenware pots.

crocodile n a large voracious tropical and sub-tropical amphibious reptile of the family *Crocodylidae* with narrower longer jaws than alligators.

croft n a small plot of arable land; a small rented farm in Scotland or Northern England.

crony n a familiar friend.

crook n a bend; a hooked staff; a shepherd's staff; a pastoral stall; a dishonest person; a swindler.

crooked adj bent; deceitful.

crop n the stomach or craw of birds; the produce of cultivated plants *esp* cereals; a riding whip; * vt to clip or cut short; to browse; to cultivate.

croquet n an open-air game played with mallets, balls and hoops.

croquette n a ball of mashed potato, meat or fish fried until brown.

cross n two straight lines crossing each other; the symbol of the Christian religion; annoyance; * vt to mark with a cross; to pass over; to intersect; to cancel; to vex or thwart; * adj peevish.

cross-examination n the examination of a witness by the opposing lawyer.

cross-purpose n a contrary purpose or aim; a misunderstanding.

crossroads npl the point where two roads cross.

cross-section n a surface exposed after cutting a solid at right angles to its length; a representative group (of people) chosen at random.

crossword n a word puzzle in which solutions to clues must be fitted into a grid.

crotch n the part of the body where the legs fork; the area of the genitals.

crotchet n a note in music; a half a minim.

crotchety adj perverse; bad-tempered.

crouch vi to bend low; to squat.

croupier n the dealer at a gaming table.

crow n a large black bird with croaking voice; the cock's cry; * vi to make the cry of a cock; to exult.

crowbar n a bar of iron used as a lever.

crowd n a throng; * vt to press together; * vi to throng.

crown n royal headgear; a king's power and symbol of office; the completion; the top of the head; a wreath or garland; a reward; the centre of a road; the upper part of a tooth; * *vt* to invest with a crown; to adorn; to perfect.

crucial *adj* decisive; critical.

crucible *n* a vessel or pot for heating substances to high temperatures.

crucifix *n* a figure of Christ upon the cross.

crucifixion *n* an execution technique whereby the victim is tied, or nailed, to a cross which causes the ribcage to crush the lungs; (when capitalised) the death of Christ.

cruciform *adj* cross-shaped.

crude *adj* raw; unripe; rough; vulgar.

cruel *adj* unmerciful; harsh; fierce.

cruet *n* a small bottle for holding oil or vinegar.

cruise *vi* to sail hither and thither; to travel at a moderate speed; * *n* a sailing to and fro; a pleasure voyage.

cruiser *n* a swift armed warship; a pleasure boat.

crumb *n* a fragment; a small piece.

crumple *vt*, *vi* to press into wrinkles; to crease; to collapse.

crunch *vt* to crush between the teeth.

crusade *n* an enterprise or serious activity to further a cause.

crush *vt* to squeeze; to bruise; to overpower; to stamp out; * *vi* to press forward; * *n* a crowding; an infatuation.

crust *n* the hard outer coating of anything; * *vt*, *vi* to cover with a crust.

crustacean *n* (*pl* crustacea) any arthropod of the subphylum *Crustacea*, *usu* aquatic with hard shells and numerous legs, *eg* crab, lobster, shrimp.

crutch *n* a stick with armpit or arm rests to support the body and allow mobility to a lame person; the crotch.

crux *n* the crucial or deciding point.

cry *vi* to utter the loud shrill sounds of weeping or joy; to weep; * *vt* to proclaim; * *n* a

shriek or scream; weeping; an appeal for help; a catchword.

crypt *n* an underground vault used as chapel or burial place.

cryptic *adj* hidden; secret; mysterious.

crystal *n* pure transparent quartz; articles made of this; highly transparent glass; articles made of this; (chemistry, physics) any substance with regularly arranged molecules which form macroscopic geometrical shapes.

cub *n* the young of the bear, fox, etc; a whelp; a junior boy scout.

cube *n* a regular solid body, with six equal square sides; the third power of a number; * *vt* to raise to the third power.

cubism *n* a style of painting representing subjects from different viewpoints at the same time by rearranging their geometrical planes.

cud *n* the partially-digested food which ruminants bring up to chew again.

cuddle *vt* to hug closely; to curl up comfortably.

cudgel *n* a short thick stick.

cue *n* the last words of an actor's speech as a sign to a following actor; catchword; hint; the straight rod used in billiards.

cuff *n* a blow; a slap; part of a sleeve near the hand; * *vt* to beat with the fist or open hand.

cuisine *n* style of cooking.

cul-de-sac *n* a blind alley.

culinary *adj* relating to cookery.

cull *vt* to gather; to reduce numbers of certain animals by killing.

culminate *vi* to reach the highest point.

culpable *adj* at fault.

culprit *n* the person who committed a specific offence.

cult *n* a system of worship often with special or secret rites.

cultivate *vt* to till; to refine; to civilise.

culture *n* refinement; appreciation of the arts; the whole range of skills of a people at a certain period; artificial rearing of organismas such as bees or bacteria.

cumbersome *adj* burdensome; awkward; heavy.

cumin *n* an umbelliferous plant, *Cuminum cyminum*, bearing aromatic seeds; these seeds used as a spice.

cummerbund *n* a girdle or waistband, *usu* worn with formal men's evening dress.

cumulate *vt* to heap together.

cumulonimbus *n* a cloud of towering masses, as in rainclouds.

cumulus *n* (*pl* **cumuli**) clouds formed in rounded masses heaped on a flat base at low altitude.

cuneiform *adj* wedge-shaped.

cunning *adj* astute; crafty; * *n* craftiness.

cup *n* a small drinking vessel with a handle; its contents; a cup-shaped trophy, often silver or ornamental.

cupboard *n* a shelved cabinet to contain household objects or food.

cupidity *n* a longing to possess; avarice.

cur *n* a mongrel dog; a despicable man.

curate *n* an assistant clergyman.

curative *adj* tending to cure.

curator *n* a superintendent; a custodian.

curb *vt* to control; to check; * *n* a check; part of a horse's bridle.

curd *n* coagulated milk; * *vt*, *vi* to curdle; to congeal.

curdle *vt*, *vi* to change into curds; to thicken.

cure *n* healing; a remedy; * *vt* to heal; to preserve food by salting, pickling or smoking.

curfew *n* a regulation restricting the free movement of the population, *usu* requiring people to stay indoors at between specified hours, *esp* at night.

curio *n* a curiosity.

curious *adj* inquisitive; strange; singular.

curl *vt* to form into ringlets; * *vi* to go into coils; * *n* a ringlet of hair; a twist.

currency *n* the money used in a particular country; *fam* the time when a something is topical, *usu* within the consensus of a group.

current *adj* running; circulating; * *n* a running; a stream; progressive motion of water or electricity.

curriculum *n* a formal course of study.

curriculum vitae *n* a (written) statement or summary of a person's career.

curry *n* a highly spiced sauce; a dish spiced with this; * *vt* to flavour with curry; to comb a horse; to seek favour.

curse *vt* to call down evil on; to blight; to torment; * *vi* to swear; * *n* an oath.

cursive *adj* running; flowing; * *n* running script.

cursory *adj* hasty; careless; superficial.

curt *adj* short; rude; abrupt.

curtail *vt* to cut short; reduce *eg* privileges.

curtain *n* a screen of draped fabric for a window, door or theatre stage; (~s *pl*, *sl*) the end; death; * *vt* to enclose with curtains.

curtsey *n* an obeisance or bow.

curve *n* a bent line; an arch; * *vt*, *vi* to bend.

cushion *n* a pillow for a seat; the padded rim of a snooker table; any buffer against shock; * *vt* to furnish with cushions; to protect; to lessen impact.

cusp *n* an apex or peak; the horn of the crescent moon; (geometry) the point at which two arcs approaching from the same direction, meet, terminating with a common tangent; (botany) a pointed end, *esp* of a leaf; a cone-shaped prominence on the surface of a tooth, *esp* of a molar or pre-molar.

custard *n* a thick sauce, *usu* for puddings, made from of corn-flour, milk, eggs, sugar and flavouring.

custodian *n* a guardian; a keeper.

custody *n* care; security; imprisonment.

custom *n* habit; fashion; business patronage; (*pl*) duties on merchandise imported or exported.

customer *n* a regular purchaser at a shop or from a business.

cut *vt* to divide into pieces; to mow; to clip; to reduce; * *vi* to make an incision; to stop filming; * *adj* gashed; * *n* a wound; form; fashion or shape of a garment; a reduction in price; a share of gains.

cuticle *n* the skin at the base of fingernails and toenails.

cutlass *n* a broad, curving sword.

cutlery *n* instruments used for eating; forks, knives and spoons.

cutlet *n* a piece of meat cut off the ribs, leg or neck; a chop.

cutter *n* a light sailing vessel; a ship's boat; one who cuts cloth.

cutting *n* a piece cut off; an incision; a passage; a piece cut off a plant for propagating; an excerpt cut from a newspaper; film editing.

cyanide *n* any of the poisonous salts or esters of hydrocyanic acid.

cyberpunk *n* a distopian style of science fiction *usu* set in large cities with high technology *eg* virtual reality.

cycle *n* a period of time; a series; a bicycle; * *vi* to ride a bicycle.

cyclic, cyclical *adj* recurring in series.

cyclone *n* a storm moving in a circle; a hurricane.

cylinder *n* a solid or hollow roller-shaped body.

cymbal *n* a musical instrument of two brass plates which are clashed together.

cynic *n* a sneering, censorious person.

cypher *n see* cipher.

cyst *n* a sac in animal bodies containing morbid matter.

czar, tsar *n* the former emperor of Russia.

D

dab *vt* to press a surface lightly with something soft or moist; * *n* a gentle blow; a small mass of anything soft or moist; an adept;

a small fish of the genus *Limanda*.

dabble *vt* to wet; to sprinkle; to move hands or feet in water; * *vi* to trifle.

dagger *n* a short sharp-pointed sword.

daily *adj* happening every day; * *adv* day by day; * *n* a newspaper published every weekday.

dainty *adj* nice; delicate; elegant; * *n* a delicacy.

dairy *n* a place where milk is sold, or converted into butter or cheese.

dais *n* a raised platform; the high table where principal guests or speakers are seated.

dale *n* a valley.

dalliance *n* lovemaking; trifling.

dally *vi* to trifle; to delay; to lose time by idleness.

dam *n* a barrier to confine water; a mother (of a four-footed animal); * *vt* to confine by a dam.

damage *n* hurt; injury; money; compensation; * *vt* to injure; to harm.

dame *n* a title given to women with the rank knight commander or a holder of the Grand Cross in the Orders of Chivalry; a comical middle-aged female pantomime character.

damn *vt* to condemn; to curse; to consign to eternal punishment.

damp *adj* moist; humid; * *n* moist air; * *vt* to moisten; to dispirit; to stifle.

damsel *n* (archaic, poetic) a young girl.

damson *n* a small dark purple plum-like fruit.

dance *vi* to move in time to music; to skip or leap lightly; * *n* a party for dancing; a dance performance of an artistic nature; music for dancing.

dandruff *n* scurf on the head under the hair.

dandy *n* a fop; a coxcomb.

danger *n* risk; hazard; peril.

dangle *vi* to hang loose; * *vt* to swing.

dank *adj* damp; moist.

dapper *adj* small and neat.

dappled *adj* spotted.

dare *vt*, *vi* to be bold; to defy; to challenge; * *n* a challenge.

dark *adj* without light; gloomy; secret; ignorant; having brown or black skin or hair; * *n* darkness; ignorance.

darling *adj* dearly beloved; * *n* one much beloved.

darn *vt* to mend holes in clothes.

dart *n* a pointed missile thrown by the hand; a sudden bound; * *vi* to move rapidly; (*pl*) an indoor game in which darts are thrown at a target.

dash *vt, vi* to shatter; to rush; to frustrate; * *n* a violent striking; a rushing or onset; a mark in writing (–); a small quantity; a tinge.

dashboard *n* an instrument panel in a car.

dashing *adj* spirited; showy; stylish.

data *see* **datum**.

date *n* the time when any event happened; an appointment, especially with a prospective partner; * *vt, vi* to note the time of; to affix a date to.

dative *adj, n* a grammatical case.

datum *n* (*pl* **data**) a fact useable as the basis for further inference.

daub *vt* to smear; to paint without skill; * *n* poor painting; a smear.

daughter *n* a female child; any thing or attribute personified as a daughter in relation to its source; (physics) the nucleotide formed after the decay of a larger nucleus; (biology) a cell formed by the division of another.

daughter-in-law *n* a son's wife.

daunt *vt* to intimidate; to scare; to cow.

dauntless *adj* fearless.

dawdle *vi* to waste time; to saunter.

dawn *vi* to grow light; * *n* the break of day; first appearance.

day *n* a period of 24 continuous hours; the time of daylight; time.

daybreak *n* the dawn.

daydream *n* a reverie.

daylight *n* the light of the sun; dawn.

daytime *n* the time of daylight.

daze *vt* to stupefy; to stun; to perplex; * *n* confusion; bewilderment especially produced by a blow or a shock.

dazzle *vt* to overpower with light or splendour; * *vi* to be intensely bright.

deacon *n* a church official.

dead *adj* without life; perfectly still; exact; * *n* stillness; gloom.

deaden *vt* to make numb; to muffle.

dead-end *n* a cul-de-sac; a hopeless situation; a job without prospects.

deadline *n* the time or date by which a thing must be done.

deadlock *n* a complete standstill; a clash of interests making progress impossible.

deadly *adj* mortal; implacable.

deadpan *adj* deliberately expressionless.

deaf *adj* unable to hear; inattentive.

deal *n* an indefinite quantity; a business transaction; the distribution of playing cards; * *vt* to distribute; to behave; to do business with; to solve.

dean *n* the head of the chapter of a cathedral; a university officer.

dear *adj* costly; valuable; beloved.

dearth *n* scarcity; want.

death *n* extinction of life; decease; the destruction of something.

débâcle *n* a sudden break-up; a crash; a rout.

debar *vt* to shut out from something.

debase *vt* to lower; to degrade.

debate *n* a discussion; a formal argument; controversy; * *vt, vi* to dispute; to deliberate.

debauch *vt* to corrupt; * *vi* to revel; * *n* excess in eating or drinking.

debilitate *vt* to enfeeble.

debility *n* weakness.

debit *n* a recorded item of debt; the left-hand page or debtor side of a ledger.

debonair *adj* suave; carefree; sprightly.

débris *n* (*sing* or *pl*) fragments; rubbish; wreckage.

debt *n* what is owing; an obligation.

début *n* a first appearance in public.

decade *n* a period of ten years.

decadence *n* a falling off; decay; deterioration *esp* of morality.

decamp *vi* to leave without notice.

decant *vt* to pour from one vessel into another.

decapitate *vt* to behead.

decay *vi* to fall away; to wither; * *n* decline; putrefaction.

deceased *adj* dead.

deceit *n* fraud; guile; treachery.

deceive *vt* to mislead; to cheat.

December *n* the twelfth month of the year.

decency *n* propriety.

decent *adj* quite good; kind; generous.

decentralise *vt* to transfer power from central to the local authority.

deception *n* the act or state of being deceived; fraud.

decide *vt*, *vi* to determine; to settle; to resolve; to give a judgment on.

deciduous *adj* (of trees) shedding all leaves annually; (of leaves or antlers) shed periodically; anything transitory.

decimal *adj* by tens; having 10 as the basis of numeration.

decimate *vt* to destroy a large number; to kill or destroy one in every ten of.

decipher *vt* to decode; to solve.

decision *n* determination of a judgment; verdict; firmness of character.

decisive *adj* conclusive; absolute.

deck *vt* to clothe; to adorn; * *n* the floor of a ship, aircraft, bus or bridge; a pack of playing cards; the turntable of a record player.

declaim *vi* to make a formal speech; to harangue.

declare *vt*, *vi* to make known; to assert; to admit possession of (dutiable goods).

declension *n* a falling off; (grammar) the variation in form of nouns.

decline *vi* to bend downwards; to fail; * *vt* to refuse; to diminish; to draw to an end; (grammar) to inflect a noun; * *n* a falling off; decay; consumption.

decode *vt* convert a coded message into intelligible language.

decompose *vt* to resolve into original elements; * *vi* to decay.

decontaminate *vt* remove pollution from an area or person.

décor *n* general decorative effect or appearance of a room or building.

decorate *vt* to adorn; to deck.

decorous *adj* seemly; becoming.

decorum *n* propriety; seemliness.

decoy *n* an animal or bird trained to lure others into a snare; one who lures others into a trap; * *vt* to lure into a snare.

decrease *vi*, *vt* to become or make less; * *n* a diminution; a reduction.

decree *n* an edict; an order or law; * *vt* to enact; to award.

decrepit *adj* broken down with age.

dedicate *vt* to consecrate; (author) to inscribe (a book) to another; * *vr* to devote oneself.

deduce *vt* to infer; to arrive at by reasoning.

deduct *vt* to subtract from.

deed *n* an act; feat; a written agreement.

deem *vt* to judge; * *vi* to be of opinion.

deep *adj* being far below the surface; involved; profound; intense; secret; artful; * *n* the sea.

deer *n* (*pl* deer) any hoofed grazing animal of the family *Cervidae*.

deface *vt* to disfigure; to erase.

defame *vt* to slander.

default *n* an omission; neglect; absence; lapse; * *vi* to fail to meet payment or keep contract.

defeat *n* overthrow; loss of battle; frustration of one's plans; loss of a game, race etc; * *vt* to frustrate; to conquer.

defect *n* a want; a blemish.

defection *n* abandonment of a person or cause.

defence *n* a protection; fortification; vindication; (sport) preventing the opposing side scoring a goal; the defending players in a team.

defend *vt* to guard; to support; to act as defendant.

defendant *n* one sued at law.

defer *vt* to postpone; * *vi* to yield to another's opinion, wishes, judgment.

deferential *adj* respectful.

defiance *n* wilful disobedience; a challenge to fight; contempt of danger.

deficient *adj* defective; lacking.

deficit *n* shortage; the amount by

which a sum falls short of what is needed; an excess of expenditure over income.

defile *vt* to pollute; * *n* a narrow pass.

define *vt* to limit; to explain exactly.

definite *adj* precise; exact.

definition *n* an explanation or description.

definitive *adj* limiting; positive; final.

deflate *vt* to release gas or air from; to reduce in size or importance; to reduce inflation in the economy.

deflect *vi* to deviate; * *vt* to turn aside.

deflower *vt* to strip of flowers; to ravish; to take the virginity of.

defoliation *n* the shedding of leaves.

deform *vt* to disfigure.

defraud *vt* to cheat.

deft *adj* apt; clever; nimble.

defunct *adj* deceased; no longer functioning; * *n* a dead person.

defuse *vt* to disarm an explosive by removing its fuse; to decrease tension in a crisis or other situation.

defy *vt* to dare; to challenge; to set at nought; to resist attempts at; to elude.

degenerate *vi* to decline in good qualities; * *adj* depraved; base; * *n* a degenerate or immoral person.

degrade *vt* to depose; to dishonour.

degree *n* a step; rank; grade; measure; the measure of an angle such that a right angle has 90 degrees; a university distinction.

dehydrate *vt* to remove water from; * *vi* to lose water *esp* from body tissue.

deify *vt* to make a god of; to idolise.

deign *vi* to condescend.

deity *n* a god.

deject *vt* to dispirit; to depress.

delay *vt, vi* to defer; to retard; to stop; to linger; * *n* a stay; a hindrance.

delectable *adj* delightful.

delegate *vt* to send as a representative; * *n* a representative; an agent.

delete *vt* to erase; to efface.

deleterious *adj* hurtful.

deliberate *vi, vt* to consider; to

debate; * *adj* cautious; well-advised; intentional.

deliberation *n* thoughtful consideration.

delicacy *n* refinement of taste; tenderness; a luxurious food.

delicate *adj* fragile; easily broken or damaged; feeling unwell.

delicious *adj* highly delightful especially to the taste.

delight *n* great joy or pleasure; * *vt, vi* to charm; to take great pleasure.

delineate *vt* to draw in outline; to sketch.

delinquent *adj* neglecting duty; * *n* an offender, *esp* a young one.

delirious *adj* raving; frenzied.

deliver *vt* to set free; to rescue; to hand over; to carry and distribute regularly; to give birth; to launch or throw.

delivery *n* childbirth; rescue; distribution (of letters); manner of speaking; the act of giving birth; the bowling of a ball in cricket.

dell *n* a small valley.

delta *n* the space between diverging mouths of a river; the fourth letter of the Greek alphabet.

delude *vt* to deceive; to trick.

deluge *n* a flood; the flood; heavy rain; * *vt* to inundate; to drown.

delusion *n* a mistaken idea; a fallacy.

delve *vt, vi* to dig.

demagogue *n* a politician deriving power from appealing to popular prejudices.

demand *vt* to claim by right; to question; * *n* a claim, often urgent; a challenging; the desire shown by consumers for particular goods or services.

demarcation *n* a boundary; a fixed limit.

demean *vt* to lower in dignity; to debase.

demeanour *n* behaviour.

demented *adj* insane; infatuated.

demise *n* death; termination.

demobilise *vt* to discharge from the armed forces; to disband.

democracy *n* government by the

people through elected representatives; political, social or
legal equality.

democrat *n* a friend to popular
government.

demolish *vt* to pull down; to defeat.

demon *n* an evil spirit; the
personification of dark passion;
(*sl*) an impressive performer.

demonstrate *vt* to prove beyond
doubt; to exhibit; * *vi* to show
support for a cause by public
protest and parades.

demoralise *vt* to corrupt; to dispirit.

demur *vi* to hesitate; to object;
* *n* pause; objection.

demure *adj* affectedly modest.

den *n* the lair of a wild beast; a
place of crime and iniquity (*eg*
opium den); a hideaway for
children; a private room for
pursuing interests.

denial *n* contradiction; refusal of
a request; reluctance to admit
the truth of something.

denim *n* a hard-wearing cloth
especially for work clothes and
jeans;(*pl*) trousers of this.

denomination *n* class; religious sect.

denominator *n* the divisor in a
vulgar fraction.

denote *vt* to indicate; to imply; to
mean.

denounce *vt* to threaten; to
condemn; to accuse publicly.

dense *adj* thick; close.

density *n* compactness; stupidity;
the ratio of mass to volume.

dent *n* a mark made by a blow or
pressure; * *vt* to mark.

dental *adj* pertaining to the teeth.

dentist *n* one qualified to treat
disorders of the teeth.

denude *vt* to make bare; to strip.

denunciation *n* the utterance of a
threat, censure or menace.

deny *vt* to contradict; to disavow.

deodorant *n* a preparation that
masks body odours.

depart *vi* to go away; to deviate; to
die.

department *n* a separate part; a
division; a branch; a place of
activity.

depend *vi* to be reliant on.

dependant *n* one who depends on
another; a retainer.

dependency *n* a subject territory;
a state of need of something.

depict *vt* to portray; to describe.

depilate *vt* to strip of hair.

deplete *vt* to empty; to exhaust.

deplore *vt* to regret deeply; to
deprecate.

deploy *vt* to open out; to distribute
and position (soldiers) strategi-
cally.

deport *vt* to expel (an alien) from a
country; *vr* to conduct (oneself).

deportment *n* carriage; behaviour.

depose *vt* to dethrone; to divest of
office.

deposit *vt* to lay down; to lodge in
a place; * *n* something deposited;
money left in a bank; money left
in security.

deposition *n* affidavit; testimony;
displacement.

depot *n* a storehouse; a warehouse;
a place for storing military
supplies; a military training
centre; a railway or bus station.

deprave *vt* to corrupt.

deprecate *vi* to disapprove of.

depreciate *vt* to lower the value of;
to undervalue; * *vi* to fall in value.

depress *vt* to press down; to deject.

depression *n* dejection; an
economic phase characterised by
stagnation and unemployment; a
lowering of atmospheric
pressure; a hollow.

deprive *vt* to take from; to dispossess.

depth *n* deepness; a deep place;
intensity; profoundness.

deputation *n* persons sent to act
for others.

deputy *n* a substitute; a representative.

derange *vt* to displace; to disorder;
to unbalance; to make insane.

derail *vt* (*usu* in passive) to cause
a train to leave the tracks; to
halt some process.

derelict *adj* abandoned; * *n* the
thing or person abandoned.

deride *vt* to ridicule; to jeer.

derision *n* mockery.

derivation *adj* source or origin.

derive *vt*, *vi* to obtain; to draw; to

trace to its origin; to come from.

dermatology *n* the study of skin and its diseases.

derogatory *adj* disparaging.

descend *vi*, *vt* to climb down; to invade; to be derived; to sink morally.

descendant *n* an heir; offspring.

descent *n* act of descending; declivity; invasion; lineage.

describe *vt* to portray; to relate.

desecrate *vt* to violate a sacred place.

desert *adj* waste; * *n* a sandy barren region; * *vt* to leave; to quit; * *vi* to run away, especially from the armed forces; * *n* virtue; merit.

deserter *n* a runaway.

deserve *vt*, *vi* to merit.

desiccate *vt* to dry.

design *vt* to plan; to propose; to make working drawings for; * *vi* to intend; * *n* a drawing or sketch; purpose; aim.

designate *vt* to point out; to name; to mark; to appoint or nominate for a position.

designedly *adv* purposely.

designer *n* one who designs; a creator of high-class fashion clothes; * *adj* of the latest fashion or trend.

desire *n* longing; craving; love; * *vt* to wish for; to covet.

desist *vi* to stop; to leave off.

desk *n* a (sloping) table designed for writer's or reader's use; the section of a newspaper or bureaucracy responsible for a particular topic.

desolate *adj* forlorn; forsaken; waste; * *vt* to lay waste.

desolation *n* ruin; gloom; loneliness.

despair *n* hopelessness; * *vi* to give up all hope.

despatch, **dispatch** *vt* to send away in haste; to kill; to perform quickly; * *n* an official message; speed.

desperate *adj* reckless; hopeless; urgently needing money; extreme; dangerous.

despicable *adj* contemptible.

despise *vt* to scorn; to disdain.

despite *prep* notwithstanding; in spite of.

despoil *vt* to rob; to rifle; to plunder.

despondent *adj* dejected; hopeless.

despot *n* a tyrant.

dessert *n* the fruit or sweet course at the end of a meal.

destination *n* a goal; the place to which one is going.

destiny *n* fate; a predetermined course of events.

destitute *adj* in want; forlorn.

destroy *vt* to pull down; to overthrow; to kill.

destroyer *n* a small swift warship to destroy submarines.

destruction *n* ruin; death; slaughter.

desultory *adj* casual; rambling.

detach *vt* to separate; to release.

detached *adj* separate; aloof; unbiased.

detachment *n* separation; a body of troops away from the main army.

detail *vt* to recount; to set apart; * *n* an individual fact; an item; a small part of a painting or sculpture; a small detachment of personnel for special duties.

detailed *adj* minute; thorough.

detain *vt* to keep back; to arrest; to place in confinement.

detect *vt* to discover; to notice.

detective *n* a police officer whose duty is to detect criminals.

detention *n* act of detaining; confinement; being kept in (school) after hours.

deter *vt* to hinder; to discourage.

detergent *adj* cleansing; purging; * *n* a cleaning agent.

deteriorate *vi* to grow worse; * *vt* to depreciate.

determinant *adj* serving to determine or define; * *n* a determining factor.

determine *vt* to bound; to fix permanently; to resolve; to bring to an end.

deterrent *n* a warning; a curb; a nuclear weapon to deter attack through fear of retaliation; * *adj* deterring.

detest *vt* to abhor; to loathe.

detestable *adj* odious.

dethrone *vt* to depose.

detonate *vt*, *vi* to explode.

detour *n* a roundabout way.

detract *vt, vi* to disparage; to defame.

detriment *n* loss; damage.

devastate *vt* to lay waste.

develop *vt* to unfold; to make visible; to make to grow; to treat a photographic film or plate to reveal an image; * *vi* to grow or expand.

development *n* growth; land or property that has been improved.

deviate *vi* to stray; to wander; to diverge.

device *n* a contrivance; an emblem.

devil *n* an evil spirit; Satan; a wicked person; (*sl*) a difficulty; * *vt* to pepper and grill; * *vi* to drudge for another, especially a barrister.

devious *adj* circuitous; deceitful; underhand.

devise *vt* to plan; to contrive; to invent.

devoid *adj* destitute; free from.

devolve *vt* to transfer; to depute.

devote *vt* to dedicate; to give or use for a particular activity or purpose.

devotion *n* consecration; attachment; strong affection; piety.

devour *vt* to eat ravenously; to swallow up; to absorb eagerly.

devout *adj* pious; sincere.

dew *n* atmospheric vapour deposited on cool surfaces at night.

dexterity *n* adroitness; skill.

diabetes *n* any metabolic disorder characterised by excessive thirst and large urine production, *esp* ~ mellitus, the type caused by insulin deficiency.

diabolic(al) *adj* fiendish.

diagnose *vt* to identify a disease from symptoms; to identify faults in mechanical devices in a similar fashion.

diagonal *adj* applied to a line drawn from corner to corner.

diagram *n* an illustrative figure in outline.

dial *n* a time recorder; the face of a clock; the numbered disc on some telephones for connecting some calls.

dialect *n* the form of a language peculiar to a province.

dialectics *npl* the art of reasoning; logical skill.

dialogue *n* a conversation between two or more.

diameter *n* the line passing through or across the centre (especially of a circle).

diamond *n* a form of carbon, used as a gemstone, the hardest known natural material; a suit of playing cards.

diaphragm *n* the midriff, a muscle separating thorax and abdomen; a disc or plate closing partly or wholly a tube; a contraceptive cap.

diarrhoea *n* looseness of the bowels.

diary *n* a daily record of events.

diastole *n* dilation of the heart in beating.

diatribe *n* a tirade.

dice *see* die.

dictate *vt* to read words for reproduction by another person or by a recording machine; to prescribe; to order.

dictator *n* one invested with absolute authority.

diction *n* a way of speaking or enunciating; a choice of words.

dictionary *n* a book with the words of a language arranged alphabetically, with their meanings and other information such as pronunciation and derivation.

didactic *adj* instructive.

die *vi* to cease to live; to expire; * *n* (*pl* dice) a cube with sides marked 1, 2, 3, 4, 5, 6, used in games of chance; a stamp.

diesel *n* (in full ~ engine) an internal combustion engine in which the temperature rise generated by the process of compression ignites the fuel-air mixture; a vehicle driven by a diesel engine; the fuel for a diesel engine; (in full ~ oil).

diet *n* food; a course of feeding; * *vt, vi* to eat or cause to eat according to special guidelines.

differ *vi* to be unlike; to disagree.

different *adj* distinct; dissimilar.

differential *adj* discriminating; variable; relating to increments in given functions; * *n* an infinitesimal difference between two states of a variable quantity; the difference in wage rates for different types of labour, especially within a particular industry.

differentiate *vt* to mark or distinguish by a difference; to calculate the rate of change of a function with respect to one of its variables.

differentiation *n* (maths) the act of calculating the rate of change of a function with respect to one of its variables.

difficult *adj* arduous; perplexing; hard to please; hard to understand.

diffident *adj* wanting confidence; bashful.

diffuse *vt* to pour out and spread; to proclaim; * *adj* widely spread; not concise.

dig *vt* to turn up with a spade; * *vi* to work with a spade; to excavate; to investigate; to nudge; to understand; to approve.

digest *vt* to assimilate; to dissolve in the stomach; * *n* a summary.

digit *n* a finger; any of the figures 0 to 9.

digital *adj* of, using digits *eg* a clock.

dignify *vt* to ennoble; to grace; to exalt.

dignitary *n* one holding high rank.

dignity *n* honour; rank; formality in manner and appearance.

digress *vi* to depart from main subject; to deviate.

dike, **dyke** *n* a ditch; an embankment.

dilapidated *adj* in a ruinous condition.

dilate *vt*, *vi* to expand; to distend.

dilator *n* a muscle which dilates an organ or aperture; a surgical instrument to do this.

dilatory *adj* tardy; slow.

dilemma *n* a fix; a quandary.

diligent *adj* industrious; persevering.

dilute *vt* to reduce in strength by adding water or some qualifying matter; * *adj* weak; diluted.

dim *adj* obscure; faint; * *vt* to dull; to make dark.

dimension *n* the measure of a thing; size, extent, capacity.

diminish *vt*, *vi* to lessen; to decrease.

diminutive *adj* small; * *n* a word denoting smallness, a pet name.

dimple *n* a small hollow on the cheek or chin.

din *n* a loud sound long continued; * *vt* to stun with noise; to teach with constant repetition.

dine *vi* to eat dinner.

dinghy *n* a small ship's boat.

dingy *adj* dull; faded.

dinner *n* the principal meal of the day.

diocese *n* the see of a bishop.

dip *vt* to plunge quickly in and out of a liquid; to immerse; * *vi* to incline; * *n* a bathe; downward slope; a mixture in which to dip something.

diphtheria *n* an infectious throat disease.

diphthong *n* the blending of two vowel sounds.

diploma *n* a document conferring a degree of honour.

diplomacy *n* the art of negotiating especially between nations; tact.

dire *adj* dreadful; urgent.

direct *adj* straight; express; sincere; * *vt* to point or aim at; to show; to conduct; to order; to instruct; to address a letter.

direction *n* course; guidance; command; management; address on a letter; the way in which one is pointing.

directly *adv* without delay; expressly.

director *n* a superintendent; a counsellor; one who directs the production of a stage or screen show.

directory *n* a book listing information classified by names, addresses, services offered.

dirt *n* any filthy substance; scandal.

disable *vt* to deprive of power; to injure.

disabled *adj* handicapped physically.

disabuse *vt* to undeceive.

disadvantage *n* inconvenience; loss.

disaffect *vt* to estrange; to make discontented.

disagree *vi* to differ; to fall out; to dissent.

disappear *vi* to vanish from sight.

disappoint *vt* to fail to fulfil the hopes of a person; to frustrate.

disapprobation *n* disapproval; censure.

disapproval *n* dislike; blame.

disapprove *vt* to censure as wrong; to blame.

disarm *vt, vi* to deprive of arms; to disband.

disarrange *vt* to derange; to upset.

disarray *vt* to throw into disorder; * *n* disorder.

disaster *n* a calamity; a failure.

disavowal *n* denial.

disband *vt* to disperse; * *vi* to break up.

disbar *vt* to deprive a barrister of the right to practise.

disbelief *n* want of belief; distrust.

disburse *vt* to pay out.

disc (computer disk) *n* the flat face of a thin, round body such as a coin, counter, or compact disk.

discard *vt* to throw away.

discern *vt, vi* to perceive; to judge.

discharge *vt* to unload; to fire; to dismiss; to perform; to acquit; * *n* a dismissal; release; matter coming from a sore or wound.

disciple *n* a learner; a follower.

disciplinarian *n* one who enforces discipline; a martinet.

discipline *n* training; order; subjection to laws; punishment; correction; * *vt* to train; to punish to enforce discipline; to bring under control.

disclaim *vt* to disown, reject.

disclaimer *n* disavowal; denial.

disclose *vt* to open; to uncover; to reveal.

disco *n* see discothèque.

discolour *vt* to change the colour; to stain.

discomfort *n* uneasiness; its cause; lack of comfort.

disconcert *vt* to embarrass.

disconnect *vt* to disunite; to separate.

disconsolate *adj* comfortless.

discontinue *vt, vi* to leave off; to cease.

discord *n* want of harmony; strife.

discordant *adj* harsh sounding.

discothèque *n* (a club for) dancing to recorded popular music.

discount *n* a sum deducted from the cost; * *vt* to cash a bill at present worth; to take away from.

discourage *vt* to dishearten; to dissuade.

discourse *n* a speech; a treatise; a sermon; * *vi* to talk.

discourteous *adj* rude.

discover *vt* to lay open to view; to detect; to find or learn about for the first time.

discredit *n* want of credit; distrust; * *vt* to damage the reputation of.

discreet *adj* prudent.

discrepancy *n* variance; a disagreement as between figures in a total.

discretion *n* prudence; judgment.

discretionary *adj* left to one's judgment.

discriminate *vt* to distinguish; to select.

discursive *adj* rambling.

discus *n* a heavy, thick-centred disc, thrown originally as a weapon, now in athletic events.

discuss *vt* to debate; to examine by argument.

disdain *vt* to scorn; * *n* contempt.

disease *n* an ailment.

disembark *vt, vi* to put or go ashore.

disembody *vt* to divest of the body.

disenchant *vt* to disillusion.

disengage *vt* to detach; to release; to extricate.

disentangle *vt* to extricate.

disfavour *n* want of approval.

disfigure *vt* to mar the appearance of.

disgorge *vt* to vomit; to discharge; to surrender.

disgrace *n* shame; dishonour.

disguise *vt* to conceal; to dissemble; to change the appearance of; * *n* a make up; a pretence; a false appearance.

disgust *n* loathing; repugnance; * *vt* to offend; to sicken.

dish *n* a vessel for serving food; the food served; * *vt* to put in a dish.

dishearten *vt* to discourage.

dishevelled *adj* disarranged; untidy.

dishonest *adj* fraudulent; untrustworthy.

dishonour *n* disgrace; * *vt* to bring shame on; to refuse payment of.

disinclined *adj* unwilling.

disinfect *vt* to cleanse of infection.

disinfectant *n* a substance that destroys infectious germs.

disingenuous *adj* crafty; cunning.

disinherit *t* to cut off from inheriting.

disintegrate *vt* to break up into parts.

disinterested *adj* impartial.

disjointed *adj* unconnected; incoherent.

disk *see* disc.

dislike *n* aversion; distaste; * *vt* to feel aversion to.

dislocate *vt* to displace a joint; to upset the working of.

dislodge *vt* to remove; to oust.

disloyal *adj* faithless; untrustworthy.

dismal *adj* dark; gloomy.

dismantle *vt* to strip; to take apart.

dismay *vt* to terrify; to appal; * *n* terror; consternation.

dismember *vt* to sever the limbs from; to partition or divide up.

dismiss *vt* to send away.

dismount *vi* to descend from a horse.

disobey *vt* to neglect or refuse to obey.

disobliging *adj* unaccommodating.

disorder *n* confusion; disease; * *vt* to disarrange.

disorganise *vt* to throw into confusion.

disown *vt* to repudiate; to refuse to acknowledge as one's own.

disparage *vt* to deprecate; to belittle.

disparate *adj* unlike.

disparity *n* inequality.

dispassionate *adj* cool; impartial.

dispel *vt* to scatter; to banish.

dispensary *n* a place where medicines are made up and dispensed.

dispensation *n* distribution; exemption.

disperse *vt*, *vi* to scatter; to diffuse; to vanish.

dispirited *adj* dejected.

displace *vt* to derange; to supersede.

display *vt* to unfold; to show; to parade; * *vi* to make a show; * *n* exhibition; parade; visual ~ unit a computer monitor for presenting information.

displease *vt* to offend; to disgust.

disport *n* pastime; * *vi* to frolic; to gambol.

disposable *adj* designed to be discarded after use; available.

dispose *vt*, *vi* to arrange; to incline; to regulate; to give, sell or transfer to another; to throw away.

disposition *n* order; character; inclination; arrangement.

dispossess *vt* to deprive of possession.

disproportion *n* inequality.

disprove *vt* to prove to be wrong; to confute.

dispute *vi* to argue; to debate; * *vt* to impugn; * *n* controversy; strife.

disqualify *vt* to make ineligible through violation of rules; to incapacitate.

disquiet *n* unrest; anxiety.

disregard *n* neglect; * *vt* to slight; to ignore.

disrepair *n* neglect.

disreputable *adj* of bad character.

disrepute *n* disgrace.

disrespect *n* discourtesy.

disrobe *vt* to undress; to uncover.

disruption *n* disorder; confusion.

dissatisfied *adj* discontented.

dissect *vt* to cut up; to examine minutely.

dissemble *vt*, *vi* to hide; to disguise.

disseminate *vt* to spread abroad especially ideas and information.

dissent *vi* to disagree; to separate from an established church;

dissertation *n* a formal discourse or treatise.

disservice *n* a bad turn.

dissident *adj* dissenting; * *n* one who disagrees with policies so strongly as to risk imprisonment.

dissimilar *adj* unlike.

dissipate *vi* to scatter; to squander.

dissipated *adj* dissolute.

dissociate *vt* to disunite; to repudiate a connection with.

dissolute *adj* profligate.

dissolution *n* melting; break up (of a parliament); death.

dissolve *vt, vi* to liquefy; to break up legally; to annul; to be overcome with emotion.

dissonant *n* (music) unharmonious; clashing.

dissuade *vt* to exhort against; to deter by argument.

distance *n* remoteness in place or time; space between two points or places; reserve; * *vt* to outstrip.

distant *adj* far off; cold; shy.

distaste *n* dislike.

distemper *n* a disordered state of mind or body; a dog disease; a kind of paint for plaster without oil.

distend *vt, vi* to stretch; to swell.

distention *n* inflation.

distil *vi, vt* to extract the essence of; to fall in drops; to rectify or purify.

distillery *n* a distilling factory.

distinct *adj* separate; clear; definite.

distinguish *vt, vi* to mark a difference; to perceive; to honour.

distinguished *adj* eminent; of elegant appearance.

distort *vt* to twist; to misrepresent.

distract *vt* to draw the attention aside; to bewilder; to confuse.

distraught *adj* distracted; agitated.

distress *n* anguish; destitution; * *vt* to afflict with pain.

distribute *vt* to deal out; to apportion; to classify.

district *n* a region.

distrust *vt* to doubt; to suspect; * *n* doubt; suspicion

disturb *vt* to throw into disorder; to agitate.

disuse *n* neglect; * *vt* to cease to use.

ditch *n* a long narrow trench.

divan *n* a sofa or bed without back or sides.

dive *vi* to plunge into water head foremost; (aircraft) to descend steeply; to submerge; to dash headlong into.

diverge *vi* to deviate; to digress

diverse *adj* different; unlike.

diversion *n* amusement; a feigned attack.

diversity *n* variety.

divert *vt* to cause to change route.

divest *vt* to strip; to unclothe.

divide *vt* to separate into parts; to share; to sever; to estrange; * *vi* to part; to vote.

dividend *n* a number to he divided; share of profit.

divider *n* a distributor; (*pl*) compasses.

divine *adj* of or belonging to God; * *n* a clergyman; * *vt, vi* to foretell; to guess; to dowse for water.

divinity *n* the science of divine things.

division *n* act of dividing; separation; a separation into two opposing sides to vote; disunion; portion; a process in arithmetic.

divisive *adj* creating division or discord.

divisor *n* the number by which the dividend is divided.

divorce *n* the dissolution of a marriage; a separation; * *vt* to dissolve a marriage.

divot *n* a piece of turf, *esp* one cut out inadvertently during a golf shot or at polo.

divulge *vt* to disclose.

dizzy *adj* giddy.

do *vt, aux* to perform; to bring about; to prepare; * *vi* to act or behave; to fare in health; to cheat; to rob; * *n* a party.

docile *adj* easily taught; tractable.

dock *n* an enclosed basin for ships; an enclosure in court for prisoners; * *vt* to cut off; to put a ship in dock.

dockyard *n* an area with docks and facilities for repairing ships.

doctor *n* a learned person; a physician.

doctorate *n* the degree of a doctor.

doctrine *n* a principle or belief; the teaching of a person, school, or church.

document *n* written evidence or proof.

dodge *vt, vi* to move nimbly aside; to evade a duty; to quibble; * *n* a trick.

doe *n* a female fallow deer, reindeer, hare or rabbit.

dog *n* a domesticated carnivorous mammal, *Canis familiaris*; a wild animal of the genus *canis*, which includes wolves, or of the family *canidae*, which includes foxes; * *vt* to follow closely.

dogged *adj* obstinate; relentless.

dogma *n* a body of opinion; authoritative belief.

doldrums *npl* the dumps; equatorial region of calms.

dole *n* that which is dealt out; *sl* benefits received from the State while unemployed; * *vt* to deal out in small quantities.

doleful *adj* woeful; gloomy; sad.

doll *n* a child's toy in human form.

dollar *n* the American unit of money.

domain *n* an estate; a province; a sphere of activity.

dome *n* an arched roof; a large cupola.

domestic *adj* belonging to the home; tame; * *n* a household servant.

domicile *n* a habitation.

dominant *adj* ruling.

dominate *vt* to rule; to cow.

domineer *vi* to assume influence over others.

dominion *n* territory with one ruler or government; authority.

domino *n* (*pl* dominoes) a masquerade dress; a half-mask; (*pl*) a game played with dotted ivory or bone rectangles.

don *vt* to put on * *n* a fellow of an Oxford college.

donate *vt* to bestow.

donation *n* a gift.

donkey *n* a domestic ass; a stupid person.

donor *n* one who gives; *usu* blood, or bequests to museums and galleries.

doom *n* fate; ruin; * *vt* to condemn to failure or ruin.

door *n* the entrance of a house, room, car; the frame closing it.

dormant *adj* sleeping; inactive.

dormitory *n* a sleeping room with many beds.

dorsal *adj* pertaining to the back.

dose *n* the quantity of medicine given at one time.

dot *n* a small point, as made with a pen; * *vt* to mark with a dot.

dotage *n* the feeble-mindedness of old age.

dote *vi* to be excessively fond of.

double *adj* twice as much; designed or intended for two; having two parts; * *adv* twice; in twos; * *n* twice as much; a person or thing identical to another; * *vt*, *vi* to make twice as much or as many; to fold onto itself; to bend.

double bass *n* the lowest-toned instrument of the violin class.

doubt *vi* to question; to suspect; * *vt* to believe to be uncertain.

doubtful *adj* feeling doubt; uncertain; suspicious.

doubtless *adv* unquestionably.

dough *n* flour moistened with water or milk and kneaded to make bread.

douse *vt*, *vi* to plunge into water.

dove *n* any bird of the family *columbidae*; an advocate of peaceful policies.

dovetail *n* (woodwork) joint of interlocking wedge shapes resembling a dove's tail.

dowager *n* a title given to the widow of a nobleman after his death.

dowdy *adj* ill-dressed; not stylish.

down *n* a hill; the fine soft feathers of birds; * *adv* towards or in a lower physical position; in a lower status or in a worse condition; * *adj* occupying a low position, especially lying on the ground; depressed, dejected; * *vt*, *vi* to defeat; to swallow.

downcast *adj* dejected.

downfall *n* ruin.

downpour *n* a heavy fall of rain.

downright *adj* plain; blunt; utter.

downtrodden *adj* oppressed.

downward(s) *adv* in a descending course; * *adj* descending.

dowry *n* a wife's marriage portion.

doze *vi* to be half-asleep; * *n* a light sleep.

dozen *n* twelve; baker's ~ thirteen.

drab *adj* of a dull brown colour; dull; uninteresting.

draconian *adj* very severe.

draft *n* a detachment of men or things; an order for money; the first sketch or outline of a composition, etc; * *vt* to sketch; to select.

draftsman *see* draughtsman.

drag *vt* to draw along slowly and with force; to search with a dragnet or a hook.

dragon *n* a fabulous winged monster.

drain *vt, vi* to draw off; to filter; to flow off, to drink the entire contents of; * *n* a sewer.

drake *n* a male duck.

dram *n* a unit of weight; a small draught of spirits.

drama *n* a stage, radio or television play.

dramatic *adj* theatrical.

drape *vt* to cover or hang with cloth.

drastic *adj* acting with strength or violence.

draught *n* the quantity drunk at once; a sketch; the depth a ship sinks in water; a current of air; (~s *pl*) a game on a squared board using 24 round pieces.

draughtsman *n* a designer.

draw *vt, vi* to pull along or towards; to cause to come; to sketch; to infer; to end a game with equal scores; to shrink; * *n* the act of drawing; a drawn game.

drawback *n* a defect; a hindrance or handicap.

drawbridge *n* a retractable (up and down or sideways) bridge, *usu* over the moat of a fortification.

drawer *n* one who draws a cheque; a sliding box in a table, chest or desk; (*pl*, archaic) an undergarment.

drawing *n* a fully-finished sketch, intended to be accurate.

drawing room *n* a reception or living room.

drawl *vi, vt* to speak slowly with drawn-out vowel sounds; * *n* such speech.

dread *n* fear; terror; * *adj* exciting great fear; terrible; * *vt* to anticipate fearfully.

dream *n* a vision in sleep; an idle fancy; an ambition; * *vt, vi* to have dreams; to fancy.

dreary *adj* cheerless.

dredge *n* a dragnet; * *vt* to scoop up, especially from the bottom of a body of water.

dregs *npl* lees; grounds.

drench *vt* to soak.

dress *vt* to clothe; to set in order; to decorate; to wash and bandage; to prepare food for cooking or stone for building work; * *n* clothes; a woman's one-piece garment; style or manner of clothing.

dressing *n* a bandage applied to a wound; a sauce.

dribble *vi* to trickle; * *vt* (sport) to move the ball little by little with the foot, hand or stick.

drift *n* a heap of snow or sand deposited by the wind; natural course, tendency; the general meaning or intention (of what is said); an aimless course.

drill *vt, vi* to bore a hole; to train (soldiers); to furrow; to sow in rows; * *n* a hole borer; a furrow; exercise; procedure; routine.

drink *vi* to swallow liquid; * *n* a beverage; alcoholic liquor.

drip *vi* to fall in drops; * *n* a liquid that falls in drops; its sound; a device for injecting a fluid slowly and continuously into a vein.

dripping *n* the fat from roasting meat.

drive *vt* (*pt* drove, *pp* driven) to urge, push or force onward; to convey in a vehicle; to propel (a ball) with hard blow; * *vi* to be forced along; to be conveyed in a vehicle; * *n* a trip in a vehicle; a stroke to drive a ball; a driveway; an intensive campaign; the transmission of power to machinery.

drizzle *vi* to rain in small fine drops; * *n* a fine rain.

droll *adj* comic; amusing; whimsical.

drone *n* the male or non-working bee; a humming sound; monotonous speech; * *vi* to hum; to speak in a monotonous tone.

droop *vi* to hang down; to languish.

drop *n* a globule of any liquid; a distance to fall; * *vt, vi* to pour or let fall in drops; to fall; to let fall; to sink; to set down from a vehicle; to mention in passing; to give up (an idea).

dropsy *n* an unnatural accumulation of water in the body.

dross *n* the scum of metals; refuse; rubbish.

drought *n* a period of very dry weather.

drove *n* a herd or flock in motion.

drown *vt, vi* to suffocate or be suffocated in water.

drowse *vi* to doze.

drudge *vi* to toil; to slave; * *n* a menial servant.

drug *n* narcotics; * *vt* to dose with drugs.

drum *n* (music) a percussion instrument; a stretched membrane in the ear.

drunk *adj* intoxicated.

drunkard *n* one given to drink.

dry *adj* free from moisture; thirsty; * *vt, vi* to free from moisture; thirsty; marked by a matter-of-fact, ironic or terse manner of speech; uninteresting.

dry rot *n* a timber disease.

dual *adj* consisting of two; twofold.

dubious *adj* wavering; uncertain; untrustworthy.

duchess *n* a noblewoman of equal rank to, or the wife of, a duke.

duchy *n* a country ruled by a duke.

duck *vt, vi* to plunge in water; to bow; * *n* any waterfowl of the family *Anatidae*; the female of these (male **drake**); its flesh as food; a score of zero in cricket.

duct *n* a narrow tube in the body; a channel or pipe for fluids or electric cables.

due *adj* owed; owing; proper; * *adv* directly; * *n* a fee; a right.

duel *n* a formally arranged fight between two persons; any contest of skill.

duet *n* a piece of music for two performers.

duke *n* the highest order of nobility.

dukedom *n* the lands or title of a duke.

dulcet *adj* sweet; melodious.

dull *adj* stupid; drowsy; cheerless; (knife) not sharp; * *vt* to make dull; to stupefy; to blunt; to sully.

duly *adv* properly; suitably.

dumb *adj* mute; silent.

dumbfound, *vt* to astonish; to confuse.

dummy *n* a stupid person; a figure used to display clothes; the

exposed hand in a game of bridge; a sham.

dump *n* a place for refuse; a temporary store; a dirty, dilapidated place; (~s *pl*) low spirits.

dunce *n* a stupid person.

dune *n* a sandhill on the sea coast.

dung *n* the excrement of animals.

dungeon *n* an underground prison.

duodenum *n* the first part of the small intestines.

dupe *n* one easily cheated; * *vt* to impose on; to deceive; to trick.

duplicate *adj* double; * *n* a copy.

duplicity *n* guile; trickery.

durable *adj* lasting; permanent.

duration *n* continuance; the period in which an event continues.

duress *n* constraint; imprisonment.

during *prep* for the time of.

dusk *n* twilight.

dusky *adj* darkish.

dust *n* fine dry particles of earth, dirt; * *vt* to free from dust.

duty *n* what one is bound to do; service; a tax on goods.

dwarf *n* one markedly under average size and with shortened limbs; * *vt* to make (or make seem) small.

dwell *vi* to live in a place; to continue; to focus the attention on; to think, talk, write at length about.

dwelling *n* habitation; abode.

dwindle *vi* to diminish gradually.

dye *vt* to stain; to give a new colour to; * *n* a colouring matter; tinge.

dynamic *adj* relating to force that produces motion; energetic.

dynamite *n* a powerful explosive.

dynamo *n* a machine for producing an electric current.

dynasty *n* a line of the same powerful family.

dysentery *n* a disorder of the intestines.

dyspepsia, *n* indigestion.

E

each *adj, pron* every one separately.

eager *adj* keen; ardent earnest.

ear *n* the organ of hearing; the power of appreciating musical sounds; heed; a spike of corn.

earache *n* a pain in the ear.

early *adv, adj* before the expected time; of or occurring in the first part of a period or series.

earn *vt* to gain by labour; to deserve.

earnest *adj* ardent; eager; serious.

earnings *npl* wages.

earring *n* an ornament worn in the ear.

earth *n* the globe we inhabit; dry land; the ground; the burrow of a fox etc; * *vt* to cover with earth.

earthenware *n* ware made of clay; pottery.

earthquake *n* a shaking or trembling of the earth.

earthwork *n* a rampart of earth.

earthy *adj* consisting of or resembling earth; crude.

earwig *n* any small elongated insect of the order *Dermaptera*.

ease *n* freedom from toil or pain; rest; comfort; * *vt* to calm.

easel *n* a stand to support pictures while they are being painted.

east *n* that part of the sky where the sun rises; the countries east of Europe; * *adj* in or towards the east.

Easter *n* the festival commemorating Christ's Resurrection.

easy *adj* free from pain or anxiety; simple; relaxed in manner; lenient; compliant; unhurried.

eat *vt* to chew and swallow, as food; to wear away; to corrode.

eaves *npl* that part of the roof overhanging the walls.

eavesdrop *vi* to try to listen to a private conversation.

ebb *n* the flowing back of the tide; decline; * *vi* to flow back; to decline.

ebony *n* a hard, heavy, dark-coloured tropical wood.

ebullient *adj* enthusiastic; boiling.

eccentric *adj* not conforming to the usual pattern; unconventional; odd; whimsical.

ecclesiastic, ecclesiastical *adj* belonging to the church or clergy.

echidna *n* an egg-laying insectivorous mammal, also called the spiny anteater, of the genus *Tachyglossus* or *Zaglossus*.

echo *n* the repetition of sound by reflection of sound waves; imitation; * *vt, vi* to repeat; to resound; to imitate.

eclectic *adj* selecting the best of everything (*esp* in philosophy and the arts).

eclipse *n* an obscuring of the light of one planet by some other body; an overshadowing; * *vt, fig* to darken; to surpass.

economics *n* the science of the application of wealth, concerned with the production, consumption and distribution of goods and services.

economise *vt, vi* to manage money with prudence to save.

economy *n* thrift; prudent management; the management of finances and resources of a business, industry or household; the economic system of a country.

ecstasy *n* rapture; enthusiasm; the hallucinogenic drug MDMA.

ecstatic *adj* entrancing.

ecumenical *adj* of the whole Christian church.

eczema *n* a skin disease.

eddy *n* a whirling current of water or air; * *vi* to move round and round.

edge *n* (knife) the sharp side; an abrupt border or margin; keenness; force; effectiveness; * *vt* to put an edge or decoration on; to move gradually.

edible *adj* eatable.

edict *n* a decree; a manifesto.

edifice *n* a large building.

edify *vt* to improve morally or mentally.

edit *vt* to prepare a text for publication; to prepare a final version of a film by selecting, cutting and arranging sequences.

edition *n* the number of copies of a book printed at one time.

editorial *n* a leading article in a newspaper expressing the opinions of its editor or owner.

educate *vt* to train and instruct; to provide schooling.

eerie *adj* awesome; weird.

efface *vt* to blot out; to erase; to

make (oneself) inconspicuous through shyness, humility or false modesty.

effect *n* a result; an impression; (*pl*) belongings; * *vt* to bring about; to accomplish.

effective *adj* efficient; making a striking impression; forceful; fruitful.

effectual *adj* producing the desired result.

effeminacy *n* a display or impression of feminine qualities in a man; weakness; timidity.

effervesce *vi* to bubble or sparkle.

effete *adj* worn out; feeble; decadent.

efficacious *adj* achieving the desired result.

efficient *adj* capable; competent.

effigy *n* a portrait; a sculpture or figure of a person, *esp* one executed to ridicule or show contempt.

effluent *adj* flowing out; * *n* a stream from a river or lake; liquid waste discharged *eg* from a sewer or an industrial plant.

effort *n* exertion; strenuous endeavour.

effrontery *n* brazen impudence.

effusive *adj* profuse; gushing.

egg *n* the shell-covered reproductive body laid by female birds, snakes, or insects, which if fertile can develop into a new individual; * *vt* to urge on.

eggshell *n* the shell of an egg; anything fragile; * *adj* (of bone china) particularly delicate; (of paint) with a slight gloss finish.

ego *n* the 'I'; the self, self-image; conceit.

ego(t)ist *n* a self-centred person.

egregious *adj* conspicuously bad.

egress *n* exit.

eiderdown *n* the down or soft feathers of the eider duck.

eight *adj, n* a cardinal number and its symbol (8); the crew of an eight-oared rowing boat.

eighteen *adj, n* eight and ten (18).

eighteenth *adj, n* the ordinal number of 18.

eighth *adj, n* the ordinal number of 8.

eightieth *adj, n* the ordinal number of 80.

eighty *adj* eight times ten (80).

either *adj, pron* one or the other; one of two; * *conj* used as correlative to or.

ejaculate *vt* to exclaim; eject fluid, *esp* semen, from the body.

eject *vt* to throw out; to expel; * *vi* to escape from an aircraft or spacecraft using an ejection seat.

eke *vt* (*with* out) to supplement; to use frugally; to make a living with difficulty.

elaborate *vt* to work out; to explain in detail; * *adj* highly detailed.

elapse *vi* to by, of time.

elastic *adj* springy; rebounding.

elation *n* joy; exultation.

elbow *n* the joint between the forearm and upper arm; a sharp turn or bend; * *vt* to push away with the elbow.

elder *adj* older; * *n* an older person; an office bearer in the Presbyterian Church; any shrub or tree of the genus *Sambuccus*.

elderly *adj* quite old

eldest *adj* oldest.

elect *vt* to choose by voting to select; * *adj* chosen.

electorate *n* the body of electors.

electric (al) *adj* containing, conveying, worked or produced by electricity.

electricity *n* the force that is developed by friction, and by chemical, thermal, or magnetic action.

electrify *vi* to charge with electricity; to thrill; to astonish.

electrocute *vt* to kill by electricity.

electrode *n* a conductor through which an electric current enters or leaves a gas discharge tube.

electrodynamics *n* the science which treats of electric currents.

electrolysis *n* chemical decomposition by electricity.

electromagnetic *adj* having electric and magnetic properties.

electron *n* a negatively charged elementary particle that forms the part of the atom outside the nucleus.

electronics *n* (*sing*) the study, development and application of electronic devices; as (*pl*) electronic circuits.

elegant *adj* graceful; refined.

elegy *n* a lament.

element *n* a constituent part; a favourable environment for a plant or animal; a wire that produces heat in a electric cooker, kettle, etc; (*pl*) atmospheric conditions (wind, rain, etc,); (*pl*) the basic principles.

elementary *adj* basic, simple.

elevate *vt* to lift up; to raise in rank; to improve in intellectual or moral stature.

elevation *n* a raised place; the height above the earth's surface or above sea level; the angle to which a gun is raised above the horizon; a drawing that shows a vertical view, *esp* of a building.

elevator *n* a cage or platform for moving something from one level to another; a moveable surface on the tailplane of an aircraft to produce motion up or down; a lift; a building for storing grain.

eleven *adj* one more than ten (11).

eleventh *adj*, *n* the ordinal number of 11.

elicit *vt* to draw out by inquiry.

eligible *adj* qualified; suitable.

eliminate *vt* to get rid of; to eradicate; to exclude a competitor from a competition by defeat.

elite *n* the pick; the best.

elixir *n* the specific sought after by alchemists to prolong life or transmute metals.

ellipse *n* an oval figure; a closed plane figure found by the plane section of a right-angled cone.

elocution *n* the art of clear and pleasing speaking.

elongate *vt* to lengthen.

elope *vi* to run away secretly, *esp* of lovers to be married.

eloquence *n* skill in speaking and the use of words.

else *adj*, *adv* other; besides.

elsewhere *adv* in some other place.

elucidate *vt* to make clear.

elude *vt* to avoid; to baffle.

elusive *adj* evasive; deceptive; difficult to contact.

emaciate *vi*, *vt* to become lean.

emanate *vi* to flow out; to issue.

emancipate *vt* to liberate, *esp* from slavery; to free from restraint.

emasculate *vi* to free from testicles; to castrate; to enfeeble.

embalm *vt* to preserve a corpse by means of chemicals.

embankment *n* a protecting mound to hold back water or to carry a roadway.

embargo *n* prohibition on ships from sailing; restraint; a restriction of commerce by law.

embark *vt*, *vi* to go or put on board; to begin an activity or enterprise.

embarrass *vt* to confuse; to harass; to burden; to make a person uncomfortable.

embassy *n* the office or residence of an ambassador.

embellish *vt* to adorn.

embers *n* live remains of a fire.

embezzle *vt* to misapply funds.

embitter *vt* to make bitter.

emblem *n* a symbol; a heraldic device.

embody *vt* to give concrete form to; to incorporate in a single book, law, or system.

emboss *vt* to mould or adorn in relief.

embrace *vt* to clasp in the arms; to accept eagerly.

embroider *vt* to adorn with patterned needlework.

embroil *vt* to involve a person (in trouble).

embryo *n* unborn or unhatched offspring.

emerald *n* a bright-green precious stone; its colour; * *adj* bright green.

emerge *vi* to come forth; to issue; to be revealed as the result of investigation.

emergency *n* a crisis requiring immediate attention.

emery *n* a coarse rock of corundum and magnetite or haematite used for smoothing metal etc.

emetic *n* a medicine that induces vomiting.

emigrant *n* one who leaves his native country to settle in another.

emigrate *vi* to go to reside in another country.

eminence *n* a height; fame; the title of a cardinal.

eminent *adj* exalted; prominent.

emissary *n* an agent sent on a mission; a messenger.

emit *vt* to send or throw out.

emollient *adj* soothing; softening.

emolument *n* salary; remuneration.

emotion *n* a strong feeling *eg* of joy, sadness, anger, fear.

emperor *n* the sovereign of an empire.

emphasis *n* a particular stress placed on anything; force, vigour.

emphatic *adj* impressive; decisive.

empire *n* dominion; sway; states ruled by an emperor.

empirical *adj* based on observation, experiment or experience.

employ *vt* to give work to.

employee *n* one who works for an employer.

employment *n* occupation or profession.

emporium *n* (*pl* emporia) a commercial centre; a large shop selling goods of all types.

empower *vt* to authorise.

empress *n* the consort of an emperor; the female ruler of an empire.

empty *adj* void; vacant; lacking in substance, value or reality; hungry; * *vt* to take everything out of.

emulate *vt* to strive to equal.

emulsion *n* a mixture of mutually insoluble liquids in which one is dispersed in droplets throughout the other; a light-sensitive coating on photographic paper or film.

enable *vt* to empower; to authorise.

enact *vt* to establish by law; to decree; to act.

enamel *n* the hard outer layer of a tooth; an ornamental or preservative glass-like coating on metals; * *vt* to cover with enamel.

enamour *vt* to inspire with love.

encampment *n* a camp.

enchant *vt* to charm; to fascinate.

encircle *vt* to encompass.

enclosure *n* a space fenced in; something enclosed with a letter in a parcel or envelope.

encompass *vt* to encircle.

encore *adv* again; once more; * *n* a call for a performance to be repeated.

encounter *n* an unexpected meeting; a conflict; * *vt*, *vi* to confront; to fight against.

encourage *vt* to inspire with hope; to urge on; to promote the development of.

encroach *vi* to trespass on rights or property of others.

encrust *vt* to cover with a crust.

encumber *vt* to burden; to hamper.

encyclopaedia, encyclopedia *n* a book or books of general knowledge.

end *n* the extreme point; the close; a terminus; stopping place; death; result; aim; * *vt* to bring to an end; * *vi* to come to an end; to result in.

endanger *vt* to imperil.

endear *vt* to make dear or more loved.

endeavour *n* effort; attempt; * *vi* to try; to strive; to aim.

endemic *adj* peculiar to a people or region.

endgame *n* the final stages of a game (*esp* chess) when few pieces remain.

endorse *vt* to write one's name on; to ratify; to support; to record an offence on a driving licence.

endow *vt* to settle money or property on; to enrich.

endurance *n* fortitude; patience.

endure *vi*, *vt* to bear patiently; to tolerate; to last; to continue in existence.

enemy *n* one who is unfriendly; an antagonist; an opponent; a hostile army; something harmful.

energy *n* power; force; vigour; capacity to do work.

enervate *vt* to enfeeble.

enforce *vt* to urge with energy; to impose; to compel compliance with threats.

enfranchise *vt* to give the right of voting to.

engage *vt* to bind by pledge; to attach; to promise to marry; to attract; to enter into; to attack; * *vi* to bind oneself.

engender *vt* to breed; to occasion.

engine *n* a power machine; a locomotive; a contrivance.

engineer *n* a maker or designer or operator of machinery; * *vt* to plan or construct; to contrive; to plan.

engrave *vt* to cut or carve on metal.

engross *vt* to absorb.

engulf *vt* to swallow up.

enhance *vt* to increase in value, importance, attractiveness.

enigma *n* a puzzle; a mystery.

enigmatic *adj* puzzling; obscure; mysterious; * ~ally *adv*.

enjoin *vt* to command; prescribe.

enjoy *vi* to take delight in; to experience.

enlarge *vt*, *vi* to make large; to grow large; to speak or write.

enlighten *vt* to make clear; to instruct.

enlist *vi* to enter on a list; to enrol (in army); * *vt* to ensure support of.

enliven *vt* to brighten; to gladden.

enmity *n* hostility; ill-will.

ennoble *vt* exalt; to dignify; to elevate to the peerage.

enormity *n* great wickedness, a serious crime.

enormous *adj* huge.

enough *adj* adequate, sufficient; * *n* a sufficiency; * *adv* tolerably.

enrage *vt* to make very angry.

enrapture *vt* to fill with delight.

enrich *vt* to make rich; to fertilise.

enrol *vt* to record; to admit as a member of a society.

enshrine *vt* to enclose; to cherish.

ensign *n* a badge; an emblem; a flag.

enslave *vt* to make a slave of; to subjugate.

ensnare *vt* to entrap.

ensue *vi* to result from.

entail *vt* to involve as a result; to settle property on individuals in succession so that all are really only life tenants.

entanglement *n* disorder; a relationship between two people considered to be unsuitable.

enter *vi* to go or come in or into; to come on stage; to begin, start.

enteric *adj* belonging to the intestines; * ~ fever *n*, same as typhoid.

enterprise *n* a venture; boldness.

entertain *vt*, *vi* to receive as a guest; to amuse; to consider; to have in mind.

enthral *vt* to enslave; to charm; to captivate.

enthusiasm *n* ardent feeling; fervent zeal; keen interest.

entice *vt* to tempt; to allure; to lure away by promise of reward.

entire *adj* whole; complete.

entitle *vt* to give a title to; to empower.

entity *n* being; existence.

entomology *n* the science of insect life.

entrails *npl* the intestines.

entrance *n* coming or going in; the place of entry; the power or authority to enter; an admission fee; * *vt* to enrapture; to fill with delight.

entreat *vt* to beg earnestly; to implore.

entrench *vt* to dig in; to establish oneself in a defensive position.

entry *n* act of entering; entrance; an item recorded in a diary, account or dictionary.

enumerate *vt* to count one by one.

enunciate *vt* to utter; to pronounce (clearly).

envelop *vt* to wrap up.

envelope *n* a cover (*eg* of letter).

enviable *adj* exciting envy.

environment *n* conditions and surroundings that influence our development and that of plants and animals.

envisage *vt* to picture to oneself.

envoy *n* one sent on a mission.

envy *n* jealousy; discontent caused by another's possessions or achievements; * *vt* to begrudge.

enzyme *n* a protein, produced naturally or artificially, which acts as a catalyst to biochemical reactions.

ephemeron *n* (*pl* ephemera) an insect living only for a day, *eg* the mayfly, hence a thing of brief interest, usefulness or short-lived.

ephemeral *adj* short-lived.

epic *adj* heroic; in the grand style; * *n* a heroic poem.

epidemic *adj* a disease affecting a whole community; * *n* a disease which attacks many people during the same period.

epidermis *n* the outer skin.

epiglottis *n* the valve which covers the larynx during swallowing.

epigram *n* a pointed, witty, or sarcastic saying.

epilepsy *n* a disorder of the nervous system characterised by fits or momentary loss of consciousness.

epilogue *n* a speech to the audience at the close of a play; the concluding section of a book.

episcopacy *n* Church government by bishops; bishops collectively.

episode *n* an incident in a sequence of events; a piece of action in a book or drama.

epistle *n* a letter.

epitaph *n* an inscription on a tomb.

epithet *n* a descriptive adjective.

epitome *n* a typical example.

epoch *n* a period of time.

equable *adj* uniform; even; not extreme; even tempered.

equal *adj* the same in all respects; * *n* one not inferior or superior to another; * *vt* to make or be equal to ; to do something equal to.

equanimity *n* evenness of temper.

equate *vt* to make equal; to make, treat or regard as compatible

equation *n* act of equalling; the state of being equal; (maths) a statement indicating that two algebraic expressions are equal; (chemistry) an expression representing a reaction in symbols.

equator *n* an imaginary circle passing round the globe, equidistant from the geographic poles.

equestrian *adj* on horseback; * *n* a horseman.

equidistant *adj* equally distant.

equilateral *adj* equal sided.

equilibrium *n* a state of balance.

equine *adj* pertaining to the horse.

equinox *n* the two times of the year at which the sun crosses the celestial equator, and day and night are of equal length.

equip *vt* to furnish; to provide with necessary tools or supplies.

equitable *adj* fair; just.

equity *n* fairness; just dealing; (*pl*) ordinary shares in a company.

equivalent *adj*, *n* equal in value; virtually identical, especially in function as effect.

equivocal *adj* ambiguous.

equivocate *vi* to quibble.

era *n* a fixed reckoning date; a period of time.

eradicate *vt* to root out; to obliterate.

erase *vt* to rub out; to remove (from magnetic tape, computer memory or storage medium).

erect *adj* upright; * *vt* to build.

erection *n* act of erecting; formation; anything erected; structure; a swelling and rigidity of the penis due to sexual excitement.

erode *vt* to wear away gradually.

erotic *adj* of or causing sexual love, arousal, excitement; amatory.

err *vi* to wander; to stray.

errand *n* a message; a short journey to carry out a task.

errant *adj* roving; wandering.

erratic *adj* irregular; eccentric; unreliable.

erratum *n* (*pl* errata) an error in printing; (*usu* in *pl*) a list in a book of such errors.

error *n* a mistake; a fault.

erstwhile *adj* former; previous.

erudite *adj* deeply read; learned.

erupt *vi* to burst out; to break out into a rash; to explode ejecting ash and lava from a volcano.

escapade *n* a piece of daring or reckless behaviour; an adventure.

escape *vt*, *vi* to get out of the way of; to avoid; to be free; * *n* a getting away by flight; a leakage *eg* of gas; a temporary respite.

escarpment *n* the steep side of a layer of rock, forming a hill or natural rampart.

eschew *vt* to shun; to avoid.

escort *n* a guard; an attendant.

esoteric *adj* private; select; understood only by elite minority.

especial *adj* distinct; chief.

espionage *n* spying.

espouse *vt* to marry; to adopt a cause.

espy *vt* to catch sight of.

essay *vt* to try; * *n* an endeavour or experiment; a short literary composition.

essence *n* the inmost nature or being of anything; a substance extracted from another without the loss of the qualities of the original; perfume.

essential *adj* vital; indispensable; (oil) volatile.

establish *vt* to fix firmly; to institute; to set up (*eg* a business); permanently to settle (a person) in a position; to have generally accepted; to place beyond doubt.

established *adj* legally confirmed (church); assured.

establishment *n* household staff; a place of business; (with *cap*) those in power, supposedly conspiring to preserve the status quo.

estate *n* landed property; a large area of residential or industrial development; a person's total possessions, especially at death; a social or political class.

ester *n* any of a class of organic compounds produced by alcohol acting with an acid, eliminating water.

esteem *vt* to value; to regard highly; to prize; * *n* judgment; estimation; regard.

estimable *adj* worthy; respected.

estimate *vt* to calculate; to appraise; * *n* valuation; an approximate calculation; a judgment or opinion.

estrangement *n* withdrawal of friendship.

estuary *n* the mouth of a river.

etch *vt* to produce printed images from metal plates engraved and treated with acids.

eternal *adj* everlasting.

eternity *n* infinite time.

ether *n* a volatile liquid used as an anaesthetic or solvent.

ethereal *adj* airy; heavenly; aerial.

ethics *n* the philosophy of morality; principles.

ethnic *adj* describing races or large groups of people sharing common ancestry and culture.

etiquette *n* code of manners.

etymology *n* the study of the history and development of words.

eulogise *vt* to praise; to extol.

eulogy *n* praise; panegyric.

euphemism *n* the use of a mild for a harsh term (*eg* 'fairy tale' for 'lie'.)

euthanasia *n* mercy killing.

evacuate *vt* to make empty; to quit; to move people from a danger to a safe area.

evade *vt* to avoid; to escape from.

evaluate *vt* to assess; to determine the value carefully.

evaporate *vi* to change into vapour; to remove water from; to disappear.

evasion *n* avoidance; an equivocal reply or excuse.

eve, even *n* evening; the evening before (*eg* Christmas Eve).

even *adj* level; smooth; equal; divisible by 2; * *vt* to equalise; to make even; to balance; adjust; exactly; fully.

evening *n* the close of the day.

event *n* an incident; a happening; contingency.

eventful *adj* memorable.

eventuality *n* a possible result.

ever *adv* always; at any time; in any case.

evergreen *n* a tree or plant always in leaf; * *adj* always green.

everlasting *adj* eternal; never ending.

every *adj* each of all.

everybody *n* every person.

everyday *adj* happening daily; commonplace; worn or used every day.

everything *pron* all things; all; of the greatest importance.

everywhere *adv* in every place.

evict *vt* to dispossess by law; to expel.

evidence *n* testimony; proof.

evident *adj* clear; plain; under-standable.

evil *adj* wicked; bad; * *n* sin; harm.

evince *vt* to show; to prove.

evoke *vt* to call forth.

evolution *n* the theory that existing types of plants and animals have developed from earlier forms; the process by which something attains its distinctive characteristics.

evolve *vt, vi* to unfold; to develop.

exacerbate *vt* to aggravate; to make something worse.

exact *adj* accurate; precise; * *vt* to compel payment.

exacting *adj* severe; greatly demanding; requiring close attention and precision.

exaggerate *vt* to overstate.

exalt *vt* to raise in power; to set aloft; to extol.

examine *vt* to scrutinise; to inquire into; to question (witness); to test.

example *n* a sample; pattern; model; a warning to others.

exasperate *vt* to enrage; to annoy intensely.

excavate *vt* to hollow out by digging; to unearth.

exceed *vt* to surpass; to overstep (the limit).

excel *vt* to surpass; * *vi* to be pre-eminent.

excellent *adj* of high quality; choice.

except *vt* to omit; to exclude.

exceptional *adj* unusual; rare.

excerpt *n* an extract; * *vt* to extract *eg* from a book.

excess *n* surplus; intemperance.

exchange *vt* to give and take (one thing in return for another); * *n* the conversion of money from one currency to another; a place where goods or services are exchanged; a centre or device in which telephone lines are interconnected.

excise *n* a tax levied on commodities; a tax levied on some licences; * *vt* to charge excise on; to compel to pay excise; remove (*eg* a passage from a book); to cut out surgically; * excision *n*.

excitable *adj* easily agitated.

excite *vt* to arouse the feelings of, especially to generate feelings of pleasurable anticipation.

exclaim *vi, vt* to call out; to declare loudly, suddenly and with emotion.

exclude *vt* to shut out.

exclusive *adj* excluding all else; reserved for particular persons; snobbishly aloof; fashionable; high-class, expensive; unobtainable or unpublished elsewhere; sole, undivided.

excommunicate *vt* to expel (someone) from the church.

excrement *n* waste matter discharged from the body.

excretion *n* ejection of waste matter.

excruciating *adj* intensely painful.

excursion *n* a pleasure trip.

excuse *vt* to let off; to forgive; to overlook; * *n* an apology; that which excuses; a reason or explanation of.

execrable *adj* hateful; detestable.

execute *vt* to perform; to carry out; to put to death; to make valid.

executive *n* a person or group administering or managing a business or organisation.

executor *n* one who carries out the provisions of a will.

exemplary *adj* model; worthy of imitation.

exemplify *vt* to show by example.

exempt *vt* to free from; excuse.

exercise *n* the use or application of a power or right; regular physical or mental exertion; something performed to develop or test a specific ability or skill; * *vt* to use, exert, employ; to engage in regular physical activity.

exert *vt* to put forth strength.

exertion *n* effort.

exeunt *vi* (*eg* stage direction to actors) leave the stage.

exhale *vt, vi* to breathe out.

exhaust *vt* to use up; to make empty; to use up; tire out; (subject) to deal with or develop completely; the waste gas or steam from an engine.

exhaustion *n* extreme weariness.

exhaustive *adj* full; thorough.

exhibit *vt* to display, especially in public; to present to a court in legal form; * *n* an act or instance of exhibiting, something exhibited.

exhibition *n* any public display.

exhilarate *vt* to elate; to enliven.

exhort *vt* to encourage; to warn.

exhume *vt* to disinter.

exigence *n* pressing necessity.

exile *n* banishment; * *vt* to banish from one's country.

exist *vi* to be; to live; to manage one's life with difficulty.

exit *n* a going out; a way out.

exonerate *vt* to free from blame.

exorbitant *adj* excessive, especially of prices.

exorcise *vi* to drive out evil spirits.

exotic *adj* foreign; excitingly different or unusual.

expand *vt, vi* to spread out; to swell; to describe in fuller detail; to become more friendly and genial.

expanse *n* a wide area.

expansion *n* enlargement; increase.

expatriate *vt* to exile oneself or banish another; * *n* (a person) living in another country, or self-exiled or banished.

expect *vt* to anticipate, to regard as likely to arrive or happen; to consider necessary, reasonable or due; to suppose.

expectorate *vt* to spit or cough out.

expedient *adj* suitable for the present time or circumstances; * *n* device; a means to an end; a means used for want of a better.

expedite *vt* assist the progress of; to accelerate; accomplish rapidly.

expedition *n* promptness; an enterprise or those who undertake it.

expeditious *adj* speedy; prompt.

expel *vt* to drive out; to banish.

expend *vt* to spend; to use up.

expenditure *n* outlay; cost.

expense *n* cost; charge; price.

expensive *adj* costly; lavish.

experience *n* personal trial; knowledge gained from contact with life or work; an effecting event; * *vt* to try; meet with.

experiment *n* a trial; a practical test.

expert adj skilful; knowledgeable through training and experience; * *n* a specialist.

expertise *n* expert knowledge or skill.

expiate *vt* to atone for.

expire *vt* to breathe out; to exhale; * *vi* to die; to end.

explain *vt* to make clear; to expound.

expletive *n* an oath.

explicable *adj* explainable.

explicit *adj* definite; expressly or frankly stated.

explode *vt, vi* to burst with a loud noise; to expose; discredit.

exploit *n* a brilliant deed; a bold achievement; * *vt* to make use of; to take unfair advantage of.

explore *vt* to search; to examine closely; to travel through for the purpose of discovery.

explosion *n* a violent detonation; an outburst (of feeling).

explosive *adj* liable to explode; * *n* material that explodes.

exponent *n* one who favours or promotes something; (maths) the argument of an exponential function.

exponential *adj* (of an increase) more and more rapid; (maths) (of a function) having a rate of increase proportional to the total * exponentially *adv*.

export *vt* to send goods abroad for sale; * *n* the commodity exported.

expose *vt* to deprive of protection; to uncover; to display; to endanger.

exposition *n* explanation; exhibition.

exposure *n* a laying open to view or weather or danger; the time during which light reaches and acts on a photographic film, paper or plate; publicity.

expound *vt* to explain.

express *vt* to declare; to utter; to make known; to squeeze out; * *adj* swift, special; explicit.

expression *n* a phrase or mode of speech; facial look; taste and feeling (music); terms or collection saving to express something in mathematics.

expressive *adj* striking; full of expression.

expressly *adv* of set purpose; explicitly.

expulsion *n* ejection; discharge.

expunge *vt* to blot out; to erase.

expurgate *vt* to purify; to cut out offensive passages *eg* from books.

exquisite *adj* beautiful; incomparable; acutely felt.

extend *vt, vi* to stretch out; to prolong in time; to spread; to accord; to reach; to hold out.

extension *n* extent, scope; an added part *eg* to a building; an extra period; a programme of extramural teaching; an additional telephone connected to the principal line.

extensive *adj* far-reaching; large.

extent *n* compass; size; range; scope.

extenuate *vt* to make excuses for.

exterior *adj* external; outside.

exterminate *vt* to destroy utterly.

external *adj* on the outside; visible.

extinct *adj* dead; extinguished.

extinguish *vt* to put out; quench.

extinguisher *n* a device for putting out a fire.

extol *vt* to exalt; glorify.

extort *vt* to exact by compulsion.

extortionate *adj* exorbitant; harsh.

extra *adj, adv* additional; something additional; a special edition of a newspaper; one who plays a non-speaking part in a film.

extract *vt* to take or pull out by force; to withdraw by chemical or physical means; to abstract; * *n* the essence of a substance obtained by extraction; a passage taken from a *eg* book.

extradite *vt* to return a fugitive to the country in which his / her alleged crime took place.

extrajudicial *adj* not legally authorised, *eg* lynching.

extramural *adj* connected with a university but not as regular students.

extraneous *adj* foreign; irrelevant; inessential.

extraordinary *adj* unusual; remarkable.

extravagant *adj* lavish in spending; excessively, high of prices; unrestrained; wasteful; profuse.

extravaganza *n* a fantastic literary or musical composition.

extreme *adj* of the highest degree or intensity; excessive, immoderate, unwarranted; very severe, stringent; outermost; * *n* the highest or furthest limit or degree.

extremist *n* a supporter of extreme measures.

extremity *n* the farthest point.

extricate *vt* to set free.

exuberant *adj* high-spirited; lively.

exude *vt, vi* to ooze out.

exult *vi* to rejoice exceedingly; to triumph.

eye *n* the organ of vision; mind; perception; a small hole; * *vt* to regard closely.

eyebrow *n* the hairy arch above the eye.

eyelash *n* the hair that edges the eyelid.

eyelid *n* the cover of the eye.

eyesight *n* power of sight.

eyesore *n* something offensive to the sight.

eye-witness *n* a person who sees an event.

eyrie *n* an eagle's nest.

F

fable *n* a short story with a moral; a falsehood.

fabled *adj* legendary.

fabric *n* frame of anything; a building; texture; cloth.

fabricate *vt* to fashion; to invent.

fabulous *adj* incredible; mythical.

façade *n* front view of an edifice.

face *n* the front part of the head; dial of a watch; * *vt* to front; to oppose.

facet *n* one particular aspect of a thing; one of many sides .

facetious *adj* flippant or inopportune humour.

facilitate *vt* to make easier.

facility *n* (*pl* ~ies) ease; dexterity; (*esp in pl*) the opportunity, equipment or the resources to do something.

facsimile *n* an exact copy; a machine transmitting one.

fact *n* a deed; event; truth.

factoid *n* an assumption or speculation which is reported and repeated so often that it gains currency as true; an imagined fact.

faction *n* a self-interested party; discord.

factor *n* an essential element; a measure of a number; an agent.

factory *n* a building where goods are made.

factotum *n* (*pl* ~ums) an employee who does all kinds of work.

faculty *n* capacity; power; special aptitude; a department of a university.

fad *n* personal habit or idiosyncrasy.

fade *vt, vi* to lose vigour or brightness or intensity gradually; to vanish gradually.

fail *vi* to weaken; to fade away; to stop operating; to become bankrupt; not to succeed; to miss; * *vt* to disappoint the expectation or hope.

faint *vi* to become feeble; to swoon; * *adj* dim; indistinct; weak; feeble; * *n* a swoon.

fair *adj* pleasing to the eye; just; (weather) favourable; moderately good or large; average; * *adv* justly; * *n* a regular market or gathering for sale of goods.

fairly *adv* honestly, justly.

fairy *n* a small, mythical, humanoid, supernatural entity.

faith *n* belief *usu* without complete proof; trust or confidence in; religious conviction; system of beliefs; fidelity to one's promises.

faithful *adj* loyal; trusty; accurate.

fake *vt* to disguise and so cheat; to pretend; to simulate; * *n* a faked article; a forgery; an impostor.

falcon *n* any diurnal bird of prey of the family *Falconidae*.

falconry *n* the breeding and training of hawks; the use of hawks for hunting.

fall *vi* to drop down; to descend; to collapse; to sin; to lose power, status, office; to be injured or die in battle; to happen; * *n* a drop; a decrease; a decline in status or position; overthrow.

fallacy *n* a false argument or idea.

fallible *adj* liable to err.

fall-out *n* a deposit of radioactive dust from a nuclear explosion.

fallow *adj* soil left uncultivated for one or more seasons.

false *adj* not true; forged.

falsehood *n* untruth; a lie.

falsetto *n* an unnaturally high-pitched voice.

falsification *n* wilful misrepresentation.

falsify *vt* to alter or copy *eg*
documents, in order to deceive.

falter *vi* to hesitate; to waver; to move unsteadily.

fame *n* reputation; renown.

familiar *adj* well-acquainted; friendly; common; well-known; presumptuous; * *n* an intimate.

familiarity *n* intimacy; presumptuous.

family *n* parents and their children; a set of relatives; the descendants of a common ancestor; a group of related plants or animals.

famine *n* extreme scarcity of food.

famish *vt, vi* to starve; to suffer extreme hunger

famous *adj* renowned.

fan *n* a device for creating a current of air; to cool by moving; to ventilate; to stir up or excite; to spread out in a fan shape; an enthusiastic follower.

fanatic *adj* frenzied, bigoted; * *n* a zealot; an over-eager person.

fancy *n* imagination; caprice; whim; delusion.

fanfare *n* a musical flourish of trumpets.

fang *n* a long, sharp, pointed tooth.

fanlight *n* a window over a door.

fantastic *adj* unrealistic; fanciful; unbelievable; imaginative.

fantasy *n* imagination; a product of this; an imaginative poem, play or novel.

far *adj* remote; extreme in political views; * *adv* very distant in space, time or degree; very much.

farce *n* absurdly futile proceedings; a ludicrous situation; a play based upon such a situation.

fare *n* food; the price of a journey on a publlic transport.

farewell *interj, n* goodbye.

farm *n* land (with buildings) on which crops and animals are raised; * *vt, vi* to cultivate; to lease out; to subcontract.

farther *adj, comp* more remote; * *adv* to a greater degree.

farthest *adj* super most distant; * *adv* at the greatest distance.

fascia *n* the instrument panel *eg* of a motor vehicle; the part of a shop front showing the name.

fascinate *vt* to charm; to captivate.

fashion *n* a current style of *eg* dress; the manner or appearance of an action; * *vt* to make in a particular form; to suit or adapt.

fast *adj* firm; fixed; steadfast; swift; lasting; * *vt* to abstain from food; * *n* a period of doing without food.

fasten *vt*, *vi* to fix firmly.

fastidious *adj* hard to please; over-refined.

fat *adj* plump; oily; rich; fertile; * *n* oily substance in animal bodies.

fatal *adj* deadly; disastrous.

fatalist *n* one who holds that all things are predetermined.

fatality *n* a fatal occurrence; a death caused by disaster or accident; a person so killed.

fate *n* destiny; necessity; death; doom; lot.

fateful *adj* having important, often unpleasant, consequences.

father *n* a male parent; an ancestor; name given to R.C. priests.

fatherhood *n* state of being a father.

father-in-law *n* the father of one's husband or wife.

fathom *n* a measure of six feet (1.82 metres), *esp* used in depth soundings; * *vt* to measure the depth of; to comprehend.

fatigue *n* tiredness from physical or mental effort; the tendency of a material to break under repeated stress; * *vt*, *vi* to make or become tired.

fatuous *adj* vacantly silly; idiotic.

fault *n* a slight offence; a flaw; a break of rock strata; an incorrect stroke in tennis.

fauna *n* collective term for the animals of a specific environment.

favour *n* goodwill; kindness; leave; a token of goodwill; a gift presented at a party; * *vt* to befriend; to show support for; to oblige with; to facilitate.

favourite *n* a person habitually preferred; a darling; a competitor expected to win; * *adj* preferred.

fawn *n* a young deer; * *vi* to flatter to gain favour; * *adj* light brown.

fear *n* dread; terror; awe; anxiety.

feasible *adj* practicable; possible.

feast *n* a sumptuous meal; a periodic religious celebration; * *vi*, *vt* to have or take part in a feast; to entertain with a feast.

feat *n* an exploit; a notable act.

feather *n* a hollow central shaft with a vane of fine barbs on each side, many of which cover the skin of a birds; * *vt* to ornament with feathers.

feature *n* any of the parts of the face; a characteristic trait of something; a special attraction or distinctive quality; a prominent newspaper article etc.

February *n* the second month in the year.

fecund *adj* prolific; fertile.

federal *adj* united in a league for national purposes, but each partner having independent powers in local affairs.

fee *n* a reward for services; a payment; charge; * *vt* to pay a fee to.

feeble *adj* weak; infirm.

feed *vt* to give food to; to fatten; * *vi* to take food; to eat; to graze.

feedback *n* a return to the input of part of the output of a system; the result of this, *esp* screeching on a public address system; information about a product or service to its supplier.

feel *n* the sense of touch; feeling; a quality as revealed by touch; * *vt*, *vi* to perceive or explore by the touch; to find one's way by touch; to be affected by; to convey a certain sensation when touched.

feeler *n* an insects' organ of touch; a remark made to prompt reaction.

feeling *adj* sensitive; sympathetic; * *n* the sense of touch; emotion; sympathy; a belief; an opinion arising from emotion (*pl*) emotions; sensibilities.

feign *vt*, *vi* to pretend; to invent.

feint *n* a pretence (of doing); a sham (attack) intended to deceive (an opponent).

felicitous *adj* happy; apt.

feline *n* a member of the cat family *felidae*; * *adj* of or related to these; cat-like, *esp* in movement or cunning.

fell *adj* cruel; savage; * *n* a stony hill; * *vt* to strike down.

fellow *n* a partner; one of a pair; a man; a member of the governing body in some colleges and universities; a member of a learned society.

fellowship *n* companionship; an association; the status of a college fellow.

felon *n* a criminal.

felony *n* a serious crime.

felt *n* a non-woven woollen fabric.

female *n* a girl or woman; * *adj* of the sex that produces the larger gamete.

feminine *adj* of women; having qualities associated with women; denoting the gender of words classified as female.

feminism *n* the movement to win political, economic and social equality for women.

femur *n* the thigh bone.

fen *n* a marsh; a bog.

fence *n* a barrier put round land to mark a boundary; (*sl*) a receiver of stolen goods.

fencing *n* material for fences; the practice of sword play.

fend *vt* to keep or ward off; (with for) to provide a livelihood for.

fender *n* a hearth guard; a buffer along a ship's side.

fenestrated *adj* (architecture) having windows; perforated.

ferment *n* tumult; agitation.

fermentation *n* the breakdown of complex molecules by micro-organisms *eg* yeasts, to produce alcohol in making beer or wine.

ferocious *adj* fierce; savage.

ferret *n* a small semi-domesticated polecat, *Mustela putorius furo*.

ferry *n* a ferrying service; a boat used for it; its location; * *vt* to convey goods or people over a stretch of water; to transport from one place to another.

fertile *adj* fruitful; inventive.

fertilise *vt* to enrich (soil) by adding nutrients; to impregnate.

fertiliser *n* natural organic or artificial substances used to enrich the soil.

fervent *adj* burning; ardent.

fervid *adj* zealous; eager.

fervour *n* zeal; earnestness.

fester *vi* to suppurate; to rankle.

festival *n* a feast; a gala day; public performances given periodically.

festive *adj* joyous; merry.

fetch *vt* to go and bring back; to heave.

fête *n* a festival; * *vt* to honour; to make much of.

fetid, foetid *adj* stinking; offensive.

fetish *n* anything excessively reverenced.

fetter *n* a shackle for feet; restraint.

feud *n* a quarrel especially between individuals, families, clans.

feudalism *n* ancient political system whereby land was held by tenants in return for rent and / or services.

fever *n* a disease marked by high temperature; restless excitement.

few *adj* not many; a small number.

fiancé(e) *n* man (woman) engaged to be married.

fiasco *n* an ignominious failure.

fibre *n* any of the threads or filaments which form animal and plant tissue and textiles; texture; strength or character; roughage.

fibreglass *n* a plastic reinforced with glass fibres.

fickle *adj* vacillating; inconstant.

fiction *n* a made-up story; novels.

fiddle *n* a violin; * *vt* to play the violin; to swindle.

fidelity *n* faithfulness; loyalty.

fidget *vi* to he restless.

field *n* enclosed cultivated land; range; sports ground; the physical area affected by electromagnetic or gravitational influence; the area visible through an optical lens; all competitors in a contest; a section of a record in a database; * *vt*, *vi* (sport) to catch and return the ball; to deflect hostile questions.

field marshal *n* an army officer of the highest rank.

fiend *n* a demon; a cruel person.

fierce *adj* wild; savage; violent.

fiery *adj* burning; passionate.

fight *vi*, *vt* to contend; to strive for

victory; * *n* a struggle; a battle.

fighter *n* a person who fights; one who does not yield easily; an aircraft designed to engage enemy aircraft.

figment *n* a fiction; a falsehood.

figuration *n* shape; form.

figurative *adj* using figures of speech; metaphorical.

figure *n* form; outline; diagram; pattern; person; statue; symbol; price.

figurehead *n* the carved figure on the bow of ships; a nominal head or leader.

filament *n* a slender thread *eg* the fine wire in a light bulb.

filch *vt* to pilfer; to steal.

file *n* a container for holding papers; an orderly arrangement of papers; a line of persons or things; (computer) a collection of related data under a specific name; a smoothing or polishing or grinding tool; * *vt, vi* to put on record; to put in a file.

filial *adj* of or relating to a son or daughter.

filigree *n* delicate tracery in gold or silver.

filings *npl* particles rubbed off by a file.

fill *vt, vi* to make or become full.

fillet *n* a thin strip (of boneless fish or meat); * *vt* to remove bones from.

filling *n* substance used to fill *eg* a tooth cavity; the contents of something: * *adj* substantial (of a meal).

filly *n* a young female horse, *usu* younger than four.

film *n* a flexible cellulose material covered with a light-sensitive substance used in photography; a fine, thin coating; a motion picture.

filter *n* a device or substance straining out solid particles or impurities; a traffic signal that allows cars to turn left or right while the main lights are red.

filth *n* dirt; pollution; obscenity.

fin *n* projecting tissue by which a fish swims and steers; similarly-shaped projection used as a stabiliser, as on an aircraft.

final *adj* last; conclusive; * *n* (often *pl*) the last of a series of contests; the final examination for an undergraduate degree.

finale *n* the last piece; end, *esp* of a public performance.

finance *n* the management of money; * *vt* to supply or raise money for.

find *vt* to come upon; to discover; to supply; to declare; * *n* a discovery.

fine *adj* slender; delicate; superior; * *n* a money penalty.

finery *n* showy apparel or jewellery.

finesse *n* delicacy or subtlety of performance; skilfullness, diplomacy in handling a situation; * *vt* to achieve by finesse.

finger *n* any one of the five digits of the hand *usu* excluding the thumb; anything finger-shaped.

fingerprint *n* the impression of the ridges on a fingertip, *esp* as used for identification purposes.

finish *n* the last part, the end; the finished effect; means or manner of completion or perfecting; a surface; polished behaviour; * *vt, vi* to bring to an end, to come to the end of; to consume entirely; to perfect; to give a desired surface effect to.

finite *adj* limited; bounded.

fire *n* the flame, heat and light of combustion.

fire alarm *n* a device that gives an audible warning of a fire.

firearm *n* a gun or rifle.

fire brigade *n* the emergency service primarily concerned with extinguishing fires.

fireplace *n* a place for a fire, especially a recess in a wall.

fireproof *adj* made incombustible.

fireside *n* the hearth; home.

firework *n* a device packed with explosive and combustible material, used to produce noisy and colourful displays.

firm *adj* steady; strong; hard; * *n* a business partnership.

firmament *n* the sky or heavens.

first *n* the initial thing; the

beginning; the winning place; the highest grade achievable (*eg* in a university undergraduate degree); * *adj* before all others; foremost; most eminent; * *adv* before anyone or anything else.

first aid *n* emergency treatment for an injury, before regular medical aid is available.

first-class *adj*, *n* of the highest quality.

first-hand *adj* obtained directly.

fiscal *adj* relating to public finance; * *n* a public prosecutor.

fish *n* a vertebrate cold-blooded animal living in water, with gills and fins; an invertebrate animal living wholly in water; their flesh as food; * *vi* to try to catch fish.

fisherman *n* one who fishes for a living or for sport.

fishery *n* the business of fishing; fishing ground.

fishmonger *n* a dealer in fish.

fishy *adj* like a fish; creating doubt or suspicion.

fission *n* a split or cleavage; (in full **nuclear fission**) the splitting of atomic nuclei to release energy.

fissure *n* a cleft; a chasm.

fist *n* the hand clenched.

fit *n* a spasm; convulsion; right size; caprice; * *adj* suitable; proper; healthy; * *vt*, *vi* to make fit; to suit; to adapt; to equip.

fitful *adj* spasmodic; uncertain.

fitter *n* one who fits things; one who puts the parts of machinery together.

fitting *adj* becoming; appropriate.

five adj, *n* the third prime number; the symbol for this (5, V, v).

fix *vt*, *vi* to make fast or firm; to settle; to appoint; to direct one's attention; to repair; to arrange or influence a result; * *n* a dilemma.

fixed *adj* firm; fast.

fixture *n* that which is fixed to anything; a fixed article of furniture; a firmly established person or thing; a fixed or appointed time or event.

fizz *vi* to make a hissing sound.

fjord, fiord *n* an inlet of the sea.

flabby *adj* soft; limp.

flaccid *adj* flabby.

flag *n* a standard; ensign; a flat paving stone; * *vi* to droop.

flagellate *vt* to whip.

flagon *n* a jug-shaped metal or pottery vessel.

flagrant *adj* glaring; shameful; notorious.

flail *n* a hand-held threshing implement.

flair *n* natural ability; aptitude; stylishness.

flake *n* a scale; (snow) a particle of frozen rain; * *vi* to peel off; * *vt* to form into flakes.

flamboyant *adj* florid; flaming; strikingly elaborate; dashing.

flame *n* ignited gas; one portion of this; a blaze; passion; * *vi* to blaze.

flan *n* an open case of pastry or sponge cake with a sweet or savoury filling.

flange *n* a raised edge.

flank *n* the fleshy part of the side; from the ribs to the hip; (military) the side; * *vt* to be at the side of; to menace on the side.

flannel *n* a soft woollen fabric; a small cloth for washing the face; nonsense; equivocation; (in *pl*) flannel trousers.

flap *n* the beat of wings; anything hanging loose (*esp* part of a garment); * *vi*, *vt* to move like wings; to flutter; agitation; panic, to panic.

flare *n* a sudden flash; a bright light used as a signal or illumination; a widened part or shape.

flash *n* a sudden gleam; a brief moment, display, news item; * *vi*, *vt* to shine out suddenly; to signal.

flashback *n* an interruption in the continuity of a narrative by an earlier illustrative episode.

flashbulb *n* a small bulb giving an intense light, used in photography.

flashlight *n* a torch.

flashy *adj* gaudy; showy.

flask *n* a kind of bottle; a vacuum flask.

flat *adj* level; prostrate; tasteless; below pitch; deflated; dull; tedious; (of a battery) no longer charged; * n a storey or set of rooms in a house.

flatter vt to praise unduly or insincerely.

flatulence n wind in the stomach.

flaunt vi, vt to show off.

flavour n distinctive taste; * vt to season; to give flavour to.

flaw n a crack; a defect.

flax n a blue flowered plant, *Linum usitatissimum*, cultivated for its textile fibres and its seed.

flaxen adj like flax; fair; pale yellow.

flay vt to strip off skin, *esp* by beating; criticise severely.

flea n a small wingless jumping insect, of the order *Siphonaptera*, that feeds on animal blood.

fleck n a spot; a streak.

fledgling n a young bird; a trainee.

flee vi to run away; to disappear.

fleece n a sheep's coat; * vt to shear the wool from; to rob; to defraud.

fleet n a squadron of ships; navy; a group of cars, ships, buses under one management; * adj swift.

fleeting adj transient; passing.

flesh n soft, *esp* the muscular, tissue between the skin and bone; the pulpy part of fruits; meat.

fleshy adj plump; fat.

flex vt to bend.

flexible adj pliable; supple; adaptable.

flick n a light, sharp, quickly retracted blow with a whip; the sudden release of a bent finger or thumb, *esp* to propel a small object; * vt to flip.

flicker vi to burn unsteadily.

flight n the act, manner, or power of flying; distance flown; an aircraft scheduled to fly a certain trip; a set of stairs; an act or instance of fleeing.

flighty adj fickle; giddy.

flimsy adj thin; slight; weak; light and thin; unconvincing.

flinch vi to shrink; to quail; to drawback.

fling vt to hurl; to scatter; * vi to move quickly or impetuously; * n a throw; a Scottish Highland dance.

flint n a hard stone; a pebble.

flip n a flick; * vt to flick; to turn something, *usu* small, over.

flippant adj saucy; heedless; frivolous.

flirt vt, vi to make insincere amorous approaches; to trifle or toy with *eg* an idea; to throw or jerk; * n one who toys amorously with the opposite sex.

flit vi to fly or dart ; to vacate premises.

float n a lighter than water device used on a fishing line to show that the bait has been taken; a low-loading vehicle decorated for exhibit in a parade; a small sum of money available for cash expenditures; * vt, vi to rest on the surface of or be suspended in liquid; (*fig*) to put into circulation.

floe n floating ice.

flog vt to whip; to thrash.

flood n a deluge; a river; abundance; * vt to overflow; to deluge.

floodlight n a strong source of light used at *eg* a sports field.

floodtide n the rising tide.

floor n the bottom surface *esp* of a room; a storey in a building; the lower limit, the base.

flop vi to sway or bounce loosely; to move in a heavy, clumsy or relaxed manner; to fail; * n a flopping movement; a collapse; (*inf*) a complete failure.

floppy disk n a magnetic disk for storing computer data.

flora n the plant life of an area.

floral adj pertaining to flowers.

florid adj flowery; ruddy of complexion.

florist n a cultivator or seller of flowers.

flotation n the act or process of floating; a launching of a business venture.

flotilla n a small fleet.

flotsam n floating wreckage.

flounce vi to move in an emphatic or impatient manner; * n a frill of material sewn to the skirt of a dress; * vt to add flounces to.

flounder n a flat fish, *Pleuronectes flesus*; * vi to move, or speak awkwardly and with difficulty.

flour *n* the meal obtained by grinding and sifting cereals, *esp* wheat.

flourish *vi* to grow luxuriantly; to thrive; to live in a specified era; * *vt* to brandish; * *n* showy expression; fanciful stroke of the pen; brandishing.

flout *vt* to disobey openly; to treat with contempt.

flow *vi* to move, as water; to issue; to glide smoothly; to hang loose; to circulate; to be plentiful; * *n* a stream; current.

flower *n* the blossom of plants; youth; the prime; * *vi* to blossom; to bloom.

fluctuate *vi* to vary in an irregular way; to waver; to be unstable.

flu *n* influenza.

flue *n* a smoke vent.

fluent *adj* flowing; voluble; able to speak and write a foreign language with ease; articulate; graceful.

fluff *n* light down or nap; a mistake.

fluid *adj* capable of flowing.

fluke *n* the barb of an anchor; a lucky stroke; a flat fish, *esp* a flounder; any parasitic flatworm of the class *Trematoda*, *esp* of the subclass *Digenea*.

fluoride *n* any of various compounds of fluorine.

flurry *n* a sudden gust of wind, rain or snow; bustle; hurry; * *vt, vi* to (cause to) become flustered.

flush *n* a rapid flow, as of water; sudden, vigorous growth; a sudden excitement; a blush; (poker) a hand of cards all of the same suit; * *vt* to make game birds fly away suddenly; * *vt, vi* to cause to blush; to excite; to flow rapidly.

fluster *vt* to agitate; to confuse.

flute *n* an orchestral woodwind instrument with finger holes and keys held horizontally and played through a hole located near one end; a decorative groove; * *vi* to play or make sounds like a flute.

flautist *n* a flute player.

flutter *vi* to flap; to quiver; to beat irregularly or spasmodically (of the heart); * *n* a tremor; stir; nervous excitement; commotion; a small bet.

fly *n* any insect of the order *Diptera*, with one pair of wings; an imitation fly attached to a fish-hook as bait; (*usu pl*) a flap on clothing that hides a fastening; this fastening; * *vi, vt* (*pt* flew, *pp* flown) to move through the air, especially on wings; to travel in an aircraft; to control an aircraft; to take flight, as a kite; to escape, flee from; to pass quickly; (*inf*) to depart quickly; * *adj* (*inf*) astute.

flyleaf *n* a blank leaf at the beginning or end of a book.

flyover *n* a bridge that carries one road or railway over another.

foal *n* the young of a horse, or related animal.

foam *n* froth or fine bubbles on the surface of liquid; * *vi* to cause or emit foam.

fob *n* a watch pocket in a trouser waistband.

focus *n* the point at which reflected or refracted rays converge; correct adjustment of the eye or of a lens to form a clear image; a centre of activity or interest.

fodder *n* food for animals.

foe *n* an enemy.

foetus *n* the unborn young of an animal.

fog *n* a thick mist.

foil *vt* to frustrate; to baffle; * *n* defeat; a sword used in fencing; a leaf of metal; a background to set things off.

foist *vt* to palm off.

fold *vt, vi* to bend something over so that one part covers another; to interlace one's arms; to incorporate (an ingredient) into a food mixture by gentle overturning; * *n* something folded; a crease made by folding; a pen for sheep.

foliage *n* leaves.

folio *n* a sheet once folded; a leaf in a ledger; a book of large size.

folk *n* a people in general; ~ lore traditional culture.

follow *vt, vi* to go or come after; to pursue; to succeed; to result from; to understand; to practise.

folly *n* foolishness; madness; an

extravagant or fanciful building serving no practical purpose.

foment *vt* to stir up strife.

fond *adj* tender; loving; doting.

fondle *vt* to caress.

font *n* the receptacle for baptismal holy water; set of type.

food *n* nourishment; provisions.

fool *n* a simpleton; a clown; a jester; a cold pudding of whipped cream and fruit purée; * *vi* to trick; * *vt* to deceive.

foolhardy *adj* rash; venturesome.

foolproof *adj* proof against failure; easy to understand; easy to use.

foolscap *n* a size of paper.

foot *n* (*pl* **feet**) that upon which anything stands; the appendages at the ends of one's legs; a measure of 12 inches(304.8mm); a group of syllables serving as a unit of metre in verse; * *vt* to pay (a bill).

football *n* a large ball; game played with it by two teams.

foothold *n* a surface irregularity offering grip for the foot when climbing; a place from which further progress may be made.

footing *n* foothold; basis; status.

footlights *n* a row of lights in front of a stage floor.

footpath *n* path for pedestrians.

footprint *n* impression of the foot.

footstep(s) *n* the sound of footfall(s).

for *prep*, because of; as a result of; as the price of, or recompense of; to serve as; on behalf of; in place of; in favour of; to the extent of; throughout the space of; during; * *conj* because.

forage *n* fodder; * *vt* to collect or go in search of provisions.

foray *vt* to pillage; * *n* a sudden raid.

forbid *vt* to prohibit; to oppose.

forbidding *adj* unfriendly; solemn; strict; repulsive.

force *n* strength, power; (physics) (the intensity of) an influence that causes the momentum of a body to change, or induces stress in it; a body of soldiers or police; violence, compulsion; * *vt* to compel by superior strength; to press or drive against resistance; to break open; to impose, inflict.

forceps *n* a pincer-like instrument for grasping and holding firmly, or exerting traction upon, objects *esp* by jewellers and surgeons.

ford *n* a crossing place in a river; * *vt* to wade across.

fore *adj* in front of; * *adv* before.

forearm *n* the arm from elbow to wrist; * *vt* to arm beforehand.

forebode *vt* to foretell; to portend.

forecast *vt* to foresee; to predict events through rational analysis; * *n* a prediction.

foreclose *vt* to preclude; to stop.

forecourt *n* an enclosed space in front of a building, as in a filling station.

forefathers *npl* ancestors.

forefront *n* the foremost part.

foregone *adj* past; preceding; unalterable.

foreground *n* the front part of a picture.

forehead *n* the brow.

foreign *adj* alien; native, belonging to another country; introduced from outside.

foreman *n* an overseer; the spokesman in a jury.

foremost *adj* first; chief; most advanced.

forensic *adj* belonging to or used in courts of law.

forensic medicine *n* the application of medical expertise to legal and criminal investigations.

forerunner *n* a herald; precursor.

foresee *vt* (*pt* **foresaw**, *pp* **foreseen**) to be aware of beforehand.

foreshadow *vt* to prophesy; to augur.

foresight *n* forethought; provision for the future.

forest *n* an extensive wood.

forestall *vt* to anticipate.

foretaste *n* a taste beforehand.

forever *adv* always; eternally.

foreword *n* a preface to a book.

forfeit *vt* to lose by fault; to be penalised; * *n* a penalty.

forge *n* a furnace; a smithy; * *vt*, *vi* to shape by heating and hammering; to falsify; to produce a counterfeit.

forgery *n* a forged copy.

forget *vt* to cease to remember.

forgive *vt* to pardon; to stop feeling resentment; * *vi* to be merciful or forgiving.

forgo *vt* to go without; to abstain from.

fork *n* a small, *usu* metal, instrument with two or more thin prongs set in a handle, used in eating and cooking; anything that divides into prongs or branches; the point of separation.

forlorn *adj* deserted; hopeless.

form *n* general structure; the figure of a person or animal; arrangement; a printed document with blanks to be filled in; a class in school; condition of mind or body; * *vt*, *vi* to shape; to train; to develop (habits); to constitute; to be formed.

formal *adj* in conformity with established rules or habits; regular; relating to outward appearance only; ceremonial; stiff.

formality *n* accordance with custom.

format *n* size, form, shape, manner; general style or presentation; (computer) the way in which data are arranged and stored.

formative *adj* pertaining to formation and development; shaping.

former *adj* past; preceding.

formidable *adj* terrifying; difficult.

formula *n* (*pl* **formulae**) a set of symbols expressing the composition of a substance; a mathematical rule expressed in algebraic form; a prescribed form; a fixed method according to which something is to be done.

formulate *vt* to express clearly, as in a formula.

forsake *vt* to abandon; to renounce.

fort *n* a fortress.

forte *adv* loudly (music); * *n* a person's strong point.

forth *adv* forward; abroad.

forthcoming *adj* about to appear.

forthright *adv* frank; straightforward; outspoken.

forthwith *adv* without delay.

fortification *n* the act of fortifying; defensive works.

fortify *vt* to strengthen; to erect defences; to add alcohol to.

fortitude *n* endurance; courage.

fortnight *n* two weeks.

fortress *n* a stronghold; a castle.

fortuitous *adj* chance; accidental.

fortunate *adj* lucky; prosperous.

fortune *n* chance; luck; fate; vast wealth; prosperity.

forum *n* an assembly or meeting to discuss topics of public concern; a medium for public debate *eg* a magazine.

forward *adv* towards the front; * *adj* in advance, ready; bold; pert; * *n* a first-line player; * *vt* to hasten; to advance; to send on.

fossil *adj* petrified and preserved in rocks; * *n* petrified remains of plants and animals.

foster *vt* to nourish; to promote; to bring up a child not one's own.

foul *adj* dirty; filthy; stormy; impure; obscene; contrary to rules; * *vt*, *vi* to defile; to dirty; to strike against; * *n* unfair play.

found *vt* to lay the base of; to establish; to institute; to cast (in a mould); * *vi* to rest on.

foundation *n* an endowment for an institution; such an institution; the base (of a wall); an underlying principle.

founder *n* an originator; one who founds metals; * *vi*, *vt* to fill with water and sink; to fall; to collapse.

foundry *n* a workshop for casting metal.

fount *n* a source; a set of printing type of one style and size.

fountain *n* a spring; an artificial jet; source.

fowl *n* a bird; poultry.

fox *n* any dog-like mammal with a bushy tail of the genus *Vulpes*; a sly person; * *vt* to deceive by cunning; to confuse.

fracas *n* an uproar.

fraction *n* (maths) a quantity less than a whole, expressed by a numerator and denominator or as a decimal; a small part.

fractious *adj* snappish; peevish.

fracture *n* breaking of a bone; a break; * *vt* to break.

fragile *adj* easily broken; frail; delicate.

fragment n a part broken off; * vt, vi to break or cause to break into fragments.

fragrance n a perfume.

fragrant adj sweet-smelling.

frail adj weak; fragile; easily broken.

frame vt to make according to a pattern; to construct; to put into words; to enclose (a picture) in a border; (sl) to falsify evidence against; * n composed of parts fitted together and united; the case enclosing a window or door; an ornamental border, as round a picture; (snooker) a single game; physical build of a human body.

franchise n the right to vote in public elections; authorisation to business in the name of another, usu in a particular area; * vt to grant a franchise.

frank adj free and direct in expressing oneself; honest, open; * vt to mark letters to show prepayment of postage; * n a mark cancelling a postage stamp; ~ness openness.

frankincense n incense; perfume.

frantic adj mad; distracted; furious; wild.

fraternal adj of or belonging to a brother or a fraternity; brotherly; friendly.

fraternise vi associate with; friendly relations with an enemy.

fratricide n murder of a brother.

fraud n criminal deception; a deceitful person; an impostor.

fraught adj full of; loaded with.

fray n an affray; a fight; * vt, vi to wear away or become worn.

freak n an unusual phenomenon; (fam) a notably unconventional person or one with a strong interest; * ~ish adj.

freckle n a brownish spot on the skin.

free adj not under the control or power of another; able to move in any direction; not exact; generous; with no cost or charge; clear of obstruction; * adv without cost; in a free manner; * vt to set free.

freehand adj drawn by hand.

freehold n land owned absolutely.

freelance(r) n a person who pursues an occupation without long-term commitment to a single employer; * vt to work as a freelance.

freeze vi, vt to be formed into or covered by ice; to be converted from a liquid to a solid by cold; to become motionless; to become formal and unfriendly.

freezer n a container that freezes and preserves food for long periods.

freight n cargo (ship); load (train); goods being moved.

frenzy n madness; passion; wild excitement.

frequent adj coming, happening often; numerous; common; * vt to visit often.

fresco n a painting made on wet plaster.

fresh adj new; brisk; unfaded; not salt; not stale; pure; cool.

fresher n a first-year student.

fret vt to eat into; to vex; * vi to be vexed; * n irritation; peevishness; one of a series of ridges along the fingerboard of a stringed instrument to guide the fingers.

fretful adj peevish; petulant.

fretwork n ornamental and perforated woodwork.

friar n a member of certain Roman Catholic religious orders.

fricassée n a dish of white meat, highly seasoned.

friction n a rubbing together; resistance offered to moving bodies; unpleasantness; conflict.

Friday n the sixth day of the week.

fridge n, abbrev of refrigerator; a cabinet which keeps food cool.

friend n a close companion; one warmly attached to another.

friendly adj kind; well-disposed; favourable; * n a sporting game played for fun, not in a competition.

frieze n a decorative band round the upper part of walls.

frigate n a warship, between a corvette and a destroyer in size, used for escort, anti-submarine, and patrol duties.

fright n sudden fear; a shock; something unsightly or ridiculous in appearance.

frigid adj cold; stiff; formal.

frill n a ruffle; a fringe; an affectation.

fringe n a decorative border of hanging threads; an outer edge; a marginal or minor part; * vt to be or make a fringe; * adj at the outer edge; additional; minor; unconventional.

frisk vi to dance, skip, gambol; * vt to search (a person) by feeling or looking for eg concealed weapons; * ~y adj lively.

fritter n fried battered food; a pancake; * vt to trifle away; to waste.

frivolity n levity; trifling act, thought or action.

fizzle vi (cookery) to sputter, hiss, sizzle; ~ out to taper off, dwindle.

fro adv from; back; backward.

frock n an outer garment; dress.

frogman n diver trained in working underwater, wearing a rubber suit, flippers, oxygen supply.

frolic adj joyous; frisky; * n a lively party; a prank; * vi to gambol.

from prep beginning at, starting with; out of; originating with.

frond n the leaf of a fern.

front n the part facing forward; an outward behaviour; the first part; the promenade of a seaside resort; the battle area in warfare; a person used to hide another's activity.

frontage n the front of a building.

frontier n the border between two countries; the limit of existing knowledge of a subject.

frontispiece n picture facing the title page of a book.

frost n a temperature at or below freezing point; a coating of powdery ice particles; coldness of manner; * vt to cover (as if) with frost or frosting; to give a frost-like opaque surface to (glass).

frostbite n injury to a part of the body due to excessive cold, often resulting in gangrene.

froth n foam; bubbles; empty talk; frivolity.

frown vi to scowl; to concentrate or look displeased by contracting the brow; * n a stern look.

frugal adj careful; thrifty; meagre.

fruit n the produce of plants; offspring; the outcome or result of any action.

fruitful adj producing much fruit; very productive.

fruition n fulfilment; realisation.

frustrate vt to foil; to prevent from achieving a goal or fulfilling a desire.

fry vt to cook over direct heat in hot fat; * n young fish.

fudge n a soft sweet made of butter, milk, sugar, flavouring; * vt, vi to fake; to refuse to commit oneself; to cheat.

fuel n material burned to supply energy, usu as heat and power; anything that serves to intensify strong feelings; * vt, vi to supply with fuel.

fugitive adj fleeting; transient; * n a runaway; a refugee.

fugue n a piece of music in which the theme is taken up by the parts in succession.

fulcrum n (pl fulcra) the point of support of a lever; the means by which influence is brought to bear.

fulfil vt to carry into effect; to carry out a promise; to satisfy; to bring to an end; to complete.

full adj having or holding all that can be contained; complete; having reached greatest size, extent etc; * ~ly adv completely, directly, exactly.

full stop n the punctuation mark (.) at the end of a sentence.

full time n (sport) the finish of a match; * adj working or lasting the whole time.

fulminate vi, vt to thunder; to explode.

fulsome adj insincere; excessively flattering.

fumble vi to handle clumsily.

fume n (often pl) smoke; vapour; rage; * vi to emit smoke; to rage.

fumigate vt to purify, disinfect by fumes.

fun n merriment; sport; amusement.

function n office; duty; work; occupation; an official ceremony or social entertainment; * vi to perform work; to act; to operate.

functional *adj* of a function or functions; practical, not ornamental.

fund *n* a stock; money set apart for a special object; a supply; (*pl*) ready money; * *vt* to provide money for; to invest.

fundamental *adj* basic; essential; * *n* an essential part.

funeral *n* the ceremony associated with the burial or cremation of the dead.

funereal *adj* dark; dismal.

fungus *n* (*pl* fungi) any of a major group of lower plants, *eg* mushrooms that lack chlorophyll and reproduce by spores.

funnel *n* a wide-mouthed utensil for conveying liquids into bottles; an air or smoke shaft; * *vt*, *vi* to (cause to) pour through a funnel.

funny *adj* droll; comical; puzzling; unwell.

fur *n* the short soft hair of mammals; a coating.

furious *adj* full of rage; violent.

furl *vt* to roll up a sail.

furlong *n* one eighth of a mile.

furlough *n* leave of absence, *esp* for military personnel.

furnace *n* a fire chamber in which powerful heat can be raised.

furnish *vt* to provide a room with furniture; to supply; to equip.

furniture *n* household effects, *eg* chairs.

furore *n* excitement; stir.

furrow *n* a trench made by a plough; a wrinkle; * *vt* to groove; to wrinkle.

further *adv* besides; farther; in addition; * *adj* more distant; additional; * *vt* to advance.

furtive *adj* stealthy.

fury *n* rage; frenzy.

fuse *n* a piece of thin wire that melts and breaks when an electric current exceeds a certain level; a tube or wick filled with combustible material for setting off an explosive charge; * *vt* to join or become joined by melting.

fuselage *n* the body of a car or aircraft.

fusillade *n* a general discharge of rifles.

fusion *n* act of melting; a blending; union; partnership.

fuss *n* excited activity; bustle; anxious state; * *vt* to worry over.

fusty *n* musty; mildewed.

futile *adj* serving no useful end.

future *adj* forthcoming; * *n* time to come; future events; likelihood of eventual success.

futuristic *adj* forward-looking.

fuzz *n* fluff; ~y *adj* fluffy; blurred.

G

gab *vi* to chatter; * *n* idle talk.

gable *n* top of the end wall of a house.

gadget *n* a small mechanical or electronic tool or device.

gag *vt* to stop the mouth; to silence; * *vi* to retch; * *n* something thrust into the mouth to stop it.

gaiety *n* mirth; high spirits, liveliness.

gain *vt*, *vi* to obtain, earn, especially by effort; to win in a contest; to attract; to get as an addition; to make an increase in; to reach; * *vi* to make progress, to increase in weight; * *n* an increase especially in profit or advantage; an acquisition.

gainsay *vt* to contradict; to deny.

gait *n* a manner of walking.

gala *n* a celebration; a festival.

galaxy *n* any of many solar systems held together by gravitation in the universe; the Milky Way.

gale *n* a strong wind.

gall *n* impudence; rancour; spite; the bile of animals; the gall bladder and its contents; a growth caused by insects or fungus on plants, *esp* on oaks; * *vt* to fret; annoy intensely; * ~ing *adj* irritating; provoking.

gallant *adj* brave; courteous; dignified; * ~ry *n*.

gall bladder *n* a membranous sac attached to the liver.

galleon *n* a (Spanish) warship.

gallery *n* a covered walk; a long balcony; a place for the exhibition of works of art; an upper floor, *esp* of seats in a theatre.

galley *n* a long, low ship with sails and oars; the cooking place on board ship; (printing) a flat, oblong tray for metal type; a proof sheet printed from such type.

gallon *n* a unit of liquid measure equal to 277.4 cubic inches 4,547.5 cm³.

gallop *vi* to go at full speed; * *n* a horse's fastest pace.

gallows *n sing* (*pl* gallows) a wooden frame from which to hang one sentenced to death.

gallstone *n* a small hard mass formed in the gall bladder.

galore *adv* in abundance (placed after the noun *eg* definitions galore).

galvanise *vt* to electrify; to electroplate; to stimulate into action.

gambit *n* any action to gain an advantage, but with some risk.

gamble *vi* to play games of chance for money.

gambol *vi* to skip; * *n* a frolic.

game *n* sport of any kind; a contest; a scheme; animals and birds hunted for sport or food; * *adj* brave; plucky; willing.

gamekeeper *n* a person who breeds and takes care of game birds and animals.

gammon *n* the lower, most fleshy, part of cured or smoked ham.

gamut *n* the musical scale; the entire range.

gang *n* a group of persons, especially labourers, working together; those acting or associating together, especially for illegal purposes; * *vt, vi* to form into or act as a gang.

gangrene *n* death of body tissue when the blood supply is obstructed.

gangster *n* a member of a criminal gang.

gangway *n* a passageway, *esp* an opening in a ship's side for loading; a gangplank.

gaol *n* a prison; a jail .

gap *n* an opening; a breach; an interruption in continuity; an interval; a mountain pass; divergence.

gape *vi* to open the mouth wide; to stare wide-eyed and open-mouthed (in astonishment); to yawn.

garage *n* an enclosed shelter for motor vehicles; a place where they are repaired and / or fuel sold; * *vt* to put or keep in a garage.

garb *n* dress; clothes.

garbage *n* waste matter; rubbish.

garble *vt* to tell a confused or jumbled story.

garden *n* an area of ground for growing herbs, fruits, flowers, or vegetables, *usu* attached to a house; a public park, laid out with plants and trees; * *vi* to make, or work in, a garden.

gargle *vt, vi* to rinse the throat by breathing air from the lungs through liquid held there; * *n* a liquid for this purpose; the sound made by gargling.

gargoyle *n* a grotesque carving on a gutter spout.

garish *adj* gaudy; showy.

garland *n* a wreath of flowers.

garlic *n* a bulbous strong-smelling herb.

garment *n* any article of clothing.

garner *vt* to store up.

garnet *n* a precious stone.

garnish *vt* to adorn; to decorate (food).

garret *n* attic.

garrison *n* the soldiers in a fortress; * *vt* to man with troops.

garrotte, garrote *vt* to throttle or strangle.

garrulous *adj* very talkative.

garter *n* an elasticated band to hold up a stocking or sock.

gas *n* an air-like substance with the capacity to expand indefinitely yet not liquefy or solidify at ordinary temperatures; (*fam*) empty talk; (USA) petrol; * *vt* to poison or disable with gas; (*fam*) to talk idly.

gash *vt* to slash; to cut; * *n* a deep cut.

gasket *n* a piece or ring *eg* of rubber sandwiched between metal surfaces to act as a seal.

gasp *vi* to labour for breath; to pant; * *vt* to utter breathlessly.

gastric *adj* belonging to the stomach.

gastronomy *n* the art of good eating.

gate *n* a movable structure controlling passage through an opening in a fence or wall; a device (as in a computer) that outputs a signal when specified input conditions are met.

gather *vt, vi* to bring together in one place or group; to collect; to harvest; to draw (parts) together; to come together in a body; to cluster around a focus of attention.

gathering *n* an assembly; folds made in a garment by gathering; an abscess.

gauche *adj* socially inept; tackless.

gaudy *adj* showy; flashy.

gauge *vt* to measure; * *n* a measuring rod; a measure; distance between rails of a railway; calibre.

gaunt *adj* emaciated; lean.

gauze *n* a light transparent cloth; a surgical dressing.

gavotte *n* a sprightly dance.

gay *adj* merry; frolicsome; colourful; homosexual.

gaze *vi* to stare; to contemplate; * *n* a fixed look.

gazette *n* a newspaper, especially an official one.

gazump *vt, vi* to force up a price (*esp* of a house) after a price has been agreed.

gear *n* clothing; equipment; a toothed wheel for meshing with another; * *vt* to connect by or furnish with gears; to adapt (one thing) to confirm with another.

gearbox *n* a metal case enclosing a system of gears.

gelatine *n* a tasteless, odourless substance extracted from bones and used in food and medicines.

gelding *n* a castrated male horse.

gem *n* a precious stone.

gender *n* sex, male or female; words, masculine or feminine.

gene *n* a unit of hereditary material forming part of the blueprint of the organism carrying it.

genealogy *n* family descent; lineage.

general *adj* not local, special, or specialised; of or for a whole genus, relating to all parts of a class or group; widespread, common to many; not specific or precise.

general election *n* a national election to choose parliamentary representatives in every constituency.

generalise *vt, vi* to form general conclusions from specific instances; to talk (about something) in general terms.

general practitioner *n* a non-specialist doctor who treats all types of illnesses in the community.

generate *vt* to beget; to produce.

generation *n* the act or process of generating; a single succession in natural descent; people of the same period.

generator *n* one who or that which generates; a machine that changes mechanical energy to electrical energy.

generic *adj* pertaining to a genus.

generous *adj* giving or given freely; magnanimous; ample; liberal.

genesis *n* origin.

genetic *adj* relating to genes, *usu* inherited features or traits.

genial *adj* cordial; cheerful; warm.

genitals, **genitalia** *npl* the external sexual organs.

genius *n* an outstanding, *usu* intellectual, ability; one blessed with such ability.

genocide *n* the mass extermination of people, *esp* of a nation or race.

genre *n* portrayal of scenes from ordinary life; a category of work, especially literary or artistic.

genteel *adj* affectedly refined or polite.

gentle *adj* well-born; refined, mild.

gentleman *n* a man of good birth; a courteous, honourable man.

gentry *n* well-born people.

genuflection *n* a bending of the knee.

genuine *adj* real; true; sincere.

genus *n* (*pl* **genera**) a taxonomic classification of organisms having common characteristics distinct from those of other genera, containing several species, and being one of several genera making up a taxonomic family.

geography *n* the science of the physical nature of the earth *eg* land and sea masses, and its interaction with the human population; the physical features of a region.

geology *n* the science of the history and the structure of the earth.

geometry *n* the branch of mathematics dealing with the properties, measurement, and relationships of points, lines, planes and solids.

germ *n* any microscopic, disease-causing organism; (*fam*) something tiny capable of growing and developing.

germane *adj* closely allied; relevant.

germinate *vi* to sprout; to start developing.

gerrymander *vt* to manipulate in one's own or party interests.

gerund *n* a verbal noun.

gestate *vt* to carry (young) in the womb during pregnancy; to develop (a plan) gradually.

gesticulate *vi, vt* to make gestures when speaking.

gesture *n* an expressive movement of the body or limbs.

get *vt, vi, aux* to obtain: to gain; to reach; to become; to catch; to persuade; to cause to be; to prepare; to understand.

geyser *n* a hot-water spring; a water heater.

ghastly *adj* deathlike; hideous.

ghetto *n* a section of a city in which members of a minority group live, especially because of social, legal or economic pressure.

ghost *n* a spirit; an apparition; a faint trace or suggestion; * *vt* to ~ write to write on behalf of another.

ghoul *n* a spirit, said to prey on corpses.

giant *n* a huge legendary being of great strength; a person or thing of great size, strength, or intellect; * *adj* incredibly large.

gibberish *n* nonsense.

gibe *vt* to taunt; to sneer.

giddy *adj* dizzy; fickle; frivolous.

gift *n* a present; talent; natural ability; * *vt* to endow; to present.

gigantic *adj* huge; colossal; immense.

giggle *n* to laugh; to snigger.

gild *vt* to cover with gold; to illuminate * gilt, gilded *adj*.

gill *n* the organ of respiration in fishes; a quarter of a pint.

gimlet *n* tool with screw point for boring.

gimmick *n* a device for attracting notice, advertising or promoting a person, product or service.

gin *n* a spirit flavoured with juniper berries; a pile-driving machine; a snare.

ginger *n* a hot spice; a reddish-brown colour; (*fam*) vigour.

gingerly *adv* cautiously.

gingham *n* a checked cotton cloth.

girder *n* large steel beam for supporting joists or forming the framework of a building.

girdle *n* a belt; * *vt* to encompass.

girl *n* a female child.

girlfriend *n* a female friend, *esp* with whom one is romantically involved.

girth *n* a saddle strap; the thickness of (the waist).

gist *n* the essence; the substance of anything.

give *vt* to bestow; to hand over; to deliver; to yield; to utter; to pledge.

gizzard *n* the muscular stomach of a bird.

glacier *n* a slowly moving ice floe.

glad *adj* pleased; cheerful.

glade *n* a clear space in a wood.

glamour *n* charm; allure; attractiveness; beauty.

glance *vi* to strike obliquely and go off at an angle; to look quickly.

gland *n* an organ that separates substances from the blood and synthesises them for further use in, or for elimination from, the body; * glandular *adj*.

glare *n* a dazzling light; a fixed, fierce stare; * *vi* to shine brightly; to look fiercely and angrily.

glass *n* a hard brittle substance, *usu* transparent; glassware; a glass article, as a drinking vessel; (*pl*) spectacles or binoculars.

glasshouse *n* a large greenhouse for the commercial cultivation of plants.

glassy *adj* smooth; expressionless, lifeless.

glaucoma *n* an eye disease.

glaze *vt, vi* to provide *eg* windows with glass; to give a hard glossy finish to ceramics; to cover foods with a glossy surface.

glazier *n* one whose business is to set window glass.

gleam *n* a ray; * *vi* to flash.

glean *vt, vi* to gather (after reapers); to pick up.

glee *n* joy and gaiety; a song in parts for three or more voices.

glen *n* a narrow valley.

glib *adj* speaking smoothly, to the point of insincerity.

glide *vt, vi* to move smoothly and effortlessly; to descend in an aircraft or glider with little or no engine power.

glider *n* an engineless aeroplane carried along by air currents.

glimmer *vi* to give a faint, flickering light; to appear faintly.

glimpse *n* a brief, momentary view; * *vt* to catch a glimpse of.

glint *n* a brief flash of light; a brief indication.

glisten *vi* to shine, as light reflected from a wet surface.

glitter *vi* to sparkle.

gloat *vi* to feast one's eyes on, with evil feelings of satisfaction.

globe *n* a sphere; a planet; a star; the earth.

globule *n* a small globe-like particle; a droplet of liquid.

gloom *n* darkness; deep sadness.

glory *n* praise; honour; renown; splendour; * *vi* to rejoice; to exult.

gloss *n* the lustre of a polished surface; a superficially attractive appearance; * *vt* to give a shiny surface; (*with* over) to hide (an error) or make seem right or inconsequential.

glossary *n* a list of *usu* technical words and their definitions.

glossy *adj* smooth and shining; highly polished; superficial; lavishly produced (of magazines).

glove *n* a cover for the hand.

glow *vi* to shine (as if) with an intense heat; to emit a steady light without flames; to be full of life and enthusiasm; * *n* a light emitted due to intense heat; a steady, even light without flames.

glower *vi* to scowl; to stare sullenly or angrily.

glucose *n* a crystalline sugar found naturally in fruits and honey.

glue *n* a sticky substance used as an adhesive; * *vt* to join with glue.

glum *adj* sullen; moody.

glut *vt* to over-supply (the market); to gorge; * *n* over-abundance.

glutinous *adj* sticky; viscous.

glutton *n* a voracious eater; a person with a great capacity.

glycerine *n* a colourless sweet liquid obtained from fats.

gnarl *n* a knot in wood.

gnash *vt* to grind (the teeth).

gnat *n* a biting insect.

gnaw *vt, vi* to nibble; to chew on; to torment as by pain or guilt.

gnome *n* a sprite; a dwarf dwelling in the earth.

go *vi, vt* to move on a course; to proceed; to work properly; to act, sound, as specified; to result; to become; to be accepted or valid; to leave; to die; to be allotted or sold; to be able to pass (through); to be capable of being divided (into); to fall asleep; to take place as planned.

goad *n* a spiked stick to prick cattle; a spur; a stimulus to action.

goal *n* the winning post; an objective; an aim.

gobble *vt* to gulp; to bolt.

go-between *n* messenger; an intermediary.

goblet *n* a drinking cup without handle.

goblin *n* a mischievous or evil sprite.

god *n* any of various beings conceived of as supernatural and immortal, especially a male deity; an idol; a person or thing deified; (*with cap*) the creator and ruler of the universe in monotheistic religions.

goddess *n* a female deity.

godfather *n* a male sponsor for a child at baptism. (Also god-mother, -son, -daughter.)

god-forsaken *adj* desolate, wretched.

godliness *n* piety.

godsend *n* anything that comes unexpectedly when needed or desired.

goggle *vi* to roll the eyes; to stare with bulging eyes; * *adj* bulging; * *npl* large spectacles.

gold *n* a precious yellow metal; coins; jewellery made of this, money; wealth.

golf *n* a game in which players attempt to hit a small ball with clubs around a turfed course into a succession of holes in the smallest number of strokes.

gondola *n* a long narrow boat used on the canals of Venice; an enclosed car suspended from a cable used to transport passengers, *esp* skiers.

gong *n* a disk-shaped percussion instrument struck with a *usu* padded hammer; (*sl*) a medal.

good *adj* having the right or proper qualities; valid; healthy or sound; virtuous, honourable; enjoyable, pleasant; * *n* something good; benefit; something that has economic utility.

good sense *n* sound judgment.

good-tempered *adj* good-natured.

goodwill *n* benevolence; the established custom and reputation of a business.

gore *n* (clotted) blood; a gusset in material to shape a garment; * *vt* to wound with tusk or horn.

gorge *n* the throat; a very narrow pass; * *vt* to eat greedily and overmuch.

gorgeous *adj* splendid; strikingly attractive; brightly coloured.

gory *adj* bloody.

gospel *n* religious teaching; (*fam*) the truth.

gossamer *n* cobweb-like threads in the air or on bushes; any very flimsy material.

gossip *n* a tattler; idle talk about others; * *vt* to tattle; * *vi* to take part in or spread gossip.

Gothic *adj* in the pointed-arch style of architecture of the Middle Ages; supernatural, grotesque, exaggerated style of literature.

gouge *n* a chisel with a grooved blade; * *vt* to scoop out.

gourmet *n* a particular eater.

gout *n* a hereditary disease affecting joints, especially the big toe.

govern *vt* to rule; to regulate.

government *n* the exercise of authority over (a state); a system of ruling or political administration; those who who exercise this authority.

governor *n* a person appointed to govern (a province); the elected head of any state of the USA.

gown *n* a loose outer garment, specifically a woman's formal dress or a long, flowing robe worn by *eg* university teachers; (hospital) overall worn in the operating theatre.

grab *vt* to seize; to snatch; to catch the interest or attention.

grace *n* favour; kindness; divine influence; mercy; the mode of address to a duke, duchess or bishop; beauty of form or movement; ease of manner; a short prayer before meals.

gradation *n* arrangement step by step.

grade *n* a stage or step in a progression; a group of people of the same rank; the degree of slope; a mark or rating in an examination.

gradient *n* degree of ascent or descent; a sloping road or railway.

gradual *adj* slow and regular.

graduate *vt*, *vi* to mark off into degrees; to receive a university degree; * *n* recipient of a degree.

graft *n* a shoot inserted in another plant; the transplanting of body tissue; work; * *vt* to insert such a shoot; to join organically.

grain *n* the seed of any cereal plant; a tiny, solid particle, as of salt or sand; the pattern of fibres of *eg* wood.

grammar *n* the study of the correct use of language; the rules for speaking and writing a language; a grammar textbook.

gramme *n* a metric unit of mass equal to one thousandth of a kilogram.

gramophone *n* an early record player.

granary *n* a storehouse for grain.

grand *adj* noble; magnificent; imposing; important; illustrious; comprehensive.

grandeur *n* greatness; splendour.

grandfather *n* one's father's or mother's father.

grandiloquence *n* pompous language.

grandiose *adj* imposing; bombastic.

grandmother *n* one's mother's or father's mother.

granite *n* a hard igneous rock.

grant *vt* to bestow; to confer on; to admit as true; to cede; * *n* a gift; money or a gift granted for a particular purpose; a conveyance in writing.

granule *n* a little grain.

grape *n* a purple or green berry growing in clusters on the vine, eaten as fruit and fermented for wine.

graph *n* a diagram representing successive changes in the value of a variable quantity of quantities.

graphic(al) *adj* described in realistic detail; pertaining to a graph; (computer) any image which is not editable text; (*fam*) particularly vivid.

grapple *vt, vi* to seize; to wrestle.

grasp *vt, vi* to grip; to lay hold of; to understand; * *n* a grip; reach; comprehension.

grasping *adj* avaricious; greedy.

grass *n* any plant of the family *Gramineae* with jointed stems and long narrow leaves; such plants grown as lawn; pasture.

grate *n* a frame of metal bars for holding fuel in a fireplace; a grating; * *vt* to grind into particles by scraping; to rub against (an object).

grateful *adj* pleasing, gratifying; appreciative.

grater *n* utensil for scraping.

gratification *n* pleasure; enjoyment.

gratify *vt* to please; delight; to indulge.

grating *n* a frame of bars; * *adj* harsh; irritating.

gratis *adv* without charge.

gratitude *n* thankfulness for favours, gifts received.

gratuity *n* a free gift; a tip.

grave *vt* to engrave; to impress deeply; * *n* a tomb; * *adj* solemn.

gravel *n* small pebble.

gravitate *vt, vi* to exert or to move under the influence of gravity; to move towards one another.

gravity *n* the mutual attraction of massive bodies; the gravitational pull the earth exerts; seriousness.

gravy *n* sauce to accompany cooked meat, made from its juices.

graze *vt, vi* to scrape (the skin) slightly; to eat grass; to supply grass.

grease *n* oily or fatty matter, *esp* used as a lubricant; * *vt* to smear with grease; to lubricate.

great *adj* large; eminent; noble; chief; intense; excellent; skilful.

greed *n* excessive desire.

green *adj* of a green colour; unripe; naive; environmentally sound; (*fig*) jealous; * *n* a grassy plot.

greengrocer *n* a dealer in vegetables and fruit.

greenhouse *n* a glass house for rearing plants.

greet *vt* to salute; to welcome.

gregarious *adj* living in flocks; sociable; fond of company.

grenade *n* a small bomb thrown by hand or projected (by a rifle etc).

grey *n* a neutral colour between black and white; * *adj* of a grey colour; grey-haired; dreary; vague.

grid *n* a grating; an electrode for controlling the flow of electrons in a valve or cathode ray tube; a network of squares on a map used for easy reference; a national network of transmission lines.

griddle *n* a flat iron plate for cooking scones.

grief *n* sorrow; deep distress.

grievance *n* injustice; hardship; a cause for complaint.

grievous *adj* heavy; distressing.

grill *vt* to cook by direct heat using a grill; (*fig*) to question relentlessly; * *n* a device on a cooker that radiates heat downward for grilling; grilled food.

grille *n* an open grate forming a screen.

grim *adj* stern; forbidding.

grimace *n* a contortion of the face.

grime *n* soot, dirt.

grin *vi* to laugh through the teeth; * *n* a broad, friendly smile.

grind *vt* to reduce to powder or fragments by crushing; to wear down, or sharpen by friction.

grip *n* a grasp; a handle.

gripe *vt*, *vi* to grasp; to pinch; to complain; * *n* a clutch; a complaint.

grisly *adj* dreadful; terrifying.

gristle *n* cartilage in meat.

grit *n* coarse particles of sand; stubborn or resolute courage; * *vt* to clench or grind the teeth; to spread grit (on icy roads).

grizzle *n* (*esp* of a child) to cry fretfully; to moan whiningly.

grizzled *adj* streaked with, grey hair.

groan *vi* to moan; * *n* a deep moan.

grocer *n* a merchant who deals in food and household supplies.

grog *n* a mixture of spirits and cold water.

groggy *adj* dazed and unsteady.

groin *n* the depression between the belly and the thigh.

groom *n* one who cares for horses; a bridegroom; * *vt* to clean and care for animals; to train someone for a specific purpose.

groove *n* a long hollow; a rut; a spiral track in a gramophone record for the stylus; a settled routine.

grope *vi* to search about blindly, as in the dark; to search uncertainly for a solution to a problem; * *vt* to find by feeling; (*sl*) to fondle.

gross *adj* thick; coarse; obscene; whole; * *n* twelve dozen; the whole; the total without deduction.

grotesque *adj* distorted or fantastic in appearance or shape; absurdly incongruous.

grotto *n* a picturesque cave.

ground *n* the solid surface of the earth; soil.

grounding *n* basic general knowledge of a subject.

groundwork *n* basis; foundation.

group *n* a number of persons or things; a collective unit.

grouse *vt* to complain; * *n* a complaint; any of various game birds of the family *Tetranodae*.

grout *n* mortar; coarse meal.

grove *n* a small wood.

grovel *vi* to beg favour or forgiveness obsequiously.

grow *vi* to increase; to make progress; to become; to develop; to accrue; * *vt* to produce; to raise; to cultivate.

growl *vi* to snarl; to make a rumbling noise as an angry animal; * *vt* to speak in a growling voice; * *n* a grumble.

grown-up *adj* adult.

growth *n* the act or process of growing; progressive increase, development; something that grows or has grown; (medical) an abnormal formation, *esp* a tumour.

grub *vi*, *vt* to root out; to work hard; * *n* the larva of an insect.

grubby *adj* dirty, soiled.

grudge *vi*, *vt* to envy; to give unwillingly; * *n* ill-will; envy.

gruel *n* food made by boiling meal in water.

gruelling *adj* exhausting.

gruesome *adj* repulsive.

gruff *adj* surly; harsh; hoarse.

grumble *vi* to mutter with discontent.

grumpy *adj* surly; gruff; bad-tempered.

grunt *vi* to make a noise like a hog.

guarantee *n* a formal assurance that an obligation will be honoured; a pledge to replace something substandard; an assurance that something will be done as specified.

guarantor *n* a person who gives a guarantee.

guard *vt*, *vi* to watch over; to defend; * *n* defence; protector; sentinel; attention.

guarded *adj* circumspect; discreet.

guardian *n* a custodian; a person legally in charge of a minor or of someone incapable of taking care of their own affairs.

guerrilla *n* a member of a force of irregular soldiers, *usu* politically motivated, *usu* fighting a larger regular force.

guess *vt* to form an opinion, hypothesis, or estimate of something with little or no measurement, calculation or information; to judge correctly by doing this; to think or suppose; * *n* an estimate based on guessing.

guest *n* a person entertained by another; any paying customer of a hotel or restaurant; a performer appearing by special invitation.

guide *vt* to point out the way for; to lead; to direct the course of; to control; * *n* a person who leads.

guidebook *n* a book containing information for tourists.

guide dog *n* a dog trained to guide people who are visually impaired.

guild *n* a society for mutual aid.

guile *n* wiliness; deceit.

guillotine *n* a machine for cutting paper; (France) an instrument for beheading persons.

guilt *n* the regret felt for having done a wrong.

guinea pig *n* a domesticated South American rodent, *Cavea porcellus*; a person or thing subject to an experiment.

guise *n* an assumed appearance.

guitar *n* a musical instrument with six strings which are plucked or strummed.

gulf *n* a stretch of sea with a deep inlet and a narrow mouth; a chasm.

gull *n* any of various long-winged sea birds of the family *Laridae*.

gullet *n* the throat; the food passage from the mouth.

gully *n* watercourse cut out by heavy rain.

gulp *vt* to swallow eagerly.

gum *n* the firm tissue surrounding the teeth; the sticky substance found in some trees.

gumption *n* shrewd good sense.

gun *n* a weapon comprising a metal tube from which a projectile is discharged by explosive action.

gunmetal *n* an alloy of copper and tin, formerly used to make cannon.

gunner *n* one who helps fire artillery; a naval warrant officer in charge of a ship's gun.

gunpowder *n* an explosive mixture used for blasting.

gunwale, gunnel *n* the upper edge of a ship's side.

gurgle *vi* to flow with a bubbling sound; to utter this sound.

gush *vi* to rush out; to be effusively sentimental in speech or writing.

gushing *adj* rushing forth; effusive.

gusset *n* a triangular piece of cloth put in a garment to strengthen or widen.

gust *n* a sudden blast of wind.

gut *n* the intestine; (*pl*) entrails; courage; daring.

gutter *n* a water channel below eaves or at the roadside.

guttural *adj* throaty.

guy *n* a rope securing a tent; an effigy of Guy Fawkes; a man or boy.

guzzle *vi, vt* to swallow greedily.

gymnasium *n* (*pl* gymnasia) a room or building with gymnastics equipment.

gynaecology *n* the branch of medicine dealing with disorders of the female reproductive system.

gypsy *n* a member of a travelling people.

gyrate *vi* to rotate, to whirl.

gyroscope, gyrostat *n* a device, used in stabilisers and navigation systems, consisting of a wheel, rapidly rotating about an axis, the orientation of which is unperturbed by changing the orientation of the mounting.

H

haberdasher *n* a draper.

habit *n* usage; custom.

habitable *adj* that may be inhabited.

habitat *n* the natural abode.

habitation *n* abode; residence.

habitué *n* a regular frequenter.

hack *n* a hired horse; a horse for

ordinary riding; a mediocre writer; * *vt* to gash; to kick; to ride a horse cross-country.

hackneyed *adj* much used; trite.

haemorrhage *n* the escape of blood from a blood vessel; heavy bleeding; * *vi* to bleed heavily.

haemorrhoids *npl* piles.

haft *n* the handle of *eg* an axe.

hag *n* an ugly old woman.

haggard *adj* wild-looking; gaunt.

haggis *n* a Scottish dish of sheep entrails and oats boiled in the stomach sac.

haggle *vt* to drive a hard bargain.

hail *n* frozen rain; a greeting; * *vi, vt* to rain hail; to call to; to greet or welcome with approval; to acclaim; to originate from.

hair *n* a thread-like covering on the skin of mammals; a mass of hair growing on the human head.

hairdresser *n* a person who cuts, styles, and colours, hair.

hairpiece *n* an additional piece of hair attached to a person's real hair.

hairpin bend *n* a sharply curving bend in a road.

hair-raising *adj* terrifying, shocking.

hair's-breadth *n* a minute distance.

hair-splitting *n* making over-fine distinctions.

halcyon *adj* calm; peaceful.

hale *adj* sound; robust.

half *n* (*pl* halves) one of two equal parts.

half-brother *n* a brother by one parent only.

half-caste *n* one born of parents of different races.

half-hearted *adj* unenthusiastic.

half-sister *n* a sister by one parent only.

hall *n* a large public room; the entrance room of a house.

hallmark *n* a mark used on precious metals to signify a standard of purity; a characteristic feature.

hallucination *n* the apparent perception of *eg* sights that are not actually present; something perceived in this manner.

halo *n* circle of light around a luminous object; such a circle round the head of a saint portrayed.

halt *vi, vt* to stop; to cease marching; * *n* a minor station.

halve *vt* to divide into two equal parts.

ham *n* the thigh of a pig salted and dried; an actor who overacts; an amateur radio operator.

hamburger *n* ground beef; a cooked patty of such meat in a bun.

hamlet *n* a small village.

hammer *n* a tool for driving nails; * *vt, vi* to beat or forge; to defeat utterly.

hammock *n* a swinging bed of cloth or netting suspended by the ends.

hamper *n* a large basket; * *vt* to hinder; to interfere; to encumber.

hamstring *n* a tendon behind the knee; * *vt* to lame by cutting.

hand *n* the part of the arm below the wrist, used for grasping; a side or direction; (often in *pl*) possession or control; skill; applause; help; a hired worker; one of a ship's crew; anything like a hand, as a pointer on a clock; the breadth of a hand, four inches (101.6mm) when measuring the height of a horse; the cards held by a player at one time; a round of card play.

handbag *n* a small bag for carrying personal items.

handbook *n* a textbook; a manual.

handcuff *n* manacles restraining a prisoner by binding the wrists together.

handful *n* as much as the hand will hold; a small quantity or number; a person difficult to control.

handicap *n* an allowance in sporting contests to make the chances more equal; a mental or physical impairment; * *vt* to give a handicap to; to hinder.

handicraft *n* manual skill.

handkerchief *n* a cloth for blowing the nose.

handle *vt* to feel, use, or hold with the hand; to deal with; to manage; to buy and sell goods; * *n* the part of anything designed to be held by the hand.

handsome *adj* good-looking.

handwriting *n* manner of writing.

handy *adj* convenient; near.

hang vi, vi to suspend; to attach by hinges to allow to swing freely; to execute by hanging; to dangle; to fix up; to exhibit works of art.

hangar n a shelter for aircraft.

hanger n a device on which something is hung, eg clothes.

hanger-on n a dependent; a parasite.

hang-glider n an unpowered aircraft consisting of a metal frame over which material is stretched, with a harness for the pilot suspended below.

hangman n a public executioner; a word-game.

hangover n the unpleasant after-effects of excessive consumption of alcohol; something, usu unwanted, surviving from an earlier time.

hang-up n an emotional preoccu-pation with something.

hank n a skein of yarn.

hanker vi to desire longingly.

haphazard adj chance; random.

hapless adj unlucky; unhappy.

happen vi to take place; to occur.

happy adj pleased; lucky; joyous.

harangue n a speech; a tirade.

harass vt to plague; to vex.

harbour n a shelter; a haven; an inlet for anchoring ships; * vt to shelter; to nurse secretly in the mind.

hard adj firm; solid; difficult to understand, accomplish, bear; unfeeling; harsh; (of drugs) addictive and injurious; (of currency) stable in value; (of news) definite, not speculative; (of drink) alcoholic.

hardback n a book bound with a stiff cover.

hardboard n a stiff board made of compressed wood chips.

harden vt, vi to make hard; to inure; to be unfeeling.

hard-hearted adj pitiless.

hardihood n boldness; audacity.

hardly adv scarcely; barely.

hardship n privation; injustice.

hardware n common metal articles, eg tools; the components that make up a computer system.

hardy adj bold, intrepid; able to withstand hardship.

hare n any of various mammals of the genus Lepus.

harebrained adj giddy; heedless.

harelip n a congenital deformity of the upper lip in the form of a vertical fissure.

harem n apartments for the women of a Moslem household; the women themselves.

haricot n a kidney bean.

hark vi to listen.

harlequin n a well-known comic pantomime figure; a buffoon.

harlot n a prostitute.

harm n hurt; damage; evil; * vt to injure.

harmonic adj pertaining to har-mony; musical; * n a secondary tone; overtone; (maths) of or relating to quantities, the reciprocals of which are in arithmetical progression; (physics) a component frequency of a wave.

harmonica n a small wind instrument that produces tones when air is blown or sucked across a series of metal reeds; a mouth-organ.

harmonium n a wind instrument resembling a small organ.

harmonise vi, vt to be in, or bring into, or sing, in harmony.

harmony n (musical) concord; accord; agreement.

harness n the leather straps and metal pieces by which a horse is fastened to a cart; any similar fastening or attachment eg for a parachute; * vt to put a harness on; to control so as to use the power of.

harp n a stringed musical instrument.

harpoon n a barbed spear.

harpsichord n a stringed instrument with a keyboard like a piano.

harrow n a large rake for breaking ploughed ground; * vt to cause mental distress to.

harrowing adj distressing.

harry vt to harass; to worry.

harsh adj grating; rough; jarring on the senses or feeling; cruel.

hart n a stag or male deer.

harvest n the reaping season; the crop reaped; the fruit of labour.

hash vt to chop; to mince.

hashish n resinous cannabis derived from the top leaves and shoots of the hemp plant, smoked, chewed or drunk, medicinally or (illegally) as an intoxicant.

hasp n a clasp for a staple.

hassock n a footstool.

haste n speed; hurry; * vt to hurry.

hat n a head covering.

hatch vt to produce (young) from eggs; to contrive; to devise; * n a brood; a trap door; a door or opening on an aircraft or ship.

hatchback n a sloping rear end on a car with a door; a car of this design.

hatchet n a small axe.

hatchment n the coat of arms of a deceased person.

hatchway n an opening in a ship's deck covered with hatches.

hate vt to detest; to abhor.

hateful adj odious.

hatter n a seller of hats.

haughty adj proud and disdainful; arrogant.

haul vt to pull; to drag; * n a catch (of fish).

haulage n the transport of goods.

haunch n the hip; the thigh.

haunt vt to frequent; to revert repeatedly to; to appear habitually as a ghost; * n a place often visited.

hauteur n a haughty manner.

have vt to hold in one's possession; to possess as an attribute; to hold in the mind; to experience; to give birth to.

haven n a harbour; a shelter.

haversack n a canvas bag worn over one's shoulder.

havoc n widespread destruction or disorder; devastation.

hawk n a bird of prey; an aggressive or ruthless person; * vt to hunt with hawks; to carry about for sale.

hawser n a small cable.

hawthorn n any thorny tree or shrub of the genus Crataegus (rose family), esp C. monogyna.

hay n grass cut and dried for fodder.

hay fever n an allergic reaction to pollen causing irritation of the nose and eyes.

hazard n a danger or risk; the source of this; venture; an obstacle on a golf course; * vt to risk.

haze n vapour; mist; smoke; slight vagueness.

hazel n any shrub or small tree of the genus Corylus, C Avellana; * adj a reddish brown colour.

hazy adj obscure; dim; vague.

he pron of the (masculine) third person; * n a male person.

head n the part of an animal or human body containing the brain, eyes, ears, nose and mouth; the top part of anything; the foremost part; the chief person.

headache n pain in the head.

headgear n covering for the head.

heading n something forming the head, top or front; the title of a chapter; the direction in which (a vehicle) is moving.

headland n a cape; a promontory.

headlight, headlamp n a light at the front of a vehicle.

headline n printed lines at the top of a newspaper article giving the topic; ~s pl a brief news summary.

headlong adj with the head first; with uncontrolled speed or force; rashly.

headquarters n the centre of operations of an organisation.

headway n progress.

heady adj (of drink) intoxicating.

heal vt to cure.

health n a sound state of body or mind * ~y adj hale; sound.

heap n a mass; a pile; * vt to amass.

hear vt, vi to perceive by the ear; to listen; to conduct a legal hearing.

hearing n one of the five senses.

hearing aid n a small electronic amplifier to aid hearing.

hearsay n gossip; rumour.

hearse n a car for conveying a coffin.

heart n the organ which pumps the blood; the kernel; spirit; strength; courage; (pl) a suit of playing cards marked with a heart-shaped symbol.

heartache n sorrow; anguish.

heartbeat n the rhythmic contraction and dilation of the heart.

heartbreak *n* overwhelming sorrow or grief.

heartburn *n* a burning sensation in the lower chest.

hearten *vt* to encourage.

hearth *n* the floor of the fireplace.

heartless *adj* unfeeling.

heartwood *n* the dense inner wood of a tree, yielding the hardest wood.

hearty *adj* warm; cordial; keen; healthy; plentiful.

heat *n* the quality of being hot; the perception of hotness; hot weather or climate; strong feeling, *esp* anger; a single bout or round in sports; the period of readiness for mating in female mammals.

heath *n* a waste or shrub-covered tract of land; heather.

heathen *n* a pagan.

heather *n* the evergreen shrub, *Calluna vulgaris*.

heating *n* a system of providing heat, as central heating.

heatwave *n* a prolonged period of very hot weather.

heave *vt*, *vi* to lift something heavy; to retch; (marine) ~ **to** come to a halt.

heaven *n* the sky; the abode of God; bliss.

heavy *adj* weighty; sad; dull; clumsy.

heavyweight *n* (sport) a contestant weighing more than a certain amount, *usu* around (176lb) 80kg; (*fam*) a very influential individual.

heckle *n*, *vt* to harass a speaker.

hectic *adj*, *vt*, *vi* feverish.

hector *vt* to intimidate.

hedge *n* a fence consisting of a dense line of bushes or small trees; a means of protection against loss; an evasive or non-committal answer or statement; * *vt* to enclose with a hedge; to place secondary bets as a precaution.

hedgehog *n* a nocturnal mammal of the family *Erinaceidae*.

heed *vt* to attend to; to notice.

heel *n* the hind part of the foot; the part of a sock or shoe covering it.

hefty *adj* heavy; large and strong.

hegira *n* the flight of Mohammed from Mecca in the year 622.

heifer *n* a young cow that has not calved, or has borne only one calf.

height *n* the distance from top to bottom; eminence; elevation.

heighten *vt* to raise higher or to make more intense.

heinous *adj* wicked.

heir(ess) *n* one who inherits.

heirloom *n* any possession which descends from generation to generation.

helicity *n* (physics) a combination of the spin and linear momentum of a particle.

helicopter *n* an aircraft lifted and propelled by large rotary blades mounted horizontally.

helium *n* a the lightest noble gas, used in balloons and deep diving.

helix *n* (*pl* **helices**) a wire coil.

hell *n* the abode of the dead or the souls of the damned, in Judaism, Christianity and Islam; any place or state of extreme misery or pain.

hello *interj* a greeting.

helm *n* a rudder, the steering wheel on a ship.

helmet, **helm** *n* head armour.

helmsman *n* the person who steers a ship.

help *vt* to make things better or easier for; to aid; to serve or wait on; assistance.

hem *n* the edge of cloth, folded over and sewn down; * *vt* to put a hem on cloth; ~ **in** to enclose; to confine.

hemisphere *n* a half sphere; half the earth.

hemlock *n* a poisonous plant, *Conium maculatum*.

hemp *n* (in full **Indian hemp**) a herbaceous plant, *Cannabis sativum*, native to Asia; its fibre, used to make rope and sailcloth; a narcotic drug obtained from the plant (*also* **cannabis**, **marijuana**).

hen *n* a female bird, *esp* of the domestic fowl; a domestic fowl of either sex.

henbane *n* a poisonous herbaceous plant, *Hyoscyamus niger*.

hence *adv* from this time; for this reason; as a result of inference.

henceforth *adv* from now on.

henchman *n* a trusted supporter;

the principle attendant of a Highland chief.

hepatic *adj* pertaining to the liver.

heptagon *n* a regular seven-sided figure.

heptahedron *n* (geometry) a solid figure with seven faces.

her *pron* the possessive and objective case of she.

herald *n* one who brings news; a forerunner; * *vt* to usher in.

heraldry *n* the study of genealogies and coats of arms; ceremony; pomp.

herb *n* any non-woody plant, the stem of which dies yearly; any plant used medicinally or as seasoning.

herbivorous *adj* an animal that feeds on plants.

herd *n* a large number of animals, *esp* cattle, living and feeding together; * *vt, vi* to assemble or move animals together.

here *adv* in this place; now; on earth.

hereabout(s) *adv* about this place.

hereafter *adv* after this time; * *n* the ~ the future; life after death.

hereby *adv* by this means; near.

hereditary *adj* descending by inheritance; transmitted to offspring.

heredity *n* the inheritance of characteristics by one genera-tion from the previous one by the transmission of genetic mate-rial; such characteristics.

heresy *n* a belief contrary to orthodox (religious) doctrines.

heretic *n* one practising heresy; the holder of unorthodox opinion.

heritable *adj* (law) capable of being inherited by heirs; capable of inheriting; (biology) trans-missible from one generation to the next.

heritage *n* anything inherited or to be inherited; inherited circumstances; a nation's traditions or historical sites.

hermaphrodite *adj* being of both sexes; * *n* a flower with both stamens and pistils.

hermetic(al) *adj* airtight; protected from outside influences.

hermit *n* a recluse.

hermitage *n* a hermit's abode; a monastery.

hernia *n* the displacement and protrusion of part of an organ through the cavity containing it, *esp* of the abdomen.

heroin *n* a derivative of morphine used as an analgesic and as a narcotic.

hero(ine) *n* a brave person; the chief character in a play, novel or film.

heroism *n* the qualities or conduct of a hero; magnanimity; bravery.

heron *n* any of various wading birds of the family *Ardeidae*.

herring *n* a small North Atlantic fish, *Clupea harengus*.

herself *pron* emphatic and reflexive form of she and her.

hesitancy *n* a hesitating.

hertz *n* the SI unit of frequency equal to one cycle per second.

hesitate *vt* to show or feel indecision; to exhibit scruples.

heterogeneous *adj* mixed; diverse.

heterosexual *adj, n* of or related to attraction to the opposite sex.

hew *vi* to cut, chop, hack; to shape.

hexagon *n* a regular geometric object with six equal sides.

hey *interj* an exclamation.

heyday *n* a period of greatest success or happiness; prime.

hiatus *n* a gap; a break.

hibernate *vt* to pass the winter in sleep; to be inactive.

hiccup *n* an involuntary spasm of the diaphragm with sudden closure of the glottis, producing a characteristic sound; (*fig*) a minor setback.

hickory *n* any North American tree of the genus *Carya*.

hide *vt, vi* to conceal; to screen; to lie hidden; * *n* the skin of an animal; camouflaged place of concealment used by hunters or bird-watchers.

hideous *adj* frightful; horrifying.

hiding *n* concealment; a thrashing.

hierarchy *n* a group of people or things arranged in order of rank.

hieroglyph *n* writing in which words or syllables are represented by pictures, as used in ancient

Egyptian; one of these pictures.

high *adj* elevated; lofty; strong; (of price) dear; sharp; (of food) not fresh; intoxicated; * *adv* greatly; in, on, or to a high degree or rank; * *n* a high level or place; a euphoric state induced by drugs or alcohol.

highbrow *n, adj* an intellectual.

high-flyer, *n* an ambitious person; a person of great ability in any profession.

highland(s) *n(pl)* a mountainous region.

highlight *n* the lightest area of an image; the most interesting or important feature; * *vt* to bring to special attention; to give highlights to.

highness *n* the title used in addressing and referring to princes and princesses.

highway *n* a public thoroughfare.

highwayman *n* one who robbed on the highway.

hike *vi* to take a long walk.

hilarious *adj* very amusing.

hill *n* a rise in the land, lower than a mountain; a slope in a road.

hilt *n* a handle, *usu* of a sword.

him *pron* the objective case of he.

himself *pron* the emphatic and reflexive form of he and him.

hind *n* a female deer; * *adj* situated at the back.

hinder *vt* to prevent; to thwart.

hindrance *n* a check; an obstruction; an obstacle.

hinge *n* a joint or flexible part on which a door or lid turns; a natural joint, as of a clam shell; * *vt, vi* to attach or hang by a hinge; to depend.

hint *vt, vi* to suggest indirectly; to insinuate; * *n* an indirect or subtle suggestion; a slight mention; a piece of advice or practical help.

hip *n* the joint of the thigh; the fruit of the dog rose; * *adj* stylish; up-to-date.

hippopotamus *n* (*pl* **hippopotami**) a large African mammal, *Hippopotamus amphibius*.

hire *vt* to engage for wages; to lease out; * *n* wages; payment for the temporary use of something.

his *pron* possessive case of he.

hiss *vt* to make a sharp sibilant sound as of the letter S; to show disapproval in this way.

historian *n* a writer of history.

history *n* a record or account of past events; the study and analysis of past events; past events in total; the past events or experiences of a specific person or thing; an unusual or significant past.

histrionic *adj* theatrically exaggerated * ~s *n* .

hit *vt, vi* to strike; not to miss; to reach; to affect strongly; to discover by accident or unexpectedly; * *n* a stroke; a blow; a collision; a successful and popular song, book etc; a lucky chance.

hit-and-run *n* a motor vehicle accident in which the driver leaves the scene without stopping or informing the authorities.

hitch *vt, vi* to fasten; to tether.

hitch-hike *vt* to travel by seeking free lifts from passing vehicles.

hither *adv* to this place.

hitherto *adv* till now.

hive *n* a shelter for a colony of bees; a beehive; a busy crowded place; a scene of great activity.

hoard *n* a hidden stock stored away for future use *esp* of money, food.

hoarding *n* a temporary fence round a building, construction site etc; a large board for pasting advertisements to.

hoarse *adj* rough-voiced; grating.

hoax *n* a practical joke; * *vt* to trick.

hob *n* a ledge at the side of a fireplace for keeping things hot; a flat surface on a cooker with hot plates or burners.

hobble *vi* to limp; to shackle (a horse).

hobby *n* an occupation pursued purely out of interest.

hobnob *vi* to get together for friendly conversation; to socialize.

hock, **hough** *n* the joint on the hind-leg, between the knee and fetlock of a quadruped.

hockey *n* game played with a ball and curved stick between two teams of eleven players each.

hod *n* a trough on a pole for carrying mortar and bricks.

hoe *n* a garden tool with a long handle, used for weeding.

hog *n* a castrated male pig raised for its meat; a selfish, greedy or dirty person; * *vt* to take more than one's share; to hoard greedily.

hogweed *n* any of various weeds of the genus *Heracleum*.

hoist *vt* to heave up; * *n* a lift.

hold *vt*, *vi* to have in one's grasp; to confine; to keep; to contain; to occupy; to carry on, *eg* a meeting; * *n* a grasp; possession; a dominance over; the lowermost inside part of a ship.

holdall *n* a portable bag.

holding *n* a small rented farm with land; (often *pl*) property, *esp* land, stocks and bonds.

hole *n* a hollow place; an aperture; a cavity; a den; a small dirty place; a difficult situation; a small bound hollow to receive a golf ball; a fairway plus tee in golf.

holiday *n* a day or period away from work etc; a time for rest or amusement.

holiness *n* sanctity; (*when cap.*) the title to address and refer to the Pope.

hollow *adj* not solid; empty; false; * *n* a cavity; * *vt* to excavate.

holly *n* *Ilex aquifolium*, an evergreen shrub, with prickly leaves.

holocaust *n* large scale destructions, *esp* by fire or nuclear war; (with *cap*) the mass murder of Jews in Europe by Nazis (1941-45).

hologram *n* physics a three dimensional image formed by interference of coherent light beams.

holograph *n* a document in one's own handwriting.

holster *n* a leather case attached to a belt for a pistol.

holy *adj* sinless; consecrated.

homage *n* duty; fealty; a demonstration of respect or honour towards someone or something.

home *n* one's own abode; residence; native place; a household; an institution for aged people, orphans etc; a private hospital.

homeland *n* the country where a person was born.

homely *adj* simple; plain; everyday.

home-made *adj* made or looking as if made at home.

homesick *adj* affected with homesickness; longing for home.

homespun *adj* coarse; rough; unsophisticated.

homestead *n* a house with the grounds and buildings attached.

homeward, **homewards** *adv* towards home.

homework *n* work, *esp* piecework, done at home; schoolwork to be done outside the classroom.

homicide *n* the killing of a person; one who does this.

homily *n* a sermon; sound advice.

hominid *n* any member of the primate family *hominidae*, humans being the only non-extinct members.

homoeopathy *n* disease treatment by administering tiny doses of drugs which wold produce the disease symptoms in a healthy individual.

homogeneous *adj* of the same kind; of uniform structure.

homonym *n* a word alike in form or sound, but not in meaning, as here, hear.

homosexual *n*,*adj* of or concerning attraction to one's own sex.

hone *n* a whetstone, *esp* for razors; * *vt* to sharpen (as) with one.

honest *adj* free from fraud; upright; truthful; trustworthy; frank.

honey *n* a sweet sticky yellowish substance made by bees out of nectar collected from flowers.

honeycomb *n* the waxy storage cells of bees.

honeymoon *n* the holiday spent together by newlyweds.

honeysuckle *n* any climbing shrub of the genus *Lonicera*.

honorarium *n* a fee paid for voluntary services.

honorary *adj* conferred as an honour; unpaid; voluntary.

honour *n* glory; good name;

integrity; distinction; a title of respect; (*pl*) university distinctions; * *vt* to esteem; pay (bill) when due.

hood *n* a cowl; a head covering; anything hood-shaped.

hoof *n* (*pl* **hooves**) the horny part of an ungulate's foot.

hook *n* a piece of metal bent so as to catch or hold; a sickle; * *vt* to catch with a hook; to ensnare; to drive a ball to the left (golf); to pass the ball backwards from a scrum in rugby; * *vi* to bend; to be curving.

hoop *n* the band of a cask; a ring.

hoot *vi* to shout in contempt; to cry as an owl; to blow a whistle.

hooter *n* something that makes a hooting sound *eg* a car horn; a nose.

hop *n* a leap on one leg; a spring; a short flight; a climbing plant, *Humulus lupulus*, cultivated for its cones; the ripe cones of this used to give a bitter flavour to beer; * *vi* to leap; to skip.

hope *vt* to desire and expect; * *vi* to trust.

hopeful *adj* filled with hope.

horde *n* a crowd; a throng; a rabble.

horizon *n* the apparent junction of the earth and sky; the limit of a person's apprehension.

horizontal *adj* level; parallel to the plane of the horizon.

hormone *n* a regulatory substance formed in one part of the organism and carried to another part, where it stimulates specific cells or tissues into action; a synthetic compound having the same purpose; * *adj* hormonal.

horn *n* a hard pointed growth on the heads of some animals; the feelers of snails, etc; anything horn-like; a wind instrument *esp* the French horn; a device blown or sounded as a warning.

hornet *n* a large wasp, *Vespa Crabro*.

horoscope *n* an observation of the heavens, by which astrologers profess to predict future events in the life of an individual.

horrible *adj* dreadful; frightful.

horrid *adj* shocking; hideous.

horror *n* dread; intense fear; a person or thing inspiring horror.

hors-d'oeuvre *n* an appetizer served at the start of a meal.

horse *n* four-legged, solid-hoofed herbivorous mammal, *Equus caballus*.

horseman *n* a rider on horseback.

horse mushroom *n* a large edible mushroom, *Agaricus arvensis*.

horseplay *n* rough, rude conduct.

horsepower *n* an imperial unit of power equal to 550 foot pounds per second (approx. 750 watts); the power of a motor or engine measured by this unit.

horseradish *n* a cruciferous plant, *Amoracia rusticana*, with a edible root; this root in sauces.

horseshoe *n* a flat, U-shaped plate nailed to a horse's hoof.

Horseshoe crab *n* a large marine arthropod, *Xiphosura polyphemus*, with a horseshoe shaped shell, a long tail-spine, and blue blood.

horticulture *n* the art or science of growing flowers, fruit and vegetables.

hose *n* *sing* or *pl* stockings; breeches; a flexible tube for conveying water etc; * *vt* to spray with a hose.

hosiery *n* stockings and socks.

hospice *n* a nursing home for the care of the terminally ill.

hospital *n* an institution for the care of the sick.

hospitality *n* kindness, generosity to guests and strangers.

host (**ess**) *n* a person who receives or entertains stranger or guest at his house; an animal or plant on or in which another lives; the presenter on a television or radio programme; a very large number of people or things; the wafer of bread used in the Eucharist or Holy Communion.

hostage *n* a person kept as a pledge to secure the performance of conditions.

hostel *n* a lodging house for the students, nurses, etc.

hostile *adj* unfriendly.

hostility *n* enmity; (*pl*) warfare.

hot *adj* (**hotter**, **hottest**) of high

temperature; very warm; giving or feeling heat; causing a burning sensation on the tongue; full of intense feeling; following closely; electrically charged; (*fam*) new; radioactive; stolen.

hotel *n* a establishment providing lodging and meals for payment.

hothead *n* an impetuous person.

hotpot *n* a casserole of meat and vegetables covered by a layer of potatoes.

hound *n* a hunting dog; * *vt* to urge on.

hour *n* a period of 3600 seconds; a special point in time; * ~ly *adj* occurring every hour.

hourglass *n* a glass containing sand for measuring time.

house *n* a building to live in, *esp* by one person or family; a household; a family or dynasty including relatives, ancestors and descendants; the audience in a theatre; a business firm; a legislative assembly.

house arrest *n* detention in one's own house, as opposed to prison.

houseboat *n* a boat furnished and used as a home.

housebreaker *n* a burglar.

household *n* the occupants of a house; * *adj* domestic; pertaining to house and family.

housekeeper *n* a person who runs a home, *esp* one hired to do so.

housekeeping *n* the daily running of a household; (*fam*) money used for domestic expenses; routine maintenance of equipment, records, etc in an organisation.

house warming *n* a party given to celebrate moving into a new house.

hovel *n* a small mean dwelling.

hover *vi* (of a bird, helicopter, etc) stay stationary in the air; linger near.

hovercraft *n* a vehicle that travels over land or water supported on a cushion of air.

how *adv* in what manner.

however *adv* in whatever manner; * *conj* yet; though.

howl *vt*, *vi* to utter the long, wailing cry, such as of wolves; to

utter a similar cry of anger or pain; to shout in pain; to laugh in amusement.

hub *n* the centre part of a wheel; a centre of activity.

huddle *vi*, *vt* to crowd together in a confined space.

hue *n* colour; tint; an outcry.

huff *n* a state of resentment; * *vi* to blow; to puff.

hug *vt* to embrace; to keep close to; to squeeze tightly; * *n* a close embrace.

huge *adj* immense; enormous.

hulk *n* the body of a dismantled ship, used as a storage vessel; a clumsy person.

hull *n* the husk or outer covering; the body of a ship; * *vt* to strip off covering.

hum *vb* (*pt* ~med) *vt*, *vi* to make a low continuous sound.

human *adj* of or relating to human beings; having the qualities of humans as opposed to animals; kind, considerate; * *n* a primate, *homo sapiens sapiens*.

humane *adj* merciful; compassion-ate.

humanity *n* the human race; the state or quality of being human or humane; philanthropy; kindness.

humble *adj* lowly; modest; * *vt* to lower in condition or rank; to humiliate.

humerus *n* the bone in the upper arm.

humid *adj* moist; damp (of air).

humiliate *vt* to humble; to mortify; to lower the pride or dignity.

humility *n* modesty; meekness.

hummingbird *n* any nectar feeding tropical American bird of the family *Trochilidae*.

hummock *n* a rounded knoll.

humour *n* disposition; mood; jocularity; * *vt* to gratify; to indulge.

hump *n* a protuberance, *esp* on the back *eg* of a camel; a lump.

humpback *n* a hunchback; a baleen whale, *Megaptera novaeangliae*.

humus *n* the organic constituent of soil, *usu* formed by the decomposition of plant matter.

hunch *n* a hump; an intuitive feeling; * *vt* to arch into a hump; * *vt* to move forward jerkily.

hunchback *n* a person with curvature of the spine.

hundred *adj* ten times ten; a symbol for this *eg* 100, C, c.

hundredweight *n* 112 lb; 1/20 ton.

hunger *n* a craving for food; any strong desire; * *vi* to feel hunger; to have a strong desire (for).

hunt *vt, vi* pursue and kill wild animals for sport or food; (of an animal) to chase prey; to search for; * *n* an instance of this.

hurdle *n* a portable frame of bars for temporary fences or for jumping over by horses or runners; an obstacle.

hurl *vt* to throw with force.

hurrah *interj* an exclamation of joy.

hurricane *n* a tropical cyclone with winds of at least 119kmph (74 mph).

hurry *vt, vi* to act or move with haste; * *n* rush; haste.

hurt *n* a wound; an injury; harm; * *vt* to pain; harm; injure; damage.

hurtle *vi* to move or throw with great speed and force.

husband *n* a male spouse; * *vt* to manage frugally; to conserve.

hush *n* stillness; * *vt, vi* to silence.

husk *n* the outer dry covering of certain fruits and seeds.

husky *adj* dry; hoarse; harsh; hefty; strong; * *n* an Arctic sled dog.

hustle *vt, vi* to jostle; to push or force hurriedly; to swindle.

hut *n* a small crude house or cabin.

hutch *n* a pen for small animals.

hyacinth *n* any bulbous plant of the genus *Hyacynthus*.

hybrid *n* the offspring of two plants or animals of different species; a mongrel; * *adj* crossbred.

hydrangea *n* any shrub of the genus *Hydrangea*.

hydrant *n* a large, valved pipe for drawing water from a main.

hydraulic *adj* (of a liquid) conveyed through pipes *usu* under pressure; (of a device) operated by liquid moving in this manner.

hydrofoil *n* a boat with planes to lift its hull out of the water.

hydrogen *n* a flammable, colour-less, odourless, tasteless, gas, the lightest chemical element, occurring in water and all organic chemicals.

hydrometer *n* an instrument for finding the specific gravity of liquids.

hydrophobia *n* a morbid fear of water, *esp* as a symptom of rabies.

hydrostatic *adj* of the equilibrium and the pressure exerted at rest of a liquid.

hyena, hyaena *n* a dog-like carnivorous mammal of the genus *Hyaenidae*.

hygiene *n* principles and practice of health and cleanliness.

hygrometer *n* an instrument for measuring humidity of air.

hymn *n* a song of praise.

hymnal *n* a collection of hymns.

hyperbola *n* one of the curves formed by the section of a cone.

hyperbole *n* an exaggeration for effect or emphasis.

hyphen *n* a mark (-) joining syllables or words.

hypnosis *n* (*pl* hypnoses) a relaxed state resembling sleep in which the mind responds to external suggestion.

hypnotise *vt* to put in a state of hypnosis; to fascinate.

hypochondria *n* chronic depres-sion; needless and anxiety about one's health.

hypocrisy *n* a falsely pretending to possess virtues; an example of this.

hypodermic *adj* introduced beneath the skin (injection).

hypotenuse *n* the side opposite the right angle of a right-angled triangle.

hypothesis *n* (*pl* hypotheses) a proposition made as a basis for reasoning, without knowledge of its truth; a conjecture made as a starting point for further investigation from known facts; groundless supposition.

hypothetical *adj* based on hypothesis, conjectural.

hysteria *n* a mental disorder marked by excitability, anxiety, imaginary organic disorders etc; frenzied emotion or excitement.

hysterical *adj* caused by hysteria; suffering from hysteria; (*fam*) extremely funny.

I

I *pron* the first person singular.

ice *n* frozen water; ice cream or water ice; * *vt*, *vi* to freeze; to cool with ice; to cover with icing.

iceberg *n* a floating mass of ice.

ice cream *n* a sweet creamy frozen food.

ice floe *n* a sheet of floating ice.

icicle *n* a hanging taper of ice formed by frozen dripping water.

icing *n* a coating of sugar mixture *usu* on a cake.

idea *n* a mental impression or notion; an opinion or belief.

ideal *adj* perfect; * *n* a perfect example; a standard for attainment or imitation; an aim or principle.

idealism *n* the practice of forming, or following after, ideals, *esp* when unrealistic.

idealist *n* a visionary.

idealise *vt* to represent as ideal.

identical *adj* exactly the same.

identification *n* act of identifying.

identify *vt* to consider to be the same; to establish the identity of.

identity *n* the distinguishing characteristics of a person, personality; the state of being the same in substance, nature, etc.

ideology *n* the doctrines, opinions or beliefs of an individual, social class, political party etc.

idiocy *n* stupidity.

idiom *n* an accepted expression with a different meaning from the literal (eg over the moon); a form of expression peculiar to a language, person, or group of people; the language of a people or of a place.

idiosyncrasy *n* a personal peculiarity; a quirk; eccentricity.

idiot *n* (*fam*) a stupid person.

idle *adj* doing nothing; lazy; out

of work; * *vt* to waste or spend time uselessly; * *vi* (of an engine) to operate without transmitting power.

idleness *n* inaction; sloth.

idly *adv* lazily; carelessly.

idol *n* a graven image or anything worshipped.

idolatry *n* the worship of idols.

idolise *vt* to love excessively.

idyl, idyll *n* a romantic or a pastoral poem.

idyllic *adj* describing an idyll; charmingly picturesque.

if *conj* on condition that; in the event that; supposing that; even though; whenever.

igneous *adj* descriptive of rocks formed from solidified magma or lava.

ignite *vt*, *vi* to kindle; to set fire to; to burn or cause to burn.

ignition *n* an act or instance of igniting; the starting of an internal combustion engine.

ignoble *adj* mean; base.

ignominy *n* public disgrace; shame.

ignoramus *n* (*pl* ignoramuses) an ignorant person.

ignorance *n* want of knowledge.

ignore *vt* to disregard.

iguana *n* any lizard of the family *Iguanidae* .

ill *adj* bad or evil; sick; * *n* unwell; evil; * *adv* not well; badly.

ill-bred *adj* not polite; rude.

illegal *adj* contrary to law.

illegible *adj* unreadable.

illegitimate *adj* born out of wedlock.

illicit *adj* improper; unlawful.

illiterate *adj* not able to read or write; ignorant.

ill-judged *adj* injudicious; unwise.

ill-mannered *adj* rude; boorish.

ill-natured *adj* bad-tempered; spiteful.

illness *n* sickness.

illogical *adj* not logical.

ill-tempered *adj* cross; morose.

ill-treat *vt* to treat unkindly, unfairly.

illuminate *vt* to light up; to adorn; to enlighten.

illusion *n* a false notion; an unreal or misleading image; deception.

illusionist n a conjuror; a magician.

illusive adj deceptive.

illusory adj fallacious.

illustrate vt to make clear by explanation or drawing.

illustration n an example, a picture, or drawing; esp in a book.

illustrative adj explanatory.

illustrious adj renowned; distinguished.

ill-will n hatred; malice.

image n a likeness; an idol; a mental picture; the visual impression of something in a lens, mirror etc.

imagery n picturesque language.

imaginary adj not real; visionary; (maths) the square root of a negative number.

imagination n fancy; the creative faculty.

imagine vt, vi to fancy; to conceive; to believe falsely.

imago n the final stage, after all metamorphoses, of an insect, eg a butterfly.

imbibe vt to drink in; to absorb.

imitate vt to copy; to mimic; to impersonate; * **imitation** n.

immaculate adj spotless; perfectly executed; free from fault; not spotted.

immaterial adj unimportant.

immature adj unripe; not mature; facile.

immeasurable adj of too great, or small, a size to be measured.

immediate adj acting or occuring without delay; next, nearest, without intervening agency; next in relationship; in close proximity; near to.

immense adj immeasurable; huge.

immerse vt to plunge into esp water.

immigrant n one who settles in a country not his own.

immigrate vi to enter a country as a settler.

imminent adj impending; about to happen; threatening.

immobile adj fixed; stable.

immoderate adj excessive.

immodest adj indelicate.

immoral adj depraved; wicked; corrupt.

immortal adj living forever; having lasting fame.

immortalise vt to make famous for ever.

immovable adj steadfast; unalterable.

immune adj not susceptible to a specified disease through vaccination or natural resistance; not subject to (arrest etc).

immutable adj unchangeable.

impact n a collision.

impair vt to make worse; to weaken.

impala n an antelope, native to southern and eastern Africa, Aepyceros melampus.

impale vt to transfix with a sharp pointed instrument.

impart vt to give; to besto; to confer.

impartial adj just; fair; unbiased.

impassable adj incapable of being travelled over or through.

impasse n a deadlock.

impassioned adj deeply felt; ardent.

impassive adj unmoved; apathetic.

impatient adj fretful; intolerant; restless; * **impatience** n.

impeach vt disparage a person's honesty; charge with a crime against the state, esp treason; (US) charge a public official (esp the president) with misconduct.

impeccable adj faultless.

impecunious adj penniless.

impede vt to hamper; to obstruct.

impel vt to drive or urge forward.

impend vi to hang over; to threaten.

impenetrable adj impervious; unable to be passed through.

imperative adj commanding; obligatory; designating or of the mood of a verb that expresses a command, entreaty etc.

imperceptible adj minute; not easily detected by the senses.

imperfect adj incomplete; faulty; designating a verb tense that indicates a past action or state as incomplete or continuous.

imperial adj pertaining to an empire; the system of imperial units (ounces, yards etc.).

imperil vt to endanger.

imperious adj commanding; arrogant.

impermeable *adj* impervious; impenetrable by liquids.

impersonal *adj* without reference to a particular person; cold; unfeeling; (of a verb) occuring only in the third person singular.

impersonate *vt* to assume the character, voice, appearance, etc of another.

impertinence *n* insolence; irrelevance; rudeness.

impervious *adj* impassable; not receptive to or affected by.

impetuous *adj* hasty; thoughtless.

impetus *n* the force with which a body moves; driving force.

impinge *vi* to encroach.

implacable *adj* not to be appeased; inexorable; unrelenting.

implant *vt* to plant; to instil.

implement *n* a tool, utensil, or instrument; * *vt* to carry out.

implication *n* entanglement; inference; deduction.

implicit *adj* implied but not stated.

implore *vti* to beseech, to entreat.

imply *vt* to suggest indirectly.

impolite *adj* rude; uncivil.

imponderable *adj* without weight; * *n* something difficult to assess.

import *vt* to bring from abroad; to signify; to imply.

important *adj* momentous; serious; powerful and authoritative.

importune *vt* to press urgently; to crave.

impose *vt* to lay on as a tax; to inflict oneself on others.

imposing *adj* impressive; stately.

imposition *n* an unfair obligation.

impossible *adj* not possible; inconceivable; unendurable.

impostor, imposter *n* a deceiver.

impotent *adj* feeble; incompetent; sexually impotent.

impound *vt* to seize legally.

impoverish *vt* to make poor.

impractical *adj* not practical; not competent in practical skills.

impregnable *adj* invincible; secure against attack.

impregnate *vt* to cause to become pregnant; to saturate; to pervade.

impress *vt* to press into; to stamp; to fix deeply (in the mind).

impression *n* an effect produced (*esp* on the mind); an impersonation; a vague idea; an imprinted mark; the number of copies of a book printed at one time.

impressionism *n* a movement in art attempting to convey emotional effect by visual impression.

imprint *vt* to impress; to stamp.

imprison *vt* to confine in prison.

improbable *adj* unlikely to be true or to happen.

improbity *n* wickedness; lack of moral integrity; dishonesty.

impromptu *adj* extempore; * *n* an unrehearsed performance.

improper *adj* indecent; erroneous.

improve *vt*, *vi* to better; to grow better; to use to good purpose.

improvident *adj* thriftless.

improvise *vt* to compose and recite off the cuff; to use whatever is at hand.

imprudent *adj* indiscreet; heedless.

impulse *n* a thrust; a motive; a sudden determination to act; (physics) the momentum imparted by a, *usu* large, force acting for a, *usu* small, time.

impulsive *adj* impetuous; hasty.

impunity *n* freedom from punishment.

impure *adj* obscene; adulterated.

impute *vt* to attribute; ascribe.

in *prep*, *adv* within; not out; during; being a member of; wearing.

inability *n* lack of ability.

inaccessible *adj* unattainable.

inaccurate *adj* incorrect; not exact.

inaction *n* idleness; rest.

inadequate *adj* defective; not capable; * inadequacy *n*.

inadmissible *adj* not allowable.

inadvertent *adj* heedless; careless.

inadvisable *adj* not advisable; inexpedient.

inalienable *adj* incapable of being transferred.

inane *adj* silly; senseless.

inanimate *adj* lifeless; spiritless.

inapplicable *adj* not applicable.

inapposite *adj* not to the point.

inappropriate *adj* unsuitable.

inapt *adj* unapt; unfit.

inarticulate *adj* incapable of

coherent or effective communication.

inattentive *adj* not attending; thoughtless.

inaudible *adj* unable to be heard.

inagurate *vt* to introduce, to install into office; to open a building etc formally to the public; to initiate.

inauspicious *adj* ill-omened.

inborn *adj* innate; inherent.

inbred *adj* innate; produced by inbreeding.

inbreed *vt, vi* to breed from closely related stock.

incalculable *adj* numberless; very great; uncertain; impossible to calculate.

incandescent *adj* white or glowing with heat.

incantation *n* a magical formula; the reciting of this.

incapable *adj* unfit to perform an activity.

incapacitate *vt* to render unfit; to disable.

incarceration *n* imprisonment.

incarnate *vt* to embody in flesh.

incautious *adj* unwary; imprudent.

incendiary *adj* (of a bomb, etc) designed to start fires; inflammatory.

incense *n* spices burnt in religious rites; the resultant smoke; * *vt* to inflame; to provoke.

incentive *adj n* an inducement.

incessant *adj* unceasing; constant.

incest *n* intercourse between close blood relations.

inch *n* a unit of length equal to one twelfth of a foot or 2.54 cm; * *vt, vi* to move by or by degrees.

incidence *n* the degree or range of occurence or effect.

incident *n* a distinct event; a minor event.

incidental *adj* casual; occasional; happening by the way.

incinerate *vt* to burn to ashes.

incipient *adj* beginning to be or appear.

incise *vt* to cut in or into; to carve.

incisor *n* a front cutting tooth.

incite *vt* to urge on; to stir up.

inclement *adj* (of the weather) severe, *esp* stormy.

inclination *n* a propensity or disposition, *esp* a liking; a deviation from the horizontal or vertical; a slope.

incline *vi* to slope; to be disposed towards an opinion or action; * *vt* to cause to bend forwards; to cause to deviate; * *n* a slope.

include *vt* to enclose; to comprise; to contain.

incognito *n, adj, adv* with one's name or identity kept secret; an assumed identity for this purpose; one who is incognito.

incoherent *adj* confused; unintelligible; (physics (of waves) of unrelated phase.

incombustible *adj* not able to be burned.

income *n* all moneys coming in for work or investments etc.

incoming *n* the act of coming in; that which comes in.

incommunicative *adj* reserved; unsocial.

incomparable *adj* matchless.

incompatible *adj* irreconcilable; unable to exist with in harmony.

incompetent *adj* unskilful.

incomplete *adj* imperfect; defective; unfinished.

incomprehensible *adj* unintelligible.

inconceivable *adj* unimaginable.

inconclusive *adj* indecisive; uncertain as to result or outcome.

incongruous *adj* discordant; inconsistent; lacking harmony or agreement of parts.

inconsequential, inconsequent *adj* not following logically; irrelevant.

inconsiderable *adj* unimportant; insignficant.

inconsiderate *adj* thoughtless.

inconsistent *adj* variable.

inconsolable *adj* grieved beyond measure.

inconspicuous *adj* not easily noticed; undistinguished.

incontestable *adj* unquestionable.

incontinent *adj* unable to control the bladder or bowels.

incontrovertible *adj* certain; indisputable.

inconvenient *adj* awkward.

incorporate *vt* to unite in one body.

incorrect *adj* untrue; improper.

incorrigible *adj* incurable; hopeless.

incorruptible *adj* incapable of physical corruption, decay or dissolution; incapable of being bribed.

increase *vi* to become greater; to augment; * *vt* to add to; * *n* a growing larger; addition; profit; interest.

incredible *adj* unbelievable.

incredulous *adj* sceptical; doubting.

increment *n* the amount of an increase.

incriminate *vi* to involve in an accusation; to accuse.

incubate *vi* to sit on eggs; to hatch.

inculcate *vt* to teach; to implant.

incur *vt* to bring upon oneself.

incurable *adj* hopeless; past cure.

incursion *n* a raid; an inroad.

indebted *n* beholden; owing.

indecent *adj* unseemly; obscene.

indecipherable *adj* incapable of being deciphered.

indecision *n* inability to take a decision; * indecisive *adj*.

indecorous *adj* unseemly; improper.

indeed *adv* certainly; * *interj* expressing irony, disbelief, surprise, etc.

indefatigable *adj* untiring; unremitting.

indefensible *adj* untenable; inexcusable.

indefinable *adj* vague; difficult to explain clearly.

indefinite *adj* uncertain; unlimited; vague.

indelible *adj* not able to be erased.

indelicate *adj* improper; coarse.

indemonstrable *adj* unprovable.

indemnify *vt* to make good a loss; to insure against loss, damage.

indent *vt* to notch; to indicate a paragraph by leaving a space at the margin.

indenture *n* a written contract between two parties.

independent *adj* free; unrstrained; not dependent upon.

indescribable *adj* unutterable; inexpressible; too beautiful, etc for words.

indestructible *adj* imperishable.

indeterminate *adj* uncertain.

index *n* an alphabetical list of names, subjects, items, etc mentioned in a printed book, *usu* at the end of the text.

index finger *n* the forefinger.

index-linked *adj* (of wages etc) linked to the retail price index.

indicate *vt* to point out; to show; to state briefly; to suggest.

indictment *n* a formal charge or accusation of a crime.

indifferent *adj* unconcerned; uninterested; mediocre.

indigenous *adj* native to a particular country, region or enviroment.

indigent *adj* needy, poor

indigestion *n* pain caused by difficulty in digesting food.

indignant *adj* angry; scornful.

indignity *n* humiliation; an insult.

indigo *n* a blue vegetable dye.

indirect *adj* roundabout.

indiscreet *adj* tactless; imprudent.

indiscriminate *adj* not making any distinction; general; confused; random.

indispensable *adj* necessary; vital.

indisposed *adj* disinclined; unwell.

indisputable *adj* unquestionable.

indistinct *adj* faint; confused.

individual *adj* existing as a seperate thing or being; of, by, for, or relating to a single person; * *n* a single thing or being.

indivisible *adj* not able to be divided.

indoctrinate *vt* to instruct systematically in a doctrine, idea or belief.

indolent *adj* lazy; idle.

indomitable *adj* unyielding; invincible.

indoors *adv* within house.

indubitable *adj* certain; evident.

induce *vt* to persuade; to draw (a conclusion) from particular facts; to cause.

inducement *n* an incentive; a motive.

induct *vt* to install; to introduce.

induction *n* introduction to office; a prologue; magnetic influence.

indulge *vt* to gratify; to humour; * *vi* to give way to one's desire.

industrialist *n* a person who owns an industrial enterprise.

industrious *adj* diligent; active.

industry *n* organised production or manufacture of goods; effort.

inebriated *adj* drunken.

inedible *adj* no fit to be eaten.

ineffable *adj* indescribable.

ineffective *adj* useless; impotent.

ineffectual *adj* fruitless; futile.

inefficacy *n* failure to produce effect.

inefficient *adj* using too much, or more than neccessary, time, resources, etc.

inelegant *adj* plain; ungraceful.

ineligible *adj* not qualified; unsuitable; * ineligibility *n*.

inept *adj* unsuitable; awkward.

inequality *n* lack of equality; unevenness of surface.

inequitable *adj* unfair; unjust.

inert *adj* lifeless; sluggish; inactive; dull with few or no properties.

inertia *n* inactivity; tendency of matter to remain in existing state of rest (or continue in a fixed direction) unless acted on by an outside force.

inestimable *adj* priceless.

inevitable *adj* unavoidable.

inexact *adj* not exactly true or correct.

inexcusable *adj* indefensible.

inexhaustible *adj* unfailing.

inexorable *adj* inflexible; relentless.

inexpedient *adj* not advisable; injudicious.

inexpensive *adj* cheap.

inexperienced *adj* unskilled; raw.

inexplicable *adj* unaccountable; without explanation.

inextricable *adj* that cannot be disentangled, or escaped from.

infallible *adj* incapable of errors reliable; * infallibility *n*.

infamy *n* public disgrace; ignominy.

infancy *n* early childhood; the early stages of anything.

infant *n* a very young child.

infanticide *n* child murder.

infantry *n* foot soldiers.

infatuate *vt* to inspire with passion; * ~d *adj* besotted.

infect *vt* to taint with disease; to corrupt.

infection *n* an instance of being infected, or having an infectious disease.

infectious *adj* able to be transmitted.

infer *vt* to conclude, to deduce.

inferior *adj* subordinate; beneath; * *n* a person lower in rank, etc.

inferno *n* intense heat; a devastating fire.

infernal *adj* diabolical; fiendish; extremely irritating.

infertility *n* barrenness.

infest *vt* to overrun in large numbers; to be parasitic on.

infidelity *n* want of faith; unfaithfulness *esp* in marriage.

infighting *n* intense competition within an organisation.

infiltrate *vt*, *vi* to permeate; to penetrate stealthily, *eg* as spies.

infinite *adj* limitless; vast.

infinitesimal *adj* microscopic; minute.

infinitive *n* the form of a verb without reference to person, number or tense.

infinity *n* immensity; a boundless number, quantity or time period.

infirm *adj* weak; sickly.

infirmary *n* a hospital.

inflame *vt* to kindle; to excite; to incense; * *vt* to grow hot.

inflammable *adj* combustible.

inflammation *n* a condition of the body marked by heat, swelling, and pain.

inflammatory *adj* tending to excite passion.

inflate *vt* to fill up with air or gas; distend; to increase beyond what is normal, *esp* the supply of money.

inflation *n* an act or instance of inflating; a state of falling currency value and rising prices.

inflection *n* modulation of voice; changes in word forms.

inflexible *adj* unbending; rigid.

inflict *vt* to impose as a penalty.

influence *n* moving or directing power; sway; affect.

influenza *n* a contagious, feverish viral disease marked by muscular pain and inflamation of the respitory system.

influx *n* a flowing in of people or things to a place.

inform vt to tell; to enlighten; to teach; to give information.

informal adj without ceremony; unofficial; casual

information n items of knowledge; news;.

informer n one who informs; a spy.

infrastructure n the basic structural foundations of a society or organisation; a nations basic economic structure, roads, bridges etc.

infrequent adj uncommon; rare.

infringe vt to break; to transgress.

infuriate vt to madden; to enrage.

infuse vt to pour in; to instil; to steep.

infusion n process of infusion; liquor (as tea) so obtained.

ingenious adj inventive, original; resourceful; * ingenuity n.

ingenuous adj open or candid.

inglorious adj unhonoured; humiliating.

ingot n a bar of cast metal, esp gold, silver, or steel.

ingrate n an ungrateful person.

ingratiate vt to get into another's favour.

ingratitude n thanklessness.

ingredient n something included with others in a mixture.

ingress n entrance.

inhabit vt, vi to live in; to reside.

inhabitable adj habitable.

inhabitant n a resident.

inhale vt to draw into the lungs.

inhaler n a respirator; an apparatus for inhaling vapours.

inharmonious adj discordant.

inherent adj inborn; ingrained.

inherit vt, vi to come into possession of as an heir.

inhibit vt to restrain; to forbid.

inhospitable adj unfriendly and ungenerous to strangers; barren.

inhuman adj cruel; merciless.

inimical adj unfriendly; hostile.

inimitable adj matchless; peerless.

iniquitous adj wicked; criminal.

initial adj primary; of or at the beginning; * n the first letters of a person's name (pl); * vt to mark or sign with initials.

initiate vt to begin; to originate; to admit as a member of a club etc.

initiation n formal introduction or admittance.

initiative n first step; lead; power of originating.

inject vt to force (fluid into the body) esp with a syringe.

injudicious adj unwise; indiscreet.

injunction n a command; exhortation; a legal writ restraining or ordering.

injure vt to hurt; to damage.

injustice n wrong; unfairness.

ink n a coloured liquid used for writing, printing etc.

inkling n a vague notion; a hint.

inland adj interior; remote from the sea; domestic.

inlay vt to decorate a surface by inserting pieces of metal, etc.

inlet n a narrow strip of water extending into a body of land; an opening.

inmate n a resident; an occupant, esp of a prison or other institution.

inn n a small hotel; a public house.

innards n entrails; the internal workings of a machine, etc

innate adj inborn; natural; instinctive.

inner adj interior; * n the part of a target adjoining the bull's eye.

innings n (pl innings) the batting period of each side (cricket).

innocence n purity; simplicity; without guilt or guile.

innocent adj not guilty of a particular crime; blameless.

innocuous adj harmless.

innovate vi to introduce new methods, ideas, etc.

innuendo n an indirect hint; a sly remark, often derogatory.

innumerable adj countless.

inoculate vt to inject a serum or a vaccine into, esp in order to create an immunity.

inopportune adj untimely; inconvenient.

inordinate adj excessive; extravagant.

inorganic adj not of living organisms; (chemistry) not containing organic compounds.

in-patient n a patient being treated

while remaining in hospital.

inquest *n* an inquiry by a coroner's court into the causes of a death.

inquire *vi* to ask about; to question; to investigate.

inquiry, **enquiry** *n* research; a question; an investigation.

inquisition *n* an inquiry; a formal search; a tribunal for trial.

inquisitive *adj* prying; inquiring; curious.

insane *adj* not sane; mentally ill.

insatiable *adj* rapacious; greedy.

inscribe *vt* to mark or engrave on a surface; to add (a person's name) to a list; to dedicate (a book) to someone.

inscrutable *adj* hard to understand; incomprehensible; enigmatic.

insect *n* any arthropod of the class *Insecta* with three pairs of legs, a head, thorax, and abdomen and two or four wings.

insecticide *n* a poison designed or used against insects.

insecure *adj* unsafe; risky; feeling anxiety; not dependable.

insensible *adj* unconscious; unaware; indifferent; unperceptible.

insensitive *adj* callous.

inseparable *adj* never apart; closely attached, *esp* romantically.

insert *vt* to put, fit, or set in.

inset *vt* to set in; to implant.

inshore *adj*, *adv* near or towards the shore.

inside *n* the inner side, surface, or part; internal; known only to insiders; secret; * *adj* on or in the inside; within; indoors; (*prep*) in or within.

insider *n* a person within a place or group; a person with access to confidential information.

insidious *adj* treacherous; stealthy.

insight *n* discernment; penetration.

insignia *npl* badges of office or honour.

insignificant *adj* without significance; unimportant.

insincere *adj* faithless; deceitful.

insinuate *vt* to introduce slowly, by degrees, etc; to hint.

insipid *adj* tasteless; flat; uninteresting.

insist *vi* to urge or press strongly.

insobriety *n* intemperance.

insolent *adj* overbearing; insulting.

insoluble *adj* incapable of being dissolved; impossible to explain.

insolvent *adj* not able to pay debts; * **insolvency** *n* bankruptcy.

insomnia *n* abnormal sleeplessness.

insouciant *n* carefree

inspect *vt* to examine; to scan carefully.

inspection *n* careful survey; examination.

inspector *n* an official who inspects in order to ensure compliance with regulations, etc.

inspiration *n* an inspiring; any stimulus to creative thought.

inspire *vt* to stimulate to creativity; to arouse (a thought or feeling) in.

instability *n* the state of being unstable; inconstancy; fickleness.

install *vt* to invest with office; to settle in a position or state.

installation *n* machinery, equipment, etc that has been installed.

instalment *n* a sum of money to be paid at regular specified times.

instance *n* an example; a step in proceeding; * *vt* to give as an example

instant *adj* immediate; (food) concentrated or precooked for quick preparation; * *n* a moment.

instead *adv* in place of.

instep *n* the upper part or arch of the foot.

instigate *vt* to; to urge; to initiate.

instil *vt* to put (an idea etc) in or into (the mind) gradually.

instinct *n* a natural impulse; a knack; * **instinctive** *adj*.

institute *vt* to set up; to found; to begin; to originate; * *n* an organisation for the promotion of scienc, art etc.

institution *n* an established law, custom etc; an organisation having a social, educational, or religious purpose; (*fam*) a long-established person or thing.

instruct *vt* to teach; to advise; to give instruction.

instrument *n* a thing by means of which something is done; any of various devices for indicating, controlling, measuring etc; any of various devices producing musical sound; a formal document.

instrumental *adj* serving as a means of doing something; helpful; of, performed on, or written for a musical instrument or instruments.

instrumentalist *n* a person who plays a musical instrument.

insubordinate *adj* disobedient.

insubordination *n* revolt.

insufferable *adj* intolerable.

insufficient *adj* not enough.

insular *adj* pertaining to an island; narrow-minded.

insulate *vt* to set apart; to isolate; to cover with a non-conducting material in order to prevent the escape of, heat, sound, etc.

insulin *n* a hormone that controls absorption of sugar by the body.

insult *n* a gross affront; indignity; * *vt, vi* to offend.

insuperable *adj* insurmountable.

insupportable *adj* intolerable.

insurance *n* a contract purchased to guarantee compensation for a specified loss by fire, death, etc.

insure *vt* to contract against loss, damage, etc.

insurgent *adj* rebellious; * *n* a rebel.

insurmountable *adj* insuperable.

insurrection *n* a revolt; a rebellion.

intact *adj* untouched; unimpaired; whole.

intangible *adj* that cannot be touched, incorporeal; indefinable.

integer *n* a whole; a whole number.

integral *adj* necessary for complete-ness; whole or complete; made up of parts forming a whole.

integrate *vt* to make up a whole; to bring parts together into a whole; (maths) to calculate the area under a curve between two limits; anti-differentiation.

integrity *n* uprightness; honesty.

intellect *n* the ability to reason or understand; high intelligence; a very intelligent person.

intelligence *n* the ability to learn, understand or to cope with information; those involved with gathering secret, *esp* military, information.

intelligent *adj* quick of mind; acute; well informed.

intelligible *adj* comprehensible.

intemperate *adj* unrestrained.

intend *vt* to design; to have in mind as an aim or purpose.

intense *adj* strained; extreme; severe; passionate; emotional.

intensify *vt* to deepen; to augment.

intensity *n* vehemence; strength; the force or energy of any physical agent.

intensive *adj* concentrated; describing the special and extensive care given to patients after serious surgery.

intent *adj* set; bent; * *n* purpose.

intention *n* purpose; design.

inter *vt* to bury.

interact *vi* to act reciprocally.

intercede *vi* to mediate; to plead for.

intercept *vt* to take or stop in its course; to obstruct; to cut off.

intercession *n* mediation.

interchange *vt* to give and receive one thing for another.

intercom *n* (*fam*) a system of intercommunication, as in an aircraft.

intercommunication *n* interchange of ideas and means for securing it.

intercostal *adj* between the ribs; * *adv* intercostally.

intercourse *n* communication or dealings between individuals, nations etc.; sexual intercourse.

interdict *vt* to forbid; to veto.

interest *n* a feeling of concern about something; anything in which one has a share; benefit; money paid for the use of money; * *vt* to excite the attention of; to cause to have a share in; to concern oneself with.

interested *adj* concerned; biased.

interesting *adj* engaging; intriguing; attractive.

interfere *vi* to meddle; to obstruct.

interference *n* intermeddling; clashing; (radio, TV) the

interruption of reception by atmospherics or by unwanted signals.

interim *n* the meantime; an intervening period of time.

interior *adj* internal; inland.

interject *vt* to throw in between; to insert; to interrupt

interjection *n* a word thrown in abruptly.

interlace *vti* to weave together.

interlock *vi, vt* to clasp together.

interloper *n* an intruder; a meddler.

interlude *n* an interval.

intermediary *n* a go-between.

intermediate *adj* intervening.

interment *n* burial.

interminable *adj* endless; boundless.

intermingle *vt* to mingle together.

intermission *n* a pause between parts of a performance; a rest.

intermittent *adj* coming and going; ebbing and flowing; periodic.

intern *vt* to confine prisoners, etc, in a prescribed area.

internal *adj* of or on the inside; inward.

international *adj* between or among nations; concerned with the relationship between nations; for the use of all nations.

internecine *adj* deadly; bloody; mutually destructive.

interpose *vt* to place between.

interpret *vt* to explain; to translate; to construe; to give one's own conception of; * *vi* to translate between speakers of different languages.

interpretation *n* an explanation.

interrogate *vt* to question.

interrupt *vi* to break in upon.

intersect *vt* to divide; to cross mutually; * intersection *n*.

intersperse to scatter; to mingle.

interstellar *adj* ocurring or situated between the stars.

intertwine *vt* to weave or twist together.

interval *n* time or distance between; the difference of pitch between two sounds; a break between parts of a theatrical or musical performance.

intervene *vi* to interpose or

interfere; to settle or hinder a matter etc.

intervention *n* a coming between; interference; mediation.

interview *n* a meeting in which a person is asked about his or her views, etc; a meeting at which a candidate for a job is questioned and assessed for a job.

intestate *adj* dying without having made a will.

intestine *n* the part of the alimentary canal between the stomach and the anus.

intimacy *n* close friendship; familiarity; close friendship.

intimate *adj* most private or personal; very close or familiar, *esp* sexually; * *n* a close friend.

intimation *n* a hint.

intimidate *vt* to overawe; to cow.

into *prep* expressing motion towards the inside; to a particular condition.

intolerable *adj* insufferable; unbearable.

intolerant *adj* illiberal; bigoted.

intonation *n* a modulation of the voice.

intone *vi* to chant in a slow monotone.

intoxicant *n* a substance used to alter mood, perception etc (*eg* alcohol).

intoxicate *vt* to make drunk; to stir up.

intracellular *adj* inside or occurring inside a cell (of an organism).

intractable *adj* ungovernable; headstrong; difficult to solve (of a problem).

intransigent *adj* irreconcilable; unwilling to compromise.

intransitive *adj* of a verb which does not take or does not require an object.

intrepid *adj* undaunted; fearless.

intricate *adj* involved; detailed.

intrigue *n* an underhand plot; * *vi* to plot secretly; to rouse curiosity.

intrinsic *adj* inherent; belonging naturally to.

introduce *vt* present; to insert; to make known; to bring into use.

introduction *n* an introducing; the presentation of one person to another; preliminary statement; preface; presentation.

introspection *n* self-examination.

introvert *n* a person who is more interested in his or her own thoughts, feelings, etc than in external objects or events.

intrude *vi* to trespass; meddle; * *vt* to force oneself on others.

intrusion *n* encroachment; trespass.

intuition *n* insight; instinctive perception; * intuitive *adj*.

inundate *vt* to flow over; to flood.

inure *vt* to harden by use.

invade *vt* to enter as an enemy; to attack; to encroach upon.

invalid *adj* void; illegal; * *n* a person who is ill or disabled; * *vt* to disable.

invaluable *adj* priceless.

invariable *adj* constant; unchangeable.

invasion *n* hostile entrance; encroachment; intrusion.

invective *n* a tirade; vituperation; * *adj* abusive.

inveigle *vt* to beguile; to decoy.

invent *vt* to originate; to devise; to concoct; to fabricate (a lie etc).

invention *n* a new contrivance.

inventory *n* an itemized list of goods, property etc as of a business; * *vt* to make an inventory of; to enter in an inventory.

inverse *adj* opposite; contrary.

invert *vt* to turn upside down; to reverse in order, position or relationship.

invertebrate *adj* without a backbone; * *n* an animal without a backbone.

invest *vt* to buy property, stocks, shares, etc, for profit; to install in office; to furnish with power, authority, etc; * *vi* to invest money.

investigate *vt* to search into; to examine; to inquire into.

investiture *n* the act or right of giving legal possession; the ceremony of investing a person with an office, robes, title, etc.

investment *n* the act of investing money productively; the amount invested; an activity in which time, effort or money has been invested.

inveterate *adj* deep-rooted.

invidious *adj* envious; causing ill-will.

invigilate *vi* to supervise an examination.

invigorate *vt* to strengthen; to enliven; to refresh.

invincible *adj* unconquerable.

inviolable *adj* sacred; not to be broken.

inviolate *adj* virgin; stainless; intact.

invisible *adj* unseen; imperceptible; hidden.

invite *vt* to ask to come somewhere or do something; to entice.

inviting *adj* attractive; enticing.

invocation *n* a prayer to God for help; an appeal to muse for aid.

invoice *n* a list of goods supplied, with prices; a bill; * *vt* to make out a bill (for goods).

invoke *vt* to call upon (God etc); to resort to (law etc) as pertinent.

involuntary *adj* done without power to choose; instinctive.

involve *vt* to roll up; include; to implicate; to complicate.

invulnerable *adj* not able to be hurt; secure.

inward *adj* situated within or directed to the inside; relating to or in the mind or spirit.

iodine *n* a nonmetallic element from the halogen group; this dissolved in alchol used as an antiseptic.

ion *n* an atom with one or more missing or extra electrons.

iota *n* the ninth letter of the Greek alphabet; a jot; a very small quantity.

irascible *adj* easily angered; irritable; * irascibility *n*.

ire *n* anger; wrath; rage.

iridescence *n* display of colours like the rainbow.

iris *n* (*pl* irises, irides) the round pigmented membrane surrounding the pupil of the eye; any herbaceous plant of the genus *Iris*

irk *vt* to weary; to vex; to annoy.

irksome *adj* wearisome; tedious.

iron n a metallic element, occurring naturally as magnetite, haematite, etc; a tool, etc of this metal; a heavy implement with a heated flat undersurface for pressing cloth; (pl) shackles of iron; firm strength; power; any of certain golf clubs with angled metal heads; * adj of iron; strong and firm; * vt, vi to press with a hot iron.

ironmonger n a dealer in hardware; metal goods, tools etc.

irony n an expression, usu sarcastic, in which the sense is conveyed by words of opposite meaning; the ill-timing of a fortuitous event; * ironic adj.

irradiate vt to subject to any form of radiation; to illuminate.

irrational adj void of reason; (maths) not expressible as a fraction.

irreconcilable adj inconsistent; implacable; incompatible.

irredeemable adj hopelessly lost; inconvertible.

irreducible adj that which cannot be reduced or simplified.

irrefutable adj unanswerable; unable to deny or disprove.

irregular adj not regular; crooked; not conforming to the rules; imperfect; not belonging to the regular armed forces.

irrelevant adj not to the point.

irreparable adj irremediable; not able to be repaired, rectified or made good.

irrepressible adj uncontrollable.

irreproachable adj faultless.

irresistible adj overwhelming.

irresolute adj undecided; wavering.

irrespective adj making no exceptions; regardless of.

irresponsible adj lacking a sense of responsibility; flighty.

irretrievable adj irreparable; hopeless.

irreverent adj not paying due respect; * irreverence n.

irreversible adj irrevocable.

irrevocable adj unalterable.

irrigate vt to supply water to land; (medicine) to wash out a wound.

irritable adj short-tempered; touchy; * irritability n.

irritate vt to provoke; to inflame.

is 3rd per. sing. pres. indic. verb to be.

Islam n the religion of Mohammed; the Moslem world.

island n land totally surrounded by water.

isle n an island.

islet n a little island.

isobar n a line on a map joining places with equal atmospheric pressure.

isolate vt to cut off; to set apart from others; to quarantine; to seperate a constituent subject from a compound.

isolation n detachment; loneliness.

isosceles adj (of a triangle) having two sides equal.

isotherm n a line on a map joining laces with equal temperature.

isotope n any of two or more forms of an element having the same atomic number but different atomic mass.

issue n offspring; a point under dispute; that which is put forth at one time (an issue of bonds, a periodical etc); * vi to go or flow out; to result (from) or end (in); to be published; * vt to let out; to discharge; to give or deal out, as supplies; to publish.

isthmus n a narrow neck of land; connecting two larger bodies of land.

it pron 3rd. per. neuter.

italic adj the name of a printing type in which the letters slant upwards to the right pl; italic type (italic); * italicize vt.

itch n an irritating sensation on the surface of the skin causing a need to scratch; an insistent desire; * vt to have or feel an irritating sensation in the skin; to feel a restless desire.

item n an article; a unit; a seperate thing; a bit of news; (fam) a couple.

itemise vt to specify the terms of; to set down by items.

iterate vt to repeat.

itinerant adj travelling from place to place; * n a traveller.

itinerary *n* a travel route; a record or detailed plan of a journey.

its *pron* 3rd per. possessive of it.

itself *n* the neuter reflexive pronoun.

ivory *n* a hard bony substance forming tusks of elephants, etc; a creamy white colour; * *adj* of or like ivory; creamy white.

ivy *n* a climbing evergreen shrub, *Hedera Helix*.

J

jab *vt, vi (pt)* to poke or thrust roughly; to punch with short blows.

jabber *vi* to gabble.

jack *n* any of various mechanical or hydraulic devices used to lift something heavy; * *vt* to raise by means of a jack.

jacket *n* a short outer garment; an outer covering.

jackknife *n* a pocket-knife; * *vi* (of an articulated lorry) to lose control so that the cab and trailer swing against one another.

jackpot *n* a large prize accumulated in *eg* a lottery.

jade *n* a hard, semiprecious stone; it's light green colour.

jaded *adj* tired, exhausted; satiated.

jag *vt* to notch; to prick; * *n* a point.

jagged *adj* ragged; notched.

jaguar *n* a big cat, *Panthera onca*.

jail *see* gaol.

jam *n* a preserve made of boiled fruit and sugar; * *vt* to press into a confmed space; to cause interference to a radio signal rendering it unintelligible.

jangle *vi* to make a discordant sound, as bells; * *vt* to cause to jangle.

janitor *n* a caretaker.

January *n* the first month of the year.

jar *vi* to clash; to grate; * *n* a harsh sound; a vase or jug; a jolt.

jargon *n* the specialised or technical vocabulary of a science, profession, etc; obscure and *usu* pretentious language.

jaundice *n* a liver disease marked by yellowness of the eyes and skin.

jaundiced *adj* disillusioned; suffering from jaundice.

jaunt *vi* to go from place to place.

jaunty *adj* sprightly.

javelin *n* a light spear for throwing.

jaw *n* one of the bones which hold the teeth.

jazz *n* a type of popular music, characterized by syncopated rhythms.

jealous *adj* suspicious of a rival; envious.

jeans *npl* trousers made from denim.

jeep *n* a small robust vehicle with heavy duty tyres and four-wheel drive.

jeer *vi* to laugh derisively; to mock.

jelly *n* the juice of fruit boiled with sugar to a glutinous state.

jeopardy *n* hazard; risk.

jeroboam *n* a wine bottle of four times the normal size.

jerk *vt, vi* to give a sudden pull, thrust, or push to; * *n* a sudden thrust; a quick pull; * jerky *adj*.

jersey *n* a knitted woollen garment.

jest *n* a joke; pleasantry; * *vi* to joke.

jet *n* a spouting forth; a nozzle for emission of fluid or gas; a hard black mineral that when polished is used for jewellery.

jet-black *adj* of the deepest black.

jetsam *n* cargo thrown overboard to lighten a ship; this when washed ashore.

jettison *vt* to throw goods overboard.

jetty *n* a small pier.

jewel *n* a precious stone.

jewellery *n* jewels in general, *eg* rings, necklaces, brooches etc.

jib *n* the triangular foremost sail of a ship; the arm of a crane.

jib *vt, vi* to shift a sail; to turn aside.

jibe *vt* to taunt; gibe; * *n* a sneer.

jig *n* a lively dance or tune; * *vi* to dance.

jigsaw *n* a picture on wood or board cut into irregular shapes for re-assembling or for amusement.

jilt *vt* to discard a lover.

jingle vi, *vt* to clink, or tinkle; * *n* a tinkling sound; a tune.

jingoism *n* belligerent patriotism.

jinx *n* someone or something thought to bring bad luck.

jitter *vi* to feel nervous; * *npl* a nervous feeling of panic.

job *n* a piece of work done for pay; a task; a duty; the thing or material being worked on; work; employment.

jockey *n* a professional racehorse rider; * *vt* to manoeuvre for position.

jocular *adj* joking; full of jokes.

jog *vt* to give a slight shake or nudge to; to rouse, as the memory; * *vi* to run at a slow pace for exercise; * *n* a slight push or nudge; a slow run.

join *vt, vi* to bring and come together (with); to connect; to unite; to unite; to become a member of (a club, etc); to participate in; * *n* a joining.

joiner *n* a worker in wood.

joint *n* a place where, or way in which, two things are joined; the part where two bones move on one another in an animal; * *adj* common to two or more; sharing with another; * *vt* to connect by a joint or joints; to divide (meat) into parts for cooking.

jointly *adv* together; in common.

joist *n* a beam supporting floorboards.

joke *n* something said or done to cause laughter; a thing said or done for fun.

jolly *adj* merry; jovial; full of fun.

jolt *vi, vt* to shake with sudden jerks; to surprise or shock suddenly.

jostle *vt, vi* to knock against; to hustle; to elbow for position.

jot *n* an iota; * *vt* to note down briefly.

jotter *n* a notebook.

journal *n* a daily record of events, as a diary; a newspaper or periodical.

journalism *n* reporting news for, a newspaper, magazine or TV programme.

journey *n* a travelling; the distance travelled; a tour; * *vi* to travel.

jovial *adj* gay; merry; jolly.

jowl *n* the jaw. cheek by jowl, side by side.

joy *n* delight; gladness.

joyful *adj* filled with, expressing, or causing joy.

joyous *adj* full of joy.

jubilant *adj* rejoicing greatly; triumphant.

Judaism *n* the religion of the Jews.

Judas *n* one who betrays, *esp* a friend; (*uncap*) a peephole.

judge *n* a public official with authority to hear and decide cases in a court of law; * *vt, vi* to hear and pass judgement on the relative worth of anything.

judiciary *adj* relating to courts of justice; * *n* judges collectively.

judicious *adj* possessing prudence; characterized by sound judgement.

jug *n* a vessel for holding and pouring liquids; a pitcher.

juggernaut *n* a terrible, irresistable force; a large heavy truck.

juggle *vi* to conjure; to manipulate.

juggler *n* a conjuror.

jugular *adj* pertaining to the throat.

juice *n* fluid of fruits, vegetables and meat.

July *n* the seventh month of the year.

jumble *vt, vi* to mix in a confused mass; * *n* a muddle; articles for a jumble sale.

jumbo *n* something very large of its kind.

jump *vi* to spring or leap from the ground, a height, etc; to jerk; a sudden transition; an obstacle; a nervous start.

jumper *n* a knitted pullover.

junction *n* a point of union; a railway centre.

juncture *n* where lines meet; link or cross each other.

June *n* the sixth month of the year.

jungle *n* a tropical rainforest.

junior *adj* younger in age; of more recent or lower status; of juniors.

junk *n* discarded rubbish or useless articles; heroin; Chinese floating vessel.

jurisdiction *n* judicial authority, its range or extent.

jurisprudence *n* the philosophy of law.

jurist *n* one versed in law.

jury *n* a number of men and women sworn to hear evidence and deliver a verdict on a case; a panel.

just *adj* fair, impartial; deserved, merited; proper, exact; conforming strictly with the facts; * *adv* exactly; nearly; only.

justice *n* justness, fairness; the use of authority to maintain what is just; the administration of law.

justification *n* a defence; vindication.

justify *vt* to prove right.

justly *adv* rightly; properly.

jut *vi* to project.

juvenile *adj* young; immature.

juxtaposition *n* a placing near or side by side.

K

kail, kale *n* a kind of cabbage which forms no compact head.

kaleidoscope *n* a small tube containing bits of coloured glass reflected by mirrors to form symmetrical patterns as the tube is rotated.

kangaroo *n* a large marsupial of the genus *Macropus*.

keel *n* the backbone of a ship.

keen *adj* shrewd; sharp; eager; low (of prices) as to be competative.

keep *vt* to hold; to preserve; to guard; to detain; to continue any state, course, or action; * *vi* not to perish; * *n* a strong tower.

keeper *n* one who guards.

keeping *n* care, charge; observance.

keepsake *n* a gift treasured because of the giver.

keg *n* a small cask or barrel.

kennel *n* a small shelter for dogs; (*pl*) where dogs are bred or kept.

kerb *n* stone edging to pavement.

kernel *n* the core (*esp* of nut).

kettle *n* a metal vessel with spout for boiling water.

kettledrum *n* a drum made of a hollow metal body with a parchment head.

key *n* a device for locking and unlocking something; a code etc.

keyboard *n* a set of levers or keys used to operate a piano, computer, etc.

keynote *n* the basic note of a musical scale; the basic idea or ruling principle.

keystone *n* the top stone of an arch, keeping it up.

khaki *adj* dull yellowish-brown; uniforms of this colour.

kick *vt, vi* to strike with the foot; to recoile; * *n* a blow with the foot or feet; recoil; a thrill; an intoxicating effect.

kidnap *vt* to carry off a person by force and hold to ransom.

kidney *n* one of two glands that secrete urine.

kill *vt* to cause the death of; to destroy; * *n* the act of killing; an animal or animals killed.

kiln *n* a stone furnace for baking or hardening lime, bricks etc.

kilogram, kilogramme *n* a measure of weight (2.204 lbs).

kilometre *n* a measure of length, 1000 metres or 0.62 mile.

kin *n* family; kindred; relatives.

kind *n* race; genus; variety; nature; * *adj* humane; friendly; sympathetic.

kindle *vt, vi* to set on fire; to arouse.

kindly *adj* friendly; genial; kind; gracious.

kindness *n* goodness; helpfulness; benevolence.

kinetic *adj* causing motion; of motion.

king *n* the male, heriditary, ruler of a state; the piece that ones opponent seeks to checkmate in chess.

kingdom *n* a state headed by a king; the highest taxinomic classification.

kink *n* a tight twist or curl in a piece of string, rope, hair etc; a painful cramp in the neck, back, etc.

kiosk *n* a light open structure for sale of papers, sweets, etc.

kipper *n* a herring split open, salted, and dried.

kirk n a church.

kiss vt, vi to touch with the lips as an expression of love, affection or in greeting; * n an act of kissing; a light, gentle touch.

kit n an outfit; equipment eg tools etc; a set of parts for assembly.

kitchen n a place where food is prepared.

kite n a light paper-covered frame for flying in air.

kith n relatives and friends.

kiwi n (pl **kiwis**) a flightless bird of the genus Apterix native to New Zealand; (colloq.) a New Zealander.

kiwi fruit n the fruit of Actinidia chinensis.

kleptomania n an irresistible impulse to steal.

knack n dexterity; a trick; a habit.

knapsack n a backpack.

knead vt to work dough; to squeeze and press with the hands.

knee n the joint between the thigh and the lower part of the human leg; anything shaped like a bent knee; * vt (pt **kneed**) to hit with the knee.

kneel vi to go down and remain on the knees.

knell n the sound of a bell (esp funeral bell); * vi to toll.

knickers npl a female undergarment covering the lower body and having separate leg holes.

knife n a cutting instrument.

knight n a rank conferring title Sir; a chessman shaped like a horse's head.

knighthood n the rank or dignity of a knight.

knit vt, vi (pt **knitted** or **knit**) to form (fabric or a garment) by interlooping yarn using knitting needles or a machine.

knob n a rounded lump or protuberance; a boss or stud or handle (of a door).

knock vt, vi to strike; to rap on a door; to criticize; * n a blow; a rap.

knocker n the device hinged against a door for knocking.

knoll n a little round hill.

knot n a lump in a thread, etc formed by a tightened loop or tangling; a fastening made by tying lengths of rope, etc.

know vt to be aware that; to be sure that; to understand; to be acquainted with; * vi to have knowledge.

knowing adj well informed; shrewd; implying a secret understanding.

knowledge n acquaintance with; learning; information.

knuckle n the joint of a finger.

Koran n the sacred book of Islam.

kudos n glory; fame; renown.

L

label n a slip of paper, cloth, metal etc attached to anything to provide information about its nature, contents.

laboratory n a building where scientific work and research is carried out.

laborious adj arduous; laboured; hardworking.

labour n exertion; toil; workers collectively; the process of childbirth; * vi to work.

labourer n a worker; esp doing heavy or manual work.

labyrinth n a place full of winding paths; a maze.

lace n a fine fabric of cotton or silk; a cord, etc used to draw together and fasten parts of a shoe, a corset etc.

lacerate vt to tear; to cut.

lack vt to want; to need; * vi to be in want; * n want; failure deficiency.

lackadaisical adj languid; showing lack of energy or interest.

lackey n footman; flunkey.

laconic adj concise; brief.

lacquer n varnish; lacquered ware.

lactic adj related to or procured from milk.

lad n a boy; a young man.

ladder n a portable metal or wooden framework for climbing up and down.

laden adj loaded; burdened.

ladle n a large long-handled spoon.

lady n a woman of rank; a title.

ladybird *n* an insect of the family *Coccinellidae*.

lag *vi* to loiter; to fall behind; to insulate pipes with insulating material.

lager *n* a light beer.

lagging *n* insulating material.

lagoon *n* a shallow saltwater lake cut off from the sea by a coral reef.

laity *n* lay people, as distinguished from the clergy.

lake *n* water wholly surrounded by land.

lame *adj* crippled; limping.

lament *vi* to weep; to grieve; * *vt* to bewail; * *n* a mournful song or tune.

lamentable *adj* distressing; deplorable.

lamentation *n* mourning; sorrow.

lamp *n* any device producing light.

lance *n* a long spear; * *vt* to cut or pierce with a lancet.

land *n* the solid part of the earth's surface; ground, soil; a country and its people; property in land; * *vt*, *vi* to go ashore from a ship; to come to port; to arrive at a specified place; to come to rest.

landing *n* act or place of disembarking; a platform or flat area at the top of a flight of stairs or between flights of stairs.

landlady *n* a female landlord.

landlocked *adj* enclosed by land.

landlord *n* owner of land or houses; owner or host of an inn, etc.

landmark *n* a prominent feature that serves as a guide or distinguishes a locality; an important event or turning point.

landscape *n* an expanse of natural scenery seen in one view; a picture of natural, inland scenery; * *vt* to make (a plot of ground) more attractive.

landslide *n* the sliding of a mass of soil or rocks down a slope; an overwhelming victory *esp* in an election.

lane *n* a narrow road, path etc.

language *n* human speech; speech peculiar to a nation.

languid *adj* faint; listless; weak.

languish *vi* to be or become faint; to droop; to pine.

languor *n* faintness; listlessness.

lank *adj* tall and thin; long and limp.

lantern *n* a portable transparent case for holding a light.

lap *n* the seat formed by knees and thighs in sitting posture; one round of a course in a race.

lapel *n* the folded back part of coat continuous with the collar.

lapse *n* a small error; a decline or drop to a lower condition, degree, or state; a moral decline.

larceny *n* the theft of personal property (replaced by statute with theft in 1968).

lard *n* melted and clarified pig fat; * *vt* to embellish.

larder *n* a store cupboard for provisions.

large *adj* great in size, number; big.

largely *adv* widely; copiously; mainly.

largess *n* a present; bounty.

lark *n* a frolic; a prank.

larva *n* (*pl* larvae) an insect in grub state.

larynx *n* the upper part of the windpipe containing the vocal cords.

lasagne *n* pasta in thin sheets, *esp* when served with mice and cheese sauce.

lascivious *adj* lewd; lecherous.

lash *n* the thong of a whip; a stroke with a whip; * *vt* to whip; to bind.

lassitude *n* faintness; weariness.

last *adj* coming after all the others; latest; final.

lasting *adj* durable; permanent.

latch *n* the catch of a door, gate etc; * *vt*, *vi* to fasten with a latch.

late *adj* behind time; long delayed; deceased; * *adv* at a late time.

latent *adj* not yet apparent.

lateral *adj* of, at, from, towards; on the side.

lathe *n* a machine for shaping wood or iron.

lather *n* froth of soap and water.

latitude *n* breadth; width; scope; freedom from restriction on action or opinions; distance north or south of the equator.

latter *adj* later; coming after; being the last mentioned of two.

lattice *n* a network of crossed laths; a trellis; a window so formed.

laudable *adj* praiseworthy.

laugh *vi* to make the sound expressive of mirth; to be gay, mirthful.

launch *vt* to throw; to propel and slide (into water); * *vi* to initiate; to put into action.

launder *vt, vi* to wash clothes; transfer funds to conceal their illegal origin.

launderette *n* an establishment equipped with coin-operated washing machines.

laundry *n* place where clothes are washed and ironed.

laureate *n* a poet laureate, the official court poet.

lava *n* molten volcanic rocks.

lavatory *n* a place for washing hands, urinating etc.

lavish *adj* profuse; generous; abundant; extravagant.

law *n* all the rules of conduct as upheld by the state.

law-abiding *adj* obeying the law.

lawbreaker *n* a person who violates the law.

lawn *n* a smooth level grass plot.

lawyer *n* a person whose profession is advising others in matters of law or representing them in a court of law.

lax *adj* loose; slack; vague.

laxative *adj* purging; * *n* a gentle purgative.

laxity *n* slackness; carelessness.

lay *vt* to cause to lie; to place; to impose; to allay, to bring forth eggs; to wager; * *n* a song; a poem.

layer *n* a stratum; a single thickness; a coat, as of paint.

layman *n* one not a clergyman; a non-specialist or professional.

layout *n* the manner in which anything is laid out.

lazy *adj* slothful; indolent.

lead *n* a soft and heavy metal; a stick of graphite.

lead *vt, vi* to guide or conduct; to direct; to precede; to entice; to influence; to be first.

leaden *adj* heavy; dull; like lead; gloomy.

leader *n* one who leads; an editorial article; the first violin.

leaf *n* one of the thin parts of a plant, *usu* green, the main organ of photosynthesis; a sheet of paper or metal; two pages of a book.

leaflet *n* a little leaf; a sheet of printed information or advertising matter.

league *n* a union for mutual help; an alliance; a treaty; an association of sports club that organizes matches between members.

leak *n* a hole which admits water or gas; confidential information made public deliberately or accidentally; * *vi* to let water in or out; to disclose.

lean *vi* to slope; to incline; to rest against; to rely on.

lean *adj* thin; barren; meagre.

leaning *n* inclination, tendency.

leap *vi, vt* to jump; to bound.

learn *vt, vi* to gain knowledge or skill; to find out; to realize.

learning *n* knowledge; scholarship.

lease *n* a letting for a term of years; * *vt* to let or lease.

lessehold *adj* held by lease; * *n* tenure by lease.

leash *n* a thong or strap for leading animals; * *vt* to hold on a leash.

least *adj* smallest; * *adv* in the smallest degree.

leather *n* tanned and dressed animal hide.

leave *n* permission; farewell; the period allowed for absence; * *vt* to let remain; to bequeath; to quit.

leaven *n* a substance, *esp* yeast, added to dough to make it ferment and rise.

lecherous *adj* lustful; lewd.

lecture *n* a discourse; a reprimand; * *vi* to deliver a lecture; * *vt* to reprove.

ledge *n* a narrow shelf; a ridge; a layer.

ledger *n* an account book.

leech *n* any worm of the class *Hirudinea*; a person who clings to or uses another.

leer *n* a sly or lewd glance.

left *adj* denoting opposite to the right; towards the west when facing north; * *n* the left side; the left hand.

left-wing *adj* of or relating to the liberal faction of a political party.

leg *n* one of the limbs on which humans and animals support themselves and walk; any of a series of games or matches in a competition.

legacy *n* money, property etc left to someone in a will.

legal *adj* of or based on law; permitted by law; of or for lawyers.

legality *n* conformity to law.

legalise *vt* to make lawful; to sanction.

legatee *n* one to whom a legacy is left.

legend *n* a *usu* mythical story handed down from the past; a notable person or the stories of his or her exploits.

leggings *npl* a leg-hugging garment for women.

legible *adj* able to be read.

legion *n* a great number.

legislate *vi* to make or pass laws.

legislator *n* one who makes laws.

legislature *n* the lawmaking body in a state.

legitimate *adj* legal; born in wedlock; genuine; valid.

leguminous *adj* pertaining to the family *Leguminosae* of plants, having seed pods, *eg* peas, pulse.

leisure *n* free time; relaxation; * ~ly *adj, adv* slowly.

lemur *n* any primate of the family *lemuridae*.

lend *vt* to grant use of a thing temporarily; to provide money at interest.

length *n* extent from end to end; duration; extension; a long expanse; a piece of specified length cut from a longer piece.

lenient *adj* merciful; forbearing.

lens *n* (*pl* lenses) a curved piece of transparent glass, plastic etc used in optical instruments to refract light rays; a similar transparent part of the eye that focuses light rays on the retina.

leopard *n* (also panther) a big cat, *Panthera pardus*.

leotard *n* a skintight one-piece garment worn by dancers and others engaged in strenuous exercise.

leper *n* one affected with leprosy.

leprosy *n* disease of the skin, mucous membranes and nerves causing disfigurement.

lesbian *n* a female homosexual.

lesion *n* an injury; a wound.

less *adj* smaller; * *adv* in a lower degree; to a smaller extent.

lessen *vt, vi* to make or become less.

lesson *n* something to be learned or studied; an example.

lest *conj* for fear that.

let *vt* to permit; to allow; to lease; to rent.

lethal *adj* deadly; fatal.

lethargy *n* a drowsy state.

letter *n* a symbol representing a phonetic value in a written language; a character of the alphabet; a written or printed message.

letter box slit in the doorway of a house or building through which letters are delivered; a postbox.

lettering *n* the act or process of inscribing with letters; letters collectively; a title; an inscription.

lettuce *n* a plant of the daisy family, *Lactuca Sativa*, used in salads.

leukaemia *n* a chronic disease characterized by an abnormal increase in the number of white blood cells.

level *n* an instrument for determining the horizontal; a horizontal line or surface; an even surface; * *adj* horizontal; even; flat; * *vt, vi* to flatten.

lever *n* a bar resting on a pivot, for raising weights; a device used to operate machinery.

leverage *n* power gained by use of a lever; power; influence.

levity *n* lightness; frivolity; lack of seriousness.

levy *vt* to collect (taxes) by the force or authority.

lewd *adj* lustful; sensual; obscene.

lexicographer *n* a dictionary compiler.

lexicon *n* a dictionary.

liability *n* an obligation; debt; a handicap; a disadvantage; *pl* debts; obligations.

liable *adj* responsible; subject to; likely to do.

liaison *n* communication, *esp* between military units; an illicit love affair.

liar *n* one who tells lies.

libel *n* a false damaging published or broadcast statement.

libellous *adj* slanderous; defamatory.

liberal *adj* generous; ample; profuse; not too strict; free.

liberality *n* generosity; breadth of view.

liberate *vt* to free; to deliver.

liberty *n* state of being free, *esp* from slavery; captivity etc.

libido *n* (*pl* **libidos**) *Psychol.* a psychic drive, *esp* sex drive.

libidinous *adj* lustful.

librarian *n* the keeper of a library.

library *n* a collection of books or the place in which they are kept.

lice *npl* of **louse**.

licence *n* authority given to do something specified; a certificate or document giving permission; excess of liberty

license *vt* to grant a licence to.

licensee *n* one to whom a licence is granted.

licentious *adj* profligate; morally unrestrained.

lichen *n* any plant organism of the group *Lichenes*.

lick *vt* to pass tongue over; to flicker, as of flames; to defeat.

lid *n* a removable cover of a box, vessel, etc; an eyelid.

lie *vi* to speak untruthfully; * *n* an untrue statement.

lie *vi* to stretch out or rest in a horizontal position; to be in a specified condition; to be situated; to exist; * *n* relative position of objects.

lieu *n* place; stead.

lieutenant *n* a deputy; an army officer ranking below a captain.

life *n* the state of living or being alive; existence; vigour; vivacity.

lifeboat *n* a small rescue boat carried by a ship.

life buoy *n* a buoyant object for keeping persons afloat.

lifeguard *n* an expert swimmer employed to prevent drownings.

lifeless *adj* dead; dull; heavy.

lifelike *adj* true to life in appearance.

lifespan *n* the duration of a life; the time for which a thing exists or works.

lift *vt, vi* to raise up; to hoist; to cheer; to steal; to disperse (of fog); to rise; * *n* a hoist; an elevation of mood; a ride in a vehicle.

liftoff *n* the point at which an aircraft, space ship etc. takes off.

ligament *n* band of tough tissue joining bones at joints.

ligature *n* a tie for blood vessels in operations.

light *n* the agent by which objects are made visible to the eye; day; that which gives or admits light; illumination of mind; * *adj* bright; clear; not heavy; active; slight; * *vt* to give light to; to enlighten; to ignite; * *vi* to brighten; to alight.

lighten *vi* to shine; to flash; * *vt* to illuminate; to make less heavy; to alleviate; to cheer.

lighter *n* a small device producing a flame to light cigarettes, etc.

lighthouse *n* a tower with a light to guide ships.

lightly *adv* easily; nimbly.

lightning *n* the vivid flash of electricity that precedes thunder.

lightweight *adj* of less than average weight; trivial, unimportant.

light year *n* the distance light travels in one year.

lignite *n* fossil wood.

like *adj* equal; similar; resembling; * *adv, prep* similarly; * *vt, vi* to be fond of; to be pleased; to approve.

likelihood *n* probability.

likely *adj* probable; suitable.

liken *vt* to compare.

likewise *adv* in like manner; also.

liking *n* inclination; fondness; affection.

limb *n* the arm or leg; a large branch of a tree.

limber *adj* flexible; * *n* the detachable front of a gun carriage.

limbo *n* a kind of purgatory; an intermediate stage between extremes.

lime *n* a substance obtained by heating limestone, and with sand and water forming cement.

limerick *n* a humorous doggerel verse of five lines.

limestone *n* a rock composed mainly of calcium carbonate of lime.

limit *n* boundary; utmost extent; restraint; * *vt* to restrict.

limited *adj* narrow; restricted; lacking imagination.

limp *vi* to walk lamely; * *n* a lameness in walking; * *adj* not firm; flabby.

limpid *adj* clear; crystal.

linchpin *n* a pin fastening a wheel to the axle; a person or thing vital to the success of an enterprise.

line *n* a length of cord, rope, or wire; a cord for measuring, making level; a system of conducting fluid, electricity etc; edge, boundary; border, outline, contour, a row of persons or things, as printed letters across a page.

lineage *n* race; descent.

linear *adj* of, made of, or using a line or lines; narrow and long.

linen *n* cloth made of flax; household articles made of linen, *eg* sheets.

liner *n* a large passenger ship or aircraft.

linesman *n* an assistant referee.

linger *vi* to delay; to loiter; to remainin the mind.

linguist *n* one skilled in languages.

lining *n* an inner covering of a garment etc.

link *n* a single loop or ring of a chain.

links *npl* flat sandy ground; a golf course, *esp* by the seaside.

linoleum *n* a floor covering of coarse fabric backing with a smooth, hard decorative coating.

linseed *n* flaxseed.

lint *n* linen specially prepared as a dressing for wounds; fluff.

lintel *n* the upper bar of a doorway or a window.

liny *adj* marked with lines

lion *n* a large carnivorous cat, *panthera leo.*

lion-hearted *adj* courageous and generous.

lip *n* either of the front edges of the mouth; the edge or rim of a jug etc.

lipstick *n* a small stick of cosmetic for colouring the lips

liquefy *vt* to melt; to dissolve.

liqueur *n* a sweet, many-flavoured alcoholic drink

liquid *adj* fluid; smooth; * *n* any fluid; * *adj* in liquid form; clear; limpid; readily convertible into cash (of assets).

liquidate *vt* to settle the accounts of; to wind up a bankrupt business; to convert into cash; to kill.

liquor *n* a drink (*esp* alcoholic).

liquorice *n* a black extract from the root of a plant, used in medicine and confectionery; a liquorice flavoured sweet.

lisp *vi* to pronounce imperfectly (*esp* 's'); * *n* lisping speech.

lissom, lissome *adj* supple.

list *n* a series of names, numbers written in order.

listen *vi* to try to hear; to give heed.

listless *adj* languid; weary; unenthusiastic.

litany *n* a series of petitions in a prayer book; any tedious recital.

literacy *n* the ability to read and write.

literal *adj* exact; word for word.

literary *adj* versed in letters and literature.

literate *adj* able to read and write; educated.

literature *n* the writings of a period or country.

lithe *adj* pliant; flexible.

lithesome *adj* supple; nimble.

lithograph *vt* to imprint on stone and transfer to paper.

litigate *vt, vi* to go to law; to contest points of law.

litigious *adj* given to litigation; unreasonably fond of suing.

litre n a unit of capacity in metric system, 1.76 pints.

litter n a portable bed; scattered rubbish; young produced at one birth; * vt, vi to strew carelessly; to make tidy.

little adj small; short; * adv in a small degree; less; slightly; not in the least; * n small in amount, degree etc.

live vi to exist; to dwell; to conduct one's self in life; to subsist; to gain a livelihood; * vt to lead; to spend; to pass; * adj alive; having life; not exploded; carrying electic current.

livelihood n means of living.

lively adj vivacious; spirited.

liver n a large lobed glandular organ in vertibrates responsible for many processes including bile secretion, regulation of toxic material etc; animal liver as food.

livestock n (farm) animals raised for use or sale.

livid adj very angry.

living n livelihood; benefice of a clergyman; a way of living.

lizard n any reptile of the suborder Lacertillia or Sauria.

load vt to charge with a load; to burden; to oppress; to put film in a camera; to install a program in a computer memory; to charge, as a gun; * n a burden.

loaf n a shaped mass of bread; * vi to idle about.

loam n a rich clayey soil.

loan n lending; something lent, esp money; * vt, vi to lend.

loath adj reluctant.

loathe vt, vi to hate; abhor.

loathsome adj disgusting.

lob n a slow, high-pitched ball (cricket, etc); * vt to bowl slowly.

lobby n an entrance hall; a person or group who try to influence (legislators) to support a cause etc.

lobe n the lower part of the car; a division of the brain, lungs, etc.

local adj pertaining to or of a particular place; of or for a particular part of the body; * n an inhabitant of a specific place; a local pub.

locale n a locality.

locality n a place; a neighbourhood.

locate vt to place the position of something.

loch n a Scottish lake.

lock n a fastening device operated by a key; the part of a canal dock in which the level of the water is regulated by the operation of gates.

locker n a small cupboard, chest etc.

locket n a small gold case worn round the neck.

locksmith n a maker of locks.

locomotive n a railway engine.

locum (tenens) n a temporary deputy.

locust n a type of grasshopper of the family Acridiae; a carob tree.

lodge n a small house at the entrance to a park or stately home; * vt, vi to live in a place for a time; to live as a paying guest.

loft n the space or room under the rafters; * vt to lift into the air.

lofty adj high; haughty; stately.

log n a section cut from a felled tree.

logarithms n maths the inverse function to exponentiation.

logbook n an official record of a ship's or aircraft's voyage or flight.

logic n the science of reasoning.

logistics n the planning and organisation of any complex activity.

loin n (in pl) the part of the body on either side of the spine, between the fase ribs and the hip bones; a joint of meat including the loin vertibrae.

loiter vi to hang about; to linger.

loll vi to lean idly; to hang out (tongue).

lone adj solitary; single; isolated.

lonesome adj solitary.

long adj not short; protracted; slow; * vt to desire earnestly; * adv for a long time; from start to finish.

longevity n great length of life.

longhand n ordinary handwriting, as opposed to shorthand.

longing n an intense desire.

longitude n length; distance east or west of fixed meridian.

longitudinal *adj* running length-wise.

look *vi* to direct the eye so as to see; to gaze; to consider; to expect; to heed; to appear; * *n* gaze; a glance; aspect; appearance.

lookout *n* a watching for; a watching post; a watcher.

loom *n* a weaving machine; * *vi* to come into view large or threateningly.

loop *n* a figure made by a curved line crossing itself; an intra-uterine contraceptive device.

loophole *n* a narrow slit for outlook, etc; a way of escape or evading obligation etc.

loose *adj* untied; free; vague; careless; not firm, tight or compact; * *vt* to untie; to set free; to discharge a bullet.

loosen *vt* to make loose.

loot *n* booty; plunder; money.

lop *vt* to cut off.

lopsided *adj* leaning to one side.

loquacious *adj* talkative.

lord *n* a master; a ruler; a nobleman.

lordly *adj* proud; haughty; of a lord.

lose *vt, vi* (*pt* lost) to have taken from one by death, accident, removal, etc; to be unable to find.

loss *n* a losing or being lost; the damage, trouble caused by losing; the person, thing, or amount lost.

lot *n* a part or share; fate which falls to one; a considerable quantity; the thing drawn at random to decide something.

lotion *n* a healing or cleansing or cosmetic liquid.

lottery *n* a system of raising money by selling numbered tickets that offer the chance of winning a prize.

lotus *n* (in Greek mythology) a plant inducing luxurious langour to the eater; any water lily of the genus *Nelumbo*.

loud *adj* easily audible; noisy; showy; obtrusive.

lounge *vi* to loiter; to loll; to spend time idly; * *n* a comfortable room.

louse *n* (*pl* lice) a parasitic insect, *Pediculus humanus*, infesting human hair and skin; any insect of the orders *Anopleura* or *Malophaga* which infest birds and mammals; a contemptible person; * **lousy** *adj* infested with lice; very bad.

lout *n* an awkward, rude fellow.

love *vt* to regard with affection; to delight in; * *vi* to be in love; * *n* warm affection; the passionate affection for another; a term of endearment.

lovely *adj* beautiful; charming.

lover *n* a person in love with another; a person having a sexual relationship.

loving *adj* fond; kind.

low *adj* situated below an given surface; not high; deep; mean.

lower *vt* to let down; to abase.

lowing *n* the bellowing of cattle.

lowland *n* comparatively low or level country.

lowly *adj* humble; meek.

loyal *adj* faithful; true.

loyalist *n* one who is true to his country.

loyalty *n* fidelity; constancy.

lubber *n* a clumsy fellow.

lubricant *n* a substance for oiling or greasing.

lubricate *vt* to smear with oil to lessen friction; to make smooth.

lucent *adj* shining; resplendent.

lucid *adj* easily understood; sane.

luck *n* chance; fortune; success.

lucky *adj* fortunate; auspicious.

lucrative *adj* paying; gainful.

ludicrous *adj* laughable; droll.

lug *vt* to haul; * *n* the ear.

luggage *n* a traveller's baggage.

lugubrious *adj* sad; doleful.

lukewarm *adj* moderately warm; indifferent.

lull *vt* to calm; to send to sleep; to allay (fears etc) *usu* by deception; * *n* a calm interval.

lullaby *n* a cradle song.

lumbago *n* rheumatism in the lower back.

lumbar *n* pertaining to the lower back.

lumber *n* rubbish; felled timber.

luminary *n* an enlightening, influential or famous person.

luminous *adj* shining; clear.

lump *n* a small shapeless mass; an abnormal swelling.

lunacy *n* mental derangement; utter folly.

lunar *adj* pertaining to the moon.

lunatic *adj* insane; * *n* a madman.

lunch, luncheon *n* a midday meal.

lung *n* either of the two organs of respiration.

lunge *n* a sword thrust; a plunge forward.

lurch *vi* to roll or sway to one side; * *n* a sudden roll.

lure *n* a bright fishing bait; something that tempts or entices.

lurid *adj* vivid; glaring; sensational; ghastly pale; wan.

lurk *vi* to lie hidden in wait; to loiter furtively.

luscious *adj* very sweet; delicious.

lush *adj* luxuriant; juicy.

lust *n* longing desire; sensual appetite; * *vi* to desire eagerly.

lustre *n* brightness; renown; a glossy surface.

lusty *adj* vigorous; robust.

luvvy *n coloq.* a familiar form of address; an actor or actress.

luxuriant *adj* profuse; abundant.

luxurious *adj* given to luxury.

luxury *n* indulgence and pleasure in sumptuous things; *pl* something cosy and enjoyable but not a necessity.

lymph *n* colourless fluid in the body contained in and collected from the tissues.

lynch *vt* to put to death by mob law.

lyre *n* an ancient stringed instument related to the harp.

lyric, lyrical *adj* of the nature of song.

M

macaroni *n* pasta rolled into tubes.

macaroon *n* a cake or biscuit of ground almonds.

mace *n* a spiked club; an ensign of office; an aromatic spice made from the outside covering of the nutmeg.

machine *n* a device using or applying mechanical power to do work; a coin operated dispenser; the controlling system in an organisation.

machine gun *n* an automatic gun which fires continuously.

machinist *n* one who works a machine.

machismo *n* excessive masculine pride.

mad *adj* insane; crazy; angry.

madam *n* a polite form of address a woman; a woman in charge of a brothel.

madcap *n, adj* reckless (person).

madden *vt* to make mad.

madman (madwoman) *n* an insane person.

madness *n* insanity; folly.

maelstrom *n* a whirlpool.

magazine *n* a storehouse; a munition depot; a periodical publication containing feature articles, fiction etc; a supply chamber as in a camera, a rifle etc.

magenta *n* a bright purplish-crimson dye or colour.

maggot *n* a soft bodied larva.

magic *n* the supposed influence of events by supernatural means; conjuring tricks.

magic mushroom *n* a mushroom producing psilocybin

magician *n* a conjurer.

magistrate *n* a public officer who administrates justice.

magnanimous *adj* noble and generous; unselfish.

magnate *n* a man of rank, wealth or influence.

magnesium *n* a white malleable metal.

magnet *n* a piece of iron or steel that has the property of attracting iron.

magnetism *n* magnetic phenomena and the laws of (electro-) magnetism; charisma.

magnificent *adj* imposing; superb.

magnify *vt* to enlarge; to extol; to glorify; to exaggerate.

magnitude *n* greatness; importance.

magnum *n* a wine bottle of twice the usual size.

mahogany *n* a hard reddish wood used for furniture.

maid *n* a young girl; a female servant.

maiden *n* a young unmarried woman; a runless over in cricket.

mail *n* letters etc conveyed and delivered by the post office; a postal system.

maim *vt* to mutilate; to disable.

main *adj* chief; leading; * *n* the greater part; the ocean.

mainland *n* the land, other than islands.

mainstay *n* the chief support.

maintain *vt, vi* to keep up; to sustain.

maintenance *n* upkeep; the provision or means to support life; alimony.

maize *n* a cereal lant, *Zea Mays*, yielding large grains on a cob.

majesty *n* grandeur; nobility; dignity.

major *adj* the greater in number, quantity, or extent; very serious; (music) higher than the corresponding minor by half a tone; * *n* an army officer one rank below a lieutenant colonel.

majority *n* the greater number.

make *vt, vi* to create; to construct; to produce; to cause to be; to perform; to force; to reach; * *n* style; brand or origin; manner of production.

makeshift *n* a temporary substitute.

maladjustment *n* poor adaptation, *esp* to social environment.

maladministration *n* bad management.

maladroit *adj* clumsy.

malady *n* illness; disease.

malaise *n* a feeling of discomfort.

malaria *n* an intermittent and remittent disease caused by a *protozoan* parasite of the genus *Plasmodium*, and transmitted by flea bites.

malcontent *n* a discontented person.

male *n* one of the individuals in a sexually reproducing species which produces the smaller gamete; a man or boy.

malefactor *n* a criminal; a felon.

malevolent *adj* spiteful; malicious.

malformation *n* deformity.

malfunction *n* faulty functioning.

malice *n* spite; ill will.

malign *adj* harmful; malignant.

malignant *adj* malevolent; (of a tumour) cancerous.

malinger *vi* to feign illness.

malleable *adj* capable of being beaten out by hammering; pliable.

mallet *n* a wooden hammer.

malnutrition *n* lack of nutrition.

malpractice *n* misconduct.

malt *n* barley which has been germinated and smoked *esp* for distilling, etc.

maltreat *vt* to abuse.

mammal *n* an animal of the class *Mammalia*; a warm-blooded vertebrate that suckle their young.

mammoth *n* an extinct species of elephant; * *adj* gigantic.

man *n* a male adult; mankind; a male servant; a husband; an ordinary soldier.

manacle *n* handcuffs; * *vi* to fettel

manage *vt* to wield; to direct.

manageable *adj* able to be managed; tractable.

management *n* direction; the directors of a business.

manager *n* a person who manages a company, organisation etc; an agent who looks after the business affairs of an actor, writer etc.

mandarin *n* any high-ranking official; (*with cap*) the Beijing dialect that is the official language of China.

mandate *n* a command; written authority to act for another.

mandatory *adj* compulsory.

mandible *n* an animal's jaw.

mane *n* the long hair on the neck of a horse, male lion etc.

manequin *n* a woman who models fashion clothes.

mangetout *n* a variety of pea eaten whole, with the pod.

mangle *vt* to mutilate; to press.

manhole *n* a hole giving entrance.

manhood *n* virility; manliness.

mania *n* grat enthusiasm; a craze.

maniac *n* a madman; an enthusiast.

manicure *n* the fingernails and care of the hands.

manifest *adj* clearly visible; evident; * *vt* to display; * *n* a list of a ship's or aircraft's cargo.

manifesto *n* a public declaration of policy issued by a goverment or a party.

manifold *adj* numerous and various.

manipulate *vt* to handle; to manage skilfully or craftily.

mankind *n* the human race.

manly *adj* brave; hardy.

man-made *adj* manufactured or created by man; synthetic.

manner *n* the mode in which anything is done; bearing or conduct; *pl* behaviour.

mannerism *n* a personal peculiarity.

manoeuvre *n* a tactical movement; a planned and controlled movement of troops, ships etc.

manor *n* the land or house belonging to a lord; a police district.

mansion *n* a large imposing house.

manslaughter *n* the killing of a person without malice.

mantelpiece *n* the ornamental work round a fireplace; the shelf above.

mantle *n* a loose sleeveless cloak.

manual *adj* done by the hand; * *n* a textbook; a book of instructions.

manufacture *n* the making of goods on large scale.

manure *n* animal dung for fertilizing soil; * *vt* to treat with manure.

manuscript *n* a paper written with the hand.

many *adj* numerous.

map *n* a plan of any part of the earth's surface.

mar *vt* to injure; impair; to spoil.

marble *n* a valuable building and monumental stone.

march *vi* to walk in step; * *vt* to cause to march; * *n* a military walk; a distance walked; a musical composition; (*cap*) the third month of a year.

marchioness *n* a noblewoman equal in rank to, or the wife of, a marquess.

mare *n* a female horse.

margarine *n* a butter substitute made from vegetable fat.

margin *n* an edge; the blank border of a printed page; surplus; the difference between the cost and the selling price.

marginal *adj* written in the margin; situated at the margin or border; close to the lower limit of acceptability; very slight, insignificant.

marina *n* a harbour for pleasure craft.

marine *adj* pertaining to the sea.

marionette *n* a puppet.

marital *adj* pertaining to marriage.

maritime *adj* relating to the sea or ships; bordering on or near the sea.

mark *n* a visible sign or stamp; eminence; aim; a cross made instead of a signature; a symbol, *eg* a punctuation mark; a grade for academic work; impression.

market *n* the arena in which trade takes place; a meeting of people for buying and selling merchandise; the place where a market is held; trade in general.

marketable *adj* fit for sale.

marketing *n* the work done to maximize sales of a commodity.

marmalade *n* a preserve made from oranges, sugar and water.

maroon *n* a brownish-crimson colour; * *vt* to be stranded.

marquee *n* a large tent used for entertainment.

marquess *n* a nobleman ranking above an earl and beneath a duke

marriage *n* wedlock; a union.

marrow *n* a soft substance in cavities of bones; a kind of gourd.

marsh *n* a swamp; boggy land.

marshal *n* one who is in charge of ceremonies etc; military officers of the highest ranks (Air marshal, Field marshal, etc).

marsupial *adj*, *n* any mammal of the order *Marsupialia*, carrying its young in a pouch.

martial *adj* warlike; military.

martyr *n* one who is tortured and suffers death for a cause.

marvel *n* a wonder; * *vi* to feel astonishment.

marvellous *adj* wonderful; miraculous; astonishing.

mascot *n* a charm.

masculine *adj* male; manly.

mash *n* a soft thick mixture of ingredients, *esp* as food for horses and cattle; mashed potatoes.

mask *n* a covering to conceal or protect the face.

mason *n* a worker or builder in stone; a freemason.

masonry *n* stonework.

masquerade *n* a fancy-dress ball at which masks are worn; a pretence.

mass *n* a lump; magnitude; a large quantity; bulk; the main part; (physics) the elementary charge associated with gravity (cf. charge and electro-magnetism) ; *pl* the common people; (*cap*) the celebration of the Eucharist.

massacre *n* ruthless slaughter.

massage *n* the rubbing and kneading of parts of body.

masseur, masseuse *n* one who gives massage professionally.

massive *adj* bulky and heavy; solid.

mast *n* an upright on which a ship's sails are set.

master *n* one who rules or directs; an employer; an owner; a ship's captain; a teacher; an expert of craftsman; a writer, painter etc regarded as pre-eminent; an original from which copies are made; a holder of an advanced academic degree.

masterpiece *n* an artist's greatest work; any extraordinary piece of work.

masterstroke *n* a supremely able act.

mastery *n* command; ascendancy.

masticate *vt* to chew and prepare for swallowing.

masturbate *vi* to manually stimulate one's, or anothers sexual organs.

mat *n* a fabric of plaited fibre, straw, etc, for protection purpose.

match *n* any person or thing which goes with another; an equal; a contest; a strip of wood or cardboard tipped with a chemical that ignites when struck.

matchless *adj* unrivalled.

mate *n* an associate; an animal's sexual partner; a companion; a spouse; a merchant ship's officer subordiate to the master.

material *n* consisting of matter; * *n* the substance of which anything is made.

materialism *n* *philos* the belief that nothing exists except for matter and *esp* that conciousness and free will are due soley to material agency; tendancey to consider possetions and comfort over spiritual matters.

materialise *vt* to give concrete form to.

maternal *adj* of, like a mother.

maternity *n* motherhood; * *adj* relating to pregnancy.

mathematics *n* the science dealing with quantities, forms, space, etc and their relationships by use of numbers and symbols.

matinée *n* an afternoon performance;

matriarch *n* a woman who rules.

matricide *n* the killing of a mother; the person guilty of it.

matriculate *vt*, *vi* to enrol or be enrolled; * matriculation *n*.

matrimonial *adj* pertaining to marriage.

matrimony *n* marriage.

matrix *n* a mould; an environment, substance etc. in which a thing is developed; a womb; fine grained rock containing fossils, gemstones etc; (maths) a rectangular array of numbers treated as a single mathematical entity.

matron *n* a woman in charge of domestic and nursing arrangements.

matted *adj* entangled.

matter *n* physical substance in general; material.

matting *n* a course material, such as woven straw or hemp.

mattress *n* a casing of strong cloth filled with cotton, foam rubber, springs, etc. used as a thing to sleep on.

mature *adj* ripe; fully developed.

maul *vt* to handle roughly; (of an animal) to tear and mulilate prey.

mausoleum *n* a large tomb.

mauve *n* a shade of pale purple.

maxim *n* an established principle.

maximum *n* the greatest quantity.

may n (cap) the fifth month of the year; hawthorn blossom; * vb, aux used to imply possibility, desire.

maybe adv perhaps.

mayhem n violent destruction, confusion.

mayonnaise n a salad dressing.

mayor, mayoress n the chief administrative officer of a municipality.

maze n a labyrinth; a perplexity.

me pers pron the objective case of I.

meadow n a piece of land where grass is grown for hay.

meagre adj thin; scanty.

meal n the food taken at one time.

mean adj selfish; ungenerous; * vt, vi to intend; to signify.

meander n a winding course.

meaning n significance.

meantime adv during the intervening time; at the same time.

meanwhile adv, n meantime.

measles n (used as sing) an acute, contagious viral disease.

measurable adj that may be measured.

measure n the extent, capacity or magnitude of a thing; a standard; a course of action; a legislative proposal; musical time; metre.

measured adj set, marked off by a standard; regular; deliberate.

measurement n dimensions.

meat n animal flesh as food; the essence of something.

mechanic n a person skilled in operating, maintaining machines.

mechanical adj of or using machinery or tools; produced or operated by machinery; done as if by a machine, lacking emotion.

mechanics n the science of motion and force; knowledge of machinery; the technical aspects of something.

mechanism n the working parts of a machine; any system of interrelated parts.

medal n a piece of metal struck to celebrate an event; a merit reward.

meddle vi to interfere in another's afeairs.

mediate vi to try to reconcile; to intercede.

medication n intercession for another.

mediator n an intercessor; an advocate.

medical adj pertaining to medicine.

medicinal adj healing.

medicine n the science of treating disease; any healing substance.

medieval, mediaeval adj pertaining to the Middle Ages.

mediocre adj of moderate quality; skill, ability, etc.

meditate vi to think deeply; reflect.

meditation n reflection; contemplation of spiritual or religious matters.

meditative adj thoughtful.

medium n (pl media, mediums) the middle state or condition; any intervening means, instrument, or agency; (pl media) means of communication, esp newspapers, television, radio; (pl mediums) a person claiming to act as an intermediary between the living and the dead.

medley n (pl medleys) a miscellany; a musical piece made up of various tunes.

meek adj patient, submissive.

meerkat n an African mongoose, Suricata suricatta.

meet vt, vi to come face to face; to encounter; to satisfy (of criteria).

melancholy n mental depression; dejection; sadness; * adj dejected.

mellifluent, mellifluous adj sweet; honeyed.

mellow adj soft and ripe; genial.

melodious adj tuneful.

melodrama n a sensational drama.

melodramatic adj over-emotional.

melody n a tuneful composition.

melon n any of several plants of the gourd family with large fruit.

melt vt, vi to liquefy; to soften; to dissolve; to fade; to disappear.

member n a limb; one of a society, company, legeslature, etc.

membership n the members of an organization, etc.

membrane n a thin flexible sheet or film. esp any such thing in an organism.

memento n a souvenir.

memoirs *npl* an autobiography.

memorabilia *npl* things worthy of record; objects, souvenirs of famous people.

memorable *adj* worthy to be remembered; easy to remember.

memorandum *n* (*pl* memorandums, memoranda) a note to help the memory; an informal letter, *esp* in business, the civil service, etc.

memorial *adj* bringing to memory; * *n* a monument; a remembrance.

memory *n* the faculty of remembering; the sum of the things remembered; an individual recollection.

menace *n* a threat; * *vt* to threaten.

mend *vt* to repair; to improve.

mendacious *adj* lying; false.

menial *adj* low; servile; descriptive of work of little skill.

meningitis *n* inflammation of the membranes enveloping the brain.

menopause *n* the time of life during which a woman's menstrual cycle ceases.

menstruation *n* the monthly discharge of blood from the uterus.

mental *adj* pertaining to the mind; occuring or performed in the mind.

mention *n* a brief reference or notice; an official recognition.

menu *n* a bill of fare.

mercantile *adj* relating to trade.

mercenary *adj* concerned with reward, *esp* financial; * *n* a soldier hired for service in a foreign army.

merchandise *n* goods; trade.

merchant *n* a trader on a large scale; a retailer.

merchant navy *n* commercial shipping.

merciful *adj* compassionate; tender.

merciless *adj* pitiless; cruel.

mercurial *adj* volatile; sprightly.

mercury *n* a heavy silvery liquid metallic element used in thermometers etc.

mercy *n* pity; compassion; pardon.

mere *adj* sole; simple.

merge *vt* to absorb; to blend.

merit *n* excellence; worth; *pl* the rights and wrongs (of a case).

merlin *n* a small falcon, *Falco columbarius*.

merry *adj* joyous; jovial, cheerful.

mesh *n* the wires of a screen etc; engagement of geared wheels.

mesmerism *n* hypnotism.

mess *n* a state of disorder or untidiness; a building where service personnel dine.

message *n* a communication; an errand; the chief idea a writer, artist etc seeks to communicate in a work.

messy *adj* dirty; confused; untidy.

metabolism *n* the total processes in living organisms by which tissue is formed, energy produced and waste products eliminated.

metal *n* any of a class of chemical elements which are ductile solids, and are good conductors of heat and electricity such as gold, iron, copper, etc.

metallurgy *n* the science concerned with the production, purification and properties of metals.

metamorphic *adj* altered in structure.

metamorphosis *n* (*pl* metamorphoses) a complete change of form.

metaphor *n* a figure of speech in which a word or phrase is used for anotherof which it is an image.

metaphoric, metaphorical *adj* figurative.

metaphysics *n* the branch of philosophy dealing with the nature of being.

meteor *n* a small object of interplanetary origin entering earths atmosphere and becoming incandesent.

meteoric *adj* brilliant but transitory.

meteorite *n* a meteor sufficiently large to impact with the ground.

meteorology *n* the study of the atmosphere and of weather-forecasting.

meter *n* an instrument for registering consumption of gas, water, time etc.

method *n* mode of procedure.

methodical *adj* systematic; orderly.

methuselah *n* a wine bottle of eight times the normal size.

methylated spirit *n* a form of alcohol, used as a solvent.

meticulous *adj* over careful; precise about small details.

metre *n* pattern in verse or music; the basic unit of length in the metric system (39.37 in.).

metric *adj* pertaining to the decimal system.

metric system *n* a decimal system of weights and measures.

metronome *n* an instrument that beats musical tempo.

metropolitan *adj* belonging to a metropolis.

mettle *n* spirit; courage.

mezzanine *n* an intermediate storey between others.

mezzo *adj* in music, middle; mean.

mezzoprano *n* a female voice, between soprano and contralto.

mice *npl* of mouse.

microbe *n* a microscopic organism.

microcosm *n* man as an epitome of the universe; a minature representation.

microfilm *n* film on which documents, etc are recorded in reduced scale.

microphone *n* an instrument for transforming sound waves into electric signals.

microscope *n* an optical instrument for magnifying.

microscopic *adj* minute; visible only through a microscope.

mid *adj* middle; intervening.

midday *n* noon.

middle *adj* equally distant from the extremes.

middle age *n* the time between youth and old age.

Middle Ages *npl* the period of European history between about AD500 and 1500.

middle class *n* people between the working classes and the bourgoisie.

midnight *n* twelve o'clock at night.

midst *prep* amidst; among.

midwife *n* a nurse specialising in childbirth.

might *n* power; strength.

migrant *n* a person or animal who migrates.

migrate *vi* to remove from one region or country to another.

migratory *adj* roving; wandering.

mild *adj* gentle; merciful; soft.

mildew *n* a mouldy deposit or coating caused by fungus.

mile *n* 1760 yards or 1.61 km.

milestone *n* a stone or post marking each mile of a road; an important event.

militant *adj* warring; combative.

militarism *n* reliance on force.

military *adj* pertaining to the armed forces.

militate *vi* (with against) to have an adverse effect on.

militia *n* an armed force composed of civilians.

milk *n* a fluid secreted by female mammals to feed their young; * *vt* to draw milk from; to extract money etc from; to exploit.

mill *n* a machine for grinding corn, etc; a factory; * *vt* to grind.

millennium *n* a period of 1000 years.

milligramme *n* the thousandth part of a gramme.

millimetre *n* the thousandth part of a metre.

million *n* a thousand thousands; 1,000,000.

millionaire *n* a person with assets worth one million pounds or more.

millstone *n* a stone used in grinding corn.

mime *n* a drama enacted through gestures.

mimic *adj* imitative; * *n* one who imitates.

mimicry *n* imitation.

mince *vt*, *vi* to chop into small pieces; to act or walk affectedly.

mincemeat *n* a mixture of chopped apples, raisins, etc used as a pie filling.

mind *n* the intellectual faculty or power; intellect; reason; understanding; inclination; opinion; memory; * *vt* to heed; to pay attention to; to take care of.

mindful *adj* attentive; heedful.

mine *pron* my; belonging to me; * *n* an excavation from which minerals are dug; a concealed explosive device.

minefield *n* an area in which mines are laid; a situation containing hidden problems.

miner *n* a person who works in a mine.

mineral *n* an inorganic substance found in or on the earth.

mineralogist *n* an expert on mineralogy.

mineralogy *n* the science of minerals.

mingle *vt* to mix together; to blend.

miniature *n* a small-scale portrait.

minim *n* a note in music.

minimise *vt* to estimate at the lowest; to disparage.

minimum *n* the smallest amount.

minister *n* a member of a government heading a department; a diplomat; a clergyman serving a church; * *vt* to give help.

ministration *n* service; a giving of aid; the work of a minister of the church.

ministry *n* service; office of a minister; clergy; a government department headed by a minister.

minor *adj* lesser; smaller; petty; * *n* a person under full legal age.

minority *n* the smaller of two or more groups; a smaller ethnic group in a country.

mint *n* the place where money is coined; a large amount of money; any aromatic plant of the genus *Mentha*.

minuet *n* a slow graceful dance.

minus *adj* less; * *n* the sign indicating subtraction

minute *adj* very small; precise; exact; * *n* the sixtieth part of an hour or a degree; *pl* a summary of proceedings; an official record of a meeting; * *vt* to make a note of.

minutiae *npl* small details.

miracle *n* a supernatural event.

miraculous *adj* marvellous.

mirage *n* an optical illusion.

mire *n* wet, muddy soil; mud.

mirror *n* a looking glass; a faithful depiction.

misadventure *n* a mishap; (law) an accident not due to a crime or negligence.

misanthrope, misanthropist *n* a hater of mankind.

misapply *vt* to apply wrongly.

misapprehend *vt* to misunderstand.

misappropriate *vt* to embezzle.

misbehave *vi* to behave badly.

miscalculate *vt* to reckon wrongly.

miscarriage *n* a failure; misman-agement; the premature expulsion of a foetus.

miscellaneous *adj* mixed; diverse.

mischance *n* ill luck; mishap.

mischief *n* wayward, prankish behaviour.

mischievous *adj* troublesome; hurtful.

misconduct *n* immoral or bad behaviour.

misconstrue *vt* to interpret wrongly.

miscount *vt, vi* to make an error in counting; a wrong counting.

misdeed *n* an evil action.

misdemeanour *n* a minor offence.

miser *n* a skinflint; a hoarder of money.

misery *n* wretchedness; sorrow.

misfit *n* a bad fit; a maladjusted person.

misfortune *n* ill fortune; calamity.

misgiving *n* a doubt; mistrust.

misguided *adj* foolish; mistaken.

mishap *n* a slight or unfortunate accident.

misinform *vt* to give wrong information to.

misinterpret *vt* to misconstrue.

misjudge *vt* to judge erroneously.

mislay *vt* to lose temporarily; to put down in the wrong place.

mislead *vi* to deceive; to misinform.

mismanage *vt* to manage badly.

misnomer *n* an incorrect or unsuitable name for someone or something.

misogamist *n* one who hates marriage.

misogynist *n* a woman-hater.

misplace *vt* to put out of place.

misprint *n* a mistake in printing.

mispronounce *vt, vi* to pronounce wrongly.

misquote *vt* to quote incorrectly.

misrepresent *vt* to represent falsely.

misrule *n* misgovernment.

miss *vt* to fail to hit, find, meet, etc; to lose; to omit; to fail to take advantage of; to feel the loss of; * *n* a failure to hit; loss; want; an unmarried woman; a girl.

misshapen *adj* ill-formed.

missile *n* an weapon which is thrown at a target or fired from a launcher.

missing *adj* lost; absent.

mission *n* a group of people sent by a church, government, etc to carry out a special duty or task.

misspell *vt* to spell wrongly.

misspend *vt* to squander; to waste.

mist *n* a mass of visible water vapour.

mistake *vt* to misunderstand or misinterpret; * *vi* to err; * *n* a blunder, an error of judgment.

mistress *n* the feminine of master; the woman with whom a man is having an affair.

mistrust *n* suspicion; * *vt* to doubt.

misunderstanding *vt* to take the wrong meaning from.

misuse *vt* to use for wrong purpose; to abuse; * *n* improper use.

mite *n* a very small arachnid of the order *Acarina*.

mitigate *vt* to lessen, to abate.

mitre *n* the headdress of a bishop.

mitten *n* a glove with two sections, one for the thumb and one for the fingers.

mix *vt, vi* to unite or blend; to mingle; to combine (ingredients).

mixture *n* a compound; a medley; a jumble.

mix-up *n* a mistake; confusion; muddle.

mnemonics *n* art of memory; rules for assisting memory.

moan *vi* to utter a mournful sound.

moat *n* a ditch round a castle or fort.

mob *n* a crowd; a rabble.

mobile *adj* movable, not fixed; having transport.

mobilise *vt* to organise troops in readiness for service.

moccasin *n* a soft leather shoe with a combined sole and heel.

mock *vt* to imitate or ridicule; to behave with scorn; to defy.

mockery *n* derision; a sham.

mock-up *n* a full-scale working model of a machine, etc.

mode *n* way of acting, doing, existing; manner; fashion; (music) any of the scales used in composition; (statistics) the most frequent element of a set.

model *n* a pattern; an ideal; a standard worth imitating; a representation on a smaller scale, *usu* three-dimensional; a person who sits for an artist or photographer; a person who displays clothes by wearing them.

moderate *vt* to restrain from excess; to temper.

moderation *n* temperance; restraint.

modern *adj* of the present or recent times; contemporary; up-to-date.

modernism *n* modern thought or practice.

modernise *vt* to make modern.

modest *adj* retiring; bashful.

modicum *n* a small quantity.

modification *n* the act of modifying.

modify *vt* to change slightly; to lessen the severity of; to limit in meaning.

modulate *vt* to measure; to vary (the voice) in tone.

module *n* a self-contained unit, *esp* in a space-craft.

moist *adj* slightly wet; damp.

moisture *n* dampness; huinidity.

moisturise *vt* to add moisture to the skin, air etc with various preparations.

mole *n* a dark spot on human skin; a spy within an organisation; (chemistry) the SI unit of amount equal to the number of atoms in 0.012kg of carbon 12; a burrowing insectivrous mammal of the family *Talpidae*.

molecule *n* (chemistry) the smallest fundamental unit of a chemical compound which can take part in a chemical reaction; amy small thing.

molest *vt* to annoy; to vex; to assault *esp* sexually.

mollify *vt* to soften; to appease; to tone down.

mollusc *n* any invertibrate of the *phylum mollusca*, *eg* oyster, clam.

molten *adj* melted by heat.

moment *n* an indefinitely brief period of time; importance.

momentary *adj* lasting only for a moment.

momentous *adj* important.

momentum *n* (*pl* **momenta**) the quantity of motion possessed by a moving body, measured as the product of its velocity and its mass.

monarch *n* a sovereign ruling by hereditary right.

monarchy *n* government headed by a monarch; a kingdom.

monastery *n* the residence of monks.

monastic *adj* of monks or monasteries.

Monday *n* the second day of the week.

money *n* current coin or its equivalent in bank notes, etc.

moneyed *adj* wealthy.

mongoose *n* any of several mammals of the family *Viveridae*.

mongrel *adj* of mixed or unknown breed.

monitor *n* a prefect; any device for regulating the performance of a machine, aircraft etc.

monk *n* a male member of a religious order in a monastery.

monkey *n* (*pl* **monkeys**) any of various primates, *usu* with long tails, of the families *Cebidae*, *Callithricidae*, and *Cercopithecidae*, *esp* the smaller, long-tailed primates; a mischievous child; slang £500.

monocle *n* a single eyeglass.

monogamy *n* marriage to one wife or husband only.

monogram *n* letters (*esp* initials) interwoven in one design.

monograph *n* an essay on one subject.

monolith *n* a standing stone or pillar.

monologue *n* a soliloquy.

monopolise *vt* to obtain entire control of.

monopoly *n* an exclusive trading privilege; exclusive use or possession.

monosyllable *n* a word of one syllable.

monotone *n* speaking without inflection; a sameness of style, colour etc.

monotony *n* an irksome sameness.

monster *n* an imagined, ferocious, creature.

monstrous *adj* unnatural; horrible.

month *n* any of the twelve divisions of the year; a calendar month; a period corresponding to the moon's revolution.

monument *n* a tomb, pillar, statue etc, erected as a memorial.

monumental *adj* of, like, or serving as a monument; colossal; lasting.

mood *n* a temporary state of mind; * **moody** *adj* temperamental.

moon *n* the natural satellite that orbits the earth and shines by reflected sunlight; any natural satellite of another planet.

moonbeam *n* a ray of light from the moon.

moonlight *n* the light of the moon; * *vi* to have a secondary (usually night-time) job.

moor *n* a heath; wasteland; * *vt* to secure a ship by cable or anchor.

mooring *n* the anchors, buoys, etc by which or to which a boat is moored.

moot *adj* debatable; undecided.

mop *n* a rag, sponge etc fixed to a handle for washing floors or dishes; a thick, unruly head of hair.

mope *vi* to be downcast.

moral *adj* of or relating to character and human behaviour, particularly as regards right and wrong; virtuous.

morale *n* the tone, spirit, or mental condition prevailing with regard to courage, discipline, confidence etc.

morality *n* the doctrine of moral duties; ethics; virtue.

moralise *vt, vi* to reflect on moral questions.

morass *n* a marsh; a bog; a fen.

moratorium *n* legal permission to defer payments due; a temporary stoppage.

morbid *adj* diseased; gruesome.

more *adj* greater in amount, extent etc; * *adv* in a greater degree.

morel *n* an edible fungus, *Morchella esculenta*, with ridged caps

morning *n* the first part of the day.

morose *adj* surly; sullen; glum.

morphine, **morphia** *n* an analgesic and narcotic drug obtained from opium.

morsel *n* a bite; a small piece.

mortal *adj* subject to death; deadly; fatal; * *n* a being that will die.

mortality *n* the state of being mortal; the death rate.

mortar *n* a bowl in which substances are pounded with a pestle; a short bore artillery piece that fires bombs at high trajectories; cement.

mortgage *n* a conveyance of property as security for loan; the deed of conveyance; * *vt* to pledge as security.

mortify *vt*, *vi* to be affected by gangrene or necrosis; to shame.

mortise lock *n* a lock set into a mortise in a door.

motuary *n* a place for temporary storage of dead bodies; a morgue.

mosaic *n* inlaid work of marble, precious stones, etc.

Moslem, Muslim *n* a Mohammedan; an adherent of Islam.

mosque *n* a Moslem place of worship.

moss *n* any small crypogamous plant of the class *Musci*,.

most *adj* (*superl* of more) greatest in any way.

motel *n* an hotel for motorists with adjacent parking.

moth *n* any *usu* nocturnal insect of the order *Lepidoptera*.

mother *n* a female parent; source or origin; the head of a nunnery, etc; * *adj* of, like a mother; * *vt* to be or care for as a mother.

mother-in-law one's spouse's mother.

motion *n* activity, movement; a formal suggestion made in a meeting, law court, or legislative assembly; evacuation of the bowels; * *vt*, *vi* to signal or direct by a gesture.

motionless *adj* not moving; still.

motive *n* something (as a need or desire) that causes a person to act.

motley *adj* composed of diverse element.

motor *n* a machine that produces motion; a motor car.

motorbike *n* a two wheeled powered vehicle.

motorboat *n* a boat propelled by an engine or motor.

motorist *n* a person who drives a car.

motorway *n* a road with controlled access for fast-moving traffic.

mottled *adj* marked with blotches of various colours.

motto *n* (*pl* mottoes) a short saying adopted as a maxim or ideal.

mould *n* a microscopic fungus producing a furry growth on the surface of organic matter; a hollow form in which something is cast; * *vt* to make in or on a mould; to form, to shape, to guide.

moulder *vt*, *vi* to decay; to crumble.

moulding *n* anything cast in a mould; omamental contour along an edge.

moult *vi* to shed or cast the hair, horns, skin, etc.

mound *n* an artificial elevation of earth or stones; a rampart.

mount *n* a hill; a mountain; a setting for photographs, etc; a backing; a horse; * *vi* to rise; to get on horseback; to provide with horses; to amount; * *vt* to climb; to fix, place in position.

mountain *n* a high hill, a vast number.

mountaineer *n* a mountain climber.

mourn *vi* to sorrow; * *vt* to grieve for.

mouse *n* (*pl* mice) any of various small rodents of the family *Muridae*; a hand-held device used to position the cursor and control software on a computer screen.

moustache *n* the hair on the upper lip.

mouth *n* the opening in the head through which food is eaten, sound uttered or words spoken; opening, entrance, as of a bottle.

mouthwatering *adj* appetizing.

movable *adj* portable; * *npl* furniture; belongings; personal property.

move *vt* to cause to change place; to set in motion; to affect; to rouse; to prevail on; to make a motion; * *vi* to stir; to go from one place to another; to walk; to change residence.

movement *n* motion; change of

position; a gesture; joint action; the policy of a group; a trend; a division of a musical work.

movies *npl* the cinema.

moving *adj* touching; pathetic.

mow *vt, vi* to cut down; to cut grass.

much *adj* (*comp* more, *superl* most) great in quantity.

mucous membrane *n* a membrane lining the nose and other cavities of the body.

mucus *n* a viscid fluid secreted by mucous membrane.

mud *n* moist soft earth; mire.

muddle *vt* to make a mess of, to mix up; to confuse; * *n* a mess; confusion.

muff *n* a fur cover for both hands.

muffin *n* a baked roll.

muffle *vt* to wrap up close; to conceal; to deaden sound.

muffler *n* a long scarf.

mug *n* a large cup; * *vt* to assault (and rob).

mule *n* the offspring of a male donkey and a female horse; an obstinate person.

mull *vt* to heat, sweeten, and spice (as wine, etc); to ponder.

multifarious *adj* many and varied.

multilateral *adj* many-sided.

multiple *adj* manifold; various; * *n* a number containing another as a factor.

multiplicity *n* great number or variety.

multiply *vt, vi* to make or become many; to increase; to find the product of by multiplication.

multistorey *adj* (of a building) with many storeys.

multitude *n* a crowd; a throng; the populace.

mumble *vi, vt* to mutter; to speak indistinctly.

mummy *n* an embalmed human body, *esp* an embalmed corpse of ancient Egypt; a diminutive form of mother.

mumps *n* a contagious and infectous viral disease with swelling of the parotid salivaray glands and risk of sterility in adult males.

munch *vt, vi* to chew steadily.

mundane *adj* routine; everyday.

municipal *adj* of or concerning a city, town, etc or its local government.

municipality *n* the corporation or governing body of a town.

munificent *adj* bountiful; generous.

mural *adj* pertaining to a wall; * *n* a picture painted onto a wall.

murder *n* unlawful and premeditated killing of another human.

murderous *adj* cruel; savage.

murky *adj* dark; gloomy; obscure.

murmur *n* a low indistinct sound; an abnormal beat made by the heart.

muscle *n* fibrous tissue that contracts and relaxes, producing body movement; strength; power.

muscular *adj* brawny; sinewy.

muse *n* poetic inspiration; * *vt, vi* to ponder; to meditate.

museum *n* a building housing a collection of curios, works of art, etc.

mushroom *n* the *usu* edible spore producing body of various fungi, *esp Agaricus campestris*.

music *n* melody or harmony; the art of producing musical compositions featuring vocal or instrumental sounds having rhythm, harmony, melody.

musical *adj* melodious; harmonious; having an interest in or talent for music; * *n* a play or film incorporating story, song and dance.

musician *n* one skilled in music.

musing *n* meditation.

Muslim *see* Moslem.

muslin *n* a fine cotton cloth.

mussel *n* any bivalve mollusc of the genus *Mytilus* living in sea water or of the genus *Margaritifer* or *Anodonta* living in fresh water and forming pearls.

must *aux vb* expressing necessity or certainty; * *n* a necessity.

mustard *n* any of various plants of the genus *brassica*, or the genus *Sinapis*.

muster *vt* to collect, as troops; * *vi* to assemble; * *n* an assembling of troops.

musty *adj* mouldy; stale; damp.

mutation *n* change; alteration.

mute *adj* silent; dumb; not pronounced; * *n* a person who cannot speak.

mutilate *vt* to cut off a part, parts.

mutineer *n* one guilty of mutiny.

mutiny *n* a revolt against authority in military service; * *vi* to rise in revolt.

mutter *vi* to mumble; to murmur to grumble; * *n* indistinct speech.

mutual *adj* reciprocal; shared alike; having the same feelings one for the other.

muzzle *n* the projecting mouth and nose of an animal; the open end of a gun; a strap fitted over an animal's jaws to prevent biting; * *vt* to gag.

my *pron* the possessive case singular of I.

myopia *n* short-sightedness.

myself *pron* emphatic and reflexive form of I; in my normal state.

mystery *n* something unexplained.

mystic *adj* having a meaning beyond normal human under-standing; magical.

mystify *vt* to perplex; to bewilder.

myth *n* a tradition or fable embodying the primitive ideas of a people.

mythology *n* a body of myths; the study of myths.

N

nab *vt* to catch; to seize or arrest.

nadir *n* the lowest point.

nag *n* a horse; a person who nags; * *vt, vi* to scold constantly.

nail *n* a horny substance covering the tip of the finger or toe; a metal spike.

naïve *adj* ingenuous; unsophisti-cated.

naïveté *n* lack of sophistication.

naked *adj* bare; nude; destitute.

name *n* the word by which a person or thing is designated; title; reputation; a family; * *vt* to give a name to.

namely *adv* that is to say.

namesake *n* one named after, or with the same name as another.

nap *n* the woolly substance on the surface of cloth, etc; a short sleep.

nape *n* the back of the neck.

naphtha *n* a volatile oil distilled from coal.

napkin *n* a serviette.

nappy *n* material wrapped around a baby to absorb or retain its excreta.

narcosis *n* a state induced by anesthetic drugs; insensibility.

narcotic *n* a sedative; (of a drug) affecting the mind; such a drug.

narrate *vt* to tell or relate; to provide a spoken commentary (of a film, etc).

narrow *adj* of little breadth; very limited; not liberal; near.

nasal *adj* pertaining to or sounded through the nose.

nascent *adj* budding; dawning; opening.

nasty *adj* malicious; indecent; disagreeable.

natal *adj* pertaining to birth.

nation *n* people *usu* under the same government and of mainly common descent, culture, language, history, etc *usu* occupying a territory.

nationalist *n* one who supports nationalism.

nationality *n* the nation to which an individual belongs.

nationalise *vt* to convert land, mines, etc into state property.

nationalism *n* a policy of national independance; patriotism, *esp* when extreme.

native *adj* pertaining to the place of one's birth.

nativity *n* birth; time, place, manner of birth.

natural *adj* pertaining to nature; native; inborn; (music) not sharp or flat.

naturalisation *n* the admission of one of foreign birth to citizenship.

naturalise *vt* to acclimatize; to confer.

naturally *adv* in a natural manner, by nature; of course.

nature *n* the essential character

of a thing or person; the phenomena of the material world (plants, snimals, volcanos, etc); the personification of these forces.

naughty *adj* bad; mischievous.

nausea *n* sickness; disgust.

nauseate *vt, vi* to arouse feelings of disgust or revulsion.

nautical *adj* pertaining to ships.

naval *adj* pertaining to ships or to a navy.

navel *n* the depression in the centre of the abdomen caused by the severing of the umbilical cord; the belly button.

navigate *vi, vt* to guide the course of a ship, aeroplane, etc; to sail.

navigation *n* the method of calculating the position of a ship, aircraft etc.

navvy *n* a labourer, who excavates roads, canals, etc.

navy *n* the warships of a nation with their crews and equipment.

near *adj* not distant; intimate; closely related; approximate.

nearly *adv* almost; closely.

neat *adj* trim; (of alcohol) undiluted.

nebula *n* (*pl* **nebulae**) (Astronomy) a cloud of gas and dust, apparent because of luminosity or opacity; a galaxy or a smaller cluster of stars.

nebulous *adj* cloudy; hazy; unclear.

necessary *adj* indispensable; essential; * *n* a proved need; *pl* essential needs.

necessity *n* urgent need; compulsion.

neck *n* the part of body connecting the head to the body; an isthmus; the narrowest part of a bottle.

necklace *n* a string of beads worn round the neck.

necrosis *n* (Medical) the death of tissue due to damage or disease.

nectar *n* a sugary substance produced by flowers, to attract insects to acilitate pollination, and made into honey by bees; (in Greek and Roman mythology) the drink of the gods; a drink compared to this.

need *n* want; necessity; poverty; * *vt, vi* to lack; to require.

needle *n* a small steel instrument for sewing; an indicator on a dial; the thin, short leaf of trees such as the pine or spruce.

negation *n* a denial; a saying no.

negative *adj* expressing denial or refusal; the opposite of positive; * *n* a photographic print from which positive prints are taken; * *vt* to veto; to contradict.

neglect *vt* to disregard; to leave uncared for; * *n* want of care.

negligée *n* a woman's loose dressing gown.

negligence *n* carelessness.

negotiate *vi* to treat; to bargain in order to reach an agreement or settlement.

negotiation *n* bargaining.

neigh *vi* to whinny.

neighbour *n* a person living near; a fellow human being; * *vt* to adjoin.

neighbourhood *n* a particular area, district or community; the vicinity.

neighbourly *adj* friendly.

neither *pron, adj* not either; * *conj* not either; also not.

nephew *n* the son of a brother or sister.

nepotism *n* favouritism to relatives shown by influential people.

nerve *n* one of the fibrous threads which convey messages to and from the brain or spinal cord; courage; audacity.

nervous *adj* timid; excitable.

nest *n* a bird's hatching place.

nestle *vi* to lie close and snug.

net *n* a meshwork of cord, twine, etc; a piece of this used to catch fish, to divide a tennis court etc; a snare; * *vt* to snare; to twine.

net, nett *adj* (*esp* of money) remaining after deductions, etc.

netball *n* a game for two teams, in which points are scored by putting a ball through an elevated horizontal ring.

nettle *n* any plant of the genus *Urtica, esp U. dioica.*

network *n* an interconnecting arrangement of lines; a group co-operating with each other; a chain of interconnected operations, computers etc.

neuralgia *n* pain in a nerve.

neuritis *n* inflammation of nerve.

neurology *n* the study of nerves.

neurone *n* a nerve cell.

neurosis *n* (*pl* neuroses) a mental disorder with symptoms such as anxiety.

neurotic *adj* suffering from neurosis; highly strung.

neuter *adj* (of nouns) neither masculine nor feminine; (biology) having no sex organs; * *vt* to castrate or spay.

neutral *adj* not aligned with either party in a dispute; having no distinctive characteristics; (chemistry) neither acid nor alkaline; (physics) uncharged; * *n* a position of a gear mechanism in which power is not transmitted.

never *adv* at no time; in no case.

nevertheless *adv* for all that; notwithstanding.

new *adj* recent; novel; fresh; unused.

news *npl* current events; recent happenings; the media's coverage of these.

newsagent *n* a retailer of newspapers.

newspaper *n* a paper published periodically giving latest news.

next *adj* nearest; immediately preceding or following; adjacent; * *adv* in the nearest time, place, rank, etc; on the first subsequent occasion.

nexus *n* tie; connexion.

nibble *vt, vi* to bite little by little.

nice *adj* fastidious; pleasant; dainty.

nicety *n* precision; exactness.

niche *n* a recess in a wall for a statue, etc.

nick *n* a notch; a score; a police station; * *vt* to make a small cut in.

nickname *n* a name given to an individual in jest or ridicule.

nicotine *n* an addictive alkaloid stimulant present in tobacco.

niece *n* the daughter of one's brother or sister.

night *n* the period from sunset to sunrise.

nightcap *n* a cap worn in bed; an alcoholic drink taken just before bedtime.

nightclub *n* a place of entertainment for drinking, dancing, etc, at night.

nightdress *n* a loose garment worn in bed by women and girls.

nightmare *n* a frightening dream; any horrible experience.

nil *n* nothing.

nimble *adj* active; agile.

nine *adj, n* the product of three and three (9 or IX).

nineteen *adj, n* nine plus ten (19 or XIX).

ninety *adj, n* nine times ten (90 or C).

ninth *adj, n* one part in nine.

nip *vt* to pinch; to snip; * *n* a pinch.

nipple *n* the small protuberance on a breast or udder through which the milk passes, a teat.

nitrogen *n* a gaseous element forming nearly 78 per cent of air.

no *adv* expressing negation; * *n* a denial; a refusal; a negative vote.

noble *adj* of high rank; famous; lofty in character; stately; * *n* a peer; a person of high rank.

nobleman *n* a noble; a peer.

nobody *n* no one; a person of no importance.

nocturnal *adj* nightly; by night.

nod *vi, vt* to make a slight bow, to incline the head quickly in assent or greeting.

nodule *n* a little knot or lump.

noise *n* a din; clamour; a harsh sound; * *vt* to make public.

noisome *adj* noxious; offensive.

nomad *n* a wanderer; one of a people or tribe who travel in search of pasture.

nomenclature *n* a system of names.

nominal *adj* formal; existing in name only; having only token worth.

nominate *vt* to name; to designate; to appoint to a office or post; to propose someone as a candidate (for election).

nominee *n* a person nominated for office, etc.

nonchalance *n* indifference; coolness.

noncommittal *adj* not revealing one's opinion.

nondescript *adj* hard to classify,

indeterminate; lacking individual characteristics.

none *n, pron* not one; not any.

nonentity *n* a person of no significance.

nonsense *n* words without meaning.

noodle *pl* pasta in thin strips.

noon *n* midday.

noose *n* a loop on a running knot.

nor *conj* and not; not either.

norm *n* a rule; a pattern; a standard.

normal *adj* according to a ride; regular.

north *n* the cardinal point opposite the midday sun; * *adj* in, of, towards, from the north.

northeast *n* the point midway between north and east.

northwest *n* the point midway between the north and west.

nose *n* the part of the face above the mouth, used for breathing and smelling, having two nostrils; the sense of smell.

nostalgia *n* yearning for past times or places.

nostalgic *adj* feeling or expressing nostalgia; longing for one's youth.

nostril *n* one of the two apertures of the nose for breathing and smelling.

not *adv* expressing denial, refusal or negation.

notable *adj* worthy of being noted or remembered; distinguished; memorable.

notation *n* act of recording anything by symbols.

notch *n* an incision; nick.

note *n* a mark, a sign or token; an explanation; an epistle; a musical sound or its symbol; the sound of a bird's call; * *vt* to mark down; to observe.

noted *adj* famous; celebrated.

notepaper *n* paper for writing down notes.

nothing *n* not anything; a trifle; a zero; thing of no importance or value; * *adv* in no way; not at all.

notice *n* heed; regard; intimation; warning; information; * *vt* to observe.

noticeable *adj* worthy of notice; remarkable; easily seen or noticed.

notification *n* intimation; warning.

notify *vt* to make known; to inform.

notion *n* a concept; an idea; an opinion.

notorious *adj* widely known, *esp* unfavourably; * notoriety *n*.

notwithstanding *prep, conj* in spite of; nevertheless; although.

nougat *n* a chewy sweet consisting of sugar paste and nuts.

nought *n* not anything; a zero.

noun *n* the name of anything.

nourish *vt* to feed; to foster.

nourishment *n* food, nutriment.

novel *adj* new and striking; * *n* a fictitious story or narrative in book form.

novelty *n* a new or strange thing; *pl* cheap, small objects for sale.

November *n* the eleventh month of the year.

novice *n* a beginner; a person in a religious order before taking vows.

now *adv* at the present time; * *conj* since; seeing that.

nowhere *adv* not in, at, or to anywhere.

noxious *adj* hurtful; pernicious.

nozzle *n* the projecting spout of something; *eg* a nose or pipe.

nuance *n* a fine shade; a delicate distinction of meaning etc.

nuclear *adj* of or relating to a nucleus; using nuclear energy.

nucleus *n* (*pl* nuclei, nucleuses) the central part or core around which something may develop, or be grouped or concentrated; the central positively charged core of an atom.

nude *adj* naked; bare; * *n* a naked human figure in a work of art.

nudge *n* a light jog with the elbow.

nugget *n* a lump, as of gold.

nuisance *n* that which annoys.

null *adj* of no force; void; invalid.

nullify *vt* to render null; to cancel out.

numb *adj* having no feeling through shock or cold; * *vt* to deaden.

number *n* a symbol or word indicating how many; a numeral identifying a person or thing by its position in a series; * *vt, vi* to count; to give a number to; to include or be included as one of a group; to limit the number of; to total.

numeral *n* a figure or symbol representing a number.

numerate *adj* able to use and understand numbers and arithmetic.

numerical *adj* denoting number; consisting of numbers.

numerous *adj* many.

nun *n* a woman belonging to a religious order.

nunnery *n* a convent.

nuptials *npl* marriage.

nurse *n* one trained to care for the sick, or infirm; * *vt* to tend.

nursery *n* a place where children may be left in temporary care; a place where young trees and plants are raised for transplanting.

nurture *n* upbringing; education; nourishment; * *vt* to nourish.

nut *n* a fruit containing a kernel in a hard covering; a screw fastening a bolt.

nutcracker *n* an instrument for cracking nuts; a bird with speckled plumage.

nutmeg *n* an evergreen tree, *Myristica fragrans*; the seed used as a spice.

nutriment *n* food; nourishment.

nutritious *adj* nourishing; health-giving.

nylon *n* any of numerous polyamide fibres used *esp* in textiles.

nymph *n* the larva of the dragon-fly, mayfly etc; any of several mythological, semi-divine spirits, personified as maidens; (poetic) a beautiful young woman.

O

oaf *n* a stupid clumsy person.

oak *n* any tree of the genus *Quercus* having acorns as fruits.

oar *n* a pole with a flat blade for rowing.

oarsman *n* a rower.

oasis *n* (*pl* oases) a fertile tract in a desert.

oat *n* a cereal, *Avena sativa*.

oath *n* a solemn affirmation.

oatmeal *n* ground oats.

obdurate *adj* unrelenting.

obedient *adj* submissive; dutiful; complaint.

obeisance *n* a bow or curtsy; an act of respect.

obese *adj* very overweight.

obey *vt, vi* to do as commanded; to yield to; to comply with.

obituary *n* an announcement of a person's death.

object *n* the end aimed at; a purpose; anything present to the senses; * *vt, vi* to oppose; to disapprove.

objection *n* the act of objecting; a ground for; or expression of, disapproval.

objective *adj* not influenced by opinions or feelings; impartial; having an independent existence of it sown, real; * *n* the thing or placed aimed at.

obligation *n* the binding power of a promise, contract, law, etc.

oblige *vt* to constrain; to compel; to do or favour; to gratify.

obliging *adj* civil; kind; agreeable.

oblique *adj* slanting; indirect.

obliterate *vt* to blot out; to destroy.

oblivion *n* the state of forgetting or being utterly forgotten.

oblivious *adj* forgetful; unaware.

oblong *adj* rectangular.

obnoxious *adj* odious; unpopular.

oboe *n* a wind instrument of wood.

obscene *adj* indecent; vile; offensive to a moral standard.

obscure *adj* darkened; dim; abstruse; unimportant; * *vt* to darken; to hide from view; to confuse; to make unclear.

obsequious *adj* cringing; fawning.

observance *n* the observing of a practice, etc; the performance of rites, etc.

observant *adj* attentive; watchful.

observation *n* the act or faculty of observing; a comment or remark.

observatory *n* a building for astronomical observations.

observe *vt, vi* to take notice of; to remark; to keep religiously.

obsess *vt* to possess or haunt the mind of.

obsession *n* the complete capture

of the mind by some idea; a persistent preoccupation.

obsolete *adj* antiquated; out of date.

obstacle *n* a hindrance.

obstetrics *n* the branch of medicine concerned with the care and treatment of women during pregnancy and childbirth.

obstinate *adj* stubborn; self-willed.

obstreperous *adj* unruly; disorderly.

obstruct *vt* to block up; to impede; to hinder; to keep light from.

obtain *vt* to acquire; to gain; to earn; * *vi* to prevail; to hold good.

obtrusive *adj* forward; interfering.

obtuse *adj* blunt; stupid; greater than a right angle.

obvious *adj* plain; evident.

occasion *n* an occurrence; an incident; an opportunity; a cause.

occasional *adj* casual; happening now and then; incidental.

occult *adj* hidden; mysterious; belonging to the supernatural; mystic.

occupancy *n* tenancy.

occupation *n* possession; tenure; business; vocation; employment.

occupy *vt* to take possession of; to fill; to employ; to engage.

occur *vi* to happen.

occurrence *n* an event, an incident.

ocean *n* the vast body of water surrounding the land or one of its divisions.

octave *n* in music, the eighth full tone above or below a given tone, the interval of eight degrees between a tone and either of its octaves.

October *n* the tenth month of the year.

ocular *adj* pertaining to the eye; visual.

odd *adj* peculiar; occasional; not divisible by two; extra or left over.

oddity *n* the state of being odd; an odd thing or person; peculiarity.

oddment *n* a remnant *esp* of fabric.

odds *n sing, pl* the ratio of the winnings to the stake in a bet; probability.

ode *n* a lyric poem.

odium *n* hatred; dislike; blame.

odour *n* any scent or smell.

oesophagus *n* the part of the alimentary canal from the mouth to the stomach.

of *prep* denoting source, cause, etc.

off *adv* away; distant; detached; out of condition; * *adj* cancelled; having gone bad (of food).

offence *n* injury; insult; displeasure; crime.

offend *vt* to displease; to affront; to shock; * *vi* to break the law.

offensive *adj* causing offence; impertinent; aggressive; * *n* an attack.

offer *vt* to present for acceptance or rejection; to tender; to bid; * *vi* to present itself; * *n* a bid; a proposal.

offering *n* a gift; a sacrifice.

office *n* duty; public employment; function; service; place of business.

officer *n* the holder of an office; a commissioned officer in the armed forces.

official *adj* pertaining to an office properly authorised; formal; * *n* an officer; one holding public office.

officious *adj* fussy; meddling; interfering.

offing *n* the near or foreseeable future.

off-peak *adj* denoting use of a service, etc in a period of lesser demand.

offshoot *n* a shoot coming off a main branch; a derivative product, idea, etc.

offside *adj, adv* an illegal position of a player in a sport, *usu* ahead of the ball.

offspring *n, sing, pl* children; progeny.

often *adv* frequently; many times.

ogle *vt, vi* to gape at; to look at lustfully.

ohm *n* the SI unit of electric resistance.

oil *n* any of several viscous, often inflammable, liquids which are insoluble in water.

oilskin *n* waterproof cloth; a garment of this.

oil slick *n* a mass of oil floating on the surface of water.

oily *adj* like or covered with oil;

greasy; too suave or smooth, unctuous.

ointment *n* a substance for applying to skin for healing or cosmetic purposes.

old *adj* aged; not new or fresh; out of date; former; not modern.

old-fashioned *adj* out of date.

olfactory *adj* pertaining to sense of smell.

oligarchy *n* government by a small group of people; a state so run.

olive *n* any evergreen tree of the genus *Olea* its edible fruit yielding oil.

omega *n* the last letter of Greek alphabet.

omelette *n* eggs beaten and cooked flat in a pan.

omen *n* a sign of a (*usu* undesirable) future event; * **ominous** *adj*.

omission *n* a failure to do something; a leaving out of something.

omit *vt* to neglect; to leave out.

omnipotent *adj* all-powerful.

omniscient *adj* all-knowing.

omnivorous *adj* feeding on many types of food, *esp* on both plants and animals.

on *prep* in contact with the upper surface of, supported by, attached to, or covering; concerning; about; using; * *adv* (so as to be) covering or in contact with something; forward; (device) switched on; continuously in progress; due to take place; (actor) on stage; on duty.

once *adv* on the occasion only; formerly; * *conj* a soon as; * *n* one time.

one *adj* single; undivided; united; the same; of a certain unspecified time; * *n* the figure 1; unity; * *pron* any single person; any individual; anything.

onerous *adj* burdensome; heavy.

one-sided *adj* partial; unfair.

one-way *adj* requiring or admitting no reciprocal action or obligation.

ongoing *adj* progressing, continuing.

onion *n* a plant, *Allium cepa*, with an edible bulb.

onlooker *n* a spectator.

only *adj* single; * *adv* for one purpose; not more than; * *conj* except that.

onomatopoeia *n* forming words by imitation of sounds, as hiss.

onset *n* an attack; an assault; a beginning.

onslaught *n* a fierce attack.

onus *n* a burden; a duty; a responsibility.

onward *adj* advancing.

ooze *n* soft mud or slime; * *vi* to issue gently; to percolate; to seep.

opaque *adj* not transparent.

open *adj* not shut; accessible; unfenced; treeless; public; candid.

opening *adj* beginning; * *n* a way in or out; a vacancy; a chance.

opera *n* a drama, set to music.

operate *vt, vi* to work; to produce an effect; to treat surgically; to control.

operation *n* action; process; procedure; surgical treatment; military action.

operative *adj* effective; functioning; * *n* a workman; factory hand.

opiate *n* a narcotic drug containing opium.

opinion *n* a belief; a notion; a judgement; an evaluation.

opium *n* a drug obtained from poppies.

opponent *n* an adversary.

opportune *adj* timely; convenient.

opportunist *n* a person who seizes opportunities for their own benefit.

oppose *vt, vi* to act against; to resist; to obstruct; to bar.

opposite *adj* facing; adverse; contrary.

opposition *n* the act of opposing; contradiction; the party opposing the government.

oppress *vt* to treat harshly; to subjugate; to weigh down in the mind.

oppressive *adj* burdensome; tyrannical; sultry, close of weather.

opt *vi* to chose or exercise an option.

optical *adj* of or relating to the eye or to optics; visual.

optician *n* one who makes or sells optical aids.

optics *n* the scientific study of sight and of the behaviour of light.

optimism *n* the tendency to take the most hopeful and cheerful view.

optimist *n* a sanguine person.

option *n* free choice.

opulence *n* wealth; riches; luxury.

or *conj* denoting; an alternative.

oral *adj* spoken; of the mouth; taken by mouth.

orange *n* a large round citrus fruit; a tree of the genus *Citrus, esp C.sinensis* or *C.aurantium* bearing this; the colour of this fruit.

oration *n* a public speech.

oratory *n* eloquence in public speaking.

orb *n* a sphere; a globe surmounted by a cross as part of royal insignia.

orbit *n* the path of a planet, etc, round the sun, etc; the eye socket; * *vt, vi* to put (a satellite) into orbit; to circle round.

orchard *n* an area planted with fruit trees.

orchestra *n* a group of musicians playing together under a conductor.

orchestral *adj* suitable for or performed by an orchestra.

ordain *vt* to consecrate (for ministry).

ordeal *n* a severe trial or test.

order *n* arrangement; method; relative position; sequence; tidiness; rules of procedure; a religious fraternity; an honour of decoration; an instruction or command; * *vt, vi* to arrange; to command.

orderly *adj* in good order; well-behaved; methodical; * *n* a hospital attendant; a soldier attending an officer.

ordinary *adj* regular; usual; normal; commonplace; unexceptional.

ordination *n* the act of ordaining or being ordained.

ore *n* rock from which metals and other minerals may be extracted.

organ *n* a musical wind instrument with pipes, stops, and a keyboard; a part of an animal or plant that performs specific vital functions.

organic *adj* pertaining to or affecting a bodily organ; of the

class of compounds that are formed from carbon; (vegetables etc) grown without the use of artificial fertilisers or pesticides.

organism *n* anything living; an organised body.

organisation *n* suitable arrange-ments for effective work; system; structure.

organise *vt* to put in working order; to establish; to institute.

orgasm *n* the climax of sexual excitement; * orgasmic *adj.*

orgy *n* a wild drunken party, *esp* with casual sexual activity.

orient, orientate *vt, vi* to adjust (one-self) to a particular situaton.

orifice *n* an opening or mouth of a cavity.

origin *n* a source; a beginning; ancestry or parentage.

original *adj* relating to the origin or beginning; novel; inventive, creative; * *n* an original work, as of art; something from which copies are made.

originate *vt, vi* to bring into being.

ornament *n* decoration; * *vt* to beautify; * ornamental *adj.*

ornate *adj* richly ornamented.

ornithology *n* the study of birds.

orphan *n, adj* a parentless child.

orphanage *n* an institution for the care of orphans.

orthodox *adj* conforming with established behaviour or opinions; not heretical.

orthopaedics *n* the study and surgical treatment of bone and joint disorders.

oscillate *vi* to swing back and forth as a pendulum.

ossify *vt, vi* to change into bone; (of habits etc) to become inflexible.

ostensible *adj* apparent; pretended.

ostentation *n* a showing off.

ostracise *vt* to exclude; to banish from society.

other *adj, pron* not the same.

ought *vi* to be bound; to be obliged.

ounce *n* a unit of weight, equal to one sixteenth of a pound or 28.34 grams.

our *adj, pron* pertaining or belonging to us.

ourselves *pron* emphatic and reflexive form of we.

oust *vt* to eject expel, *esp* by underhand means; to remove forcibly.

out *adv* not in; outside; in the open air; beyond bounds; no longer considered; on strike; extinguished; published; * *prep* outside; * *adj* external; outward; * *n* means of escape.

outbid *vt* to bid more than another.

outboard *n* an engine attached to the outside of a boat.

outbreak *n* a sudden eruption of anger, war, disease, etc.

outburst *n* an explosion of anger etc.

outcast *n* a person rejected by society.

outclass *vt* to surpass or excel greatly.

outcome *n* the issue; the result.

outcrop *n* the exposure of strata at the surface.

outcry *n* clamour; protest.

outdo *vt* to excel; to surpass.

outdoors *adv* in or into the open air.

outer *adj* external.

outfit *n* the equipment used in an activity; clothes worn together, an ensemble.

outhouse *n* a small building.

outing *n* a short excursion for pleasure.

outlaw *vt* to declare illegal; * *n* a notorious criminal.

outlay *n* expenditure.

outlet *n* an opening.

outline *n* a profile; a draft.

outlook *n* a view; a prospect.

outlying *adj* detached; remote, distant.

outmanoeuvre *vt* to surpass in strategy.

outmoded *adj* old-fashioned.

outnumber *vt* to exceed in number.

outpost *n* a military post or detachent at a distance from a main force.

output *n* the quantity (of goods, etc) produced, *esp* over a given period; information delivered by a computer; *esp* to a printer.

outrage *vt* to injure; to ravish; * *n* a gross offence, injury or insult.

outright *adv* completely; utterly.

outset *n* the beginning.

outside *n* the external surface; the exterior; * *adj* outer; outdoor.

outsider *n* a person or thing not included in a set, group, etc; a contestant not thought to have a chance in a race.

outskirts *npl* districts remote from the centre, as of a city.

outspoken *adj* frank; candid; blunt.

outstanding *adj* excellent; distinguished, prominent; unpaid; unresolved.

outstrip *vt* to outrun; to excel.

outward *adj* directed towards the outside; external.

outweigh *vt* to count for more than, to exceed in value, weight, or importance.

outwit *vt* to defeat by cunning.

oval *adj* egg-shaped.

ovary *n* one of the two female reproductive organs producing eggs.

ovation *n* an enthusiastic applause.

oven *n* an enclosed cooking or baking compartment.

over *prep* higher than; on top of, across; to the other side of; above; more than; concerning; * *adv* above; across; in every part; completed; up and down; in addition; too; * *adj* upper; excessive; surplus; finished; remaining.

overall *adj* including everything; * *adv* as a whole; generally; * *n* a loose protective garment.

overbalance *vt* to lose balance and fall.

overbearing *adj* haughty; domineering.

overboard *adv* over the side of a ship; to extremes of enthusiasm.

overcast *adj* clouded over.

overcoat *n* a warm topcoat.

overcome *vt* to subdue; to conquer; to get the better of; to render helpless or powerless, as by tears, laughter etc.

overdo *vt* to do to excess; to overcook.

overdose *n* too great a dose of a drug, etc.

overdraft *n* an overdrawing, an amount overdrawn, at a bank.

overdue *adj* past the time fixed.

overflow *vt*, *vi* to flood; to abound (with emotion etc); * *n* surplus; excess; an outlet for surplus water etc.

overflowing *adj* abundant, copious.

overgrown *adj* grown beyond the normal size; rank; ungainly.

overhang *vt*, *vi* to project over.

overhaul *vt* to examine thoroughly with a view to repairs; to overtake.

overhead *adj*, *adv* above the head; in the sky; * *n* (often *pl*) the continuing costs of a business, as of rent, light, etc.

overhear *vt* to hear by accident.

overjoyed *adj* highly delighted.

overlap *vt* (*pt* overlapped) to extend over so as to coincide in part.

overlay *vt* to coat; to smother.

overload *vt* to overburden.

overlook *vt* to superintend; to pardon; to fail to notice.

overpower *vt* to overcome; to subdue.

overreach *vt* to fail by attempting too much or going too far.

overrule *vt* prevail over.

overrun *vi* to ravage; to outrun, to swarm over; * *vi* to overflow.

overseas *adj*, *adv* abroad.

overshadow *vt* to cast into the shade; to outdo.

overshoot *vt* (*pt* overshoot) to shoot or send beyond (a target, etc); (aircraft) to fly or taxi beyond the end of a runway.

oversight *n* a mistake; an omission.

oversleep *vi* (*pt* overslept) to sleep beyond the intended time.

overstate *vt* to exaggerate.

overstep *vt* to exceed.

overt *adj* public; openly done; unconcealed; deliberate.

overtake *vt* to catch and pass.

overthrow *vt* to overturn; to defeat; * *n* ruin; defeat.

overtime *n* time beyond the regular hours; (payment for) extra time work.

overtone *n* an additional subtle meaning; an implicit quality.

overture *n* a proposal; an offer; a musical introduction to an opera.

overturn *vt* to capsize; to overthrow.

overwhelm *vt* to overpower; * overwhelming *adj* irresistible.

overwork *vt* to work beyond one's strength or too long.

owe *vt* to be indebted to; to feel the need to do or give out of gratitude.

own *adj* belonging to oneself or itself; * *vt* to possess by right.

owner *n* one who owns or possesses, a proprietor.

oxide *n* a compound of oxygen with another element.

oxygen *n* a colourless, odourless, tasteless, highly reactive gaseous element forming part of air, water, etc, and essential to life and combustion.

ozone *n* a form of oxygen with three oxygen atoms per molecule rather than two.

ozone layer *n* a layer of ozone in the upper atmosphere that absorbs ultraviolet rays from the sun.

P

pace *n* the measure of a single stride; rate of progress; * *vi* to step; to walk slowly; * *vt* to walk up and down.

pacify *vt* to calm; to allay; to restore peace to.

pack *n* a set of cards; a set of hounds; a gang; * *vt* to make up into a bundle; to fill; to crowd; * *vi* to form into a hard mass, to assemble.

package *n* a parcel; a wrapped bundle.

packet *n* a small parcel.

packing *n* wrapping material; stuffing.

pact *n* a contract; an agreement.

pad *n* a piece of stuffing, *esp* absorbent material; block of writing paper.

padding *n* anything added to achieve length or amount, *esp* in a book.

paddle *vi* to wade in shallow water; to row; * *vt* to propel by an oar or paddle; * *n* a broad short oar.

paddock *n* a grassy enclosure for horses.

paddy *n* threshed, unmilled rice; a rice field.

padlock *n* a detachable lock.

page n an attendant at a formal function; a sheet of paper in a book, newspaper, etc.

pail n a bucket.

pain n bodily suffering; distress; labour; effort; * vt to cause pain to.

painstaking adj laborious and careful.

paint vt to coat with colour; to portray; * vi to make a picture.

pair n two things of like kind; a couple; a man and his wife; * vi to join in pairs.

palace n a royal residence.

palatable adj having a pleasant taste; pleasant and acceptable.

palate n the roof of the mouth.

palatial adj spacious; magnificent.

pale n a pointed stake; a boundary; * vi to grow pale; * adj light in colour.

palette n an artist's mixing board.

pall n a mantle, as of smoke; covering on a coffin; * vi to shroud.

pallet n a portable platform used in bulk storage.

palliate vt to alleviate; to excuse.

palliative adj mitigating; * n something that eases pain.

pallor n paleness; * pallid adj.

palm n the underside of hand; a tropical tree; symbol of victory.

palpable adj perceptible by the touch; plain, obvious.

palpitate vi to throb; to tremble.

palpitation n violent pulsation of the heart.

paltry adj mean; trifling.

pamper vt to indulge to excess.

pamphlet n a small unbound book.

pan n a broad shallow vessel for cooking; the bowl of a lavatory.

panacea n a remedy for all ills.

panache n stylish behaviour.

pancake n a thin cake of cooked batter.

pancreas n a fleshy gland secreting digestive juice.

pandemonium n chaos; scene of disorder and noise.

pander vi to gratify or exploit the weaknesses of others.

pane n a plate of glass in a window.

panel n a rectangular section of door, ceiling, etc; a group of selected persons; a board for instruments or controls.

pang n a sudden pain or feeling.

panic n a sudden blind fear.

panorama n a complete view.

pant vi to gasp; to long for.

pantry n a small cupboard for provisions.

papacy n the office of the pope.

paper n thin sheets used for writing, printing, etc, a newspaper; an essay; * adj made of paper; * vt to cover with paper.

par n state of equality; normal.

parable n a religious allegory; a story with a moral lesson.

parachute n a fabric canopy used to retard speed of fall from an aircraft.

parade n display; show, muster; a promenade; * vt, vi to show off; to marshal; to walk up and down.

paradise n the garden of Eden; heaven; supreme bliss.

paradox n something containing seeming contradictory qualities or phrases.

paraffin n a distilled oil used as fuel.

paragon n a model of excellene.

paragraph n a subdivision in a piece of writing, marked by a new line.

parallax n the apparent relative change of position of objects when viewed from different points at a distance.

parallel adj equidistant at all points; * n a circle of latitude.

parallelogram n a quadrilateral, whose opposite sides are parallel.

paralyse vt to affect with paralysis; to render helpless.

paralysis n the loss of sensation and movement in any part of the body.

parapet n a wall breast-high.

paraphernalia npl belongings; trappings.

paraphrase n a restatement of a passage for clarity; * vt to interpret.

parasite n a hanger-on; a plant or animal that lives on another.

parasol n a sun shade.

parboil vt to boil partly.

parcel n a small bundle or packet.

parch vt to become hot, dry or thirsty; to scorch.

parchment *n* an animal skin prepared for writing on.

pardon *vt* to forgive; * *n* forgiveness; remission of penalty.

pare *vt* to trim by cutting; to peel.

parent *n* a father or mother; a progenitor; a source.

parentage *n* extraction; birth.

parenthesis *n* (*pl* parentheses) a written explanatory 'aside', *usu* in brackets thus ( ).

pariah *n* an outcast.

parish *n* a district served by one clergyman; * *adj* parochial.

parity *n* equality; a likeness.

park *n* a recreation field; a grass field; * *vt* to enclose; to store.

parlance *n* conversation; talk.

parley *vi* to confer, to discuss; * *n* conference, *esp* with an enemy during cessation of hostilities.

parliament *n* a legislative assembly made up of representatives of a nation.

parochial *adj* provincial in outlook; narrow-minded.

parody *n* a humorous initiation of a literary or musical work or style.

parole *n* word of honour; conditional release of a prisoner.

paroxysm *n* a fit (of rage, grief, etc).

parse *vt* to tell the parts of speech and their relations in a sentence.

parsimony *n* stinginess.

parson *n* a parish minister; a clergyman.

part *n* a portion; a section; a share; a role; (in *pl*) ability; a region; * *vi* to divide; share; break; separate; depart.

partake *vi*, *vt* to get a share of; to have or take a share in a meal.

partial *adj* only; incomplete; biased; fond of.

participate *vi*, *vt* to share in.

participle *n* a word partly verb and partly adjective.

particle *n* a minute bit of matter; the least possible amount; a minor part of speech; a prefix; a suffix.

particular *adj* single; careful; fastidious; * *n* a single item.

parting *adj* separating; final; * *n* departure; a division; a shed of the hair.

partisan *adj* biased; one-sided.

partition *n* division; a dividing wall or screen; * *vt* to divide up.

partner *n* a sharer in business, etc; either of a couple, married or unmarried.

partnership *n* fellowship; joint interest.

party *n* a company; faction; a social entertainment; a side; a political group.

pass *vi* to go past; to die; to elapse; to be enacted; to succeed in an examination; to cross; to utter.

passage *n* a way through; transit; channel; journey; part of book.

passenger *n* a traveller in a conveyance.

passing *adj* current; fleeting.

passion *n* strong feeling; great suffering; anger; love.

passionate *adj* moved by passion.

passive *adj* submissive; inert; acted on.

passport *n* an identity document issued by a state enabling foreign travel.

password *n* a secret word which gives ready entrance.

past *adj* gone by; spent; ended; * *n* former time; * *prep* beyond; * *adv* by.

paste *n* a soft plastic mass.

pasteurise *vt* to inoculate; to sterilise (milk etc).

pastime *n* recreation; play.

pastor *n* a minister of a church.

pastoral *adj* rustic; rural; relating to a pastor; * *n* a poem of rural life.

pastry *n* crust of pies, tarts, etc.

pasture *n* grass for cattle; grass land.

pasty *adj* like paste; pallid appearance.

pat *n* a tap; a small lump; * *vt* to tap.

patch *n* a repair piece; a small piece of ground; * *vt* to mend.

patchwork *n* something made of various bits, *esp* in needlework.

patella *n* the kneecap.

patent *n* grant of sole right to make or sell patented article; * *adj* open; obvious; secured by patent; * *vt* to obtain patent for.

paternal *adj* fatherly; hereditary.

path *n* a footway; a track; a course; a direction.

pathetic *adj* inspiring pity.

pathologist *n* a medical specialist in pathology.

pathology *n* the study of diseases.

patience *n* endurance; composure under trial; a card game.

patient *adj* uncomplaining; calm; * *n* an invalid.

patriarch *n* the chief of a tribe or family.

patrician *adj* high born; aristocratic; * *n* a nobleman.

patriot *n* a lover of his country.

patrol *n* a unit of persons, *esp* employed for security; their going of the rounds; * *vt*, *vi* to go the rounds, inspect, etc.

patron *n* one who encourages, helps, or protects.

patronage *n* support.

patronise *vt* to act as patron of; to favour; to treat with condescension.

patter *vi* to make a sound like that of rain or hail, or feet; * *n* chatter.

pattern *n* a model; a design.

paucity *n* scarcity; poverty.

paunch *n* the belly; *esp* of a potbelly.

pauper *n* a very poor person.

pause *n* a temporary stop.

pave *vt* to make a smooth roadway with blocks, flags, etc.

pavement *n* paved path for walkers.

pavilion *n* a large tent; a clubhouse; temporary building for exhibitions.

paw *n* the foot of animals with claws.

pawn *n* a security; piece of least value (chess); * *vt* to give in pledge.

pawnbroker *n* a person licensed to lend money on pledged goods.

pay *vt*, *vi* to give money for goods, service etc; to reward; to bestow (attention, etc); * *n* wages; salary.

payable *adj* due on a certain date.

payee *n* one to whom money is to be paid.

payment *n* what is paid.

peace *n* quiet; calm; freedom from war or disorder.

peaceable *adj* disposed to peace.

peaceful *adj* quiet; calm; mild.

peak *n* pointed top of hill; projection on cap; highest point.

peal *n* a loud clash; a clang; chime; loud laughter; * *vi* to ring out.

pearl *n* a *usu* white hard mass formed within the shell of oysters and other bi-valves prized as a gem.

peasant *n* a rural labourer.

peat *n* partly carbonised turf used as fuel.

pebble *n* small water-worn stone.

peccadillo *n* a petty fault or sin.

peck *n* a quick kiss; * *vi*, *vt* to strike or pick up with the beak.

peckish *adj* hungry.

pectoral *adj* pertaining to the breast or chest; thoracic.

peculiar *adj* one's own; particular; special; odd; * **peculiarity** *n*.

pecuniary *adj* financial; relating to money.

pedal *adj* pertaining to a foot; * *n* any of various foot operated levers or controls; * *vt*, *vi* to work a pedal.

pedestal *n* the base of a column, etc.

pedestrian *n* a person who walks.

pedigree *n* lineage; ancestry.

peddler *n* one who sells small goods from place to place.

peel *vt* to strip off skin, *esp* of fruit; to bare; * *vi* to lose the skin, bark, or rind; * *n* the skin or rind.

peep *vi* to look through a slit; * *n* a furtive or hurried glance.

peer *n* an equal; a nobleman; * *vi* to peep out; to look closely or with difficulty.

peerage *n* the rank or title of a peer.

peerless *adj* matchless.

peevish *adj* fretful; querulous.

peg *n* a wooden nail, pin, or bolt.

pellet *n* a little ball; a pill; small shot.

pelt *n* a raw hide; a blow; * *vt*, *vi* to assault (with stones, etc); to fall heavily (as rain); to hurry; to rush.

pelvis *n* the bony framework which joins the lower limbs to the body.

pen *n* an instrument for writing, drawing, etc; enclosure for livestock; * *vt* to write; to coop up.

penal *adj* involving punishment.

penalty *n* due punishment; a fine.

pence *n* plural of penny.

penchant *n* bias; liking.

pencil *n* an instrument for drawing; a fine paintbrush.

pendant *n* a hanging ornament.

pendent *adj* hanging; pendulous.

pendulous *adj* hanging; swinging.

pendulum *n* a weight suspended
and swinging (as in a clock).

penetrate *vt, vi* to enter or pierce.

penetrating *adj* sharp; discerning.

peninsula *n* land almost surrounded by water.

penitent *adj* repentant; contrite.

pennant *n* a long pointed flag at
masthead.

penny *n* (*pl* pennies or pence)
pennies denotes the number of
coins (pence the value); a copper
coin equal in value to one one
hundredth of a pound sterling.

pension *n* a periodic payment for
past services or old age; a
boarding house.

pensioner *n* one in receipt of a
pension.

pensive *adj* thoughtful; grave.

pentagon *n* a plane figure having
five sides.

penthouse *n* a top floor apartment.

penultimate *adj* the last but one.

penury *n* poverty; want.

people *n* human beings; a nation; a
race; a person's family; *pl* persons;
the masses; * *vt* to populate.

pepper *n* a hot aromatic spice
made from the dried berries of
various plants; any climbing
vine of the genus *Piper, esp
P.nigrum*, which yields this berry.

perambulate *vt* to walk up and down.

perceive *vt* to apprehend; understand.

percentage *n* the duty, rate, etc,
on each hundred.

perceptible *adj* discernible.

perch *n* any edible freshwater fish
of the genus *Perca, esp P.fluviatis*,
with spiny fins; a roost for fowls;
an elevated position.

percolate *vt* to filter through.

percolator *n* a strainer or filter.

percussion *n* collision; impact;
sounding (medical); musical
instruments *usu* played with
sticks or hammers.

peremptory *adj* urgent; dictatorial.

perennial *adj* lasting through the
year; never-ending.

perfect *adj* complete; flawless.

perfidy *n* treachery.

perforate *vt* tto pierce.

perform *vt* to do; * *vi* to act a part.

performance *n* achievement; deed;
entertainment (musical, etc).

perfume *n* a pleasant scent;
fragrance; * *vt* to scent.

perfunctory *adj* careless; half-
hearted; indifferent.

perhaps *adv* it may be; possibly.

peril *n* risk; danger.

perimeter *n* a boundary around.

period *n* a portion of time; an age;
full stop (.); menstruation.

periodic *adj* regular.

periodical *n* a publication issued
weekly, monthly, etc.

periphery *n* the boundary line of a
figure.

perish *vi* to die; to decay.

perjure *vt* to bear false witness.

perjury *n* false evidence duration.

permanent *adj* lasting; abiding.

permeable *adj* allowing the
passage of fluid, gases, etc.

permeate *vt* to pass through the
pores; to pervade.

permission *n* leave; consent.

permissive *adj* allowing but not
compelled.

permit *vt, vi* to allow; to grant; to
concede; * *n* a written permission.

permutation *n* interchange;
(maths), all the possible
reorderings of a set.

pernicious *adj* deadly; noxious.

perpendicular *adj* upright; at
right angles; * *n* a line at right
angles to another.

perpetrate *vt* to commit.

perpetual *adj* unending; eternal.

perpetuate *vt* to make lasting.

perpetuity *n* endless duration; an
annuity payable forever.

perplex *vt* to confuse; to puzzle.

persecute *vt* to harrass a person,
esp on the grounds of their belief.

persevere *vi* to pursue steadily
any design.

persist *vi* to persevere; stand firm.

person *n* a human being; the body;
a verb inflexion.

personal *adj* individual; private;
one's own; unkind (remarks).

personality *n* one's individual
characteristics; a celebrity.

personification *n* embodiment; a

metaphor ascribing life to inanimate objects.

personify *vt* to embody; to endow with human qualities.

personnel *n* the staff.

perspective *n* the art of representing objects on a flat surface as they are to the eye; objectivity.

perspire *vi* to sweat.

persuade *vt* to influence by argument, etc; to induce.

persuasive *adj* convincing; winning.

pert *adj* lively; saucy; forward.

pertain *vi* to belong; to concern.

pertinent *adj* to the point.

perturb *vt* to disturb; to disquiet.

perturbation *n* uneasiness; disquiet; (maths, physics) a small change to a system.

perusal *n* reading; study.

peruse *vt* to read through; to examine carefully.

pervade *vt* to permeate; to spread throughout.

perversion *n* corruption; misuse; * **perverse** *adj* obstinate in being wrong.

perversity *n* obstinacy; wickedness.

pervert *vt* to corrupt; to misapply; * *n* a person who is perverted.

pessimism *n* tendency to make or expect the worst of everything.

pest *n* a plague; a nuisance.

pestilence *n* a deadly epidemic.

pestle *n* an instrument for grinding material.

pet *n* a darling; a favourite; a domestic animal kept as a companion; * *adj* cherished; * *vt* to fondle.

petal *n* a flower leaf.

petite *adj* tiny; dainty.

petition *n* an entreaty; a written demand for government action etc signed by many.

petrify *vt* to turn into stone; to paralyse or stupefy with terror.

petrol *n* refined petroleum.

petroleum *n* natural mineral oil.

petty *adj* small; trivial; small minded.

petulant *adj* irritable; fretful.

pew *n* a seat in a church.

pewter *n* an alloy of tin and lead.

phantom *n* an apparition; a spectre.

pharmaceutical *adj* pertaining to the dispensing of drugs.

pharmacy *n* the preparation and dispensing of drugs; a drug store.

phase *n* a stage; an aspect.

phenomenal *adj* astounding.

phenomenon *n* (*pl* **phenomena**) an occurrence that is perceived, *esp* when the cause is unknown; a remarkable thing or person.

phial *n* a small glass bottle.

philanthropic *adj* benevolent.

philanthropy *n* the love of mankind; benevolence; charitable actions.

philately *n* stamp collecting.

philology *n* the study of language, linguistic science.

philosopher *n* a person who studies philosophy.

philosophically *adv* calmly; wisely; serenely.

philosophy *n* the application of reason to in seeking knowledge of reality, *esp* the nature of things and the principles governing existence; a particular system of ethics.

phlegm *n* the secretion of the mucous membrane discharged in coughing, etc.

phlegmatic *adj* stolidly calm; unemotional.

phone *n* a contraction of telephone.

phonetic *adj* pertaining to vocal sound.

phosphate *n* a salt of phosphoric acid.

phosphorescence *n* emission of light without combustion.

phosphorus *n* a non-metallic element.

photograph *n* a picture obtained by photography.

photography *n* the art of recording images permanently and visibly by action of light on prepared plates.

phrase *n* a related group of words; diction; style.

phrenetic *adj* frantic.

physical *adj* relating to matter and energy, the human body, or natural science; * *n* a general medical examination.

physician *n* a doctor of medicine.

physicist *n* a specialist in physics.

physics *n* the science dealing with the properties and interactions of matter and energy.

physiology *n* the science of bodily structures, organs, and functions.

physique *n* physical frame.

pianist *n* a performer on the piano.

piano *n* a large stringed keyboard instrument.

piazza *n* a square surrounded by colonnades.

piccolo *n* a small flute.

pick *vt*, *vi* to pluck; to choose; to nibble; * *n* a pickaxe; choice.

pickaxe *n* an excavating axe.

picket *n* a pointed stake; a military guard; a preventive guard against strikebreakers; * *vt* to post (soldiers, etc); to tether.

pickle *n* brine; vegetables preserved in vinegar; plight.

picnic *n* an informal meal taken on an outing and eaten outdoors.

picture *n* a painting, drawing, motion picture; * *vt* to portray.

picturesque *adj* striking, vivid, *usu* pleasing.

pie *n* meat or fruit with pastry covering baked; unsorted type.

piece *n* a portion; a distinct part; a short composition or writing; a coin.

piecemeal *adv* in or by pieces.

piecework *n* work paid by quantity; not by time.

pier *n* stone column supporting arch, etc; a wharf or landing stage.

pierce *vt* to perforate.

piercing *adj* penetrating; cutting.

piety *n* religious devoutness.

pig *n* a hog; a bar of smelted iron.

pigeon *n* a bird with a small head and a large body.

pigment *n* colouring matter.

pile *n* a heap; a large amount; a massive building; a supporting pillar driven into the ground; * *vt* to heap.

piles *npl* see haemorrhoids.

pilfer *vi* to steal on a small scale.

pilgrim *n* a person who makes a pilgrimage.

pilgrimage *n* a journey, *esp* to a holy place.

pill *n* a medicine in a tablet form; an oral contraceptive.

pillage *n* spoil; * *vt* to plunder.

pillar *n* a supporting column,

pillion *n* a cushion on back of saddle for a passenger.

pillow *n* a cushion for the head while sleeping.

pilot *n* a person who operates a ship or an aircraft; a guide; * *vt* to direct the course of; to act as a pilot; to guide.

pimp *n* a prostitute's agent.

pimple *n* a small red swelling on skin.

pin *n* a short pointed piece of metal for fastening clothes; a peg; a bolt; * *vi* to fasten.

pincers *npl* nippers; gripping claws.

pinch *vt* to cramp; to be sparing; * *n* a nip; distress; need; small portion.

pine *n* any coniferous tree of the genus *pinus*; * *vi* to languish.

pink *n* a garden flower; a pale red colour; excellence; * *vt* to stab.

pinnacle *n* a turret; pointed peak; the highest point; climax.

pint *n* a liquid measure equal to one eighth of a gallon.

pioneer *n* a person who explores new areas of enterprise, research, etc; an explorer; * *vt* to initiate.

pious *adj* devout; religious; sanctimonious.

pip *n* the seed of a fleshy fruit; spot on cards, dice, etc.

pipe *n* a musical instrument; long tube conveying gas, water, etc; shrill voice; tobacco-smoking apparatus; * *vt* (musical) to play on a pipe.

piquant *adj* sharp; pungent.

pique *n* irritation; resentment; * *vt*, *vi* to cause resentment in; to offend.

piracy *n* a robbery at sea; infringement of copyright.

pirate *n* one who commits piracy; an breaker of copyright.

pirouette *n* spinning round on toe in ballet.

piscatorial *adj* of or relating to fish or fishing.

pistil *n* the seed-bearing organ of a flower.

pistol *n* a mall firearm fired with one hand.

piston *n* a metal plug which slides to and fro in the cylinder of an engine, pump, etc.

pit *n* a hollow in the earth; a mine; a depression in skin; orchestra space in a theatre; * *vt* to mark with little hollows.

pitch *vt* to fix in ground; to throw; to set the keynote of; * *vi* to fall headlong; to encamp; to rise and fall, as a ship; * *n* a throw; highest rise; elevation of a note; a thick dark substance obtained from tar.

pitcher *n* a vessel for carrying liquids.

pitchfork *n* a fork for pitching hay.

piteous *adj* arousing pity.

pitfall *n* concealed danger; a trap.

pith *n* the soft centre of stem of plant; marrow; essence.

pitiable *adj* deserving pity.

pittance *n* a small quantity or allowance of money.

pity *n* sympathy or compassion; * *vt* to grieve for.

pivot *n* that on which something turns or depends.

placard *n* a poster or notice for public display.

placate *vt* to appease.

place *n* an open space in a town; a locality; position; room; passage in book; rank; office; * *vt* to put or set; to locate.

placid *adj* calm; tranquil.

plagiarism *n* the act of taking and using (the words, thoughts, etc of another) as one's own.

plague *n* a deadly epidemic; pestilence; nuisance.

plain *adj* smooth; level; evident; un-flavoured; * *n* a tract of level land.

plaintiff *n* a person who brings a lawsuit against another.

plaintive *adj* mournful.

plait *n* a fold; a braid, as of hair, etc; * *vt* to fold; to braid.

plan *n* the ground shape of an object; scheme; process; method; * *vt* to scheme; to design.

plane *adj* level; flat; * *n* smooth surface; joiner's smoothing tool; an aeroplane; * *vt* to make smooth.

planet *n* a celestial body orbiting a star.

planetary *adj* under the influence of one of the planets.

plank *n* a flat broad piece of timber.

plant *n* a vegetable organism; an herb; a shoot; industrial machinery and equipment; * *vt* to set in ground; to establish.

plantation *n* a cultivated planting of trees; a tropical estate.

plaque *n* an ornamental plate; a deposit on teeth that harbours bacteria.

plasma *n* the colourless liquid part of blood, milk or lymph.

plaster *n* a cement for covering walls; a preparation for casts, etc; adhesive dressing for wounds or relief of pain.

plastic *adj* easily shaped or moulded; any of various non-metallic compounds, syntheti-cally produced.

plasticine *n* a modelling clay.

plate *n* a flat piece of metal, glass, etc; a shallow dish for meals; * *vt* to coat with gold, etc.

plateau *n* a flat, elevated piece of land; a stable period.

platform *n* a raised structure for speaking from, entering trains.

plating *n* the art of covering articles with metal.

platinum *n* a lustrous precious silvery-white metal.

platitude *n* a dull truism; a commonplace remark.

platonic *adj* free from physical desire.

platoon *n* a military unit divided into squads or sections.

platter *n* a large, oval serving dish.

plaudit *n* a commendation.

plausible *adj* apparently truthful or reasonable.

play *vi*, *vt* to sport; frolic; gamble; act; engage in games; perform upon; * *n* free movement; a game; sport; gaming; a drama.

player *n* an actor; musician; sportsman, sportswoman.

playschool *n* a nursery for pre-school children.

plaything *n* a toy.

playwright *n* a writer of plays.

plea *n* an answer to a charge; an entreaty; a request.

plead *vi, vt* to argue for or against; to answer to a charge; to urge; to beg earnestly; to urge in excuse.

pleading *n* statement of facts for or against a claim.

pleasant *adj* pleasing; agreeable.

pleasantry *n* a polite or amusing remark.

please *vt, vi* to satisfy; to give pleasure to; to be willing; * *adv* a word to expressing a request; an expression of polite affirmation.

pleasing *adj* agreeable; giving pleasure.

pleasure *n* enjoyment; recreation; preference.

plebian adj, *n* relating to the common people; base; vulgar.

plebiscite *n* a vote of the whole electorate on a political issue.

plectrum *n* a thin piece of metal, etc for plucking strings of guitar, etc.

pledge *n* something given in security; a surety; a toast.

plenary *adj* full; complete; attended by all members.

plenitude *n* fullness; abundance.

plentiful *adj* ample; abundant.

plenty *n* more than enough.

plethora *n* overabundance.

pleura *n (pl pleurae)* the membrane enveloping the lungs.

pleurisy *n* an inflammation of the pleura.

pliable *adj* supple; pliant.

pliant *adj* flexible.

pliers *npl* a hand tool for cutting, shaping wire.

plight *vt* a pledge; predicament.

plinth *n* square slab forming the base of a column.

plot *n* a small piece of ground; a plan; a conspiracy; the story of a play, novel, etc; * *vt* to devise; to conspire; to mark on a map.

plough *n* an implement for turning up the soil; * *vt, vi* to furrow.

pluck *vt* to pick or gather; to snatch; to strip off feathers; * *n* courage.

plug *n* a stopper used for filling a hole; a device for connecting an appliance to an electrical supply; a cake of tobacco; * *vt* to stop with a plug.

plumage *n* the feathers of a bird.

plumb *n* a lead weight attached to a line used to determine the vertical; * *adv* vertically.

plumber *n* a person who installs and repairs water or gas pipes.

plumbing *n* the system of pipes used in water or gas supply, or drainage.

plume *n* a bird's feather.

plummet *vt* to fall in a perpendicular manner; to drop abruptly.

plump *adj* rounded; chubby.

plunder *vt* to steal goods by force; to loot; * *n* plundering; booty.

plunge *vt* to thrust into water; to immerse; to penetrate quickly; * *vi* to dive into water, etc; to rush into; * *n* a dive.

plunger *n* a large rubber suction cup used to free clogged drains.

plural *adj* denoting more than one; * *n (gr)* the form referring to more than one person or thing.

plus *prep* added to; in addition to.

plush *n* a velvety fabric; * *adj (inj)* luxurious.

ply *vt, vi* to work at; to wield skilfully; to press hard; to voyage or journey regularly; (goods) to sell; * *n* a layer or thickness.

pneumatic *adj* concerning wind, air or gas; operated by or filled with compressed air.

pneumonia *n* an acute inflammation of the lungs.

poach *vt* to cook (eggs) by breaking into boiling water; * *vi* take game illegally.

pocket *n* a small pouch in a garment, etc; a deposit, as of gas, minerals, etc; an isolated or closed area; * *vt* to put in one's pocket; to take dishonestly.

pod *n* the seed vessel of plants; a protective container.

poem *n* an imaginative arrangement of words, *esp* in meter, often rhymed.

poet *n* the author of a poem.

poetry *n* poems collectively.

pogrom *n* an organised extermination of a minority group.

poignant *adj* incisive; deeply moving.

point *n* the sharp end of anything; a headland; a dot; a moment in time; purpose; essence; railway switch; * *vt, vi* to indicate; to sharpen; to aim.

point-blank *adj* aimed straight at a mark; direct, blunt.

pointed *adj* sharp; personal.

pointer *n* an indicator.

poise *n* a balanced state; bearing; carriage; * *vt* to balance; to put into readiness; * *vi* to hover.

poison *n* a substance which when absorbed is fatal or injurious to an organism; any corrupt influence; * *vt* to give poison to; to taint; to corrupt.

poke *n* a bag or sack; a prod or nudge; * *vt* to prod; to hit; * *vi* (~ about, ~ around) to pry or search.

poker *n* an iron rod for poking a fire; a card game.

polar *adj* of or near the North or South pole; of a pole; having positive and negative charge; directly opposite.

pole *n* a long slender piece of wood, metal, etc; each extremity of the earth or any other rotating body; the points on a magnet at which the field is strongest.

police *n* the government department for maintaining public order.

policy *n* system or manner of government; principle or course of action; an insurance contract.

polish *vt, vi* to make smooth and glossy; to refine; * *n* gloss; elegance.

polite *adj* polished in manners; refined; elegant.

politic *adj* prudent; astute.

politician *n* a person engaged in politics.

politics *n* the science and art of government; political activities.

poll *n* a counting, listing, etc of persons; the number of votes recorded; an opinion survey; * *vt* to cast a vote.

pollen *n* the fine, powder-like material found in the anthers of flowers, containing the male gametes.

pollinate *vt* to fertilise (a flower) with pollen.

pollute *vt* to contaminate with harmful substances; to make corrupt.

pollution *n* contamination by chemicals, noise, etc.

polo *n* a game resembling hockey, played on horseback.

polygamy *n* the practice of being married to more than one person at a time.

polyglot *adj* having command of many languages; composed of several languages; * *n* a person who speaks several languages.

polygon *n* a plane figure of three or more sides.

polystyrene *n* a rigid plastic material used for packing, insulation, etc.

polytechnic *n* an institution that provides instruction in many applied sciences and technical subjects.

polyurethane *n* any of various polymers that are used *esp* in flexible and rigid foams, resins, etc.

pompous *adj* pretentious; self-important; * pomposity *n*.

pond *n* a body of standing water smaller than a lake.

ponder *vt* to consider carefully.

ponderous *adj* heavy; awkward; dull.

pontiff *n* the Pope; a bishop.

pontoon *n* a boat or float forming a support for a bridge.

pony *n* a small horse.

pool *n* a small pond; a swimming pool; a puddle; a combination of resources for a common purpose; a form of billiards.

poor *adj* having little money; needy; unfortunate; deficient.

pop *n* a short, explosive sound; any carbonated beverage; a shot; * *adj* in a popular modern style.

Pope *n* the head of the Roman Catholic church.

populace *n* the common people; all the people in a country, region, etc.

popular *adj* well-liked; common.

population *n* the inhabitants; total number of people in an area.

populous *adj* densely inhabited.

porcelain *n* the variety of ceramic ware.

porch *n* a covered entry to a building.

pore *n* a minute opening in the skin; a small interstice; * *vi* to examine or study with care.

pork *n* the flesh of a pig, used as food.

pornography *n* pictures, films, etc, intended primarily to arouse sexual desire, and *usu* considered obscene.

porridge *n* a food made from oatmeal boiled in water or milk.

port *n* a harbour; a gate; a porthole; the left side of a ship; a circuit in a computer for the transferring of data; a Portuguese fortified red wine.

portable *adj* able to be carried.

portal *n* a door or gate.

portend *vt* to give warning of; to foreshadow.

portent *n* an omen; a warning.

porter *n* a doorkeeper; a carrier.

portfolio *n* a case for drawings, papers etc; office of minister of state; a list of stocks, shares, etc.

portion *n* a part; a share; fate; * *vt* to divide.

portrait *n* a picture of a person; a vivid description.

portray *vt* to depict.

pose *n* attitude or position; * *vi, vt* to strike an attitude; to assert; to sit for a painting, photograph, etc.

poser *n* a difficult problem; a person who poses.

position *n* place; situation; posture; rank; a job; point of view.

positive *adj* explicit; absolute; confident; affirmative; noting the simple form of an adjective; a form of electricity; greater than zero.

possess *vt* to have and hold; to own.

possession *n* ownership; occupancy.

possessive *adj* denoting possession; * *n* the possessive case.

possible *adj* that may be or exist; practicable.

post *n* a piece of timber, etc, set upright; a place assigned.

postage *n* the charge for conveyance by post.

postcard *n* a card on which a short message is written, send by post.

poster *n* a large printed bill for advertising.

posterior *adj* later or subsequent; * *n* the buttocks.

posterity *n* future generations.

postgraduate *n* a person persuing further study after a first degree.

posthaste *adv* with all speed.

posthumous *adj* given or occurring after one's death.

postman *n* a mail carrier.

postmortem *adj* an autopsy; after death

post office *n* a place where postal business is conducted.

postpone *vt* to delay; defer.

postscript *n* an addition to a letter after signature.

postulate *n* self-evident truth; assumption; * *vt* to state; assume.

posture *n* an attitude; a body position; a stand.

pot *n* a vessel for holding or boiling liquids; vessel for holding plants; frame for catching fish, lobsters, etc; * *vt* to plant in pot; to shoot.

potash *n* potassium carbonate.

potassium *n* a metallic element.

potato *n* a starchy plant tuber used as food; the plant *Solanum tuberosum.*

potency *n* power; force.

potentate *n* one who possesses great power; a monarch.

potential *adj* unrealised ability.

potion *n* a mixture of liquids.

potpourri *n* a mixture of scented, dried flowers; a medley.

pottery *n* earthenware; workshop where it is made.

pouch *n* a pocket; a small bag.

poultice *n* a moist dressing applied to sore parts of the body.

poultry *n* domestic birds kept for meat or eggs.

pounce *n* to fall on suddenly.

pound *n* a monetary unit; a place of confinement or temporary holding; * *vt* to beat; to pulverise; * *vi* to strike repeatedly; to throb; to work hard.

pour *vi* to flow continuously; to rain heavily; to serve liquid refreshment.

pout *vi* to thrust out the lips; to look sulky; * *n* a sullen look.

poverty *n* want; the condition of being poor.

powder *n* fine particles; dust; gunpowder; * *vt, vi* to reduce to, or sprinkle with, powder; to salt.

power *n* ability to act or do; strength; influence; talent; command; authority; a state or government; warrant; a mechanical advantage or effect.

practicable *adj* feasible; possible.

practical *adj* skilful in work; useful; handy.

practice *n* custom; habit; exercise of any profession; training; drill.

practise *vt, vi* to do frequently or habitually; to act in a profession.

practitioner *n* one who practises a profession (*esp* medicine).

pragmatic *adj* practical; testing all concepts by their practical results.

prairie *n* an extensive tract of grassy land.

praise *vt* to express approval of; to commend; to worship.

pram *n* four-wheeled carriage for a baby.

prance *vi* to spring on the hind legs.

prank *n* a mischievous trick or joke.

prattle *vi* to talk much and idly.

pray *vi, vt* to ask reverently.

prayer *n* supplication; entreaty; praise or give thanks to God.

preach *vi* to deliver a sermon; to give earnest advice; * *vt* to proclaim.

preamble *n* introductory part of a story, speech, etc.

precarious *adj* uncertain; insecure.

precaution *n* a preventative measure; careful foresight.

precede *vt* to go before; to preface.

precedence *n* priority; order according to rank.

precedent *n* a parallel case serving as example.

precept *n* rule of conduct; maxim.

precious *adj* of great worth or value; very fastidious; affected.

precipice *n* a cliff or overhanging rock face.

precipitate *vt, vi* to hurl headlong; to sink to the bottom of a vessel; to bring down (moisture); * *adj*

headlong; overhasty; * *n* a deposit from a liquid.

precipitation *n* rash haste; rain, snow, etc.

precipitous *adj* very steep.

précis *n* a summary; abstract.

precise *adj* exact; definite; punctilious; particular.

precision *n* exactness; accuracy.

preclude *vt* to shut out; to prevent; to make impossible.

precocious *adj* prematurely ripe; forward.

precocity *n* too early development.

preconceive *vt* to form an opinion beforehand.

precursor *n* a forerunner; omen.

predator *n* a person who preys, plunders or devours.

predecessor *n* one who was in office before another.

predetermine *vt, vi* to determine beforehand.

predicament *n* a quandary; critical position.

predict *vt* to foretell.

predilection *n* a previous preference.

predispose *vt* to incline beforehand.

predominant *adj* outstanding; superior.

preen *vt* (birds) to trim the feathers; to groom oneself.

preface *n* an introduction; foreword; * *vt* to introduce by preliminary remarks.

prefect *n* person placed in authority; a senior pupil in a school.

prefer *vt* to like better; to advance.

preferable *adj* more desirable.

preference *n* choice; favour; prior claim.

preferential *adj* implying preference.

preferment *n* promotion.

prefix *vt* to put at the beginning; * *n* a letter or syllable put at beginning of a word.

pregnant *adj* having a foetus in the womb; significant; filled with.

prehistoric *adj* prior to time of written records.

prejudge *vt* to condemn beforehand.

prejudice *n* bias; prejudgement; intolerance; * *vt* to affect through prejudice.

preliminary *adj* introductory.

prelude *vt* to preface; * *n* a musical introduction.

premature *adj* too early; untimely.

premeditate *vt*, *vi* to plan beforehand.

premier *adj* first; principal; * *n* a head of state.

premiere *n* the first public performance of a play, film, etc.

premise *n* a proposition on which reasoning is based; something assumed.

premises *n* a building and its adjuncts.

premium *n* a reward; a bonus; sum paid for insurance.

premonition *n* a foreboding; a feeling that something is about to happen.

preoccupied *adj* engrossed; lost on thought.

preparatory *adj* introductory.

prepare *vt*, *vi* to make ready.

preponderant *adj* superior in power, influence, etc.

preposition *n* a word used before a noun or pronoun to show its relation to mother part of the sentence.

prepossess *vt* to influence in advance; to prejudice.

prepossessing *adj* attractive.

prepossession *n* preconceived opinion; prejudice.

preposterous *adj* absurd; utterly ridiculous.

prerogative *n* a prior claim; an exclusive privilege; hereditary right.

presage *n* omen; * *vi* to betoken; to forebode.

prescience *n* foreknowledge.

prescribe *vi* to lay down authoritatively; to direct medically.

prescription *n* a written direction for preparing a medicine; a claim or title based on long use.

prescriptive *adj* based on and acquired by long use.

presence *n* state of being visible; appearance; personality; something (as a spirit) felt or believed to be present.

present *adj* being at hand, in view; now existing; ready at hand;

quick; * at ~ *n* now; a gift; *pl* law term for document itself (these presents); * *vt* to introduce; to show; to give or bestow; to nominate to a benefice; to point or aim.

presentable *adj* suitable for presenting.

presently *adv* in a short while; soon.

preservation *n* the act of preserving.

preservative *adj* tending to preserve; * *n* something that preserves, *esp* a food additive.

preserve *vt* to save from injury; to keep in a sound state; to maintain; * *n* fruit, vegetables, etc, treated with a preservative; jam; a restricted area.

preside *vi* to direct or control (a meeting); to take the chair.

presidency *n* the office of president.

president *n* the head of state of a republic; chairman.

press *vt* to weigh down; to urge; to enforce; to emphasise; to embrace; * *vi* to push with force; * *n* a pressing; a crowd; a machine for crushing or squeezing; a printing machine; printing; newspapers.

pressing *adj* urgent.

pressure *n* a weighing down; force; influence; urgency.

prestige *n* influence based on character or conduct.

presume *vt*, *vi* to take for granted; to infer; to act in a forward way.

presumption *n* arrogance; supposition.

pretence *n* act of pretending.

pretend *vt*, *vi* to claim, represent, or assert falsely; to feign.

pretentious *adj* claiming great importance; ostentatious.

pretext *n* a pretence; excuse.

pretty *adj* attractive; pleasing; * *adv* moderately; fairly.

prevail *vi* to overcome; to be in force; to succeed; to persuade.

prevalence *n* superior strength or influence; general diffusion.

prevalent *adj* prevailing; dominant; widespread.

prevaricate *vi* to make evasive or misleading statements.

prevent *vt* to stop or impede.
previous *adj* antecedent; prior.
prey *n* a victim; animal killed for food by another; * *vi* to victimise.
price *n* the value of a commodity; cost; worth.
priceless *adj* invaluable.
prick *n* a sharp point; puncture or piercing; * *vt* to puncture.
pride *n* self-esteem; conceit; delight; * *vt* to be proud of.
priest *n* in various churches, a person authorised to perform sacred rites.
prim *adj* formal; demure.
primacy *n* the office of primate or archbishop.
primal *adj* primary; primitive; fundamental.
primary *adj* first; chief, elementary; first in order of time.
primate *n* any animal of the order *Primates*, the highest order of mammals, including lemurs, monkeys, apes and humans.
prime *adj* original; not divisible by any smaller number; best quality.
primer *n* child's first reader; first coat of paint; a detonating device.
primeval *adj* primitive; original.
primitive *adj* original; antiquated; primary.
primordial *adj* first of all; original.
prince *n* the son of a king or emperor; * **princely** *adj*.
principal *n* head of a school, firm, etc; chief in authority; capital sum lent at interest; * *adj* first; chief; most important.
principality *n* a state whose head is a prince; the government of a prince.
principle *n* cause or origin; a general truth; a fundamental law; a rule of conduct; uprightness.
print *vt* to mark by pressure; to stamp; to copy by pressure; * *vi* to publish; * *n* a mark made by pressure; an engraving, etc; a newspaper; printed calico.
printing *n* the art or process of making impressions on paper, cloth, etc.
prior *adj* preceding; earlier; * *n* a monk next in rank to an abbot.

priority *n* precedence; first claim.
priory *n* a religious house ruled by a prior(ess).
prise *vt* to force up.
prism *n* a solid whose ends are any identical, and parallel plane figures; a lens of this shape for decomposing light.
prison *n* a place of confinement; a jail; * *vt* to imprison.
pristine *adj* original; first.
privacy *n* seclusion; secrecy.
private *adj* separate from others; personal; secret; * *n* a common soldier.
privation *n* destitution; hardship.
privilege *n* a prerogative, benefit, or right; * *vt* to authorise; to exempt.
privy *adj* private; clandestine; admitted to the knowledge of (*with* to).
prize *n* that which is seized from an enemy; a reward of merit; * *vi* to value highly.
probability *n* likelihood.
probable *adj* likely; credible.
probate *n* the official proof of a will; confirmation.
probation *n* proof; period of trial.
probe *vt* to explore; to examine carefully.
probity *n* uprightness; honesty.
problem *n* a question for solution; a knotty point.
proboscis *n* the trunk of an elephant, etc; the sucking tube of insects.
procedure *n* mode of conducting business; conduct.
proceed *vi* to go forward; to issue.
proceeding *n* transaction; procedure.
proceeds *npl* money brought in by a transaction.
process *n* progressive course; method of operation; legal proceedings; a writ.
procession *n* a body of people on the march.
processional *adj* relating to a procession; * *n* a service book as guide for religious processions.
proclaim *vt* to announce publicly; to publish.
proclamation *n* an official public announcement.

proclivity n inclination; tendency.

procrastinate vt, vi to put off; to postpone unduly.

procreation n the begetting of young.

procurator n the manager of another's affairs; legal agent or prosecutor.

procure vt to obtain; to cause.

prod n a goad; a nudge; a stab.

prodigal adj lavish; wasteful; * n a waster; a spendthrift.

prodigious adj portentous; enormous.

prodigy n a gifted child; an extraordinary person, thing or act.

produce vt, vi to bring forward; to exhibit; to bear, yield; to cause; to extend; * n outcome; yield.

product n result; effect.

production n fruit; product; performance.

productive adj fertile; fruitful.

profane adj blasphemous; impure; * vt to treat with irreverence; to pollute.

profanity n profane language or conduct.

profess vt to avow; to acknowledge; to pretend; * vi to declare openly.

profession n open avowal; vocation; calling; members of a profession.

professional adj pertaining to a profession; * n one who makes his living by arts, sports, etc, as distinguished from an amateur.

professor n a member of staff of a university holding a chair.

proffer vt to offer for acceptance.

proficiency n expertness; degree of advancement.

proficient adj fully versed; competent; * n an adept or expert.

profile n an outline; the side face or outline of it.

profit n any advantage, benefit, or gain; * vt to benefit; * vi to derive profit; to improve.

profitable adj lucrative; useful.

profligate adj dissolute; openly vicious; * n a depraved man.

profound adj deep; deep in skill or knowledge; far-reaching.

profundity n depth.

profuse adj lavish; exuberant.

progeny n offspring; descendants.

prognosis n a forecast of the course of a disease.

prognosticate vt to foretell; to predict.

programme n a plan of proceedings; list of items at a concert, etc.

progress n a going forward; a journey of state; advance; * vi to advance; to improve.

progressive adj forward; liberal; increasing by degrees.

prohibit vt to forbid; to prevent.

prohibition n an interdict; veto on sale of intoxicants.

prohibitive adj excessive.

project vt, vi to hurl; to scheme; to delineate; to jut; * n a scheme, plan.

projectile adj throwing forward; * n a missile; a bullet or shell.

projection n a prominence; plan or outline on a plane surface.

projector n a company promoter.

prolapse n a displacement of an internal organ.

proletariat n the toiling masses.

prolific adj fruitful.

prologue n introduction; speech, usu in verse, introducing a drama.

prolong vt to lengthen out.

prominent adj jutting out; eminent.

promiscuous adj indiscriminate, esp in sexual relations.

promise n an undertaking to do or not do something; pledge; * vt, vi to give one's word; to show promise of; * **promissory** adj.

promote vt to forward; to encourage; to exalt; to form (a company).

promotion n advancement; furtherance.

prompt adj ready; unhesitating; * vi to incite to action; to whisper (words to actor, etc).

prone adj lying face-downwards; inclined; apt.

prong n a spike, as of a fork.

pronoun n a word used instead of a noun; * **pronominal** adj.

pronounce vt to articulate; to utter; to affirm.

pronouncement n a definite statement of policy.

pronunciation n articulation.

proof n convincing evidence;

argument; test; standard strength (spirit); print copy for revision.

prop *n* a support; * *vt* to hold up.

propaganda *n* methods or system of spreading beliefs, doctrines, etc.

propagate *vt* to multiply; to diffuse; * *vi* to have young.

propel *vt* to drive or thrust forward.

propeller *n* a screw for propelling aeroplanes, etc.

propensity *n* natural tendency.

proper *adj* one's own; peculiar, correct; real.

property *n* a quality or attribute; characteristic; ownership; goods; estate.

prophecy *n* a prediction; inspired utterance.

prophet *n* a seer; inspired preacher.

prophylactic *adj*, *n* preventive of disease.

propitious *adj* favourable; merciful.

proportion *n* comparative relation; symmetry; equal share; lot; ratio.

proposal *n* proposition; offer (*esp* of marriage).

propose *vt* to offer for consideration; * *vi* to make a proposal.

proposition *n* a proposal; offer of terms; a statement or assertion.

propound *vt* to propose; to put, as a question.

proprietary *adj* belonging to a proprietor.

proprietor *n* an owner.

propriety *n* fitness; justness.

propulsion *n* the driving forward (as of an engine).

prosaic *adj* like prose; commonplace.

proscribe *vt* to outlaw; to forbid.

prose *n* ordinary speech.

prosecute *vt*, *vi* to carry on; to pursue at law.

prosecution *n* a suit at law; the party prosecuting.

proselytise *vt*, *vi* to make or seek to make converts.

prospect *n* a distant view; scene; outlook; expectation; * *vt*, *vi* to search, explore (for metals, oil, etc).

prospectus *n* a statement or outline of some enterprise.

prosper *vi*, *vt* to thrive or cause to thrive.

prosperity *n* success; a thriving state; good fortune.

prostitute *n* a person who performs sex acts for money.

prostrate *adj* lying flat; * *vt* to lie flat, to humble oneself.

protagonist *n* chief actor in a drama; the principal leader in an affair.

protean *adj* assuming different shapes; changeable.

protect *vt* to shield from danger.

protection *n* defence; shelter.

protégé (*m*), protégée (*f*) *n* one under the care of another.

protein *n* a class of organic molecules formed by chains of amino acids forming one of the vital constituents of living matter.

protest *vi* to affirm with solemnity; * *vt* to assert; to mark for non-payment, as a bill; * *n* a formal declaration of dissent.

protestation *n* a solemn affirmation; a strong protest.

protocol *n* first draft of a treaty; ceremonial etiquette.

protoplasm *n* the material comprising living cells.

prototype *n* model; pattern.

protract *vt* to prolong; to delay.

protractor *n* an instrument for measuring or plotting angles.

protrude *vt*, *vi* to thrust forward to project.

protrusion *n* a sticking out.

protuberance *n* a prominence; a knob.

proud *adj* haughty; arrogant; high-spirited.

prove *vt*, *vi* to test; to establish the truth of, to demonstrate; to obtain probate of; to turn out to be.

proverb *n* a popular saying; an adage; a maxim.

proverbial *adj* well-known; notorious.

provide *vt*, *vi* to make ready beforehand; to prepare; to supply.

provided *conj* on condition.

providence *n* foresight; divine foresight and care.

provident *adj* prudent; frugal.

providential *adj* due to divine providence.

province *n* a division of a country; sphere of action.

provincial *adj* rustic; countrified.

provision *n* preparation; stores provided; proviso; *pl* food.

provisional *adj* temporary.

proviso *n* a stipulation; condition.

provocation *n* cause of resentment.

provocative *adj* inciting; rousing.

provoke *vt, vi* to incite; to irritate.

prow *n* the forepart of a ship.

prowess *n* bravery; skill.

prowl *vi, vt* to sneak around.

proximate *adj* nearest; next.

proxy *n* a deputy; a warrant to act or vote for another.

prude *n* a person who affects excessive modesty.

prudent *adj* provident; cautious; discreet; * prudence *n*.

prune *vt* to trim; to lop off; * *n* a dried plum.

prurient *adj* lustful; filthy-minded.

pry *vi* to scan closely; to peel.

psalm *n* a sacred song or hymn.

pseudo *pref* signifying false or spurious.

pseudonym *n* a name assumed by a writer.

psychiatry *n* treatment of mental disease.

psychic *adj* belonging to the soul; spiritualistic.

psychology *n* the science concerned with the human mind and behaviour.

puberty *n* beginning of manhood and womanhood; sex maturity.

public *adj* not private; pertaining to a whole community; open to all; * *n* the people; in open view.

publican *n* keeper of a public house.

publication *n* act of publishing; book, etc, published.

publicity *n* any information or action that brings a person or cause to public notice; work concerned with such matters.

publish *vt* to make public; to proclaim; to print and offer for sale.

pucker *vt, vi* to wrinkle; * *n* a fold or wrinkle.

pudding *n* a dessert dish.

puddle *n* a small pool of dirty water.

puerile *adj* boyish; childish.

puff *n* whiff of wind or breath; a puffball; light pastry; * *vt, vi* to breathe hard; to praise overmuch.

pugnacious *adj* quarrelsome.

pull *vt, vi* to draw towards one; to tug; to rend; to pluck; to gather; * *n* act of pulling; an effort.

pulley *n* a grooved wheel with running cord for raising weights.

pulmonary *adj* pertaining to the lungs.

pulp *n* the fleshy part of fruit, etc; soft substance obtained by mashing down cloth, wood, etc.

pulpit *n* preacher's raised desk or platform.

pulsate *vi* to beat or throb.

pulse *n* the rhythmical throbbing of arteries as blood is propelled through them; a single, isolated, cycle of a wave; a musical beat; the edible seeds of various leguminous plants, beans, lentils, etc.

pulverise *vi* to reduce to dust.

pumice *n* a porous stone, used for polishing.

pummel *vt* to strike with fists.

pump *n* a machine for raising water or extracting air; a shoe used in dancing; * *vi* to work a pump; * *vt* to raise with a pump; to quiz.

pun *n* a play upon words.

punch *n* a tool for perforating; a blow; a spirituous beverage; a puppet show figure; * *vt* to stamp or perforate; to strike.

punctilious *adj* formal; precise.

punctual *adj* exact; prompt.

punctuate *vt* to mark with points or stops.

punctuation *n* the art of inserting stops in sentence.

puncture *n* hole made by sharp point; * *vt* to pierce.

pungent *adj* biting; acrid; caustic.

punish *vt* to inflict pain as a penalty; to chastise.

punishment *n* pain, loss, or penalty.

punitive *adj* penal; designed to punish.

punt *n* a flat-bottomed boat.

puny *adj* small and weak.

pup *n* a young dog, seal, fox, etc.

pupa *n* (*pl* pupae) the chrysalis form of an insect.

pupil *n* a learner; a scholar; the opening in centre of eye.

puppet *n* a mechanical figure moved by strings; a person who is a mere tool.

purchase *vt* to buy; to acquire.

pure *adj* clean; clear; chaste.

purge *vt, vi* to make pure or clean; to clear from accusation.

purification *n* a cleansing from guilt.

purify *vt* to make pure or clear.

purity *n* cleanness; innocence; freedom from adulteration.

purloin *vt* to steal or pilfer.

purple *n* a colour; red and blue blended.

purport *n* meaning; * *vt* to signify; to intend.

purpose *n* end or aim; design; intention; * *vt* to propose.

purse *n* a small pouch for money.

purser *n* the ship's officer in charge of accounts.

pursuance *n* the carrying out (of a plan, etc).

pursuant *adv* conforming to; * *adj* following; * pursuantly *adv*.

pursue *vt, vi* to follow for some end; to chase.

pursuit *n* chase; quest; business occupation.

purvey *vt, vi* to provide; to supply provisions.

purveyor *n* a caterer.

pus *n* thick yellowish or greenish liquid produced from infected tissue containing dead germs, leukocytes, tissue, etc.

push *vt, vi* to press against with force; to shove; to urge; * *n* vigorous effort.

put *vt* to place or set; to ask; to apply; to state.

put, putt *vt* to throw (a heavy stone) from the shoulder; in golf, to play the ball into the hole.

putative *adj* supposed; reputed.

putrefaction *n* decay; rottenness.

putrefy *vt* to render putrid; * *vi* to decay; to rot.

putrid *adj* rotten; corrupt.

putter *n* a golf club for putting with.

putty *n* a paste made of whiting and linseed oil.

puzzle *vt* to perplex; * *vi* to be bewildered; * *n* perplexity.

pyjamas *npl* sleeping clothes.

pylon *n* a tower like structure supporting electric power lines.

pyramid *n* a solid body having triangular sides meeting in a point at the top.

pyre *n* a funeral pile.

pyrotechnics *n* the art of making or the use of fireworks.

Q

quack *vi* to cry like a duck; * *n* the cry of a duck; an untrained person who practising medicine fraudulently; * *adj* sham.

quadrangle *n* an inner square or court of a building.

quadrant *n* the fourth part of a circle or its circumference; a sextant.

quadratic *adj* (of a maths equation) having terms which are squared.

quadrilateral *n* a plane figure having four sides.

quadruped *n* an animal with four feet.

quadruple *adj* fourfold; * *vt* to make fourfold; * *vi* to become fourfold.

quaff *vt, vi* to drink deep.

quagmire *n* wet boggy ground.

quail *vi* to flinch; to cower; * *n* any short tailed game bird of the genus *Coturnix*.

quaint *adj* attractive or pleasant in an old-fashioned style.

quake *vi* to shake; to tremble.

Quaker *n* a member of the Society of Friends.

qualification *n* quality which fits a person for office or occupation; ability; capability; restriction.

qualify *vt* to render or to become fit for office, etc; to modify or limit.

qualitative *adj* determining the nature of the component parts of bodies.

quality *n* sort, kind, or character; attribute; high rank.

qualm *n* a sudden fit of nausea; a scruple.

quandary *n* a state of perplexity; a predicament.

quantitative *adj* relating to the size or amount.

quantity *n* measure; amount.

quantum *n* a discrete amount of energy proportional to the frequency of the radiation it is associated with; an analogous discrete uantity; a small bit.

quarantine *n* isolation period imposed to prevent the spread of disease.

quarrel *n* an angry dispute; a brawl; * *vi* to dispute violently.

quarrelsome *adj* apt to quarrel; contentious.

quarry *n* an excavation for the extraction of stone, slate, etc; a place from which stone is excavated.

quart *n* 2 pints or one-fourth of a gallon.

quarter *n* the fourth part of any-thing; any point of the compass; a district; locality; proper position; mercy to a beaten foe; (in *pl*) shelter or lodging; * *vt* to divide into four equal parts; to cut to pieces; lodge.

quarterly *adj* recurring each quarter; * *adv* once in a quarter; * *n* a periodical published quarterly.

quartermaster *n* a petty officer in charge of steering, signals, etc (navy); an officer in charge of stores, rations, etc (army).

quartet *n* a musical composition in four parts; the four performers.

quartz *n* silica in crystalline form.

quash *vt* to quell; to suppress; to make void.

quasi *pref* meaning sort of, sham, almost, as quasi-religious.

quaver *vi, vt* to shake; to tremble; to quiver; * *n* half a crotchet.

quay *n* a landing stage for vessels.

queasy *adj* squeamish.

queen *n* the wife of a king; a female sovereign; * **queenly** *adj*.

queer *adj* odd; droll; peculiar.

quell *vt* to subdue; to allay.

quench *vt* to put out, as fire; to slake, as thirst.

querulous *adj* complaining; peevish.

query *n* a question; the mark of interrogation (?); * *vi* to ask questions; * *vt* to question.

quest *n* search; pursuit; inquiry.

question *n* an interrogation; inquiry; discussion; * *vi* to ask a question; to doubt; * *vt* to interrogate.

questionable *adj* doubtful.

questionnaire *n* a series of questions designed to collect statistical information.

queue *n* a line of people, vehicles, etc awaiting entry, a turn etc.

quibble *n* a minor objection or criticism; * *vi* to evade the question by play on words; to prevaricate.

quick *adj* alive; brisk; swift; keen.

quicken *vt, vi* to give life to; to vivify; to cheer; to speed up.

quicklime *n* lime burned but unslaked.

quicksand *n* a sandbank yielding under pressure, therefore dangerous.

quicksilver *n* mercury.

quiescent *adj* resting; still; tranquil.

quiet *adj* at rest; calm; peaceful; secluded; * *n* rest peace; * *vt* to calm; to lull; to allay.

quill *n* the hollow stem of a feather; anything made of this as a pen; the spine of a porcupine; * *vt* to plait.

quilt *n* a padded bedcover.

quince *n* any shrub or tree of the genus *Cydonia*.

quinine *n* a bitter drug from bark of the cinchona tree, used as an anti-malarial agent, and a flavouring in tonic water.

quinsy *n* inflammation of tonsils or throat.

quintessence *n* purest form of a substance; vital part.

quintet *n* a musical composition in five parts.

quintuple *adj* fivefold.

quintuplet *adj* one of five offspring produced at one birth.

quip *n* a gibe; retort.

quirk *n* an unexpected twist; a peculiarity of mannerism.

quit *adj* discharged; fierce; * *vt, vi* to discharge; to depart; to acquit.

quite *adv* competely; wholly.

quiver *n* a sheath for arrows; * *vi* to shake; to shiver.

quixotic *adj* romantic or chivalrous to extravagance.

quiz *n* a short written or oral test; a form of entertainment where players are asked questions of general knowledge.

quorum *n* minimum number needed to constitute a meeting.

quota *n* share assigned to each.

quotation *n* passage quoted; estimated price.

quote *vt* to cite (from writings or speeches); to give prices of articles.

quotient *n maths* the result of division.

R

rabbi *n* (*pl* rabbis) the religious and spiritual leader of a Jewish congregation.

rabble *n* a noisy crowd; a mob.

rabid *adj* infected with rabies; fanatical.

rabies *n* an acute viral disease transmitted by the bite of an infected animal.

race *n* any of the divisions of human kind; a contest in speed; a course or career; a rapid current; * *vt* to run swiftly; to compete in speed.

racecourse *n* a track on which races are run.

raceine *n* a flower cluster on common stem.

racial *adj* characteristic of race.

rack *vt* to stretch unduly; to torture; * *n* a frame for holding or stretching articles; a frame for setting up snooker balls for play, anguish; instrument of torture.

racket *n* a din; clamour; the bat in tennis, etc; (*pl*) a game like tennis.

racy *adj* strongly flavoured; risqué.

radial *adj* branching from a common centre.

radiant *adj* emitting rays; brilliant; beaming; * radiance *n*.

radiate *vi*, *vt* to emit rays; to broadcast; to spread; to shine.

radiation *n* emission of rays.

radiator *n* apparatus for warming a room.

radical *adj* pertaining to the root; original; fundamental; inherent.

radicle *n* the first rootlet of a seed.

radioactivity *adj* the emission of nuclear particles by some substances.

radiography *n* process of taking pictures by X-rays for use in medicine.

radium *n* a highly radioactive metallic element.

radius *n* (*pl* radii) distance from the centre of a circle to the circumference; a bone of the forearm.

raffle *n* a kind of lottery.

raft *n* logs fastened together and floated; a floating structure.

rafter *n* one of several sloping beams supporting a roof.

rag *n* a tattered cloth; a shred; a sensational newspaper.

rage *n* violent anger; fury.

ragged *adj* tattered.

raid *n* a hostile incursion; a sudden foray; * *vt* to make a raid on.

rail *n* a bar of wood or metal; a connected series of posts.

railing *n* a fence.

raillery *n* banter; chaff.

railroad *n* a railway.

railway *n* a road or track with parallel rails along which vehicles travel.

rain *n* moisture falling in drops.

rainbow *n* a many-coloured bow that often appears in the sky during sunshine and showers containing the colours of the spectrum.

rainfall *n* the quantity of rain that falls.

raise *vt* to cause to rise; to lift upward; to excite; to stir up; to levy; to breed; to abandon (siege).

rake *n* a toothed implement for scraping ground; * *vt* to glean.

rakish *adj* dissolute; sloping, as masts; jaunty.

rally *vt* to reunite, as disordered troops; to collect; a large gathering of people; * *vi* to recover strength; * *n* a stand; recovery of health.

ram *n* a male sheep; a battering engine; pile-driving machine; * *vt* to batter; to charge.

ramble *vi* to roam about; to talk incoherently; * *n* an aimless walk.

rambler *n* a climbing plant; a person who rambles.

rambling *adj* unsettled; discon- nected.

ramification *n* a branching; a network of parts; a consequence.

ramp *n* a sloping walk or runway.

rampage *vi* to prance; to rage and storm.

rampant *adj* in heraldry, standing on hind legs; unchecked; unrestrained.

rampart *n* a defensive earthwork.

ramshackle *adj* broken-down; shaky.

ranch *n* a large cattle or sheep farm.

rancid *adj* rank; tainted.

rancorous *adj* spiteful; virulent.

rancour *n* deep-seated hatred.

random *n* chance; without aim.

range *vt*, *vi* to set in a row; to place in order; to roam over; to rank; * *n* a row; a series of mountains; compass or extent; a place for gun practice.

ranger *n* a park warder.

rank *n* a row; a line; a social class; dignity; * *vt*, *vi* to classify; to place in line; * *adj* tainted.

rankle *vi*, *vt* to grow bitter; to irritate.

ransack *vt* to plunder; to search thoroughly.

ransom *n* release from captivity by payment; price paid for release.

rant *vi* to rave, declaim.

ranter *n* a voluble speaker.

ranunculus *n* a genus of plants, including buttercups.

rap *n* a smart blow; a knock; * *vi*, *vt* to strike smartly; *(fam)* talk, conversation.

rapacious *adj* greedy of plunder; grasping; * rapacity *n*.

rape *n* to have sexual intercourse with (someone) without (their) consent; a plundering.

rapid *adj* very swift; speedy.

rapt *adj* transported; enraptured.

rapture *n* extreme joy; ecstasy.

rare *adj* sparse; uncommon.

rarefy *vt*, *vi* to make or become less dense.

rarity *n* scarceness; thinness; a rare article.

rascal *n* a scoundrel; a rogue.

rase *vt* to wipe out; to destroy; to level to the ground.

rash *adj* precipitate; hasty; * *n* an eruption on the skin.

rasher *n* a thin slice of bacon.

rasp *vt* to rub with something rough; to grate; * *n* a coarse file

raspberry *n* a bramble, *Rubus idaeus*, with red berry fruits.

rat *n* a small rodent.

ratchet *n* a catch which cheeks a toothed wheel and moves only one way.

rate *n* proportion; standard; degree of speed; price; a tax; assess- ment; * *vt* to fix the value, rank, etc, of; to reprove; * *vi* to classify.

rather *adv* more readily; preferably.

ratification *n* sanction.

ratify *vt* to approve and sanction.

ratio *n* proportion of two classes of objects to each other.

ration *n* a fixed amount allowed.

rational *adj* endowed with reason; wise; judicious.

rationale *n* exposition of reasons for any opinion or action.

rattle *vi*, *vt* to clatter; to chatter; * *n* a clattering noise; a toy which makes a clatter.

rattlesnake *n* any of several venomous snakes of the family *Viperidae*.

raucous *adj* hoarse; harsh; loud.

ravage *n* havoc; devastation; * *vt* to lay waste.

rave *vi* to be delirious; to dote.

raven *n* a large crow, *Corvus corax*.

ravenous *adj* excessively hungry.

ravine *n* a gorge or pass.

ravioli *n* small cases of pasta filled with seasoned chopped meat or vegetables.

ravish *vt* to carry off by force; to captivate; to rape.

ravishing *adj* enchanting.

raw *adj* uncooked; in natural state; crude; unripe; cold and damp; sore.

ray *n* a line of light; a gleam of intelligence; a radius; a flatfish.

raze vt to blot out; to demolish.

razor n an instrument for shaving off hair.

reach vt to extend; to hand; to stretch out; to arrive at; to gain; * vi to extend; * n extent; scope.

react vi, vt to act in return; to return an impulse.

reaction n an action in response to a stimulus; (chemistry) an action set up by one substance in another.

reactionary adj retrograde; * n one who opposes progress.

read vt to peruse; to utter aloud; to explain; * vi to peruse; to study; to stand written or printed; to make sense; * adj well-informed, well-read.

readily adv promptly; cheerfully.

reading adj bookish; studious; * n perusal; study of books; inter- pretation; rendering.

ready adj prepared; prompt; willing.

reagent n (chemistry) a substance used to cause a reaction, esp to detect the presence of other specific substances.

real adj actual; true; genuine; in law, applied to things fixed as land, houses, etc.

realism n doctrine that the things of sense are the only reality; truth to nature in art; the practical as opposed to the ideal.

realist n one who believes in realism.

realistic adj life-like; vivid.

reality n fact; truth.

realise vt to make real; to convert into money; to gain.

really adv actually; in truth.

realm n kingdom; domain.

realty n real property.

ream n 20 quires or 500 sheets of paper.

reap vt, vi to harvest; to gather in; to receive as a reward.

reappear vi to appear anew.

reappoint vt to appoint again.

rear n the part behind; the part of army or fleet behind van; * vt, vi to raise; to educate; to breed, as cattle; to stand on hind legs.

reason n mental faculty; power of thinking; a motive or cause; justice; moderation; * vi, vt to use reason; to argue.

reasonable adj rational; just; moderate.

reasoning n the exercise of faculty of reason; arguments used.

reassurance n act of reassuring; a second assurance against loss.

reassure vt to give confidence.

rebate vt to blunt; to diminish; to make a discount from; * n abatement in price; deduction; discount.

rebel n one who fights against, or refuses to cooperate with the established government; * adj rebellious; * vi to revolt.

rebellion n an uprising against the state.

rebound n a recoil; * vi to spring back; to bounce back.

rebuke vt to reprimand; * n a reproof.

rebut vt to repel; to refute by argument.

recalcitrant adj obstinate.

recall vt to call back; to revive in memory.

recant vt, vi to withdraw or retract; to abjure.

recantation n withdrawal of previous statements or beliefs.

recapitulate vt to summarise; to go over chief points.

recast vt to mould anew.

recede vi to go back; to grow less; * vt to give back.

receipt n a written acknowledge- ment of something received.

receive vt to take, as a thing offered; to accept; to welcome; to take in.

receiver n a person who receives; one who knowingly takes stolen goods from a thief; equipment that receives radio signals; (law) a person appointed to manage or hold in trust property in a bankruptcy or lawsuit.

recent adj new; late; fresh.

receptacle n a place or vessel for holding articles.

reception n welcome; a formal receiving of guests; admission.

receptionist n a person employed to receive visitors in an office, hospital, hotel, etc.

receptive *adj* quick to absorb knowledge.

recess *n* withdrawal; a nook or alcove; holiday.

recession *n* a time of severe economic downturn.

recipe *n* a list of ingredients and directions for preparing food; a method for achieving an end.

recipient *n* a person who receives.

reciprocal *adj* mutual; alternating.

reciprocate *vi* to move backward and forward; to give in return.

reciprocity *n* equality of tariffs; fair trade.

recital *n* a narration; musical entertainment, *esp* by one performer.

recite *vt, vi* to repeat aloud from memory; to relate.

reckless *adj* heedless; rash.

reckon *vt, vi* to count; consider; to calculate.

reckoning *n* calculation; a statement of accounts.

reclaim *vt* to claim back; to reform.

recline *vt, vi* to lean backwards; to lean down on one side.

recluse *adj* retired; solitary; * *n* a hermit.

recognition *n* identification; acknowledgement.

recognise *vt* to know again; to acknowledge.

recoil *vi* to start back; to shrink; to rebound; * *n* a rebound, as from a gun.

recollect *vt* to remember.

recommend *vt* to praise to another; to advise.

recommendation *n* a favourable notice; repute.

reconcile *vt* to make friendly again; to settle.

reconnaissance *n* a survey for military purposes.

reconsider *vt* to consider again.

reconstruct *vt* to rebuild.

record *vt* to preserve in writing; to chronicle; * *n* a written memorial; a register; best result in contests; gramophone disc.

recorder *n* an official registrar; a device that records; a tape recorder.

recount *vt* to relate in detail; to count again.

recoup *vt* to make good; to indemnify.

recourse *n* a going to for help or protection.

recover *vt* to get back; to regain; to revive; to obtain as compensation; * *vi* to grow well.

recovery *n* restoration from sickness, etc; a winning back.

recreant *adj* craven; cowardly; * *n* a coward; renegade.

recreate *vt* to revive; to amuse.

re-create *vt* to create anew.

recreation *n* relaxation after toil; amusement or sport.

recrimination *n* mutual accusations.

recruit *vt* to enlist new soldiers; * *vi* to gain new supplies; * *n* a soldier newly enlisted; a beginner.

rectangle *n* a quadrilateral with four right angles.

rectify *vt* to set right; to correct.

rector *n* a clergyman in charge of a parish; a headmaster.

rectory *n* a clergyman's house.

recumbent *adj* leaning; reclining.

recuperate *vt, vi* to recover health.

recuperative *adj* strengthening.

recur *vi* to return; to happen again and again.

recurrent *adj* returning repeatedly.

red *adj* blood-coloured; * *n* a primary colour.

Red Cross *n* a red cross on a white background; the symbol of the International Red Cross, a society for the relief of suffering in time of war and disaster.

redden *vt* to make red; * *vi* to blush.

redeem *vt* to buy back; to ransom; to save; to atone for; to perform (a promise).

redemption *n* ransom; release.

redolent *adj* fragrant; reminiscent.

redoubtable *adj* formidable; valiant.

redress *vt* to set right; to adjust; to relieve; * *n* relief; compensation.

red tape *n* excessive official formality.

reduce *vt* to bring down; to decrease; to degrade; to subdue.

reduction *n* act of reducing; diminution; conversion into another state or from; subjugation.

redundant *adj* superfluous to requirements; deprived of one's job as being no longer necessary.

reed *n* a tall grass with jointed hollow stem; a pastoral pipe.

reedy *adj* harsh and thin, as a voice.

reef *n* a fold in a sail; a low line of rocks in sea; a vein of ore; * *vt* to reduce sail.

reel *n* a bobbin; an appliance for winding a fishing line; a lively Scottish dance; a length of film; * *vt* to wind upon a reel; to stagger.

re-entry *n* the resuming possession of lost lands.

re-examine *vt* to examine anew.

refectory *n* a dining hall of a college.

refer *vt* to trace back; to submit (a matter) to another person; to assign; * *vi* to appeal; to allude.

referee *n* an umpire; a judge.

reference *n* allusion; relation; scope.

referendum *n* the settling of a national question by a poll of the electorate.

refill *vt* to fill again.

refine *vt, vi* to purify; to polish.

refinement *n* fineness of manners or taste; an improvement.

refinery *n* a place for refining sugar, metals, oil, etc.

refit *vt, vi* to fit anew; to repair; * *n* repair.

reflect *vt, vi* to throw back, *esp* rays of light; to mirror; to meditate; to consider.

reflection *n* act of reflecting; a reflected image; * **reflective** *adj*.

reflector *n* a polished surface for reflecting light, etc.

reflex *adj* bent or directed back; involuntary response to a stimulus; * *n* a reflex action.

reflexive *adj* in grammar, referring back to subject.

refold *vt* to fold again.

reform *vt, vi* to improve; to better; to amend; to form anew; * *n* a beneficial change; amendment.

reformation *n* improvement; the Protestant revolution of the 16th century.

reformer *n* one who effects

reforms in religion, politics, etc.

refract *vt* to bend back sharply; to deflect (a ray of light).

refraction *n* deflection of rays on passing from one medium to another.

refrain *vt* to restrain; * *vi* to forbear; * *n* the chorus of a song.

refresh *vt* to revive; to freshen.

refreshment *n* that which refreshes, as food and drink.

refrigerate *vt* to cool.

refrigerator *n* an apparatus for keeping things cool.

refuge *n* protection from danger or distress; a retreat; a shelter.

refugee *n* one who seeks refuge in another land; to escape persecution.

refund *vt* to repay.

refusal *n* rejection; option.

refuse *vt, vi* to deny what is asked; to say 'no'.

refuse *adj* worthless; * *n* waste matter; rubbish.

refutation *n* disproof.

refute *vt* to disprove; to rebut.

regain *vt* to recover possession of; to reach again.

regal *adj* royal; relating to a king or queen.

regale *vt, vi* to entertain sumptuously.

regalia *npl* ensigns of royalty, as crown, sceptre, etc.

regard *vt* to notice carefully; to observe to heed; to consider; to value; * *n* look or gaze; respect; deference; attention; (*pl*) good wishes.

regarding *prep* respecting; concerning.

regardless *adj* heedless; careless.

regatta *n* a yacht (or boat) race.

regency *n* government of a regent.

regenerate *vt* to produce anew; to produce again in the original form.

regent *adj* ruling; * *n* a ruler; one who governs during minority, illness, or absence of king.

regicide *n* the murder, or murderer, of a king.

regime *n* mode or system of government; administration.

regimen *n* orderly government;

regulation of diet, exercise, etc.

regiment n a military unit smaller than a division; * vt to organise in a strict manner.

region n a tract of land; country.

register n an official record; a roll of voters; a recording machine.

registered adj enrolled; insured.

registrar n official keeper of records.

registration n act of registering; enrolment.

registry n place where a register is kept.

registry office n an office where civil marriages are held, and births and deaths recorded.

regret n grief; remorse; * vt to grieve at; lament.

regrettable adj deplorable; unwelcome.

regular adj according to rule, law, etc; normal; constant; uniform; * n a professional, as opposed to a reserve, soldier.

regularity n evenness; uniformity.

regulate vt to adjust by rule; to direct.

regulation n a rule; order.

regurgitate vt, vi to pour or cause to surge back.

rehabilitate vt to put back in good condition.

rehearsal n a trial performance.

rehearse vt to repeat; to recite; to perform (by way of practice).

reign vi to be sovereign; to rule; to prevail; * n royal authority; duration of kingship.

reimburse vt to refund.

reimbursement n repayment.

rein n the strap of a bridle; restraint; * vt to govern by a bridle; * vi to obey the reins.

reindeer n a subarctic deer, Rangifer tarandus, both sexes of which have antlers.

reinforce vt to supply with fresh strength or assistance.

reinstate vt to restore to a former position.

reinvest vt to invest anew.

reissue vt to issue a second time.

reiterate vt to repeat again and again.

reject vt to cast off; to forsake; to decline; to refuse to accept.

rejoice vi, vt to be glad; to exult; to cheer.

rejoin vt to join again; to answer.

rejoinder n an answer to a reply.

rejuvenate vt to make young again.

relapse vi to deteriorate back into a worse state; * n such a deterioration.

relate vt to tell; to narrate; * vi to refer.

related adj connected by blood or by some common bond.

relation n act of relating; account; connexion; kindred; a relative; proportion.

relative adj comparative; pertinent; relating to a word, clause, etc; * n a kinsman; a relating word, esp relative pronoun.

relatively adv comparatively.

relax vt to slacken; to unbend; * vi to become feeble or languid.

relaxation n recreation; the condition of being relaxed.

relay n supply of horses to relieve jaded ones; fresh supply of men or materials; a relayed broadcast; * vt to broadcast signals.

release vt to set free; to deliver from; * n liberation from.

relegate vt to send away; to move to an inferior position; to demote.

relent vi to relax severity; to grow milder.

relentless adj unmerciful; pitiless.

relevant adj applicable; to the purpose; * relevance n.

reliable adj trustworthy; dependable.

reliant adj confident; self-reliant.

relic n something treasured for connexion with a saint or hero; a memento; pl the mortal remains of saints.

relief n ease of pain; remedy; redress; assistance given to the poor, disaster victims, etc; raised design in sculpture; relief from duty by another person.

relieve vt to ease or lessen pain; to succour; to release from duty.

religion n a system of faith or worship; a belief in God or gods.

relinquish vt to give up; to renounce.

relish *vt* to enjoy the taste of; to have a taste for; * *vi* to have a pleasing taste; * *n* taste; flavour; savour.

reluctant *adj* loath; averse.

rely *vt* to depend upon; to trust in.

remain *vi* to stay in a place; to survive; to be left; to last; * *npl* a dead body; what is left over, *esp* after decay, etc, *eg* the remains of the house.

remainder *n* residue; remnant.

remand *vt* to recommit to jail for further enquiries.

remark *n* notice; a comment; * *vt* to observe; to note; to utter.

remarkable *adj* noteworthy; uncommon; striking.

remedy *n* a care; redress; a specific; * *vt* to cure; to repair; to put right.

remember *vt*, *vi* to recollect; recall; observe; bear in mind.

remembrance *n* memory; recollection; memorial; keepsake.

remind *vt* to put in mind.

reminder *n* a jog to memory.

reminisce *vi* to write, think or talk about past events.

reminiscence *n* recollections; what is recalled; (*pl*) personal recollections .

reminiscent *adj* recalling the past.

remiss *adj* careless; heedless.

remission *n* pardon; abatement.

remit *vt* to send payment; to relinquish; to forgive; * *vi* to slacken.

remittance *n* sum of money remitted.

remnant *n* a scrap; fragment.

remonstrate *vi* to protest against; to warn.

remorse *n* sorrow for a fault; compunction; bitter regret.

remorseless *adj* ruthless; merciless.

remote *adj* distant; foreign; slight.

removable *adj* able to be removed.

removal *n* change of place; dismissal.

remove *vt*, *vi* to move from its place; to take away; to dismiss; * *n* a removal; departure; a stage in gradation.

remunerate *vt* to reward for service; to recompense.

remuneration *n* pay for service; reward; * **remunerative** *adj*.

renaissance *n* revival; the revival of art and literature in the 15th century.

renal *adj* pertaining to the kidneys.

read *vt*, *vi* to tear away and apart; to split; to rive.

render *vt* to give in return; to give back; to afford; to furnish; to translate; to boil down.

rendering *n* translation; interpretation.

rendezvous *n* appointed meeting place.

renegade *n* a deserter; a person who is faithless to a principle, party, religion, or cause.

renew *vt*, *vi* to make new again; to restore; to repair.

renewal *n* a revival; a repetition.

rennin *n* a preparation for curdling milk in cheese-making.

renounce *vt* to disown; to forsake; * *vi* to revoke.

renovate *vt* to renew; to make like new.

renovation *n* act of renovating; renewal.

renown *n* fame; glory; celebrity.

renowned *adj* famous; eminent.

rent *n* money paid for use of lands or houses; a tear; a schism; * *vt*, *vi* to let or hire for rent.

renunciation *n* act of disowning or rejecting; disavowal.

reorganise *vt* to organise anew.

repair *vt* to restore; to mend; * *n* return to good condition.

reparation *n* amends; compensation.

repartee *n* a witty retort.

repast *n* a meal; food.

repatriate *vt* restore (a person) to their native country.

repay *vt* to pay back; to refund; to require.

repeal *vt* to revoke; to annul; to abrogate; * *n* a cancelling.

repeat *vt* to do or utter again; to recite; to recapitulate; * *n* repetition.

repeatedly *adv* again and again.

repeating *adj* recurring again and again indefinitely.

repel *vt*, *vi* to drive back; to repulse; to shock.

repellent *adj* repulsive; unattractive.

repent *vi, vt* to feel regret for one's conduct; to be penitent.

repentant *adj* feeling or showing sorrow; * **repentance** *n*.

repercussion *n* reverberation; echo; an indirect consequence of an event.

repertoire *n* actor's or company's stock of plays, etc.

repertory *n* a treasury; a storehouse.

repetition *n* repeating; saying from memory; recitation.

replace *vt* to put back in place; substitute; supersede.

replenish *vt* to fill again; to stock anew.

replete *adj* filled up; stuffed; gorged.

repletion *n* surfeit; plethora.

replica *n* an exact copy; a reproduction.

replication *n* an answer; echo; plaintiff's answer to defendant's plea.

reply *vt* to answer; to respond; * *n* an answer; a rejoinder.

report *vt, vi* to bring back as answer; to relate; to give an account of; to inform against; * *n* an official statement; account; rumour; loud noise.

reporter *n* one who reports for newspaper, radio or television.

repose *vt* to lay at rest; * *vt, vi* lie at rest; to rely; * *n* sleep; quiet; composure; serenity.

repository *n* a storehouse.

reprehend *vt* to reprove; to censure.

reprehensible *adj* deserving censure; culpable.

reprehension *n* reproof; blame.

represent *vt* to show; to typify; to describe; to act as the elected delegate of a constituency in parliament.

representation *n* an image or likeness; dramatic performance; a remonstrance; the representing of a constituency.

representative *adj* typical; representing; acting as delegate; * *n* a member of parliament; an agent, delegate.

repress *vt* to check; to quell; to keep under control.

reprieve *vt* to grant a respite to;

suspension of the punishment of a convict.

reprimand *n* a severe reproof; * *vt* to rebuke sharply.

reprint *vt* to print again; * *n* a new edition.

reprisal *n* something done by way of retaliation.

reproach *vt* to reprove, rebuke; * *n* censure; blame; disgrace.

reproachful *adj* abusive; upbraiding.

reprobate *adj* dissolute; profligate; * *n* a hardened sinner; * *vt* to condemn strongly; to cast off.

reproduce *vt* to generate, as offspring; to make copies of.

reproduction *n* a copy; a facsimile; to produce offspring.

reproof *n* rebuke; censure.

reprove *vt* to censure; to reprimand.

reptile *n* any of the class *Reptilia* of scaly, cold-blooded, air-breathing vertebrates; a grovelling or despised person.

reptilian *adj* like reptiles.

republic *n* a state governed by rulers popularly elected.

republican *adj* pertaining to a republic; * *n* one who favours republican government.

repudiate *vt* to reject; to deny.

repudiation *n* rejection; disavowal.

repugnant *adj* offensive; highly distasteful; * **repugnance** *n*.

repulse *n* a check or defeat; a refusal; a rebuff; * *vt* to repel.

repulsion *n* aversion; the tendency of certain bodies to repel each other.

repulsive *adj* forbidding; disgusting.

reputable *adj* held in esteem; respectable.

reputation *n* good name; repute; character.

repute *vt* to estimate; to deem; * *n* reputation; character.

reputed *adj* supposed; seeming.

request *n* an expressed desire; a petition; * *vt* to ask, to beg.

requiem *n* a mass for the dead; music for this mass.

require *vt* to ask as of right; to demand; to exact.

requirement *n* demand; an essential condition.

requisite *adj* necessary; essential.

requisition *n* a demand, *esp* for supplies.

requite *vt* to repay; to reward; to avenge.

rescind *vt* to annul; to revoke.

rescue *vt* to free from danger or harm; * *n* deliverance.

research *n* careful investigation; a scientific study.

resemblance *n* likeness.

resemble *vt* to be like; to compare.

resent *vt* to be indignant about; to begrudge; to take badly.

reservation *n* something kept back; doubt; scepticism; land reserved for special purpose, as big game, etc; a proviso.

reserve *vt* to keep in store; to retain; * *n* that which is retained; stiffness of manner; caution; limitation; shyness; (in *pl*) emergency troops.

reserved *adj* shy; distant.

reservoir *n* an artificial lake where water is stored for use.

reside *vi* to dwell; to live.

residence *n* abode; dwelling.

residual *adj* left after part is taken.

residue *n* remainder; part of estate left after paying all charges.

resign *vt* to give up; to renounce; to submit calmly.

resignation *n* calm submission; surrender; giving up of office.

resigned *adj* submissive; patient.

resilient *adj* rebounding; elastic.

resin *n* a sticky substance that oozes from trees and plants etc.

resinous *adj* pertaining to or obtained from resin.

resist *vt, vi* to withstand; to oppose.

resistance *n* opposition; stopping power or effect.

resolute *adj* determined; bold.

resolution *n* firmness of purpose; formal decision; the picture definition of a television.

resolve *vt, vi* to split up into elements; analyse; solve; determine; * *n* fixed purpose.

resonant *adj* resounding; ringing.

resort *vi* to have recourse; * *n* recourse; a popular holiday destination.

resource *n* any source of aid; an expedient; (in *pl*) funds; means.

respect *vt* to regard; to esteem; to concern; * *n* regard; deference.

respectable *adj* worthy of respect; decent; moderate.

respectful *adj* civil; courteous.

respective *adj* relating severally each to each.

respiration *n* act of breathing.

respite *n* temporary intermission; interval; reprieve; * *vt* to reprieve.

resplendent *adj* very bright.

respond *vi* to answer.

respondent *adj* answering; corresponding; * *n* a defendant in civil proceedings.

response *n* an answer; to reply.

responsible *adj* answerable; liable; important; * **responsibility** *n*.

responsive *adj* responding; sensitive to influence or stimulus; sympathetic.

rest *n* cessation of action; peace; sleep; a pause; remainder; * *vi* to cease from action; to repose; to die; to remain; * *vt* to lean or place for support.

restaurant *n* a place where meals can be bought or eaten.

restaurateur *n* the keeper of a restaurant.

restful *adj* giving rest; quiet; peaceful.

restitution *n* a giving back; reparation; amends.

restive *adj* fidgety; restless; impatient under control.

restless *adj* always on the move; uneasy; anxious.

restoration *n* act of restoring; renewal; repair; the re-establishment of mnarchy in Britain, 1660.

restorative *adj* having power to renew strength.

restore *vt* to make strong again; to cure; to give back.

restrain *vt* to hold back; to curb; to check.

restraint *n* the ability to hold back, something that restrains; control of emotions, impulses, etc.

restrict *vt* to limit; to curb.

result *vi* to follow as a consequence; to ensue; * *n* consequence; outcome.

resultant *adj* following as a result or consequence.

resume *vt* to begin again; to continue after stopping.

resumé *n* a recapitulation; a summary.

resumption *n* act of resuming.

resurgent *adj* rising again.

resurrection *n* a rising again; (with *cap*) the return to life of Christ after crucifiction.

resuscitate *vt, vi* to revive.

retail *vt* to sell directly to the consumer in small quantities; * *n, adj* the sale of goods in small quantities.

retain *vt* to hold back; to keep in possession; to engage (a barrister) for a law case.

retainer *n* a follower; a dependant; a retaining or preliminary fee paid to barrister for his services.

retaliate *vi, vt* to take revenge.

retaliation *n* the return of like for like.

retard *vt* to render slower; to impede; to delay.

retardation *n* delay; a slowing down; obstruction.

retch *vi* to strain in vomiting.

retention *n* a holding back; memory.

reticent *adj* uncommunicative; reserved; * reticence *n*.

retina *n* the light sensitive cells at the bask of the eye.

retinue *n* a body of attendants.

retire *vi, vt* to go back; to withdraw from active working life; to go to bed.

retired *adj* secluded; private; withdrawn from business.

retirement *n* retired life; seclusion.

retiring *adj* reserved; unobtrusive; shy.

retort *vt* to retaliate; to make a smart reply; * *n* a ready answer; a repartee; a vessel used in distilling.

retouch *vt* to improve by new touches, as a picture.

retrace *vt* to trace back; to trace over again.

retract *vt, vi* to take back; to recant; to unsay.

retreat *n* seclusion; a shelter; the flight of an army from an enemy;

* *vi* to draw back; to retire from an enemy.

retrench *vt* to cut down; * *vi* to economise.

retrial *n* a second trial.

retribution *n* just punishment; vengeance.

retrievable *adj* that may be retrieved or recovered.

retrieve *vt* to recover; to regain.

retriever *n* a dog trained to fetch game when shot.

retrograde *adj* going backwards; declining morally.

retrospect *n* a review of the past.

retrospective *adj* looking back; affecting things past.

return *vi* to come or go back; * *vi* to send back; to elect; * *n* repayment; yield on investment; election of representative; (*pl*) tabulated statistics.

returning officer *n* the presiding officer at an electon.

reunion *n* a social gathering, *esp* of old associates.

reunite *vt, vi* to bring together again after separation.

reveal *vt* to disclose; to divulge.

revel *n* a noisy feast; * *vi* to carouse; to make merry.

revelation *n* act of making known; an illuminating experience.

revelry *n* noisy festivity; jollity.

revenge *vt, vi* to take vengeance for; to avenge; * *n* retaliation.

revenue *n* income from lands, etc; the yearly income of a state, produced by taxation.

reverberate *vt, vi* (of sound) to be echoed, returned or reflected repeatedly.

revere *vt* to regard with respect.

reverence *n* awe combined with respect; veneration; a title of the clergy; * *vt* to revere.

reverend *adj* worthy of reverence; a title given to clergymen

reverent *adj* expressing reverence.

reverie *n* a daydream.

reversal *n* the act of reversing.

reverse *vt* to alter to the opposite; to annul; to move backwards; * *n* a defeat; a set back; the rear surface (of coin, medal, etc); * *adj* opposite.

reversible *adj* able to be reversed, turned outside in, etc.

reversion *n* a return to a former condition, type, ownership, etc.

revert *vt* to go back; * *vi* to return to a former position, habit, etc.

review *vt* to re-examine; reconsider; inspect; * *vi* to write reviews; * *n* a survey; a criticism; a magazine which reviews books; inspection of troops.

reviewer *n* one who writes reviews.

revile *vi* to vilify; to abuse.

revise *vt* to go over carefully and correct.

revival *n* a reawakening; a religious awakening.

revive *vi* to recover new vigour; * *vt* to refresh; to reproduce (a play, etc).

revocation *n* annulment; repeal.

revoke *vt* to repeal; to annul; * *vi* in card play, to neglect to follow suit.

revolt *vi* to rebel; to be disgusted; * *vt* to disgust; * *n* rebellion.

revolting *adj* exciting extreme disgust; shocking.

revolution *n* act of revolving; rotation; circuit; a radical change in government as from a monarchy to a republic; any radical change, *eg* in the theories believed to describe nature like the quantum revolution, etc .

revolutionary *adj* involving radical changes; * *n* a revolutionist.

revolutionise *vt* to bring about a complete change in.

revolve *vi, vt* to turn round an axis or centre; to consider attentively.

revolver *n* a pistol, with a rotating chambers.

revue *n* a topical play *usu* interspersed with music.

revulsion *n* disgust; aversion.

reward *n* recompense; * *vt* to repay.

rhapsody *n* an enthusiastic speech or writing; a piece of music in one extended movement.

rhetoric *n* the art of speaking or writing correctly and effectively; eloquence; declamation.

rhetorical question *n* a question asked for effect to which no answer is expected.

rheum *n* watery fluid secreted by mucous glands of the nose etc.

rheumatism *n* any disease marked by inflammation and pain in the joints, muscles and fibrous tissue, *eg* rheumatoid arthritis.

rhinoceros *n* any of various large thick-skinned ungulates with one or two horns on the nose.

rhododendron *n* any shrub of the genus *Rhododendron*.

rhubarb *n* a plant of the genus *Rheum*.

rhyme *n* the repetition of like endings in words or verse lines; * *vt* (of a poem, etc) to do this.

rhythm *n* regular recurrence of accent in music and poetry.

rib *n* one of the curved bones protecting the thoracic cavity and its organs, attached, to the spine; something resembling a rib, as in an umbrella.

ribald *adj* irreverent; humorously vulgar.

ribbon *n* a narrow band of silk, satin, etc.

rice *n* a swamp grass, *Oryza sativa*, cultivated for its grain; the grain.

rich *adj* wealthy; costly; fertile; plentiful; bright; highly flavoured.

rickets *npl* a disease of children caused by vitamin D deficiency, marked by softening and distortion of the bones.

rickety *adj* ramshackle; shaky.

ricochet *n* a rebounding from a surface.

rid *vt* to free (from something objectionable); to disencumber; * *adj* free; clear.

riddance *n* deliverance; clearance.

riddle *n* a puzzling question; an enigma; a coarse sieve; * *vt* to sift; to perforate with shot.

ride *vi* to be borne on horseback, in a vehicle, etc; to practise horsemanship; * *vt* to sit on, so as to be carried; to domineer over; * *n* an excursion on horseback, or in a vehicle.

ridge *n* a narrow elevation as crest of hill, or edge of roof.

ridicule *n* laughter with contempt; mockery; * *vt* to make sport of.

ridiculous *adj* absurd; laughable.

rife *adj* abundant; prevalent; widespread.

rifle *n* a gun with a long rifled barrel, *usu* fired from the shoulder; * *vt* to plunder; to make helical grooves a gun barrel to make the bullet spin.

rift *n* an opening; a cleft; a split.

rig *vt* to manipulate fraudulently; to fit with tackling; * *n* the masts, sails, etc of a ship; special equipment; an oil rig.

rigging *n* a ship's spars, ropes, etc.

right *adj* straight; just; correct; opposite of left; perpendicular; * *adv* justly; very; to the right hand; * *n* truth; justice; * *vt, vi* to put right.

righteous *adj* moral; virtuous; just.

rightful *adj* lawful.

rightly *adv* properly; justly.

right-wing *adj* of or relating to the conservative faction of a political party, organisation, etc.

rigid *adj* stiff; unyielding; stem.

rigmarole *n* confused or disconnected talk.

rigour *n* stiffness; austerity; severity; stringency.

rim *n* border; edge; margin.

rind *n* outer coat of fruits, trees, etc; bark.

ring *n* anything in the form of a circle; a gold, silver, etc hoop for decorating fingers; a circular area for contests; a group with mutual interests; sound of bell; * *vt* to encircle; to cause to sound; * *vi* to sound.

ringleader *n* the leader of a faction.

ringlet *n* a small ring; a curl.

ringworm *n* any of several fungal skin disease characterised by circular patches.

rink *n* a space on the ice reserved for curling; a place for roller-skating.

rinse *vt* to flush under clean water to remove soap.

riot *n* an uproar; a tumult; noisy revelry; * *vi* to revel.

riotous *adj* noisy; turbulent; disorderly.

rip *vt* to tear or cut open; * *n* a rent.

ripe *adj* ready for harvest; mature.

ripple *n* a little wave on the surface of water.

rise *vi* to ascend; to stand up; to swell; to slope upwards; to rebel; * *n* ascent; elevation; source; increase (in price).

risible *adj* prone to laugh; laughable.

rising *adj* increasing in power, etc; approaching; * *n* a mounting up; an insurrection; a prominence.

risk *n* hazard; jeopardy; * *vt* to hazard; to venture; * risky *adj.*

rite *n* a solemn religious act; form; ceremony.

ritual *n* a fixed (religious) ceremony.

rival *n* a competitor for same goal; * *adj* competing.

rivalry *n* competition.

river *n* a large running stream of water.

rivet *n* a fastening bolt clinched by hammering; * *vt* to clinch; to fasten firmly.

rivulet *n* a small stream.

road *n* a public highway for travellers, vehicles, etc; a highway; a surfaced track for travelling.

roam *vi* to wander; to travel.

roan *adj* (of an animal, *esp* a horse) having a coat in which the prevailing colour is thickly interspersed with hair of another colour, *esp* chestnut interspersed with grey or white; * *n* a animal with such a coat.

roar *vi* to cry with a loud voice; to bellow; * *n* the full loud cry of large animal; a shout.

roaring *adj* boisterous; noisy; brisk.

roast *vt* to cook with little or no moisture; to expose to great heat; * *n* roasted meat.

rob *vt* to take by force; to steal from.

robbery *n* theft with violence.

robe *n* a gown, or long, loose garment; * *vt* to invest with robes.

robot *n* a mechanical device that acts in a seemingly human fashion; a mechanism guided by automatic controls.

robust *adj* sturdy; healthy and strong.

rock *vt* to move to and fro; to swing; * *vi* to reel; * *n* a large mass of stone; a reef; a boiled sweet.

rockery n an artificial mound of earth and stones for growing ferns, etc, on.

rocket n any device driven forward by gases escaping through a rear vent; * vi to move in or like a rocket; to soar.

rod n a straight slender stick; a wand; a fishing rod.

rodent adj gnawing; * n any mammal of the order Rodentia.

roe n the spawn of fish.

roll n a scroll; anything wound into cylindrical form; a list or register; a rolling movement; a small cake of bread; an undulation; the sound of thunder; the beating of drumsticks; * vt, vi to move by turning over or from side to side; to move like a wheel; to press wth a roller.

roller n a cylinder for smoothing, crushing, etc; a long, swelling wave.

rolling adj revolving; undulating.

rolling pin n a roller for kneading dough.

rolling stock n the carriages, engines, etc, of a railway.

Roman Catholic adj belonging to the Christian church that is headed by the Pope.

romance n a tale in prose or verse; a novel of adventures; a love story; a love affair.

romantic adj fanciful; picturesque; pertaining to love affairs.

romp n a noisy game; a frolic; * vi to play boisterously.

roof n the cover of any building; a canopy; an upper limit.

rook n a kind of crow; a cheat; a piece in chess; * vi, vt to rob.

room n space; scope; opportunity; stead; a part of a building enclosed by walls, etc; *roomy adj spacious.

roost n a bird's perch or sleeping place.

rooster n the male of the domestic fowl; a cockerel.

root n that part of a plant which fixes itself in the ground foundation; origin; a form from which words are derived.

rooted adj fixed; deep; radical.

rope n a stout cord; a series of things connected; a cable; * vi, vt to fasten with a rope; to curb.

rose n any bush of the genus Rosa, family Rosaceae; knot of ribbons; a perforated nozzle.

rosemary n an evergreen fragrant shrub, Rosmarinus officinalis.

rosette n an ornamental knot of ribbons.

rosewood n any of several fragrant woods used in making furniture; a tree yielding such wood, esp a tropical tree of the genus Dalbergia.

rosin n resin.

roster n a list showing order in which officers, etc, are to take up certain duties (army).

rostrum n a platform for public speaking.

rosy adj red; blooming; hopeful.

rot vi, vt to decompose; to decay; * n putrid decay; nonsense.

rota n a turn in succession; a list or roster of duties.

rotary adj turning on an axle.

rotate vi to revolve round a centre or axis; to act in turn.

rotation n motion round a centre or axis; regular succession (as of crops).

rotten adj decomposed; decayed.

rotund adj round; spherical; plump.

rouge n a red cosmetic for tinting cheeks and lips.

rough adj not smooth; rugged; harsh; rude; uneven; ill-mannered.

roughen vt to make rough; * vi to become rough.

roulette n a game of chance played with a revolving disc and a ball.

round adj circular; spherical; plump; curved; not minutely accurate, as a number; * n ammunition; a turn or bout; * vt to make round; to encircle; * vi to make a circuit; * adv in a circle; around; * prep about; around.

roundabout adj indirect; circuitous; * n a merry-go-round.

rounders n a ball game played by two sides.

roundhead n a member of the parliamentary party in the English Civil War.

roundly adv openly; plainy.

rouse *vt* to arouse; to awaken; * *vi* to awake.

rout *n* a disorderly retreat.

route *n* a course or way.

routine *n* regular habit or practice.

rove *vi* to roam; to wander.

row *n* a line of objects; a line of seats; a noisy disturbance; a riot; * *vt* to propel (a boat) with oars.

rowdy *n* a turbulent fellow; a rough; * *adj* disreputable.

royal *adj* regal; relating to a king or queen.

royalist *n* an adherent of a king or queen.

royalty *n* state of being royal; a royal personage; share paid to an inventor, author, etc.

rub *vt*, *vi* to move one thing along surface of another with pressure or friction; to scour; to chafe; * *n* impediment; friction; pinch; gibe.

rubber *n* that which rubs; an eraser.

rubbish *n* refuse; debris; nonsense.

rubble *n* broken stones of irregular shapes.

rubric *n* headings entered on margin of page, worked out in red.

ruby *n* a valuable gem of various shades of red.

rucksack *n* a bag worn on the back by hikers.

rudder *n* the steering apparatus of a ship.

ruddy *adj* reddish; a healthy red.

rude *adj* rough-hewn; uncivilised; ill-mannered; vulgar.

rudimentary *adj* undeveloped; primitive.

rue *vt* to feel remorse for.

rueful *adj* piteous; remorseful.

ruff *n* a plaited collar or frill; a ruffle; act of trumping at whist and related card games; * *vt* to trump in card games.

ruffian *n* a brutal lawless person.

ruffle *vt* to rumple; to derange; * *vi* to bluster; * *n* a frill for the neck or wrist; agitation.

rug *n* a heavy fabric used as a mat.

rugged *adj* rough; uncouth; rocky.

rugby *n* a football game for two teams of fifteen players (rugby union) of thirteen (rugby league) played with an oval ball.

ruin *n* destruction; fall; overthrow; (*pl*) remains of old buildings; * *vt* to destroy; to impoverish.

ruinous *adj* fallen to ruin; disastrous.

rule *n* a ruler or measure; a guiding principle; a precept, law, maxim; government; method; * *vt*, *vi* to govern; to manage; to mark with lines; to decide; to reign.

ruling *adj* reigning; predominant; * *n* a point in law settled by a judge.

rum *n* spirit distilled from molasses.

rumble *vi* to make a dull, continued sound; * *n* a low, continued sound.

ruminant *n* an animal that chews the cud.

ruminate *vi* to regurgitate food after it has been swallowed; to meditate.

rummage *vt* to search narrowly but roughly; to ransack; * *n* a careful search.

rumour *n* an unconfirmed report.

rump *n* end of an animal's backbone; buttocks.

rumple *vt* to wrinkle; to ruffle.

rumpus *n* a great disturbance; a din.

run *vi* to move rapidly; to take part in a race; to flee; to spread or flow; * *vt* to incur; to smuggle; to melt; * *n* act of running; course run; trip; general demand; distance sailed or travelled.

runaway *n* a deserter; fugitive; * *adj* effected by fleeing or eloping.

rung *n* the round or step of a ladder.

runner *n* a messenger; an athlete; a creeping plant; that on which anything slides.

running *adj* moving swiftly.

runway *n* a landing strip for aircraft.

rupture *n* a break; fracture; breach; disagreement; quarrel.

rural *adj* pertaining to the country; rustic.

ruse *n* artifice; trick; deception.

rush *vi* to dash forward; * *n* a headlong advance; hurry; a reed.

rusk *n* a light hard cake or biscuit.

rust *n* the red oxide formed on iron exposed to moisture; a parasitic fungus of the class *Urediniomycetes*.

rustic *adj* rural; homely; unpolished.

rustle *vi, vt* to make a sound as of rubbing of dry leaves; * *n* the crinkling sound of blown leaves.

rusty *adj* covered with rust; impaired by inaction.

rut *n* the track of a wheel; a groove; routine.

ruthless *adj* cruel; pitiless.

rye *n* a cereal plant, *Secale cereale*; its grain; a whiskey made from rye.

S

sabbath *n* a day of rest and worship, observed on a Saturday by Jews, Sunday by Christians and Friday by Muslims.

sabbatical *n* a year's leave from a teaching post, often paid, for research.

sabotage *n* the deliberate damage of machinery, or disruption of public services, by enemy agents, disgruntled employees, etc, to prevent their effective operation; * *vt* to spoil, disrupt.

saccharin *n* a non-fattening sugar substitute.

sachet *n* a small bag for perfume, etc.

sack *n* a bag made of coarse cloth used as a container; pillage of a town; * *vt* to pillage; to dismiss.

sacrament *n* a solemn religious ordinance; a sacred symbol.

sacred *adj* set apart for a holy purpose; consecrated; religious.

sacrifice *n* something given up in the interests of another; loss; the thing offered up; * *vt* to give up.

sacrum *n* the bone at base of vertebral column.

sad *adj* sorrowful; gloomy.

sadden *vt* to make sad; * *vi* to become sad.

saddle *n* a seat for a rider on a horse or bicycle; * *vt* to put a saddle on.

sadism *n* sexual pleasure obtained by inflicting cruelty on another.

safe *adj* secure; free from danger; trustworthy; * *n* a strong box for securing valuables; a burglar-proof chamber; a cupboard.

safeguard *n* a defence; protection; * *vt* to guard.

safety *n* freedom from danger, hurt, or loss.

safety belt *n* a belt worn by a person working at great height to prevent falling; a seatbelt in a car.

safety valve *n* a valve which opens when the pressure of steam in boiler, etc, becomes too great.

sag *vi* to sink in the middle; to droop.

sagacity *n* shrewdness; high intelligence.

sage *adj* wise; grave; * *n* a wise man; an aromatic plant, *Sativa officinalis*.

sail *n* a canvas spread to catch the wind; a voyage in a sailing vessel; * *vi, vt* to move by means of sails; to glide; to navigate.

sailor *n* a seaman; a mariner.

saint *n* one eminent for piety.

sake *n* behalf; benefit; interest.

salad *n* a dish of raw herbs, lettuce, cress, tomatoes, etc.

salary *n* a fixed, regular payment for work.

sale *n* act of selling; market; auction.

salesman *n* one employed to sell goods.

salient *adj* springing; projecting; conspicuous; * **salience** *n*.

saline *adj* consisting of salt; salt.

saliva *n* the fluid secreted by glands of mouth that aids digestion.

sallow *adj* having a sickly, yellowish colour.

salon *n* a reception room; a gallery.

saloon *n* a spacious apartment; main cabin of a steamer.

salt *n* a substance, sodium chloride, for seasoning and preserving food; a compound produced by the combination of a base with an acid; savour; an old sailor; * *vt* to sprinkle with salt.

salutary *adj* beneficial, wholesome.

salutation *n* a greeting; a salute.

salute *vt* to greet; to welcome; the formalised military greeting whereby ones hand is placed above ones left eye; * *vi* to make a salute.

salvage *n* the saving of a ship or its cargo at sea; the saving of property from fire; payment for such service.

salve *n* a healing ointment; remedy; * *vt* to apply salve to.

salvo *n* a salute of guns; a sudden burst.

same *adj* identical; exactly similar; unchanged; uniform; monotonous.

sample *n* a specimen; a small part representative of the whole.

sanctify *vt* to make holy.

sanctimonious *adj* making a show of sanctity; hypocritical.

sanction *n* permission; authority; a penalty by which a law is enforced; * *vt* to ratify; to authorise.

sanctity *n* saintliness; holiness.

sanctuary *n* a sacred place; part of a church where the altar is placed; a sure refuge.

sand *n* fine particles of stone; (in *pl*) tracts of sand on the seashore, etc.

sandal *n* a shoe consisting of a sole strapped to the foot.

sandpaper *n* paper coated with sand for smoothing and polishing.

sandstone *n* a stone composed of compressed sand.

sandwich *n* slices of bread, with meat or savoury between; * *vt* to fit between two other pieces.

sane *adj* sound in mind; sensible.

sanguine *adj* full of blood; hopeful.

sanitary *adj* healthful; hygienic.

sanitation *n* measures for securing good health in a community; hygiene; drainage and disposal of sewage.

sanity *n* soundness of mind.

sanskrit *n*, *adj* the ancient language of Hindus.

sap *vt*, *vi* to undermine; * *n* a trench; vital juice of plants.

sapient *adj* wise; sage; discerning.

sapling *n* a young tree.

sapphire *n* a precious stone of a rich blue colour.

sarcasm *n* biting irony.

sarcastic *adj* bitingly ironic; satirical.

sarcophagus *n* (*pl* sarcophagi) a coffin of stone.

sardonic *adj* bitter; mocking; grimly jocular.

sarorial *adj* pertaining to a tailor.

sash *n* a long band or scarf worn for ornament; a window frame.

satan *n* the devil; the adversary of God.

satchel *n* a little bag for carrying books, papers, etc.

sate *vt* to satisfy the appetite of; to glut.

satellite *n* a small planet like body orbiting a larger planet; a man-made object orbiting the earth to gather scientific information, etc.

satiate *vt* to satisfy fully; to surfeit.

satin *n* a glossy close-woven silk cloth.

satire *n* a composition in prose or verse, ridiculing or censuring manners and customs of the time.

satirise *vt* to ridicule; to hold up to scorn.

satisfaction *n* pleasure; content-ment; atonement; payment.

satisfactory *adj* adequate; up to expectation.

satisfy *vt*, *vi* to gratify fully; to convince.

saturate *vt* to soak thoroughly.

saturation *n* state of being soaked with another substance to the utmost limit.

Saturday *n* the seventh day of the week.

saturn *n* the sixth planet out from the sun with conspicuous rings.

sauce *n* a liquid relish or season-ing for food.

saucepan *n* a deep cooking pan with a handle and a lid.

saucer *n* a curved plate in which cup is set.

saucy *adj* pert; impudent; rude.

sausage *n* minced seasoned meat, *esp* pork, packed into animal gut.

savage *adj* wild; barbarous; brutal; * *n* a barbarian.

savagery *n* cruelty; barbarity.

save *vt* to preserve; to protect; to rescue; to spare; * *vi* to be economical; * *prep* except.

saving *adj* thrifty; preserving; * *n* that which is saved.

saviour *n* a preserver; rescuer.

savour *n* flavour; a distinctive quality; * *vi* to have a particular taste.

savoury *adj* tasty; palatable; spicy rather than sweet.

saw *n* a cutting instrument with toothed edge; * *vt, vi* to cut with a saw.

say *vt, vi* to utter in words; to speak; to declare; to relate.

saying *n* a proverb; maxim.

scab *n* crust formed over a sore on healing; itch; mange.

scabbard *n* the sheath of a sword.

scabies *n* contagious itching skin disease, caused by the itch mite.

scaffolding *n* a framework to aid in building houses, etc.

scald *vt* to burn with hot liquid; * *n* a burn from hot liquid or steam.

scale *n* a thin flake on the skin of some animals; (in *pl*) instrument for weighing; gradation; a measure; series of musical notes; * *vt* to weigh; to strip of scales; to climb; * *vi* to peel.

scalp *n* the skin and hair of top of head; * *vt* to cut off scalp.

scalpel *n* a short, thin, sharp knife.

scamper *vi* to scurry; * *n* a hurried run.

scan *vt* to look through quickly; to examine with a radiological device; to mark the rhythm of verse.

scandal *n* a disgraceful event or action; * scandalous *adj*.

scant *adj* limited; meagre; * *vt* to stint; to grudge; * *adv* scarcely.

scapegoat *n* one who bears the blame of others.

scapula *n* the shoulder blade.

scar *n* the mark of a wound; a blemish; a cliff; a steep bare bank; * *vt* to form a scar; to wound.

scarce *adj* rare; deficient; hard to find; * scarcity *n*.

scare *vt* to terrify; to scare; * *n* a causeless alarm; panic.

scarf *n* a broad band or sash for neck wear; a joint in timber.

scarlet *n, adj* a bright red colour.

scathing *adj* severe; bitterly critical; withering.

scatter *vt* to disperse; to throw about loosely; * *vi* to straggle apart.

scatterbrain *n* a forgetful person.

scattered *adj* thinly spread; dispersed.

scenario *n* summary of leading incidents in a play.

scene *n* a stage; a distinct part of a play; a painted device on the stage; place of action; a view; display of emotion.

scenery *n* the painted scenes and hangings of the stage; landscape; view.

scenic *adj* picturesque.

scent *n* an odour left by an animal, by which it can be tracked, a perfume; sense of smell; * *vt* to discern by smell.

sceptic *n* a doubter; disbeliever.

scepticism *n* doubt; incredulity.

sceptre *n* the rod borne by a ruler as a symbol of power.

schedule *n* a timetable; a list or inventory; * *vt* to plan.

scheme *n* a plan of proceedings; a project; * *vt, vi* to plan; project; plot.

scholar *n* a school pupil; a learned person.

scholarship *n* learning; an annual grant to a student, *usu* won by competitive examination.

school *n* a place of instruction; a body of pupils; disciples; sect or body; a shoal (of fishes); * *vt* to instruct; to train.

schooner *n* a vessel with two masts.

science *n* a branch of knowledge based upon the systematic observation of and experiment upon natural phenomena.

scientific *adj* systematic; of or related to science; using a method prescribed by science for experiments, etc.

scientist *n* a specialist in a branch of science.

scintillate *vi* to sparkle; to twinkle.

scion *n* a cutting; a young shoot; a descendant.

scissors *npl* a cutting instrument of two blades, the edges of which slide past each other.

sclerosis *n* a hardening of tissue.

scoff *n* an expression of scorn; * *vi* to jeer; to mock; * *vt* to mock at.

scold *vi, vt* to rebuke angrily; to find fault with harshly; to tell off.

scoop *n* a short-handled shovel for grain, etc; a coal scuttle; a hollowing out spoon or gouge for cheese, etc; * *vt* to hollow out.

scope *n* an aim or end; range; opportunity.

scorch *vt, vi* to singe; parch; shrivel; to drive at reckless speed.

score *n* a notch; a line; a furrow; an account or reckoning; runs, points, etc, made in games; twenty; reason; copy of concerted musical piece; * *vt* to mark; record; register.

scorn *n* extreme contempt; * *vt* to deride; * *vi* to feel or show scorn.

scornful *adj* disdainful; mocking; contemptuous.

scotch *vt* to stamp out; (in full Scotch whisky) whisky distilled in Scotland.

scoundrel *n* a rogue, rascal.

scour *vt, vi* to clean by rubbing; to purge iolently; to pass swiftly over.

scourge *n* a lash; a whip; a grievous affliction; a plague; * *vt* to lash; to afflict sorely.

scout *n* an exploring or reconnoitring messenger; a person employed to find new talent.

scowl *vi* to frown in anger; * *n* a sullen frowning look.

scraggy *adj* lean and bony; gaunt.

scramble *vi* to clamber on all fours; to break and stir eggs; to make (a message) unintelligible in transmission; * *n* an eager struggle.

scrambling *adj* irregular; straggling.

scrap *n* a small piece; a fragment; a cut-out picture.

scrape *vt, vi* to rub with something hard; to grate; to gather money laboriously; to make a grating noise; * *n* a rasping sound; serious trouble.

scratch *vt, vi* to tear or mark with something sharp; to tear with nails; to erase or cancel; * *n* a slight mark or wound; starting line; * *adj* haphazard.

scrawl *vt, vi* to scribble; * *n* slovenly writing.

scream *vi* to shriek; * *n* a shrill cry.

screen *n* a shield from draughts, heat, etc; a partition in a church; a sheet on which pictures are projected; an electronic display; * *vt* to shelter; to conceal; to sift.

screw *n* a cylinder with a spiral ridge; a screw propeller; a twist or turn; * *vt* to fasten by a screw; to twist; to oppress.

screwdriver *n* an instrument for turning screw nails.

scribble *vt, vi* to write carelessly; * *n* a scrawl.

scribe *n* a writer; copyist.

script *n* handwriting; type imitating handwriting; the text of a play, etc.

scripture *n* any sacred writing.

scroll *n* a roll of paper; a first draft; a spiral design.

scrotum *n* the bag which contains the testicles.

scrounge *vt, vi* to seek or obtain (something) for nothing.

scrub *vt* to rub hard; to make clean or bright; * *n* vegetation mainly of brushwood and stunted forest growth.

scruple *n* (*usu pl*) a moral principle or belief causing one to doubt or hesitate about a course of action; * *vt, vi* to hesitate owing to scruples.

scrupulous *adj* conscientious; exact.

scrutinise *vt, vi* to examine closely; to investigate.

scrutiny *n* close search; careful investigation.

scull *n* a short oar, used in pairs; * *vt* to propel by sculls.

scullery *n* a back kitchen where dishes, etc, are washed.

sculptor *n* an artist in stone, wood, clay, etc.

sculpture *n* the art of carving wood or stone into images; such an image.

scum *n* impurities which rise to the surface of liquids; offscourings.

scupper *n* hole to carry off water from ship's deck, to sink deliberately.

scurry *vt* to hurry; * *n* haste.

scurvy *n* a disease caused by insufficiency of vitamin C; * *adj* vile; mean.

scythe *n* an implement for mowing grass, etc.

sea *n* an expanse of salt water, ocean or part of it.

seagoing *adj* applied to vessels going to foreign ports.

seal *n* a stamp with motto or device; wax with stamp impression; guarantee; carnivorous marine animal; * *vt* to set a seal to; to confirm; to close.

sea level *n* the level of the sea's surface.

seam *n* the joining line of edges of cloth; a vein of metal; a scar.

séance *n* to try to communicate with the dead; a meeting of spiritualists.

scar *vt* to brand; to burn; to deaden.

search *vt* to look or rummage for; to explore, examine; * *n* quest; pursuit; inquiry.

searching *adj* penetrating; severe; testing.

seashore *n* land beside the sea or between high and low water marks; the beach.

seasick *adj* affected with sickness by rolling of ship.

seaside *n* the sea coast.

season *n* a division of the year; a suitable time; time of greatest activity; * *vt* to accustom; to acclimatise; to flavour.

seasonable *adj* opportune; timely.

seasoning *n* salt, spices, etc used to enhance the flavour of food.

seat *n* that on which one sits; a chair, stool, etc; residence; station; manner of sitting; * *vt* to place on a seat; to settle.

seaward *adj*, *adv* toward the sea.

seaweed *n* a mass of plants growing in or under water; a sea plant, *esp* a marine alga.

sebaceous *adj* fatty.

secede *vi* to withdraw from fellowship; * **secession** *n*.

secluded *adj* retired; remote; private.

second *adj* next after the first; inferior; other; * *n* one who comes next after first; one who supports another; to place in temporary service elsewhere; sixtieth part of a minute; * *vt* to support.

secondary *adj* subordinate; not elementary; inferior.

secrecy *n* concealment; seclusion; habit of keeping secrets.

secret *adj* not made public; concealed from others; hidden;

private; * *n* something hidden; a mystery; a hidden cause.

secretariat *n* an administrative office or staff, as in a government.

secretary *n* a person employed to deal with correspondence, filing, answering telephone calls etc; head of a state department; executive officer of company.

secrete *vt* to hide; to produce and release (a substance) out of blood or sap.

secretion *n* act or process of secreting; matter secreted, as bile, etc.

secretive *adj* given to secrecy; reticent.

sect *n* a body of persons united in doctrine; a denomination.

sectarian *adj* pertaining to a sect; bigoted; * *n* member of a sect.

section *n* a cutting; part cut off; subdivision of chapter, etc; slice; distinct part; the plane figure formed when solid is cut through.

sectional *adj* made up of sections; partial.

sector *n* part of circle between two radii; a mathematical instrument.

secular *adj* worldly; temporal; not sacred.

secure *adj* free from care or danger; safe; confident; * *vi* to make safe; to seize and confine; to guarantee; to fasten.

security *n* safety; confidence; protection; a guarantee; a surety; *pl* bonds, stocks, etc.

sedate *adj* staid; sober; calm; composed; * **sedately** *adv*.

sedative *adj* soothing; * *n* an opiate; a soothing drug.

sedentary *adj* inactive; requiring much sitting.

sediment *n* that which settle to bottom of liquids; matter deposited by water or wind.

sedition *n* action or speech against law and order.

seduce *vt* tempt or entice into sexual activity; tempt into anything; to lead astray; to corrupt.

seduction *n* allurement; temptation; attraction; * **seductive** *adj*.

see *vt* to perceive by the eye; to notice; to understand; * *vi* to have

the power of sight; * *interj* look!
* *n* diocese or sphere of a bishop.

seed *n* a plants reproductive unit
from which a new plant grows;
descendant; * *vt, vi* to sow; to
produce seed.

seedy *adj* shabby; out of sorts.

seeing *n* vision, sight; * *adj* having
sight; observant; * *conj* in view of
the fact that; since.

seek *vt, vi* to search for; to ask for;
to resort to.

seem *vi* to appear; to look as if, to
pretend.

seemingly *adv* apparently.

seemly *adj* becoming; decent.

seesaw *n* a swinging movement up
and down; children's playground
equipment, consisting of a long
plank on a pivot; vacillation.

seethe *vi* to be very angry outwardly.

segment *n* a section; part of circle
cut off by straight line; a portion.

segregate *vt* to set apart or
separate from others; to isolate.

seismic *adj* related to earthquakes
and other vibrations of the
earth's crust.

seismology *n* the study of seismic
activity.

seize *vt, vi* to lay hold of forcibly;
to apprehend; to be gripped by
fear, illness, etc.

seizure *n* act of seizing; a sudden
attack of illness.

seldom *adv* rarely; not often.

select *vt* to choose; to pick out;
* *adj* chosen.

selection *n* process of choosing;
things chosen.

self *n* (*pl* selves) one's individual
person or interest; * *adj* uniform.

self-conscious *adj* thinking about
one's self overmuch; shy.

self-denial *n* the forbearing to
gratify one's desires; unselfishness.

self-esteem *n* one's opinion of
one's self; vanity.

self-evident *adj* obvious; needing
no proof.

self-important *adj* pompous.

self-imposed *adj* voluntarily
undertaken.

selfish *adj* absorbed in one's self;
ungenerous.

self-respect *n* proper pride.

self-righteous *adj* stressing one's
own goodness; pharisaic.

self-sufficient *adj* needing no help.

sell *vt* to give for a price; to betray;
* *vi* to practise selling; to be sold.

semblance *n* similarity; appearance.

semibreve *n* a musical note = 2
minims.

semicircle *n* half a circle.

semicolon *n* the point (;) marking
a longer pause than a comma.

seminal *adj* pertaining to seed;
germinal.

seminar *n* a small class for
university students for research,
discussion, etc; any group meetng
to discuss ideas, research, etc.

semiquaver *n* half a quaver in music.

senate *n* a legislative or delibera-
tive council; governing body in
some universities.

senator *n* a member of a senate.

send *vt* to cause to go or be
carried; to transmit; to dispatch.

senile *adj* aged; doting; tottering.

senility *n* a state of being
mentally weakened by old age.

senior *adj* older; higher in rank or
standing; * *n* one older in age or
office.

seniority *n* priority in rank or office.

sensation *n* perception through
the senses; feeling; a thrill.

sensational *adj* causing excited
feeling; emotional.

sense *n* one of the five senses, sight,
hearing, taste, smell, touch;
understanding; good judgement;
discernment; meaning.

senseless *adj* stupid; foolish;
meaningless; purposeless.

sensibility *n* acuteness of
perception; delicacy of feeling.

sensible *adj* having good sense;
judicious; reasonable; appreciable.

sensitive *adj* easily affected;
touchy; tender.

sensitise *vt* to make (paper)
susceptible to rays of light.

sensory *adj* relating to the senses;
conveying sensation.

sensual *adj* bodily, relating to the
senses rather than the mind;
arousing sexual desire.

sentence *n* opinion; judgement of a court; a number of words containing complete sense; * *vt* to pass sentence upon; to condemn.

sentient *adj* making use of the senses.

sentiment *n* tenderness of feeling; thought prompted by emotion; a toast.

sentimental *adj* apt to be swayed by feelings; romantic.

sentry *n* a soldier on guard to give warning of danger.

separate *vt* to put or set apart; to sever; to divide apart; * *vi* to go apart; * *adj* detached; distinct.

separation *n* the act of separating or the state of being separate; a formal arrangement of husband and wife to live apart.

separatist *n* one who advocates separation; a seceder.

sepsis *n* the state of being septic; blood poisoning

September *n* the ninth month of the year.

septic *adj* (of a festering wound) contaminated by bacteria; putrefaction.

septicaemia *n* blood poisoning.

septuagenarian *n* a person seventy years of age.

septum *n* (*pl* **septa**) a membrane separating organs or cavities.

sepulchre *n* a tomb; * *vt* to bury.

sequel *n* that which follows; a consequence; issue.

sequence *n* a coming after; succession; series.

sequester *vt* to set apart; to withdraw; to seize goods till debt is paid; to confiscate.

sequestrate *vt* to seize and dispose of goods for benefit of creditors.

sequestration *n* confiscation of debtor's goods in interest of creditors.

serene *adj* clear; bright; calm; unruffled; * **serenity** *n*.

sergeant *n* a non-commissioned officer above Corporal in the army etc; a police officer one rank up from constable.

serial *adj* appearing periodically; * *n* a story issued in parts.

series *n* a succession of things; sequence.

serious *adj* grave; earnest; attended with danger; important; critical.

sermon *n* a religious discourse; an admonition.

serpentine *adj* spiral; winding; crafty; * *n* a mineral.

serrated *adj* notched; toothed,

serum *n* the watery part of bodily fluid, *esp* liquid that separates out from the blood when it coagulates; such fluid taken from the blood of an animal immune to a disease, used as an anti-toxin.

servant *n* a domestic; an attendant.

serve *vt* to work for and meet the needs of; to minister to; to deliver or execute; to supply with (food); * *vi* to be a servant; to suit.

service *n* work of servant; employment; kindness; official duties; liturgy; table dishes; the services, army, navy, etc.

serviceable *adj* useful; beneficial.

servile *adj* slavish; fawning; subservient; * **servility** *n*.

servitude *n* slavery; bondage.

session *n* the meeting of a court; a series of such meetings; a period of study; a university year.

set *vt* to place in position; to fix; to regulate or adjust; to fit to music; to spread (sails); * *vi* to sink below horizon; to solidify; * *n* direction; tendency; attitude; bent; collection of things; a group of games; persons associated.

setting *n* descent below horizon; hardening of plaster; the mounting of a gem; fitting to music; a background scene; environment.

settle *vt*, *vi* to fix permanently; to quiet; to decide; to pay; to agree; to subside; to become calm; to clarify; to take up residence.

settled *adj* established; steadfast.

settlement *n* an arrangement; a newly established colony; subsidence (of buildings).

settler *n* a colonist.

seven *adj* the fourth prime number; 7.

seventeenth *adj*, *n* the ordinal of seventeen.

seventh *adj* the ordinal of seven.

seventieth *adj, n* the ordinal of seventy.

seventy *adj, n* seven times ten.

sever *vt* to separate; to divide into parts; to break off.

several *adj* separate; more than two, but not very many.

severally *adv* separately.

severance *n* separation.

severe *adj* serious; grave; harsh; searching; austere; * severity *n*.

sew *vt, vi* to make by needle and thread.

sewage *n* waste matter carried off by sewers.

sewer *n* a subterranean drain, to carry off water, filth, etc.

sex *n* the characteristics that distinguish male and female organisms on the basis of their reproductive function; the fact of being one of these; one of these groups; sexual intercourse.

sexagenarian *n* a person sixty years of age.

sexism *n* discrimination on the basis of sex.

sexual *adj* pertaining to sex.

sexual intercourse *n* the act of copulation.

sexuality *n* state of being sexual.

shabbily *adv* in a shabby manner; with shabby clothes; meanly.

shabby *adj* threadbare; mean; stingy.

shackle *n* a fetter; a manacle; * *vt* to fetter; hamper.

shade *n* interception of light; obscurity; darkness; a shady place; a screen; dimness; gradation of light; a ghost.

shading *n* light and shade in a picture.

shadow *adj* a figure projected by interception of light; shade; an inseparable companion; a spirit; * *vi* to shade; to cloud; to follow closely.

shadowy *adj* faint; dim; insub-stantial.

shady *adj* abounding in shade; of doubtful character.

shaft *n* the handle of a tool, etc; body of a column; pole of carriage; a critical remark or attack; well-like entrance to mine.

shaggy *adj* long and unkempt; rough; untidy.

shake *vt* to move quickly to and fro; to agitate; * *vi* to tremble; * *n* a tremor; shock; a trill.

shaky *adj* unsteady; feeble.

shale *n* a clay rock having a slaty structure.

shall *vb, aux* in first person it is a future tense; in the second and third it implies authority.

shallow *adj* not deep; superficial; simple.

sham *n* a pretence; a fraud; * *adj* false; * *vt, vi* to feign; pretend.

shambles *npl* a place of great disorder.

shambling *adj* walking with awkward, unsteady gait.

shame *n* a painful emotion excited by guilt, disgrace, etc; * *vt* to make ashamed; to disgrace.

shameful *adj* disgraceful; infamous.

shameless *adj* immodest; unblushing.

shampoo *n* a liquid cleansing agent for washing the hair; * *vt* to wash the hair with shampoo.

shandy *n* beer diluted with lemonade, etc.

shank *n* the leg; the shinbone; the stem or shaft of tool, anchor, etc.

shanty *n* a hut or mean dwelling; sailors' song.

shape *vt* to form; to mould; * *vi* to suit; * *n* form or figure; make; a model.

shapely *adj* well-proportioned.

shard *n* a fragment.

share *n* a part, lot, or portion; ploughshare; one of equal parts of company's capital; * *vt, vi* to divide; to apportion among others; to have part.

shareholder *n* owner of shares in company.

shark *n* any of various *usu* voracious marine fish with a cartilaginous skeleton; a swindler.

sharp *adj* having a cutting edge or point; keen; shrewd; piercing; biting; * *n* a note raised a semitone.

sharpen *vt* to make sharp; to whet.

shatter *vt, vi* to break in pieces.

shave *vt* to cut hair closely with a razor; to pare; to miss narrowly; to graze; * *n* a cutting off of the beard; a narrow escape.

shaving *n* a thin slice pared off.

shawl *n* a loose covering for the shoulders.

she *pron nominative* third person singular feminine.

sheaf *n* (*pl* sheaves) a bundle of stalks of wheat, etc.

shear *vt*, *vi* to clip or eat through; to remove (a sheep's fleece) by clipping; to break off; mechanics the strain produced in an object when layers are laterally shifted relative to one another.

sheath *n* a close fitting cover; a condom.

sheathe *vt* to put into sheath; to protect by a casing.

sheathing *n* covering of metal to protect ship's bottom.

shed *vi* to cast off; to let fall in drops; to spill; * *n* a hut.

sheen *n* brightness; gloss.

sheer *adj* mere; downright; precipitous; * *vi* to swerve; to shy.

sheet *n* a broad, thin piece of anything; broad expanse; bed linen; a single piece of paper.

shelf *n* (*pl* shelves) a horizontal board fixed in position to support books, etc; a ledge.

shell *n* hard outer case; an explosive projectile; * *vt* to fire shells at.

shellfish *n* an aquatic shelled mollusc (*eg* oyster); a crustacean (*eg* crab).

shelter *n* a protection; asylum; refuge; * *vt* shelter to protect; * *vi* to take shelter.

shelve *vt* to place on a shelf; to defer consideration; * *vi* to slope.

shelving *n* shelves collectively.

shepherd *n* a person who looks after sheep.

sheriff *n* the chief executive officer of the crown in a county administrating justice, etc.

sherry *n* a fortified wine of southern Spain.

shield *n* a protective covering or guard; a piece of armour carried for defence on the left arm; * *vt* to protect; to screen.

shift *vi* to change; to move; to contrive; to manage; * *n* a change; expedient; a dodge; relay time.

shiftless *adj* improvident; useless; without resource.

shifty *adj* unreliable; changeable; tricky,

shimmer *vi* to glisten softly; * *n* a flicker.

shin *n* the front of lower leg.

shine *vi* to emit light; to beam; to be bright, lively, conspicuous.

shingle *n* thin wood used in roofing; loose gravel; * *vt* to roof with shingles.

shingles *n* a viral disease marked by a painful rash of red spots.

shining *adj* bright; illustrious.

ship *n* a large seagoing vessel; * *vt*, *vi* to put or take on board; to transport for service in a ship; to fix in place.

shipmate *n* a fellow sailor.

shipment *n* a consignment; goods shipped.

shipper *n* one who exports or imports goods by sea.

shipping *n* ships in general; the business of transporting goods.

shipshape *adj* sea worthy; trim.

shipwreck *n* the wreck of a ship; the loss of a vessel at sea.

shipyard *n* a shipbuilding establishment.

shirk *vt*, *vi* to try to evade a duty.

shirt *n* a sleeved garment of cotton etc for the upper body.

shiver *vt* to shatter; * *vi* to tremble, as from cold; to shudder; * *n* a splinter; shaking fit.

shoal *n* a large number of fish swimming together.

shock *n* a violent collision; a sudden emotional disturbance; the effect of an electrical charge on the body; * *vt* to horrify; to disgust.

shocking *adj* dreadful; offensive.

shoddy *n* of inferior quality; * *adj* trashy.

shoe *n* outer covering for foot; metal plate on hoof of horse.

shoehorn *n* a curved piece of horn to help the putting on of shoes.

shoot *vt* to discharge with force; to hit or kill with missile; to propel quickly; * *vi* to dart along; to sprout; * *n* a young branch or bud; a chute.

shop *n* a place where goods are sold by retail; * *vi* to visit shops.

shore *n* land along edge of sea; coast; a prop; * *vt* to prop up.

short *adj* not long or tall; scanty; concise; curt; * *npl* short trousers.

shortage *n* a deficit.

shorten *vt* to make short; to reduce amount.

shorthand *n* abbreviated writing.

short-sighted *n* able to see far; wanting foresight.

shot *n* act of shooting; a projectile; a bullet; range or reach; a marksman.

shoulder *n* the joint connecting arm, foreleg, or wing to body; * *vt* to jostle; to put on one's shoulder.

shout *vi* to utter a loud cry; * *n* a loud cry.

shove *vt, vi* to push forward; to jostle; * *n* a push.

shovel *n* a kind of spade with slightly curved blade.

show *vt* to display; to exhibit; to demonstrate; to prove; * *vi* to appear; * *n* display; pageant; pretence; a theatrical performance.

shower *n* a brief fail of rain, etc; a copious supply; * *vt, vi* to rain; to pour down; to bestow liberally.

showroom *n* a room in which goods are exhibited.

shred *vt* to tear into small pieces; * *n* a fragment or scrap.

shrew *n* a small mouse-like mammal of the family *Soricidae*.

shrewd *adj* astute; clever.

shriek *vi* to scream; * *n* a shrill cry.

shrill *adj* piercing in sound; strident.

shrine *n* a hallowed place; an altar; a tomb.

shrink *vi* to contract; to shrivel; to flinch.

shrive *vt* to confess and absolve.

shrivel *vi, vt* to shrink into wrinkles; to wither up.

shroud *n* a burial cloth; anything that covers or conceals.

shrub *n* a bush with separate stems from same root.

shrubbery *n* a plantation of shrubs.

shrug *vt, vi* to raise one's shoulders in surprise, doubt, indifference, etc.

shudder *vi* to tremble with fear; to quake; * *n* a tremor.

shuffle *vt* to shove one way and the other; to confuse; to mix cards; * *vi* to quibble; to drag one's feet; * *n* an evasion; a shuffling gait or step.

shuffling *adj* moving with irregular gait; evasive.

shun *vt* to avoid; to refrain from.

shunt *vi, vt* in railways, to switch from one track to another.

shut *vt, vi* to close or stop up; to bar.

shutter *n* a movable screen for a window.

shuttle *n* a boat-shaped contrivance for shooting cross threads in loom; an aircraft, spacecraft, etc, making back-and-forth trips over a given route.

shuttlecock *n* a cork stuck with feathers, used instead of a ball in badminton.

shy *adj* timid; retiring; very self-conscious; coy; * *vi, vt* to refuse a jump (of a horse); * *n* a throw.

sibilant *adj* hissing; * *n* a letter uttered with a hissing as s and z.

sick *adj* ill; disgusted; unhealthy; vomiting.

sicken *vt* to make sick; to disgust; * *vi* to become sick.

sickening *adj* disgusting.

sickness *n* disease; ill-health.

side *n* the broad or long surface of a body; edge, border; slope (of hill); bias (of ball); * *vi* to support; espouse (a cause).

sideboard *n* a piece of furniture used to hold dining utensils, etc.

sidetrack *vt* to prevent action by diversionary tactics; to shunt aside.

sideways *adv* toward one side; on one side.

siding *n* a short line of rails for shunting purposes.

siege *n* the surrounding of a fortified place to cut off supplies and compel its surrender; the act of besieging; a coninued attempt to gain something.

sieve n a strainer; sifter.

sift vt to separate coarser parts from finer with a sieve.

sifter n a sieve.

sigh vi to draw a deep and audible breath, as in grief, weariness or relief; * n a long and deep breath.

sight n the act or power of seeing; a view; visibility; * vt to see.

sightless adj unable to see.

sign n a mark, token, stamp, or symbol; an emblem; indication; gesture; * vt, vi to affix one's signature; to make a sign.

signal n a sign to give information, orders, etc, at a distance; * adj notable; * vt, vi to convey by signs.

signally adv remarkably; notably.

signatory n party to signing a treaty or other agreement.

signature n one's name, initials or mark written at the bottom of a document, letter, etc, as a formal assent to the contents of the document.

signboard n a board marked with person's name or business.

significant adj weighty; important; highly expressive; momentous.

signify vt to make known; to mean; to imply.

silence n quiet; secrecy; absence of sound; * vt to cause to be quiet.

silent adj mute; taciturn; making no noise.

silhouette n a shadow outline of a shape against light.

silicon n a non-metallic element whose oxide is silica.

silk n the fine thread produced by silkworm; cloth made of silk.

sill n the timber or stone at foot of window.

silly adj foolish; unwise; frivolous; being stunned or dazed.

silo n a pit or tower for storage (fodder).

silt n sediment from moving water.

silver n a ductile, malleable, precious metal of a white colour used in jewellery, cutlery etc; * vt, vi to coat with silver.

silversmith n a worker or dealer in silver.

similar adj like; resembling.

simile n a figure of speech containing a comparison.

simmer vi to boil gently.

simper vi to smile in a silly manner; * n an affected smile.

simple adj not complex; single; artless; plain; silly; easy to understand or solve; * n a medicinal herb.

simplicity n sincerity; artlessness; innocence; folly.

simplify vt to make simple.

simulate vt to pretend to have or feel; to feign.

simulation n reproducing specific conditions or conduct.

simultaneous adj taking place at the same time.

sin n a transgression of a religious rule; an offence; * vi to do wrong.

since adv from that time; ago; * prep after; * conj because that.

sincere adj genuine, real, not pretended; honest; straightforward.

sincerity n honesty of mind; freedom from pretence.

sinecure n a paid office with nominal duties usu given for reasons of courtesy.

sinew n the fibrous cord which joins muscle to bone.

sinful adj wicked; erring.

sing vi, vt to utter melodious sounds; to celebrate in song.

singe vt to burn surface; * n a slight burn.

single adj being one or a unit; individual; unmarried; sincere; * vt to select individually (with out).

singular adj denoting only one person or thing; remarkable; quaint; rare.

singularly adv peculiarly; remarkably.

sinister adj left; evil; malevolent; ominous.

sink vi to fall below the surface (water); to subside; to fall in value, strength, etc; * vt to immerse; to dig (shaft); to degrade; * n a drain or receptacle to carry off dirty water.

sinner *n* a transgressor; offender; a person who sins.

sinus *n* an bone cavity in the skull that connects with the nostrils.

sip *vt* to drink in small quantities; * *n* a drop; a taste.

siphon *n* a bent tube for drawing off liquids.

sir *n* a word of respect used to men; a title.

siren *n* a device producing a loud wailing sound as a warning signal; (myth) a sea nymph who lured sailors to destruction.

sirloin *n* the upper part of loin of beef.

sister *n* the daughter of one's parents; a member of a religious sisterhood.

sister-in-law *n* a husband or wife's sister.

sit *vi* to rest oneself on the buttocks, as on a chair; to incubate; to have a seat (in Parliament); to take an examination.

site *n* situation; a building plot; the scene of something.

sitting *n* a session, *eg* of a court.

situated *adj* placed; located.

situation *n* position; station; post; a position on which one finds oneself.

six *adj, n* one more than five.

sixfold *adj, adv* six times.

sixteen *adj, n* six and ten.

sixteenth *adj* the ordinal of sixteen.

sixth *adj* the ordinal of six.

sixtieth *adj, n* the ordinal of sixty.

sixty *adj, n* six times ten.

size *n* magnitude; the dimensions or proportion,; of something; * *vt* to arrange according to size.

skate *n* a steel bar fastened to boots for skating across ice on; a cartilaginous flat fish, *Raja batis*; * *vt* to go on skates.

skateboard *n* a short oblong board with two wheels at each end for standing on and riding.

skeleton *n* the bony framework of an animal; outline.

sketch *n* an outline; a first rough draught; * *vt* to draw; to outline.

skewer *n* a pin for fastening meat.

ski *n* (*pl* **skis**) a long narrow runner of wood, metal or plastic that is fastened to a boot to enable movement across snow; * *vi* to travel on skis.

skid *vt, vi* to slide; to slide uncontrollably (of a person, car, etc).

skill *n* ability; expertness; aptitude; proficiency.

skim *vt* to remove the scum from the surface of; to glance over a book, document, etc; * *vi* to glide along (water).

skin *n* the natural outer covering of animals; a hide; rind; * *vt* to strip the skin from; flay.

skinny *adj* very thin.

skip *vi* to leap; to bound; to spring; * *vt* to omit; * *n* a light leap.

skipper *n* the captain of a ship.

skirmish *n* a minor fight in a war; * *vi* to fight when reconnoitring.

skirt *n* lower part of a coat; woman's garment that hangs from the waist; border; * *vt, vi* to border; to pass along edge.

skit *n* a short humorous sketch.

skittish *adj* excitable; frisky; fickle.

skulk *vi* to lurk; to keep out of sight; to shirk duty.

skull *n* the bone case which contains the brain; the cranium.

sky *n* that which one sees outside and looking upwards.

skylight *n* a window in a roof.

slab *n* a flat piece of stone, wood, etc; * *adj* thick and slimy.

slack *adj* loose; easy-going; not busy; relaxed; * *n* loose part of a rope, etc; * *vt, vi* to idle; less active; to slacken.

slacken *vi* to become slack; * *vt* to relax; to reduce; to loosen.

slag *n* fused dross of metal; clinkers.

slake *vt* to quench; to mix (lime) with water.

slam *vt, vi* to shut with a bang; * *n* winning of all tricks at bridge.

slander *n* a false and injurious report; * *vt* to vilify; to defame.

slang *n, adj* expressions in common use, regarded as very informal; jargon.

slant *adj* sloping; * *vt, vi* to slope; to incline; to tell in such a way as to have a bias; * *n* a slope.

slap n a blow with the open hand; * vt to strike with the open hand.

slash vt to strike at wildly with knife, sword, etc; to slit, as a sleeve; * n a long cut; slit.

slate n rock which splits into thin layers; a thin roofing slab; a writing plate; * vt to cover with slates; to criticise harshly.

slaughter n a slaying; carnage; massacre; * vt to slay; to kill for market.

slave n a person who is the property of another.

slay vt to kill by violence; to murder.

sledgehammer n a large, heavy hammer for two hands.

sledge n a vehicle on runners used over snow; a sleigh.

sleek adj smooth and glossy; plausible.

sleep vi, vt to rest with mind and body inactive; to slumber; to lie dormant; * n slumber; repose; death; * sleepy adj.

sleet n hail or snow mingled with rain.

sleeve n part of a garment enclosing arm.

sleight n manual dexterity.

slender adj thin; slim; scanty.

slice vt to cut into thin pieces; * n a thin piece cut off.

slide vi, vt to slip or glide over surface, as ice; * n a slope or track for sliding on.

slight adj small; trifling; frail; * n intentional disregard; * vt to treat as of no account.

slim adj slight; slender; cunning

slime n oozy sticky mud; mucus

sling vt to hurl; to suspend; to place in a sling; * n a contrivance for hurling stones; a hanging bandage for an injured arm.

slip vi to move smoothly along; to glide; to miss one's foothold; to err; * n act of slipping; omission; error; * n a loose garment.

slipper n a light soft shoe for household wear.

slipshod adj slovenly.

slit vi to cut lengthways; * n a long cut or opening.

slogan n a catchy phrase used in advertising or as a motto by a political party etc.

slop vt to spill; * n unappetising; semi-liquid food; (pl) dirty or waste water.

slope n a slant; * vt, vi to incline.

sloppy adj careless; untidy; slovenly.

slot n a long narrow opening; a slit; * vt to fit into a slot.

sloth n indolence; laziness.

slouch n to sit or move in a drooping or ungainly manner; * vi, vt to move with drooping gait.

slovenly adj untidy; dirty; careless.

slow adj not rapid; tardy; dull; stupid.

sludge n mire; soft mud; sediment.

sluggish adj lazy; slothful; slow.

sluice n a gate for regulating flow of water in canal, etc.

slum n an overcrowded and squalid area.

slumber vi to sleep; to doze; * n a light sleep.

slump n sudden fall in value or slacking in demand; a severe recession; * vt, vi to collapse in such a way.

slur vt to speak indistinctly; to run together (words); * n a stain, stigma.

slush n sludge or soft mud; half-melted snow.

sly adj cunning; crafty; wily.

smack vi to make a sharp noise with lips; to taste; * vt to slap; * n a loud kiss; a slap; a fishing vessel.

small adj little; petty; short; narrow-minded; mean.

smallpox n a contagious disease, now eradicated, marked by pustules on skin.

smart n a quick, keen pain; * adj keen; clever; quick; brisk; witty; spruce; * vi to feel a sharp pain.

smash vt to dash or go to pieces; * n a crash; ruin; failure.

smattering n a superficial amount of.

smear vt to daub with anything greasy.

smell vt, vi to perceive by the nose; to give out an odour; * n sense of smell; scent; odour.

smelt vt to melt ore to extract

metal; * *n* a small green or silver fish of the genus *Osmerus*.

smile *vi* to show joy by the features of the face; * *n* a look of pleasure.

smirk *vi* to smile affectedly; * *n* an inane smile; simper.

smite *vt, vi* to strike; to slay; to afflict.

smock *n* a chemise; a smock frock.

smoke *n* sooty vapour from burning substance; vapour; act of smoking (pipe, etc); * *vi, vt* to emit smoke; to use tobacco; to fumigate.

smoking *n* the use of tobacco; * *adj* emitting smoke.

smoky *adj* giving out smoke; filled with smoke.

smooth *adj* even on the surface; glossy; * *vt* to make smooth; to level.

smother *n* to cover over quickly; * *vt, vi* to stifle; to suffocate.

smoulder *vi* to burn and smoke without flame.

smudge *vt* to stain with dirt; * *n* a stain; a smear.

smug *n* complacent; self-satisfied.

smuggle *vt* to import or export secretly without paying duty.

smuggling *n* the importing or exporting goods without paying duty.

smut *n* a spot or stain; a flake of soot; obscene language.

snack *n* a light meal between regular meals.

snag *n* a short projecting stump; a knot; a stumbling block.

snake *n* any limbless, scaly reptile of the suborder *Ophidia* with a long tapering body, often with salivary glands modified to produce venom.

snap *vt, vi* to bite or seize suddenly; to break with a sharp sound; * *n* a sudden bite; spring catch; sharp noise.

snare *n* a running noose for catching animals; a pitfall; a trap; * *vt* to catch in snare; to trap.

snarl *vi* to growl with bared teeth; to speak rudely; to become entangled.

snatch *vt* to seize abruptly or without permission; * *vi* to grasp (at); * *n* a sudden seizing.

sneak *vi, vt* to proceed stealthily; to steal off; * *n* a telltale.

sneer *vi* to show contempt by a look; to jeer; * *n* a scoff; a jeer.

sneeze *vi* to emit air violently and audibly through the nose.

sniff *vi* to smell; to inhale through the nose audibly.

snigger *vi* to giggle; to laugh in sly fashion; * *n* a partly suppressed laugh.

snip *vt* to cut off at a stroke; * *n* a single cut; small piece; a certainty.

snipe *vt* to lie in wait and pick off enemy by rifle fire.

snippet *n* a small part cut off; *pl* odds and ends.

snivelling *adj* whining; tearful.

snooze *n* a short sleep; * *vi* to take a short nap.

snore *vi* to breathe noisily in sleep; noisy breathing in sleep.

snorkel *n* a breathing tube extending above the water, used in swimming just below the surface; * *vi* to swim using a snorkel.

snort *vi* to eject air violently through the nose; * *n* such a sound.

snout *n* animal's nose or muzzle.

snow *n* vapour frozen in the air and falling in flakes.

snowball *n* a ball of snow pressed together for throwing.

snowdrift *n* a bank of drifted snow.

snowdrop *n* an early spring flower, *Galanthus nivalis*.

snowplough *n* an implement for clearing snow from roads.

snub *vt* to humiliate with words or look; to slight; * *n* a check; rebuke.

snuff *vt, vi* to sniff; to smell; to take snuff; to extinguish; * *n* charred part of wick; powdered tobacco.

snug *adj* neat; trim; cosy.

snuggle *vi* to lie close for warmth; to nestle.

so *adv* in this or that manner; to that degree; thus; very; * *conj* provided that; therefore.

soak *vt, vi* to become saturated; to wet thoroughly.

soap *n* a compound of fat with an alkali, used in washing; * *vt* to rub with soap.

soar *vi* to fly upwards; to tower.

sob *vi* to weep convulsively; * *n* a short choking sigh.

sober *adj* temperate; not drunk, staid; grave; thoughtful.

soccer *n* a football game played on a field by two teams of eleven players with a round inflated ball.

sociable *adj* fond of companions; social.

social *adj* living or organised in a community, not solitary; genial; affable.

socialism *n* a theory of social organisation aiming at co-operative action and the nationalisation of capital and land.

socialist *n* one who advocates socialism.

social security *n* financial assistance for the unemployed, the disabled, etc to alleviate economic distress.

society *n* the social relationship between human beings or animals organised collectively.

sociologist *n* a specialist in social science.

sociology *n* the science of human society; social science.

sock *n* a short stocking covering the foot and lower leg.

socket *n* a cavity into which anything is fitted.

sod *n* small square piece of turf.

soda *n* the alkali, carbonate of sodium.

sodden *adj* saturated; soaked and soft.

sofa *n* a couch with cushioned seat, back, and arms.

soft *adj* yielding easily to pressure; delicate; smooth; not harsh; quiet.

soften *vt, vi* to make or become soft; to tone down; to melt; to relent.

softly *adv* gently; tenderly.

soil *vt, vi* to make dirty; to tarnish; * *n* dirt; top layer of earth; mould; country.

solace *vt* to cheer or console; * *n* consolation; comfort.

solar *adj* pertaining to or proceeding from sun.

solder *vt* to unite metals by a metal alloy; * *n* an alloy capable when fused of cementing metals together.

soldier *n* a person in military service.

sole *n* the under side of the foot; the bottom of a shoe; any flatfish of the family *Soleidae*; * *vt* to furnish with a sole; * *adj* single; only; alone.

solely *adv* singly; alone; only.

solemn *adj* grave; formal; impressive; awe inspiring.

solicit *vt, vi* to ask earnestly; to invite.

solicitation *n* supplication; entreaty.

solicitor *n* a lawyer.

solid *adj* resisting pressure; not liquid or gaseous; not hollow; compact; firm; strongly constructed; * *n* a compact body.

solidarity *n* unity of interest and action.

solitaire *n* a gem in a single setting; a stud; a game for one player.

solitary *adj* being alone; lonely; unfrequented.

solitude *n* loneliness; a lonely place.

solo *n* a tune or air for a single performer; * *vi* to perform by oneself.

soloist *n* a solo singer or performer.

solstice *n* the time when the sun is farthest north or south of equator, 21 June and 21 December respectively.

solubility *n* quality of being soluble.

soluble *adj* capable of being dissolved in a fluid; capable of solution, as a problem.

solution *n* the dissolving of a solid in a liquid; explanation; result.

solve *vt* to explain; to make clear; to unravel.

solvency *n* ability to pay debts.

solvent *adj* having the power of dissolving; able to pay all debts; * *n* a fluid that dissolves another substance.

sombre *adj* dark, gloomy; dismal.

some *adj* an indefinite number; considerable; more or less; * *pron* an indefinite part, quantity, or number; certain individuals.

somebody *n* some person; a person of importance.

somehow *adv* one way or another.

somersault *n* a leap in which the heels turn over the head.

something *n* a thing unspecified; part or portion; * *adv* to some degree.

sometime *adv* once; by and by; * *adj* former.

sometimes *adv* now and then; at times.

somewhat *n* more or less; * *adv* in some degree.

somewhere *adv* in some place.

somnolent *adj* sleepy; drowsy.

son *n* a male child or descendant.

song *n* that which is sung; vocal music; a lyric; the call of certain birds.

sonic *adj* of, producing, or involving sound waves.

son-in-law *n* a daughter's husband.

soon *adv* in a short time; quickly; readily.

soot *n* a black substance formed from burning matter.

soothe *vt* to calm; to comfort; to relieve pain.

soothsayer *n* one who foretells the future.

sop *n* something dipped in broth or liquid food; bribe given to pacify.

sophism *n* false reasoning but with appearance of truth.

soporific *adj* causing sleep; * *n* a drug that induces sleep.

soprano *n* the highest female voice; a singer with such a voice.

sorcerer, **sorceress** *n* a wizard; a person who uses magic powers.

sorcery *n* magic; witchcraft.

sordid *adj* mean; vile; base; squalid.

sore *adj* painful; tender; * *n* an ulcer, wound, etc.

sorely *adv* seriously; grievously.

sorrow *n* grief, distress of mind; sadness; regret; * *vi* to grieve.

sorrowful *adj* full of sorrow.

sorry *adj* feeling sorrow or pity; grieved; wretched.

sort *n* nature or character; kind; a set; * *vt* to arrange in order; to sort.

soufflé *n* a light dish of baked egg whites.

soul *n* the spiritual element in man; conscience; essence; a person.

sound *adj* whole; firm; healthy; orthodox; just; * *n* a narrow channel of water; a strait; that which is heard; noise; * *vt, vi* to measure the depth of; to try to discover the opinion, etc, of; to make a noise; to probe.

sounding *adj* resounding; * *n* the ascertaining depth of water.

soundings *npl* the depths of water in rivers, harbours, etc.

soundtrack *n* the sound accompanying a film; the area on cinema film that carries the sound recording.

soup *n* a kind of broth.

sour *adj* acid to the taste; tart; peevish; distasteful or unpleasant; * *vt* to make sour; to embitter.

source *n* that from which anything rises; the fountainhead; origin.

south *n* one of four compass points; the position of the sun at noon; * *adj* being in or toward the south.

southeast *n* the point midway between south and east; * *adj* pertaining to or from the southeast.

southerly *adj* lying toward the south; coming from the south.

southern *adj* belonging to the south; southerly.

southward *adv, adj* toward the south.

southwest *n* the point midway between south and west; * *adj* pertaining to or from the southwest.

souvenir *n* a keepsake; a momento.

sovereign *adj* supreme in power; chief; * *n* a monarch; a ruler.

sovereignty *n* supreme power; dominion.

sow *vt, vi* to scatter seed over; to spread abroad.

spa *n* a resort for medicinal water.

space *n* the limitless three-dimensional expanse within which all objects exist; outer space; a specific area; an interval; empty area; room; an unoccupied area or seat; * *vt* to arrange at intervals.

spacious *adj* roomy; capacious.

spade *n* an instrument for digging; one of the suits of cards.

span *n* reach or space from thumb to extended little finger; short space of time; * *vt* to extend across; to measure with the fingers extended.

spank *vt* to slap with the flat of the hand, *esp* on the buttocks.

spanner *n* a tool with a hole or jaws to grip and turn nuts or bolts.

spar *n* a long piece of timber; a pole; * *vi* to box; to bandy words.

spare *adj* scanty; thin; held in reserve; * *vt, vi* to use frugally; to dispense with; to be saving; to forbear; to have mercy on.

sparing *adj* frugal; economical.

spark *n* a particle of burning matter; a flash of light from an electrical discharge; * *vi* to emit fiery particles.

sparkle *n* a little spark; lustre; * *vi* to emit sparks; to glitter.

sparkling *adj* glittering; lively.

sparse *adj* thinly scattered; scanty.

spartan *adj* rigorously severe.

spasm *n* a violent contraction of muscles; a convulsive fit.

spasmodic *adj* intermittently.

spate *n* a sudden heavy flood; a large amount.

spatial *adj* pertaining to space.

spatter *vt* to scatter a liquid on; to sprinkle.

spatula *n* a broad thin blade, used in spreading plasters, paints, etc.

speak *vi, vt* to utter words; to talk; to deliver a speech; to pronounce.

speaker *n* one who speaks; the presiding official in a legislative assembly.

spear *n* a long, pointed weapon; a lance; * *vt* to pierce with a spear.

special *adj* particular; distinctive; uncommon.

specialist *n* one who devotes himself to some particular subject; an expert.

speciality *n* something made or sold exclusively by certain traders.

specialise *vt, vi* to apply one's self to a particular subject.

species *n, sing, pl* a kind, sort, or variety; a class of organisms capable of interbreeding, or exchanging genetic material.

specific *adj* pertaining to a species; definite; precise; * *n* a remedy for a special disease.

specification *n* a requirement; detailed statement of particulars for carrying out contracts, etc.

specify *vt* to make specific; to state in detail.

specimen *n* a sample; a part to typify the whole.

specious *adj* superficially correct; plausible.

speck *n* a small spot; a flaw; a particle; * speckled *adj*.

spectacle *n* a show; an exhibition; a pageant; *pl* glasses to assist vision.

spectacular *adj* impressive; astounding.

spectator *n* an onlooker.

spectre *n* an apparition; a ghost.

spectroscope *n* the instrument employed in decomposition of rays of light.

spectrum *n* (*pl* spectra) the coloured bands produced by passing light through a prism.

speculate *vi* to theorise; to conjecture; to gamble in stocks, land, etc.

speculation *n* act of speculating; theory; hazardous financial transactions.

speculative *adj* risky; contemplative.

speech *n* the faculty of speaking; language; talk; a formal discourse; oration.

speechless *adj* silent; unable to speak.

sped *n* success; velocity; haste.

speedometer *n* indicator for showing speed of motors, cycles, etc.

spell *n* a charm; fascination; a period of work; * *vt* to give in correct order the letters of words.

spend *vt, vi* to pay out, as money; to pass, as time; to exhaust.

spent *adj* wearied; exhausted.

sperm *n* semen; the male reproductive cell.

spew *vt, vi* to vomit; to gush forth.

sphere *n* an orb; a ball; a sun, star, or planet; extent of influence.

spherical *adj* globular.

sphincter *n* a ring-like muscle closing an opening an orifice.

spice *n* an aromatic seasoning for food; * *vt* to flavour; to season.

spicy *adj* pungent; piquant; racy.

spider *n* a small wingless arthropod of the order *Araneae* with eight legs and abdominal spinnerets for spinning silk threads to make webs.

spike *n* a piece of pointed iron; * *vt* to impale with a spike.

spill *vt, vi* to let rim out or overfow; to shed; * *n* a piece of wood or twisted paper for lighting candles, etc; a fall.

spin *vt, vi* to draw out and twist into threads; to whirl; to rotate swiftly.

spinach *n* a plant, *Spinacia oleracea* with large dark green edible leaves.

spinal *adj* pertaining to the spine.

spinal cord *n* the cord of nerves enclosed by the spinal column.

spindle *n* a tapering rod on which thread is wound; an axis; a yarn measure; a slender stalk.

spine *n* a prickle; a pointed spike in animals; the backbone.

spinster *n* an unmarried woman.

spiral *adj* winding like thread of screw; * *n* a helix or coil.

spire *n* a cone-like structure; a steeple.

spirit *n* the breath of life; the soul; a spectre; vivacity; courage; mood; essence; a volatile liquid; *pl* alcoholic liquor.

spirited *adj* lively; animated.

spiritless *adj* dejected; depressed.

spiritual *adj* not material; mental; holy; divine.

spirituality *n* quality of being spiritual; spiritual nature.

spit *n* a prong on which meat is roasted; a protrusion of the land into the sea; * *vt* to put on a spit; to pierce.

spit *vt, vi* to eject from the mouth.

spite *n* ill-will; rancour; malice.

spittle *n* saliva.

splash *vt, vi* to bespatter with liquid matter; * *n* water or mud thrown on anything; noise of heavy body striking water; a spot of mud.

splay *vt* to slope or form with an angle; * *adj* turned outward.

spleen *n* a large lymphatic organ in the upper left part of the abdomen which helps produce and remove blood cells; spitefulness; ill humour.

splendid *adj* brilliant; showy; famous; * splendour *n*.

splice *vt* to unite by interweaving; * *n* union by interweaving or joining.

splint *n* a rigid structure to keep a broken limb in position.

splinter *n* a piece of wood split off; * *vt* to split into small pieces.

split *vt, vi* to cleave; to separate; * *n* fissure; breach; * *adj* divided.

splutter *n* a confused noise; * *vi* to speak incoherently; to spit when speaking.

spoil *n* pillage; booty; plunder; * *vt* to plunder; to impair; to over indulge a child, etc; * *vi* to grow useless; to decay.

spoke *n* one of bars or rays of a wheel; rung (of ladder); * *vi, pret* of speak.

spoken *adj* oral; speaking (as in fair-spoken).

spokesman *n* one who speaks on behalf of others.

sponge *n* a plantlike marine animal of the phylum *Porifera* with an internal elastic skeleton; a piece of natural or manmade sponge for washing with; * *vt* to wipe with a sponge; * *vi (fam)* to scrounge.

sponger *n* one who lives on others; a parasite.

sponsor *n* a person or organisation that funds an athlete, competition, student, charity, etc; * *vt* to act as sponsor for.

spontaneous *adj* arising naturally; instinctive; unstilted.

spook *n* a ghost; an apparition; * *vt* to frighten.

spool *n* a reel, *esp* to wind thread or yarn on.

spoon *n* a domestic utensil used in feeding or cooking.

sporadic *adj* scattered; occurring here and there.

spore *n* the reproductive body of many plants, fungi, etc.

sport *n* a game; out-of-door recreation; jest; * *vt, vi* to play; to wear publicly.

sporting *adj* indulging in sport; belonging to sport; competing fairly.

spot *n* a speck, a blemish; a flaw; a locality; * *vt* to stain; to note.

spotless *adj* blameless; stainless.

spouse *n* a husband or wife.

spout *n* a nozzle; a waterspout; * *vt, vi* to gush forth.

sprain *vt* to overstrain muscles, ligaments or a joint; * *n* a violent strain of a joint.

sprawl *vi* to spread the limbs untidily.

spray *n* a twig; collection of small branches; windblown water; * *vt* to sprinkle with a fluid.

spread *vt, vi* to stretch or expand; to distribute; to apply a coating; to emit; to diffuse; * *n* extent; a meal or banquet.

sprig *n* a small shoot or spray; a twig with leaves on it.

spring *vi* to leap; to start up; * *vt* to cease to operate suddenly; to start or rouse; * *n* a leap; an elastic spiral; an issue of water; source of supply; season of the year.

sprinkle *vt, vi* to scatter; in small drops.

sprint *n* a short foot race; a spurt.

sprite *n* a spirit; a goblin; a dainty person.

sprout *vi* to bud; to push out new shoots; * *n* a shoot of a plant; *pl* brussels sprouts.

spruce *adj* neat; trim; * *n* a coniferous tree of the genus *Picea*.

spry *adj* nimble; active; lively.

spur *n* a spike worn on horsemen's heels; a stimulus; an incentive; an outgrowth; a ridge running off from main range; * *vt* to prick with a spur.

spurious *adj* counterfeit; false.

spurn *vt* to drive away, as with the foot; to reject or treat with disdain.

spurt *n* a gush of liquid; a special effort.

sputum *n* spittle.

spy *vt* to gain sight of; * *vi* to pry; * *n* a secret agent; an informer.

squabble *vi* to wrangle; to quarrel noisily; * *n* a scuffle; a brawl.

squad *n* a small group of soldiers.

squadron *n* a unit of cavalry or of a fleet.

squalid *adj* sordid; wretched; dirty.

squall *vi* to scream loudly; * *n* a loud scream; a violent gust of wind.

squalor *n* wretchedness; foulness.

squander *vt* to spend lavishly; to waste.

square *adj* having four equal sides and four right angles; forming a right angle; * *n* a quadrilateral having four equal sides and right angles; the product of a number with itself; * *vt, vi* to make square; to settle (accounts).

squash *vt* to crush.

squat *vi* to crouch down on the heels ; to settle on land without authority.

squatter *n* one who settles on land or property without a title.

squawk *vi* to cry with a harsh voice; as of a bird.

squeak *vi* to utter a high pitched sound; * *n* a high pitched sound.

squeal *vi* to cry with a sharp, shrill voice; * *n* a shrill, sharp cry.

squeeze *vt* to subject to pressure; to hug; * *vi* to press; to crowd; * *n* pressure; an embrace.

squint *adj* looking obliquely; * *n* a oblique look; * *vi* to half close or cross the eyes.

squirm *vi* to wriggle; to writhe.

squirrel *n* a rodent of the family *Sciuridae* with a long bushy tail.

squirt *vt* to throw out in jets; * *vi* to spurt; * *n* a syringe; a jet.

stab *vt, vi* to pierce with a pointed weapon; * *n* a thrust with dagger.

stability *n* steadiness; firmness.

stable *adj* firm; steadfast; * *n* a building for horses, etc; * *vt* to put or keep in a stable.

staccato *adj* in music, a sign for separate emphasis on each note.

stack *n* a large, regularly built pile of hay, records, papers, etc; a chimney head; a tall chimney; * *vt* to pile together.

stadium *n* an arena.

staff *n* (*pl* **staves**, **staffs**) a stick or rod; a prop or support; a baton; the five parallel lines on which musical notes are written; the executive members of an organisation.

stag *n* a full grown male deer.

stage *n* a raised platform, *esp* for actors; a theatre; field of action; degree of progress; * *vt* to put on the stage.

stagger *vi*, *vt* to reel; to totter; to amaze; * *n* a lurch; an involuntary swaying of body.

stagnant *adj* not flowing; motionless; with a foul smell; sluggish.

stagnate *vi* to cease to flow; to become foul.

stagnation *n* state of being motionless; sluggishness.

staid *adj* sober; grave; sedate.

stain *vt* to discolour; to soil; to disgrace; to dye; * *n* a discoloration; disgrace.

stainless *adj* untarnished; pure.

stair *n* a series of connected steps.

staircase *n* a flight of stairs; space occupied by stairs.

stake *n* a sharpened piece of wood; a post; that which is pledged or wagered; hazard (at ~); * *vt* to mark with stakes; to pledge; to wager

stalactite *n* a mass of calcareous matter hanging from the roof of a cave.

stalagmite *n* a spike-like calcareous mass rising from the floor of a cave.

stale *adj* not fresh; musty; trite; * *vt* to make stale.

stalemate *n* a draw in chess; a deadlock.

stalk *n* the stem of a plant; a strut; * *vi*, *vt* to walk in stately fashion; to follow game warily.

stall *n* a compartment in a stable; a bench or shed where goods are exposed for sale; a seat near orchestra in theatre; * *vt*, *vi* to play for time; to postpone.

stallion *n* a male, uncastrated horse.

stamen *n* the organ of flower that produces pollen.

stamina *n* staying power; strength.

stammer *vi*, *vt* to stutter; to halt in speech; * *n* a stutter.

stamp *vt*, *vi* to strike by thrusting foot down; to impress; to imprint; to affix a postage stamp to; to coin; * *n* an instrument for crushing or for making impressions; mark imprinted; a postage stamp; character; sort.

stampede *n* a sudden panicky rush (*esp* of cattle); * *vt*, *vi* to do this.

stance *n* posture; the attitude taken in a particular situation.

stand *vi*, *vt* to be erect; stop; endure; be on end; become a candidate; pay for; * *n* small table; booth for exhibiting; tiered platform for spectators.

standard *n* a flag; an ensign; a rule or measure; a test; a grade; an upright.

standing *adj* upright; erect; permanent; stagnant; * *n* rank; position.

stanza *n* a verse or connected number of lines of poetry.

staple *n* a principle food of a region, etc; a main constituent; a U-shaped thin piece of wire for fastening; * *vt* to fasten with a staple.

star *n* a large, luminous celestial body; a figure with radiating points; a badge of honour; an asterisk, thus * ; a famous artiste; * *vt* to adorn with stars; to bespangle; * *vi* to shine as a star; to be pre-eminent.

starboard *n*, *adj* the right-hand side of a ship; that direction.

starch *n* a vegetable substance, employed for stiffening linen, etc.

starched *adj* stiffened with starch; precise; formal.

stare *vi* to look fixedly; * *vt* to affect by staring; * *n* a fixed look.

stark *adj* bare; plain; blunt; * *adv* wholly.

start *vi*, *vt* to spring up; to set out; to begin; to wince; to startle; * *n* a sudden movement; a jump; a handicap; outset.

starter *n* a device for starting motor engine; one who gives signal for setting off; the first course of a meal.

startle *vi* to move suddenly; * *vt* to frighten.

startling *adj* surprising; alarming.

starvation *n* state of being starved.

starve *vi* to suffer or die through lack of food; * *vt* deprive (a person) of food; to deprive (of) anything necessary.

state *n* condition; situation; rank; pomp; a nation; * *adj* national; public; * *vt* to narrate.

stated *adj* fixed; regular.

stately *adj* imposing; dignified.

statement *n* something stated; narrative.

statesman *n* a well-known and experienced politician.

static *adj* fixed; stationary; at rest; * *n* electrical interference causing noise on radio or TV.

station *n* position; situation; rank; class; a stopping place for trains, etc; * *vt* to assign a position to.

stationary *adj* fixed; not moving.

stationery *n* paper, pens, etc.

statistic *n* a fact about a population, etc, regarding rates of a trait, etc.

statistician *n* one versed in statistics.

statue *n* a solid image of a person or animal of marble, bronze, etc.

statuesque *n* statue-like.

stature *n* height; tallness.

status *n* social position; rank; state of affairs.

statute *n* a law enacted by parliament.

statutory *n* enacted by statute.

staunch *adj* loyal, dependable; * *vt* to stop (blood) from running.

stave *n* a pole; one of segments in side of cask; a stanza, in music, the staff; * *vt* to make a hole in.

stay *vt* to prop; to stop; to delay; * *vt* to remain; to reside; * *n* sojourn; stop; obstacle; a prop; support; in place.

steadfast *adj* firm; constant; resolute.

steady *adj* firm; constant; regular; * *vt* to make or keep firm.

steak *n* a slice of beef or fish for grilling or frying.

steal *vt, vi* to gain secretly; to take from someone.

stealth *n* a manner of moving quietly and secretly.

steam *n* the vapour of boiling water; *fig* energy; * *vt, vi* to emit steam; to expose to steam.

steamy *adj* damp; misty; full of condensation; racy.

steel *n* iron hardened by addition of carbon; a knife sharpener; sternness; * *adj* made of steel; hard; * *vt* to harden; to temper.

steep *adj* sloping greatly; precipitous; * *n* a cliff; * *vt* to soak.

steeple *n* a spire; a pointed tower; *usu* of a church.

steer *vt, vi* to control the direction of a vehicle, etc; to guide; * *n* a young ox; a bullock.

stellar *adj* pertaining to stars.

stem *n* the stalk of a tree, shrub, etc; stock of a family; the prow of a vessel; * *vt* to dam up; to check.

stench *n* a foul smell.

stencil *n* a thin plate with a pattern cut through it, used for marking surface beneath; * *vt* to paint by means of a stencil.

stenographer *n* one who is skilled at writing in shorthand.

step *vi* to walk; * *n* a pace; a grade; a rise; footprint; rung of ladder; (*prefix*) related to by remarriage.

stepladder *n* a portable self-supporting ladder.

stepping stone *n* a stone to raise the feet above a stream or mud; a means of advancement.

stereo *n* a hi-fi or record player with two loudspeakers; * *adj* stereophonic sound.

stereophonic *adj* (sound reproduction system) using two separate channels for recording and transmission to create a spatial effect.

stereotype *n* a fixed general image of a person or thing shared by many people.

sterile *adj* barren; unfruitful; free from bacteria; * sterility *n*.

sterilise *vt* to make sterile; to rid of bacteria by boiling, etc.

sterling *adj* genuine; pure; denoting standard British money.

stern *adj* austere; harsh; * *n* the hind part of a ship.

sternum *n* the breastbone.

stethoscope *n* an instrument for sounding the chest, lungs, etc.

stew *vt* to boil slowly in a closed vessel; * *vi* to be cooked slowly; * *n* food made this way; state of anxiety.

steward, stewardess *n* one who manages affairs for another; one who helps to manage a public function; an attendant on ship or aeroplane passengers.

stick *vt*, *vi* to pierce or stab; to fasten; to adhere; * *n* a rod or wand; a staff.

sticky *adj* adhesive; gluey.

stiff *ad* rigid; formal in manner; stubborn; difficult; not flexible.

stiffening *n* substance used to make anything stiff.

stifle *vt*, *vi* to suppress; to smother.

stigma *n* (*pl* stigmas, stigmata) a mark or brand; a mark of infamy; top of pistil of a flower.

stigmatise *vt* to hold up to reproach.

stiletto *n* a small dagger; a pointed instrument for making eyelet holes; a high heel shoe with a particularly long pointed heel.

still *adj* at rest; calm; silent; not carbonated; * *vt* to make still; to appease or allay; * *adv* to this time; yet; * *n* a distilling apparatus.

stillborn *adj* dead at birth.

stilt *n* either of a pair of poles, with a rest for the foot on which one can walk.

stilted *adj* pompous; unnaturally formal.

stimulant *n* a drug that increases energy for a time; an intoxicant.

stimulate *vt* to rouse up; to incite; to spur on.

stimulating *adj* rousing; invigorating.

stimulus *n* (*pl* stimuli) an incentive to action; a spur.

sting *vt* to insert the sting of an insect; * *n* a sharp-pointed defensive organ of certain animals; secreting poison (plants); any acute mental or physical pain.

stinging *adj* sharp; keen; painful.

stingy *adj* very niggardly; scanty; mean.

stink *vi* to emit a strong offensive smell; * *n* a foul smell.

stipend *n* yearly allowance; salary.

stipple *vt* to engrave by means of dots.

stipulate *vi* to specify as terms of an agreement.

stipulation *n* a condition; item in a contract.

stir *vt* to set in motion; to agitate; to rouse; * *vi* to be in motion; to be up and doing; * *n* bustle; noise.

stirring *adj* rousing; exciting.

stirrup *n* a foot support in riding.

stitch *n* a sharp pain; movement of a needle in sewing; * *vt*, *vi* to join by stitches.

stock *adj* a post; wooden piece of a rifle; lineage; capital; shares in state funds; goods in hand; cattle; *pl* an old instrument of torture for offenders; shares; frame on which a ship is built; * *adj* standing; permanent.

stockbroker *n* one who deals in stocks and shares.

stockbroking *n* the business of a stockbroker.

stocking *n* a close-fitting covering for foot and leg.

stock market, stock exchange *n* place where shares are bought and sold.

stocktaking *n* a periodical valuation of goods in a shop, etc.

stodgy *adj* damp; heavy; indigestible.

stoic *n* one indifferent to pleasure or pain; one imperturbable and serene whatever fortune brings.

stoicism *n* impassiveness; serenity of spirit.

stoke *vt* to stir and keep supplied with fuel, as a fire.

stolid *adj* dull; unresponsive.

stomach *n* the principal organ of digestion; appetite.

stone *n* a hard mass of earthy or mineral matter; a pebble; concretion in the kidneys or bladder; the nut of a fruit; a measure of 14 lbs (6.35kg); * *vt* to pelt with stones; to remove stones from fruit.

stony *adj* abounding in or like stone; hard; frigid; unfeeling.

stool *n* a portable seat, without a back, for one person; matter evacuated from the bowels.

stop *vt, vi* to halt; to hinder or check; to suspend; to close up; to stay.

stopcock *n* a tap to regulate flow of water, gas, etc.

stopgap *n* a temporary expedient.

stoppage *n* a halt.

stopper *n* that which closes a small vent or hole.

stopwatch *n* a watch that can be started and stopped instantaneously.

storage *n* act of storing; charge for storing goods.

store *n* a large quantity for supply; a warehouse; abundance; * *vt* to amass; to hoard up.

storeroom *n* a room for reception of stores.

storey *n* a floor of a building, also story.

storm *n* a heavy fall of rain, snow etc, with strong winds; a tempest; a tumult; * *vt, vi* to assail; to take by assault; to rage.

story *n* a narrative; a tale; a fiction; a falsehood.

stout *adj* bold; valiant; corpulent; * *n* a dark-brown malt liquor.

stove *n* an apparatus for warming a room, cooking, etc.

stow *vt* to store; to pack closely.

stowaway *n* one who hides himself on a ship to avoid paying the fare.

straddle *vt* to have one leg or support on either side of something.

straggle *vi* to stray; to be scattered.

straggler *n* one who wanders from main body; a laggard.

straight *adj* continuing in one direction, not curved or bent; not crooked; upright.

straighten *vt* to make straight.

straightforward *adj* honest; open.

strain *vt, vi* to stretch tightly; to exert to the utmost; to sprain; to filter; * *n* violent effort; tenor; theme; a poem; tune; race.

strained *adj* overstretched; forced or unnatural.

strainer *n* a filter or sieve.

strait *adj* confined; narrow; strict; * *n* a narrow passage of water.

straiten *vt* to make narrow; to embarrass; to distress.

straitjacket *n* a restraint used to bind the arms of prisoners to their bodies.

strand *n* the shore; a single piece of thread or wire twisted to make a rope or cable; * *vt, vi* to drive or be driven ashore; to leave without transport.

strange *adj* foreign; wonderful; odd.

stranger *n* a foreigner; an alien; a visitor.

strangle *vt* to choke; to throttle.

strangulation *n* compression of the windpipe; constriction.

strap *n* a narrow band of leather, metal, cloth, etc; * *vt* to fasten with strap.

strapping *adj* tall and well made.

stratagem *n* a device or plan to deceive an enemy; a ruse.

strategic *adj* pertaining to strategy.

strategy *n* the planning and conduct of war, etc; a policy.

stratification *n* arrangement in layers.

stratum *n* (*pl* **strata**) a layer of rock, earth, etc.

stratus *n* a cloud formed as a continuous grey sheet.

straw *n* the stalk of threshed grain.

stray *vi* to wander; to err; * *adj* strayed; straggling.

streak *n* a long mark of contrasting colour; a stripe; * *vt* to mark with streaks.

stream *n* a small river or brook; a current; * *vi, vt* to move in a stream; issue forth.

streamer *n* a banner; a long decorative ribbon.

streamline *vt* to shape (a car, boat etc) in a way that lessens resistance through air or water; to make more efficient; to simplify.

street *n* a road in a town, village or city lined with trees.

strength *n* force or energy; power; numbers of an army, fleet, etc; on the strength of, in reliance upon.

strenuous *adj* earnest; energetic; vigorous.

stress *vt* to emphasise; * *n* pressure; mental or physical tension; emphasis.

stretch *vt*, *vi* to draw out tight; to extend; to strain; to exaggerate; * *n* strain; scope; expanse.

stretcher *n* a portable frame for carrying sick or wounded.

strew *vt* to spread by scattering; to scatter loosely.

strict *adj* rigid in enforcing rules; exact; severe.

stride *vi* to walk with long steps; * *n* a long step.

strident *adj* harsh; grating.

strife *n* conflict; discord; quarrel.

strike *vi* to hit with force; to sound (clock); to cease work to enforce a demand for better conditions, pay, etc; * *vt* to smite; to mint; to come sharply against; to lower (flag); to take down (tent); * *n* a cessation of work; a military attack.

striking *adj* surprising; impressive.

string *n* a slender cord; twine; a series; cord or wire of musical instrument; * *vt* to thread on a string.

stringent *adj* strict; severe; binding.

strip *vt* to lay bare; to skin; * *vi* to undress; * *n* a long narrow piece.

stripe *n* a streak; a band; a lash; a weal.

strive *vi* to endeavour; to struggle; to vie.

stroke *n* a blow; calamity; attack; striking of a clock; touch; a line; a gentle rub; the sweep of an oar; * *vt* to rub gently with hand.

stroll *vi* to ramble; to saunter; * *n* a short leisurely walk.

strong *adj* powerful; robust; firm; forcible; ardent.

strongroom *n* a room where valuables are kept.

structural *adj* pertaining to structure.

structure *n* a building of any kind; make; form; organisation.

struggle *vi* to strive; to contend; * *n* a violent effort; contest; strife.

strum *vi*, *vt* to play noisily on a stringed instrument.

strut *vi* to walk with affected dignity; * *n* a pompous gait; a support for a rafter or framework.

strychnine *n* a highly poisonous alkaloid.

stubble *n* the stumps of cornstalks left after reaping.

stubborn *adj* obstinate; wilful; mulish; dogged.

stuck-up *adj* giving one's self airs; proud; pompous.

stud *n* a post; a nail with a large head; an ornamental button; a set of breeding horses.

student *n* a scholar; one given to study.

studied *adj* deliberate; well-considered.

studio *n* the workplace of a painter or sculptor; a building or room where motion pictures are made or TV and radio programmes are recorded.

studious *adj* given to study; earnest.

study *n* application to learning; subject studied; room set apart for study; thought, reflection; * *vt*, *vi* to apply mind to; to investigate; to reflect on.

stuff *n* material; textile fabrics; trash; * *vt*, *vi* to pack; to cram.

stuffing *n* padding; seasoning packed into meat, fowls, etc, in cookng.

stuffy *adj* close; stifling; poorly ventilated.

stultify *vi*, *vt* to make ineffectual or foolish.

stumble *vi* to trip; to err; to light on by chance; * *n* a stagger; trip.

stump *n* part of felled tree left standing; the part of a limb left after amputation; a wicket (cricket); * *vt* to lop; to dismiss batsman off his ground; to pay (up).

stun *vt* to make senseless; to stupefy; to amaze.

stunning *adj* strikingly attractive.

stunt *n* a check in growth; a showy turn; a feat of strength or skill.

stunted *adj* underdeveloped.

stupid *adj* foolish; dull-witted.

stupor *n* torpor; insensibility.

sturdy *adj* stout; strong; hardy.

stutter *vi* to stammer; * *n* a stammer.

sty n a pen for swine; a foul place; a small swelling on edge of eyelid.

style n manner of doing anything; title; fashion; * vt to designate; to term.

stylish adj fashionable.

stylus n the component in a record player which contacts with the grove of a record and transmits sound to the amplifier.

suave adj gracious in manner; pleasant.

sub n (fam) a submarine; a substitute; a subscription; a subeditor; * prefix under, below; subordinate, next in rank to.

subconscious adj happening without one's awareness; * n the part of the mind that is active without one's conscious awareness.

subcutaneous adj immediately below the skin.

subdivide vt to divide into smaller parts.

subdue vt to overcome; to overpower; to tone down.

subeditor n an under or assistant editor.

subject adj ruled by another; liable; * n one who owes allegiance to a ruler or government; topic; the nominative of a verb; * vt to subdue; to expose.

subjection n authority; control.

subjective adj relating to the conscious subject; opposed to objective.

subjugate vt to subdue; to conquer.

subjunctive adj, n the mood of a verb which expresses condition, hypothesis, doubt, etc.

sublet vt to let to another person what oneself holds as tenant.

sublime adj awe-inspiring; noble; majestic; * n the ~, the awe-inspiring in the works of nature or of art, as opposed to the beautiful.

subliminal adj under the threshold of consciousness; subconscious.

submarine adj being under surface of the sea; * n a submersible boat.

submerge vt, vi to put under water; to sink.

submersible adj capable of being submerged and propelled under water; * n a submarine.

submission n surrender; obedience; resignation.

submit vt, vi to yield or surrender; to refer to another's judgement; to suffer without complaint.

subordinate adj secondary; lower in rank; * n one who ranks below another; * vt to place in a lower rank.

subpoena n a summons to give evidence in law court.

subscribe vt to pay to receive regular copies (of a magazine, etc); to donate money (to a charity, campaign); to support or agree with (an opinion, faith).

subscriber n a contributor.

subscript adj written below.

subscription n sum subscribed to receive copies (of a magazine) or to be a member of a club.

subsequent adj following; next.

subservience n servility; obsequiousness.

subservient adj serving to further some end; helpful; servile; inferior.

subside vi to sink or fall to the bottom; to abate; to settle.

subsidence n a sinking down of land or sea; a landslide.

subsidiary adj minor; subordinate; supplementary.

subsidy n government financial aid to a private person or company to assist an enterprise.

subsist vi to have existence; to live.

subsistence n existence; livelihood.

substance n that of which a thing consists; material; a body; essence.

substantial adj of considerable value or style; real; solid; strong.

substantiate vt to give proof for; to verify.

substantive adj expressing existence; real.

substitute vt to put in the place of another; to exchange; * n a deputy.

substructure n a foundation; basis.

subterfuge n an artifice; evasion.

subterranean adj underground.

subtitle n an explanatory, usu secondary, title of a book; a printed translation superimposed on a foreign language film.

subtle *adj* thin; acute; sly; artful.

subtlety *n* nicety of distinction.

subtract *vt* to take from; to deduct.

subtraction *n* the taking of a number from a greater.

suburb *n* an outlying residential part of a city; * suburban *adj*.

subversion *n* the act of undermining the authority of a government or institution.

subvert *vt* to ruin utterly; to overturn.

subway *n* an underground passage.

succeed *vt* to follow in order; to come after; * *vi* to ensue; to become heir, to accomplish what is attempted.

success *n* favourable result; good fortune.

successful *adj* prosperous; fortunate.

succession *n* a following in order; lineage.

successive *adj* coming in succession; consecutive.

successor *n* one who succeeds or follows another.

succinct *adj* brief; concise.

succour *vt* to help when in difficulty; to aid; * *n* aid; help.

succulent *adj* full of sap; juicy.

succumb *vi* to yield; to submit.

such *adj* of like kind or degree; similar.

suck *vt*, *vi* to draw (liquid, etc) into the mouth.

sucker *n* a person who is easily taken in or deceived.

suckle *vt* to nurse at the breast.

suckling *n* an unweaned child or animal.

suction *n* act of sucking; the sucking up of a fluid by exhaustion of air.

sucrose *n* (chemistry) sugar.

sudden *adj* happening without warning; abrupt.

sue *vt* to bring a legal action against.

suet *n* white, solid fat in animal tissue, used in cooking.

suffer *vt* to endure; to permit; * *vi* to undergo pain.

suffering *n* the bearing of pain; distress.

suffice *vi* to be sufficient; * *vt* to satisfy.

sufficient *adj* adequate; enough.

suffix *n* a letter or syllable affixed to the end of a word.

suffocate *vt*, *vi* to stifle; to choke; to be stifled.

suffrage *n* a vote; right of voting; the franchise.

suffuse *vt* to spread over or fill, as with colour or light.

sugar *n* a sweet granular substance, manufactured from sugar cane, maple, beet, etc; * *vt* to sweeten.

sugary *adj* sweet; flattering.

suggest *vt* to hint; to propose; to intimate.

suggestion *n* a hint; a tentative proposal; * suggestive *adj*.

suicidal *adj* fatal; self-destructive.

suicide *n* self-murder or self-murderer.

suit *n* a petition; a courtship; an action at law; a set of matching garments; * *vt*, *vi* to adapt; to fit; to satisfy.

suitable *adj* fitting; appropriate; becoming.

suite *n* a retinue; a set of rooms.

suitor *n* a wooer.

sulk *vi* to be sullen or pettish.

sullen *adj* ill-natured; morose; sour; dismal.

sully *vt*, *vi* to soil; to tarnish.

sulphur *n* brimstone; a yellow non-metallic element.

sulphurous *adj* impregnated with sulphur; like sulphur.

sultry *adj* very hot; oppressive.

sum *n* the whole; aggregate; essence; substance; quantity of money; arithmetical problem; * *vt* to add up; to review main facts.

summarise *vt* to set forth main facts; to make an abstract or outline.

summary *adj* concise; brief; dispensing with formalities; * *n* an abridged account; an abstract.

summation *n* addition; aggregate.

summer *n* the warmest season of year; between spring and autumn.

summit *n* the top; highest point.

summon *vt* to call by authority; to cite to appear in court.

summons *n* a notice to appear, *esp* in court; an earnest call.

sun *n* the star around which the earth and other planets; the heat and light at earth's; sunny weather; * *vt* to expose oneself to the sun's rays.

sunbeam *n* a ray of the sun.

sunburn *vt* inflammation of the skin from exposure to the sun.

Sunday *n* the day after Saturday; the Christian day of worship; the Christian Sabbath.

sundial *n* an instrument to show time by shadow cast by sun.

sundry *adj* miscellaneous; various.

sunglasses *npl* tinted glasses to protect the eyes from sunlight.

sunlit *adj* lit by the sun.

sunny *adj* like the sun; brilliant; bright or cheerful.

sunrise *n* first appearance of sun in morning.

sunset *n* descent of sun below horizon.

sunshine *n* the light of the sun; warmth; brightness.

sunstroke *n* acute illness caused by over exposure to sun's rays.

sup *vt* to sip; to imbibe; * *vi* to take supper; * *n* a small mouthful.

super *adj* (*fam*) fantastic; excellent; * *n* a varety of high octane fuel.

superannuation *n* regular contributions from one's wages towards a pension.

superb *adj* magnificent; grand; of the highest quality.

superficial *adj* being on the surface; shallow.

superfluous *adj* needless; redundant.

superhuman *adj* more than human.

superimpose *vt* to lay upon something else.

superintend *vt* to supervise; direct; manage.

superior *adj* higher; better; preferable; * *n* one higher in rank; head of monastery, convent.

superiority *n* pre-eminence.

superlative *adj* highest in degree; supreme; * *n* the highest degree of adjectives or adverbs.

supermarket *n* a large, self-service shop selling food and household goods.

superpower *n* a nation with great economic and military strength.

superscribe *vt* to write upon or over.

supersede *vt* to set aside; displace; supplant.

supersonic *adj* faster than the speed of sound.

superstition *n* credulity in regard to the supernatural; a belief without reason.

superstitious *adj* credulous.

superstructure *n* anything resting on a foundation; a building.

supervise *vt* to oversee and direct; to superintend.

supervision *n* oversight.

supine *adj* lying on the back; indo-lent; * *n* a part of the Latin verb.

supper *n* the evening meal.

supplant *vi* to supersede; to oust, *esp* by craft.

supple *adj* pliant; flexible.

supplement *n* an addition; appendix; * *vt* to make additions to.

supplicant *adj* suppliant; * *n* one who begs earnestly for some favour.

supplication *n* earnest prayer; entreaty.

supply *vt* to furnish; to satisfy; * *n* store; *pl* stores; money provided for government expenses; a substitute.

support *vt* to uphold; to prop; to maintain; to endure; to back up; * *n* a prop; aid; maintenance.

supporter *n* a defender; adherent.

suppose *vt* to assume; to imagine; to imply; to expect.

supposition *n* assumption; surmise.

suppress *vt* to put down; to quell; to conceal; to crush.

suppression *n* concealment; stoppage; * suppressive *adj*.

supreme *adj* highest in authority; sovereign; paramount.

surcharge *vt* to overload; * *n* an excessive load; an overcharge; unauthorised expenditure of public bodies and charged against members.

sure *adj* certain; positive; unfailing; stable.

surety n security against loss, etc;
guarantee; bail.

surf n the swell of sea breaking on
shore.

surface n the outside part of
anything; external appearance.

surfeit n an excess of food or
drink; satiety.

surge n the swelling of a wave; a
billow; * vi to swell; to heave.

surgeon n a medical man skilled
in surgery.

surgery n the operative branch of
medical practice; a doctor's
consulting room; * surgical adj.

surly adj morose; churlish.

surmount vt to rise above; to
overcome.

surname nthe family name of an
individual.

surpass vt to go beyond; to excel.

surplus n, adj excess beyond what
is required; balance.

surprise n act of taking unawares;
astonishment; * vt to take
unawares; to startle; to astonish.

surprising adj amazing; remarkable.

surrender vt to deliver up; to
resign; to cede; * n a yielding or
giving up; * vt to yield.

surreptitious adj done by stealth;
underhand.

surround vt to encompass.

surrounding n an environment;
(usu pl).

surveillance n a keeping watch
over; oversight.

survey vt to oversee; to inspect; to
measure and value as land, etc; * n
a general view; examination; plan.

surveying n the art or practice of
measuring land.

surveyor n a measurer; an inspector.

survival n a living or continuing
longer; a relic or custom of the
past.

survive vt to outlive; to outlast; to
endure.

susceptible adj easily affected;
sensitive.

suspect vt to mistrust; to conjecture; * n a suspected person.

suspend vt to hang; to postpone;
to discontinue; to debar temporarily from work, etc.

suspender n a supporting strap or
brace.

suspense n uncertainty; anxiety.

suspension n abeyance; temporary
cessation of office; postpone-
ment; (chemistry) a dispersion
of fine particles in a liquid.

suspicion n act of suspecting;
mistrust; a belief held or formed
without sure proof; a trace.

suspicious adj doubtful.

sustain vt to hold up or support;
maintain; endure.

sustenance n nourishment.

suture n a seam; the stitching of a
wound.

swab n a wad of absorbent material,
usu cotton, used to clean wounds,
take specimens, etc; a mop; * vt
to clean with a swab.

swagger vt to strut; to bluster; * n
swinging gait.

swallow vt to receive through the
gullet into the stomach; to engulf;
to accept without question; * n
any migratory bird of the family
Hirundinidae, esp Hirundo
rustica, with a forked tail; gullet.

swamp n a bog; a fen; * vt to
overwhelm; to capsize, as a boat.

swap vt to barter; to exchange.

swarm n a multitude, esp of
insects; * vi to throng together;
to leave hive in a body; to climb a
tree, etc.

sway vi to move backwards and
forwards; to vacillate in judgement
or opinion; * n influence; control.

swear vi, vt to make a solemn
declaration; to curse; to use
obscene language.

sweat n perspiration; labour; * vi, vt
to emit moisture through pores.

sweater n a knitted pullover.

sweep vt to remove (rubbish, dirt)
with a brush; to carry along; * vi
to pass with swiftness or pomp;
to move with a long reach; * n
reach; range; rapid survey; one
who sweeps chimneys.

sweet adj agreeable to the taste;
having taste of honey or sugar;
fragrant; melodious; kind; gentle;
* n a dessert; pl confectionery.

swell vi to grow larger, to heave; to

bulge out; * *vt* to expand; * *n* gradual increase; a rise of ground; a wave of surge.

swerve *vi* to turn aside; to alter course suddenly.

swift *adj* speedy; fleet; * *n* any swift flying bird of the family *Apodidae*.

swig *n* a long drink, *esp* from a bottle.

swill *vi* to drink greedily; to rinse with a large amount of water; * *n* a liquid refuse fed to pigs.

swim *vi* to float; to move through water; to be dizzy; * *n* act of swimming.

swindle *vt* to cheat; * *n* a gross fraud.

swine *n sing*, *pl* a pig; *pl* pigs collectively.

swing *vi* to move to and fro; to turn round at anchor; to change opinion or preference; * *vt* to achieve; to bring about; * *n* sweep of a body; rhythm; apparatus for swinging on; free course; a form of jazz.

swipe *vt*, *vi* to strike with sweeping blow; * *n* a sweeping blow.

switch *n* a sudden change; a swap; a device for changing the course of an electric current; * *vt* to change.

swivel *n* a coupling that permits parts to rotate; * *vt* to turn as if on a pivot.

swoon *vi* to faint.

swoop *vi* to dart upon prey from a height; * *n* the pounce or dart as of a hawk.

sword *n* a weapon with a long blade and a handle at one end.

sworn *adj* bound by oath.

syllable *n* a sound or combination of sounds uttered with one effort.

syllabus *n* an outline or summary, *esp* of a course of study.

symbol *n* a sign; an emblem; a type; a figure.

symbolise *vt* to represent by a symbol; to typify.

symmetry *n* the corresponding arrangement of one part to another in size, shape and position.

sympathetic *adj* compassionate; showing sympathy.

sympathy *n* fellow feeling; compassion.

symphonist *n* a composer of symphonies.

symphony *n* unison of sound; an orchestral piece of music.

symposium *n* (*pl* symposia) a discussion (oral or written) on some subject by experts.

symptom *n* a bodily sensation indicative of a particular disease; an indication.

symptomatic *adj* indicative; relating to symptoms.

synagogue *n* a place where Jews assemble for worship.

synchronise *vi*, *vt* to agree or make to agree in time.

synchronous *adj* happening at the same time; simultaneous.

syndicate *n* a company formed for a special purpose.

synonym *n* a word having the same meaning as another.

syntax *n* correct arrangement of words in sentences.

synthesis *n* the combining of parts to make a whole.

synthetic *adj* inflectional; artificially produced.

syringe *n* a hollow tube with a plunger and a sharp needle at either end by which liquids are injected or withdrawn, *esp* in medicine; * *vt* to inject or cleanse with a syringe.

syrup *n* a thick sweet substance made by boiling sugar with water; the concentrated juice of a fruit or plant.

system *n* a method of working or organising by following a set of rules; the body as a functional unity; a plan; method.

T

tab *n* a small flap; a tag.

table *n* an article of furniture with flat surface set on legs; fare; persons round the table; a list or index; * *vt* to lay on a table.

tablet *n* a set of ivory or paper slips for memoranda; a slab bearing an inscription; a small cake, as of soap, etc.

tabloid *n* a small format newspaper.

taboo *n* a ban or prohibition; * *vt* to forbid approach to or use of.

tabular *adj* in form of a table; flat.

tacit *adj* implied, but not expressed; silent.

taciturn *adj* of few words; silent.

tack *n* a small nail; a stitch; course of a ship as regards the wind; * *vt* to fasten by tacks; * *vi* to change course of a ship to catch the wind.

tackle *n* equipment; pulleys, ropes, rigging, etc; * *vt* to grapple with.

tact *n* fineness of touch; judgement; taste; adroitness.

tactical *adj* pertaining to tactics.

tactics *npl* stratagem; ploy; the science and art of military manoeuvring.

tactile *adj* having the sense of touch.

tactless *adj* lacking tact.

tag *n* a metallic point to end of a lace; an appendage; a catchword.

tail *n* a appendage at the back of some animal's body; reverse of a coin.

tailor *n* a maker of clothes, *esp* for men.

taint *vt* to defile; to infect; * *vi* to be infected; * *n* infection; a stain.

take *vt, vi* to receive or accept; to capture; to understand; to employ; to be infected; to bear; to conduct.

taking *adj* alluring; attracting.

talc *n* a smooth mineral used in ceramics and talcum powder.

talent *n* any innate or special aptitude.

talisman *n* a charm; a mascot.

talk *vi* to utter words; to converse; * *vt* to discuss; * *n* familiar conversation; rumour; discussion.

talkative *adj* garrulous; fond of talking.

tall *adj* high in stature; lofty.

talon *n* the claw of a bird of prey.

tame *adj* domesticated; spiritless; insipid; * *vt* to make tame; to subdue.

tamper *vi* to meddle or interfere; to use bribery.

tampon *n* a plug of absorbent material inserted in the vagina during menstruation.

tan *vt* to convert into leather; to make sunburnt; * *n* bark used for tanning.

tandem *adv* one behind another; * *n* a pair of horses yoked single file; a bicycle with riders single file.

tang *n* a taste; characteristic flavour; part of tool which fits into handle.

tangent *n* a straight line touching a curve but not cutting it.

tangible *adj* perceptible to touch; real; actual.

tangle *vt* to interweave; to involve; * *n* a knot; a muddle; complication.

tank *n* a large cistern; a reservoir; a covered armoured car with caterpillar wheels and containing men and weaponry.

tanning *n* the process of converting hides into leather.

tantalise *vt* to torment by raising false hopes.

tantamount *adj* equal; equivalent.

tantrum *n* a fit of bad temper.

tap *n* pipe for drawing off liquor; a stopper or plug; a touch; * *vt, vi* to broach; to strike lightly.

tape *n* a narrow band of linen; magnetic tape, as in an audio cassette or videotape.

tapestry *n* rich woven hangings of wool and silk, with pictorial representations.

tapeworm *n* any parasitic flatworm of the class *Cestoda*, living in the intestines.

taproot *n* main root of a plant.

tar *n* a thick, dark, viscous substance obtained from pine, coal, etc; a sailor; * *vt* to smear with tar.

tardy *adj* slow; late; backward.

target *n* the thing that a projectile, attack, etc is intended to hit; a shooting mark or butt.

tariff *n* a schedule of dutiable goods; a scale of charges.

tarnish *vt, vi* to sully; to dim.

tarpaulin *n* canvas covered with tar.

tarry *vi* to stay; to delay; * *vt* to wait for.

tart *adj* sharp to the taste; acid; snappish; * *n* a small fruit pie.

tartan *n* a woollen checked cloth of many colours.

task *n* a piece of work to do; lesson to be learned; toil; * *vt* to burden.

taste *vt, vi* to perceive flavour of by tongue or palate; to partake slightly of; to experience; to have a flavour; * *n* flavour; sample; discernment.

tasteful *adj* showing good taste.

tasteless *adj* stale; void of taste.

tasty *adj* savoury; palatable.

tatter *n* a loose hanging rag.

tattoo *n* military call to quarters; military exhibition; * *vt* to prick ink into skin.

taunt *vt* to reproach; to upbraid; * *n* a bitter reproach.

taut *adj* tight; stretched.

tautology *n* repetition of same meaning in a sentence, as a fault of style.

tavern *n* an inn.

tawny *adj* tan-coloured; yellowish-brown.

tax *n* a charge made by government on property, income, etc; a burdensome duty; * *vt* to place tax on; to accuse.

taxation *n* act of levying taxes; the aggregate of taxes.

tea *n* an evergreen shrub, *Camellia sinensis*; its dried leaves; a drink made by infusing them in boiling water.

teach *vt, vi* to instruct; to inform; to give instruction.

teacher *n* one who teaches; a schoolmaster.

teaching *n* act or business of instructing.

team *n* a brood; a litter; two or more draught animals harnessed together; a side in a game, etc.

tear *n* a drop of water appearing in, or falling from, the eye.

tear *vt, vi* to pull in pieces; to wound; to pull with violence; * *n* a rent.

tease *vt* to pull apart fibres of; to torment.

teat *n* a nipple.

technical *adj* pertaining to arts, crafts, or sciences.

technicality *n* something peculiar to a special art, craft, etc.

technique *n* manner of artistic execution; manipulative skill.

technology *n* the study or use of applied science.

tedious *adj* tiresome; fatiguing.

tee *n* the starting place for each hole in golf.

teem *vi* to pour (with rain); to be prolific; * *teeming adj*.

teens *npl* the years of one's age having ending teen.

teeth *npl* of tooth.

teethe *vi* to cut one's first teeth.

telegram *n* a telegraphic message.

telegraph *n* a contrivance for sending messages to a distance, *esp* by electricity, and with or without wires; * *vt* to send a telegraph.

telepathy *n* the communication of thought without aid of the senses.

telephone *n* an instrument transmitting sound to a distance by electricity; * *vt* to transmit by telephone.

telescope *n* an optical instrument for viewing distant objects.

television *n* the transmission of visual images and sound via electrical and sound waves; a television receiving set; television broadcasting.

tell *vt, vi* to number; to relate; to explain; to report; to inform; to bid.

teller *n* a bank clerk in charge of cash; one appointed to count votes.

telling *adj* very effective.

telltale *adj* revealing; informative; * *n* a blabber; a betrayer of secrets.

temerity *n* contempt of danger; rashness.

temper *vi* to mix in due proportion; to moderate; to harden; * *n* disposition of mind; passion; mood; quality.

temperament *n* disposition; nature.

temperate *adj* moderate; calm.

temperature *n* degree of heat or cold.

tempered *adj* disposed; hardened, as steel.

tempest *n* a violent storm.

temple *n* a place of worship; a church; side of head above either cheekbone.

tempo *n* musical time.

temporal *adj* pertaining to time; secular; worldly; civil, secular.

temporary *adj* impermanent; provisional; * temporarily *adv.*

tempt *vt* to entice; to put to test; to allure into evil.

temptation *n* enticement to evil.

tempting *adj* attractive; alluring.

ten *adj*, *n* the number next after nine.

tenable *adj* able to be held; defensible; sound.

tenacious *adj* holding fast; unyielding; tough; stubborn.

tenacity *n* doggedness; toughness.

tenancy *n* a holding land, etc, as a tenant.

tenant *n* an occupier who pays rent.

tend *vi* to incline; trend; aim; * *vt* to attend; guard; to look after.

tendency *n* inclination; bias; proneness.

tender *n* the part of a steam locomotive carrying fuel and water; an offer; an estimate; * *vt* to offer or present; to send in an estimate; * *adj* fragile; delicate; sensitive; compassionate; weak.

tendon *n* a sinew; fibrous band joining muscles to bones.

tendril *n* a slender, twining shoot by which some plants cling or climb.

tenement *n* block of buildings divided into separate houses.

tenet *n* a doctrine, opinion, or dogma.

tenfold *adj* ten times more.

tennis *n* a game with balls and rackets.

tenor *n* a prevailing course; purport; drift; higher of two kinds of men's voices; one with tenor voice.

tense *n* verbal inflection to express time; * *adj* stretched tight; strained.

tensile *adj* of or relating to tension; stretchable.

tension *n* act of stretching; tightness; strain; anxiety.

tensor *n* a muscle that extends or tightens a part.

tent *n* a portable shelter of canvas.

tentacle *n* a thread-like organ of various animals, serving as limb or feeler.

tentative *adj* experimental.

tenterhook *n* one of hooks on cloth-stretching frame; * *adj* (in *pl* with on) in a state of anxiety or suspense.

tenth *adj* the ordinal of ten.

tenuous *adj* thin; slender.

tenure *n* a holding or conditions of holding land, office etc.

tepid *adj* lukewarm.

term *n* a limit; boundary; period of session, etc; rent day; a word; *pl* conditions; * *vt* to name; to call.

terminable *adj* capable of being ended or bounded.

terminal *adj* pertaining to the end; * *n* an extremity; the clamping screw at each end of a voltaic battery; computer keyboard and monitor.

terminate *vt*, *vi* to bound; to end.

terminology *n* the terms special to a science, art, etc.

terminus *n* (*pl* termini) a boundary; a limit; end of a transport line.

terrace *n* a raised level bank of earth; a row of houses.

terrestrial *adj* pertaining to the earth; worldly.

terrible *adj* awful; terrifying.

terrific *adj* terrifying; dreadful.

terrify *vt* to scare; to frighten considerably.

territory *n* a large tract of land; a region.

terror *n* extreme fear; dread.

terrorism *n* the use of violence to achieve political ends.

terrorise *vt* to intimidate by means of terror.

terse *adj* concise; pointed.

tertiary *adj* third; applied to a geological formation.

test *n* a putting to the proof; examination; trial; * *vt* to try.

testament *n* in law, a person's will; (with cap) one of two divisions of Bible.

testator *n* (*f* testatrix) *n* one who leaves a will at death.

testicle *n* one of the two sperm producing glands.

testify *vi, vt* to bear witness; to affirm on oath.

testimonial *n* a recommendation of one's character or abilities.

testimony *n* evidence; declaration.

testy *adj* fretful; peevish.

tether *n* a rope confining animal within certain limits; * *vt* to confine with a tether.

text *n* a main part of a printed work; a topic; a textbook.

textbook *n* a standard book of instruction; a manual.

textile *adj* woven; * *n* a fabric made by weaving.

texture *n* the grain or feel of a thing.

than *conj* introduces second member of comparison.

thank *n* almost always in *pl* expression of gratitude; * *vt* to give thanks to.

thanksgiving *n* act of giving thanks, *esp* to God.

that *adj, demons pron* (*pl* those) pointing out a person or thing at a distance; the farther of two; * *rel pron*; *sing, pl* equivalent to who or which; * *conj* introducing noun clause; in order that.

thatch *n* straw used as cover for roofs or stacks; * *vt* to put thatch on.

thaw *vi, vt* to melt, as ice or snow; to become genial; * *n* the melting of ice or snow.

the *def art* denoting particular person or thing.

theatre *n* a playhouse; an operating room; sphere of action.

theatrical *adj* artificial; showy; pompous.

theft *n* an act of stealing.

their *poss adj, pron* belonging to them; **theirs** possessive case of they, used without noun.

them *per pron* the objective case of they.

theme *n* a subject or topic.

themselves *per pron pl* of himself, herself, etc.

then *adv* at that time; * *conj* from that place or time; therefore.

theocracy *n* government by priests; a state so governed.

theologian *n* a person well versed in theology.

theology *n* the study of religious doctrine and divine things.

theorem *n* a proposition capable of being proved.

theoretical *adj* not practical; hypothetical.

theorise *vi* to conjecture; to speculate.

theory *n* speculation; hypothesis to explain something.

therapeutic *adj* pertaining to the healing art; curative.

there *adv* in or at that place.

thereafter *adv* after that; accordingly.

thereby *adv* by that means.

therefore *adv, conj* for that or this reason; consequently.

thereupon *adv* upon that or this; immediately.

thermal *adj* pertaining to heat; hot.

thermodynamics *npl* the science of heat.

thermometer *n* an instrument for measuring degree of temperature.

thermos *n* a vacuum flask used to keep liquids warm.

thermostat *n* an appliance for regulating steam pressure and temperature.

thesaurus *n* a reference book of synonyms and antonyms.

these *pronominal adj pl* of this.

thesis *n* (*pl* theses) a subject for discussion; a theme; an essay.

thespian *adj* relating to dramatic acting; * *n* an actor.

they *per pron pl* the plural of he, she or it.

thick *adj* dense; close; foggy; crowded; dull.

thicket *n* a copse; a tangle of shrubs.

thickset *adj* thickly planted; stumpy.

thief *n* (*pl* thieves) a person who steals.

thieve *vi, vt* to steal.

thigh *n* the leg above the knee.

thimble *n* a metal cover for finger in sewing.

thin *adj* not thick; sparse; slim; lean; poor; * *vt, vi* to make or become thin.

thing *n* an inanimate object; any separate entity; *pl* clothes; baggage, etc.

think *vi, vt* to have the mind working; to reflect; to judge; to believe.

third *adj* ordinal of three.

thirst *n* the desire or distress occasioned by want of water; eager desire after anything; * *vi* to feel thirst; to desire vehemently.

thirteen *adj, n* ten and three.

thirty *adj, n* thrice ten.

this *adj, pron* (*pl* these) that which is near or present.

thorax *n* the human chest.

thorn *n* a prickly tree or shrub.

thorough *adj* complete; entire.

thoroughfare *n* a public or open road.

those *adj, pron pl* of that.

though *conj* notwithstanding.

thought *n* the power of thinking; opinion; judgement; care.

thousand *adj, n* ten hundred.

thread *n* a fine cord; any fine filament; spiral part of a screw; general purpose; * *vt* to pass thread through; tomake one's way through.

threadbare *adj* worn out; trite.

threat *n* declaration of intention to punish or hurt.

threaten *vt* to use threats towards.

three *adj, n* the number next after two.

thresh *vt* to beat out grain from husks.

threshold *n* a door sill; entrance.

thrice *adv* three times.

thrift *n* frugality.

thrifty *adj* frugal; saving.

thrill *vt, vi* to excite; * *n* a thing which excites.

thrilling *adj* exciting.

thrive *vi* to prosper; to flourish.

throat *n* the opening downward at back of mouth.

throb *vi* to beat, as the heart; to palpitate.

throne *n* a royal seat.

throng *n* a crowd; * *vi, vt* to crowd together.

throttle *n* the windpipe; the gullet; engine's steam or petrol regulator.

through *prep* from end to end of; by means of; * *adj, adv* from end to end.

throw *vt, vi* to fling or cast; to propel; to twist or wind; to utter; a cast at dice, etc; a venture.

thrush *n* a singing bird; a vaginal fungal infection.

thrust *vt, vi* to push with force; to shove; to intrude; * *n* a violent push; a stab.

thumb *n* the short thick digit of hand; * *vt* to soil with fingers.

thump *n* a dull, heavy blow; * *vt, vi* to strike with something heavy.

thunder *n* the sound which follows lightning; any loud noise; * *vi* to make a loud noise.

thunderbolt *n* a shaft of lightning.

thunderclap *n* a peal of thunder.

thundering *adj* resounding.

thunderstruck *adj* amazed.

Thursday *n* the fifth day of the week.

thus *adv* in this manner.

thwart *adj* transverse; * *vt* to cross; to frustrate.

thyme *n* any small aromatic herb or shrub of the genus *Thymus, esp T.vulgaris.*

tibia *n* the shin bone.

tick *n* the beat of watch or clock; a tapping; a dot; * *n* insect; * *vt, vi* to mark with a dot; to sound, as watch.

ticket *n* a label; a piece of cardboard giving right of entry, travel, etc.

tickle *vi, vt* to touch lightly in certain places and cause involuntary laughter; to please; to puzzle.

ticklish *adj* difficult; critical; susceptible to tickling.

tidal *adj* pertaining to tides.

tide *n* time; season; the ebb and flow of sea.

tidy *adj* clean and orderly; neat; trim; * *vt* to make tidy.

tie *vt* to fasten; to constrain; * *n* a fastening; a necktie; bond.

tier *n* a row; a rank.

tiff *n* a slight quarrel.

tight *adj* compact; well-knit; fitting close or too close; scarce; tipsy.

tights *npl* a one-piece garment covering the legs and lower body.

tile *n* a slab of baked clay for

roofing, flooring, etc; a drain pipe; * vt to cover with tiles.

till n a money drawer in shop counter; * prep until; * vt to cultivate; to plough and prepare for seed.

tilt vi to joust; to lean or slope; * n a slant; a joust; an awning for cart or bat.

timber n wood for building purposes.

timbre n characteristic quality of musical note.

time n the measure of duration; a point of duration; occasion; season; epoch; present life; rhythm; * vt to measure.

timely adj opportune; * adv early.

timetable n a table of school hours and classes; a schedule.

timid adj fearful; shy.

timorous adj full of fear.

tin n a malleable white metal.

tincture n a solution of drug in alcohol.

tinder n an inflammable sub-stance used for kindling fire from a spark.

tinge vt to tint; to imbue; * n a tint; a slight colour.

tingle vi to feel a thrilling sensation.

tinker n a mender of kettles, etc; * vt, vi to mend; to patch up.

tinkle vi to make small, sharp sounds; to clink; * n a sharp, ringing sound.

tinplate n thin sheet iron coated with tin.

tinsel n glittering thread or foil; something gaudy but of little value; mere glitter.

tint n a tinge; hue; * vt to tinge.

tiny adj very small; puny.

tip n a small end or point; a tap; a gratuity; a dump; a hint; * vt to give gratuity to.

tipple vi, vt to drink strong liquors frequently; to imbibe often.

tipsy adj mildly intoxicated.

tiptoe vi to walk very quietly.

tirade n a violent speech, denunciation.

tire n band or hoop of iron or rubber round wheels; headdress; * vt to fatigue; to weary; to attire.

tiresome adj wearisome; tedious.

tissue n delicate fabric; thin paper sheet; substance (muscle, fat, etc) composing parts of animals and plants; a fabrication.

titanic adj huge; gigantic.

titillation n a pleasant feeling, a teasing, esp sexual.

title n an inscription; heading; name; appellation of dignity; a right.

titled adj having a title.

titter vi to giggle; * n a half-suppressed laugh.

titular adj nominal.

to prep denoting motion towards.

toadstool n the spore bearing body of various mushroom-like, fungus.

toast vt to dry and brown before the fire; to drink health of; * n toasted bread; person or sentiment whose health is drunk.

tobacco n a narcotic plant whose leaves when dried are used for smoking.

toboggan n a snow sledge.

toddle vi to walk with uncertain steps, as a child.

toddy n a mixture of spirit, hot water, and sugar.

toe n one of the five digits of the foot.

toffee n a sweet made of butter and sugar.

together adv in company.

toil vi to labour; to drudge; * n hard work; a snare.

toilet n the lavatory; the act of washing and dressing oneself.

token n a mark; symbol; keepsake.

tolerable adj passable; middling.

tolerance n forbearance.

tolerant adj indulgent; broad-minded.

tolerate vt to allow or permit; to put up with.

toll n a tax charged for use of road, bridge, etc; sound of a bell; * vi to ring bell slowly.

tomb n a grave; burial vault.

tombstone n a stone erected over a grave.

tome n a volume; a large book.

tomorrow n the day after the present.

tone *n* sound or character of sound; timbre; temper; colour scheme; * *vt, vi* to tone down, to soften.

tongs *npl* an appliance for lifting coal, sugar, etc.

tongue *n* the organ of speech and taste; speech; language; clapper of bell.

tonic *adj* strengthening; * *n* a medicine; keynote.

tonight *n* the present night.

tonnage *n* weight of ship's freight; duty on ships.

tonne *n* a metric ton, 1,000 kg.

tonsil *n* one of glands on each side of the throat.

tonsillitis *n* inflammation of the tonsils.

too *adv* over; as well; also.

tool *n* an instrument to work with.

tooling *n* skilled work with a tool.

tooth *n* (*pl* teeth) one of the bony projections from gums used for chewing.

toothache *n* a pain in teeth.

toothed *adj* jagged; indented.

top *n* the highest part; summit; toy for spinning; * *vi* to excel; to be at top.

topic *n* a theme or text.

topical *adj* relevant.

topple *vi* to fall over; overbalance.

torch *n* a light to be carried in the hand.

torment *n* torture; anguish; * *vt* to torture; to tease.

tornado *n* (*pl* tornadoes) a violent vortex of wind of small extent.

torpedo *n* (*pl* torpedoes) a self-propelled explosive submarine projectile.

torpid *adj* numb; inactive.

torpor *n* apathy; numbness.

torrent *n* a rushing stream.

torrid *adj* parched; violently hot.

torso *n* a headless, limbless trunk, *esp* of statue.

toil *n* wrong; injury.

tortuous *adj* crooked; winding.

torture *n* extreme pain; agony; * *vt* to rack; to harass.

toss *vt, vi* to throw upward; to jerk; to roll about; * *n* a throw; a fall.

tot *n* anything small; a sum in addition; * *vt* to add.

total *adj, n* whole; complete.

totter *vi* to stagger; to reel.

touch *vt, vi* to come in contact with; to handle lightly; to reach; to move feelings of; * *n* contact; feeling; skill in some art.

touching *adj* affecting; * *prep* concerning.

touchy *adj* irritable; sensitive.

tough *adj* tenacious; stubborn.

tour *n* a long trip, *esp* for pleasure; * *vt* to make a tour.

tourist *n* one who makes a tour.

tourniquet *n* an appliance for stopping flow from cut artery.

tousle *vt* to ruffle; to disarrange.

tout *vi* to seek for custom openly; to canvas obtrusively; * *n* a shameless canvasser.

tow *vt* to haul by a rope; * *n* haulage; fibres of flax or hemp.

toward, towards *prep* in the direction of.

towel *n* a cloth for drying.

tower *n* a lofty narrow building; a fortress; * *vi* to soar.

town *n* an urban centre, smaller than a city and larger than a village.

toxic *adj* poisonous.

toxin *n* a poisonous substance.

toy *n* a plaything; a trifle; * *vi* to dally; to trifle.

trace *n* a mark left by anything; footstep; track; one of straps by which a carriage is drawn; * *vt* to track out; to copy by marking over.

trachea *n* the windpipe.

track *n* a footprint; rut made by wheel; beaten path; course; * *vt* to trace; to follow step by step.

tract *n* wide region; a short treatise.

traction *n* grip.

trade *n* employment; commerce; traffic; * *vi, vt* to buy and sell.

trademark *n* a distinctive mark put by manufacturer on his goods.

trades union *n* a union of workers in a trade to protect their interests.

tradition *n* knowledge handed down orally; a custom.

traffic *n* trade; commerce; intercourse; conveyance of passengers or goods on railways, roads, etc; * *vi* to trade.

tragedy *n* an elevated drama with fatal ending; any dreadful event.

tragic *adj* fatal; disastrous.

trail *n* a track or scent; * *vt* to drag along the ground; to hang downwards.

trailer *n* a climbing plant; a vehicle towed by another.

train *vt* to draw along; to drill; to exercise; to teach; to take aim; * *n* something drawn along; a series of railway carriages coupled with engine; trailing part of skirt; a retinue; process.

training *n* exercise; education; practice.

trait *n* a distinguishing feature.

traitor *n* one guilty of treason.

trajectory *n* the path of a moving body, as bullet, comet, etc.

tram *n* a tramway line; a tramcar.

tramp *vt, vi* to tread under foot; travel on foot; * *n* a journey on foot; a vagrant.

trample *vt* to tread on heavily; to ride roughshod over.

trance *n* a state of insensibility; a swoon.

tranquil *adj* calm; serene.

transact *vt, vi* to carry through.

transaction *n* management; performance; *pl* report of proceedings of societies.

transcribe *vt* to copy.

transcript *n* a written copy.

transcription *n* act of transcribing; a copy.

transfer *vt* to convey from one place or person to another; * *n* conveyance of titles, etc, from one to another.

transfigure *vt* to change in form or shape.

transfix *vt* to piece through.

transform *vt* to change the form of; to convert.

transformation *n* a complete change of appearance or nature.

transfuse *vt* to transfer, as blood, from one person to another.

transgress *vt* to break or violate; * *vi* to do wrong.

transgression *n* fault; offence.

transient *adj* passing quickly; fleeting.

transit *n* a passing across; passage of planet across sun's disc or of star across meridian of a place; conveyance.

transition *n* passage from one place or state to another.

transitive *adj* (grammar) taking a direct object; passing over.

transitory *adj* fleeting.

translate *vt* to remove from one place to another; to render into another language.

translation *n* removal; a turning into another language; a version.

translucent *adj* semi-transparent.

transmissible *adj* able to be passed through or along.

transmission *n* a passing through; act of sending.

transmit *vt* to convey or effect conveyance of news, light, etc; to hand down.

transmute *vt* to change from one form into another.

transparency *n* clarity; picture visible only when light passes through.

transparent *adj* clear; not opaque.

transpiration *n* emission of vapour or moisture through pores.

transpire *vt* to emit through pores of skin; * *vt* to exhale; to become known.

transplant *vt* to remove and plant in another place, *esp* an organ.

transport *vt* to carry from one place to another; to banish; to enrapture; * *n* conveyance for goods; a ship for carrying troops, etc; rapture.

transpose *vt* to change the order of things.

transposition *n* change in order of words for effect.

transverse *adj* lying across; crosswise.

trap *n* a device for catching animals; an ambush; a device in drains to prevent foul air rising; a light uncovered vehicle; * *vt, vi* to snare; to take unawares.

trapeze *n* a swing for gymnastic exercises.

trappings *npl* finery; adornment, *esp* for horses.

trash n rubbish; refuse.

travel n journey to a distant country; * vi to journey.

traverse adj transverse; * n a crosspiece; denial of a plea in lawsuit; barrier across a trench; * vt to cross; to journey through; to deny; * adv crosswise.

travesty n a wilful misrepresentation.

trawl vi to fish by trailing a net; * n a large net for deep-sea fishing.

trawler n a fishing vessel with a trawl net.

tray n a broad, flat, rimmed utensil for carrying dishes, etc. faithless; deceitful.

treachery n betrayal of trust; perfidy; treason.

treacle n the syrup obtained in the refining of sugar.

tread vi to step or walk; * vt to trample; dance; * n step; the part of a shoe, tyre, etc that touches the ground.

treason n treachery; disloyalty to king or country.

treasonable adj involving treason.

treasure n great wealth; something greatly valued; * vt to prize highly.

treasurer n one who has the charge of funds.

treasury n place where public money is stored; government department that controls finance.

treat vt, vi to handle; to act towards; to discourse on; * n an entertainment; a rare pleasure.

treatise n an essay; pamphlet.

treatment n mode of dealing with.

treaty n an agreement between nations.

treble adj threefold; * n highest part in music; soprano.

tree n a perennial woody plant with trunk and branches.

trek vi to migrate by wagon.

trellis n a lattice-work structure. tremble; * vi to shake; to quiver.

tremendous adj terrible; huge.

tremor n an involuntary trembling; a shivering.

trench vt, vi to dig a ditch in; to turn over and mix; * n a long

narrow cutting; a deep ditch with rampart.

trend vi to incline towards; * n direction; tendency.

trepidation n consternation; fear.

trespass vi to intrude on another's land; to transgress; to sin; * n a sin; offence; intrusion on another's property.

tress n a lock of hair.

trestle n a frame for supporting things.

trial n a putting to the test; ordeal; attempt; hardship.

triangle n a figure having three sides and three angles.

tribe n a division of a people; family; race.

tribulation n deep affliction; suffering.

tribuneral n a court of justice.

tributary adj paying tribute; subordinate; * n a stream flowing into another.

tribute n merited praise.

trick n an artifice; fraud; a knack; a prank; * vt to deceive; to cheat.

trickery n cheating; fraud.

trickle vi to fall in drops.

tried adj approved; reliable.

trifle n thing of little value; a confection or pudding; * vi to toy; to idle.

trifling adj trivial; frivolous.

trigger n the catch by which a gun is fired.

trill n a tremor of voice in singing; * vt to warble.

trilogy n a series of three connected dramas, poems, etc.

trim vt to put in order; to prune; to adjust (cargo); * adj spruce; neat; * n readiness; good condition.

trimming n an embellishment, esp of garment; pl accessories; parings.

trinity n a union of three in one.

trio n a set of three; composition for three performers.

trip vi to step lightly; to skip; to stumble; * vt to cause to stumble; * n a stumble; an excursion or jaunt.

tripe n stomach of sheep, cow, etc, prepared as food.

triple adj threefold; treble.

triplet n three of a kind; pl three children at one birth.

triplicate adj threefold.

tripod n a three-legged stand.

trite adj commonplace; well-worn.

triumph n a great victory; * vi to gain a victory; to exult.

triumphal adj pertaining to a triumph.

triumphant adj victorious; exultant.

trivial adj common; trifling.

trod, trodden v. past t and pp of tread.

trombone n a deep-toned wind instrument.

troop n a collection of people or animals; a cavalry company; pl soldiers in general; * vi to gather in large numbers.

troopship n a ship used for transport of military forces.

trophy n a token of victory.

tropic n one of the two parallel lines of latitude on either side of the equator; (pl) the regions lying between these lines.

tropical adj excessively hot; relating to the tropics.

trot to run with small steps; * n a medium pace.

troth n truth; faith.

trouble vt to disturb; to distress; * n distress; affliction.

troublesome adj annoying; tiresome.

trough n a long shallow drinking vessel; a hollow.

troupe n a company of performers.

trousers npl a garment with tubes for legs.

trowel n a hand tool for spreading mortar, etc.

truant n one who stays from school without leave.

truce n a temporary stoppage of fighting; armistice.

truck n a heavy motor vehicle for transporting goods; * vt to convey by truck; * vi to drive a truck.

truculent adj aggressive; over-bearing; * truculence n.

true adj conformable to fact; genuine; loyal; honest; exact.

truffle n any edible fungus of the order Tuberales growing underground.

truly adv really; according to truth.

trump n a winning card; one of the favoured suit for time being; a real good fellow; * vt to take with a trump card; to concoct (with up).

trumpet n a metal wind instrument; * vt to proclaim; to sound.

truncate vt to cut off; to lop.

truncheon n a short staff; a baton of authority.

trundle vi to roll or bowl; * n a little wheel.

trunk n the stem of a tree; body of an animal; chest for containing clothes, etc; proboscis of an elephant, etc.

trust n reliance; confidence; hope; credit; a business combine; money or property entrusted to individuals (trustees) for use in specified ways; * vt, vi to rely upon; to credit; to entrust.

trustee n one appointed to hold property for benefit of others.

trustworthy adj faithful; honest.

trusty adj reliable; staunch.

truth n conformity to fact or reality; integrity; constancy; reality.

try vt to test; to afflict; to examine judicially; to attempt.

trying adj severe; searching.

tub n an open wooden vessel; a small bath.

tube n a pipe; a hollow cylinder.

tuber n an underground fleshy stem or root.

tuberculosis n a disease marked by presence of tubercles in tissues; consumption.

tubing n material for tubes series of tubes.

tubular adj like a tube; consisting of tubes.

tuck vt to gather in a fold; * n a fold in a garment; eatables.

Tuesday n the second work day of the week.

tuft n a cluster; clump.

tug vt, vi to pull with jerks; * n a strong pull; strong towing vessel.

tuition n instruction; business of teaching.

tumble vi to roll about; to fall; * vt to overturn; * n a fall.

tumbler *n* an acrobat; a drinking glass.

tumour *n* an abnormal growth of tissue in any part of the body.

tumult *n* uproar; riot.

tundra *n* flat, treeless arctic plain.

tune *n* a short air or melody; harmony; correct intonation; frame of mind; mood; * *vt* to put into tune; to adapt.

tunnel *n* an arched underground passage; vt to dig a tunnel.

turbine *n* a rotary motor driven, or driving by steam, water, etc.

turbulence *n* disorder; tumult.

turbulent *adj* disorderly; riotous.

turf *n* the grassy layer on surface of ground; a sod; the ~, the business of horse racing.

turgid *adj* swelling; bombastic.

turmeric *n* a tropical Asian plant, *Curcuma longa*, whose root is used as a dye, a drug, and a flavour.

turmoil *n* uproar; disorder.

turn *vt* to cause to move round; to shape by a lathe; to alter course; to reverse; to change; * *vi* to revolve; to bend or curve; to become sour; * *n* a revolution; a bend; a short walk; purpose; short spell.

turncoat *n* one who deserts his party or principles.

turning *n* a turn; bend; art of shaping articles on a lathe.

turnstile *n* a revolving barrier that serves as entrance gate.

turpentine *n* resin from certain trees; oil distilled from this.

turret *n* a little tower forming part of a building; rotary iron tower to protect guns and gunners on warship.

tusk *n* a long pointed tooth projecting from mouth as in elephant, boar.

tussle *n* a struggle; scuffle.

tussock *n* a clump of grass.

tutelage *n* guardianship.

tutor *n* a teacher.

twaddle *vi* to prate; to chatter; * *n* silly talk.

twang *vi* to pluck a taut string or wire; * *n* sound of a taut string plucked.

tweak *vt* to pinch; twist.

tweed *n* a twilled woollen fabric.

tweezers *npl* small pincers to pluck out hairs, etc.

twelfth *adj* the ordinal of twelve.

twelve *adj*, *n* ten and two.

twentieth *adj* the ordinal of twenty.

twenty *adj*, *n* twice ten.

twice *adv* two times.

twig *n* a small shoot or branch.

twilight *n* the faint light after sunset and before dawn.

twin *n* one of two born at a birth; * *adj* double.

twine *n* strong thread or cord; * *vt*, *vi* to twist; to coil.

twinge *n* a sudden darting pain.

twinkle *vi* to sparkle; to blink; * *n* a sparkle.

twirl *vt*, *vi* to turn round rapidly; to rotate; * *n* a curl; a flourish.

twist *n* something twined, as a thread; roll of tobacco; a wrench; a turn; * *vt*, *vi* to twine; to writhe; to pervert.

twitch *vt* to pluck; to jerk; * *n* a quick pull; a muscular jerk.

two *adj*, *n* the number next above one.

tympanum *n* (*pl* **tympana**) the eardrum.

type *n* a distinguishing mark; emblem; model; letter used in printing; such letters collectively.

typewriter *n* a machine for producing printed letters by inked type.

typhoid *n* enteric fever; a low fever with acute intestinal pain.

typhoon *n* a violent hurricane.

typical *adj* characteristic; symbolic.

typify *vt* to represent; exemplify.

tyrannical *adj* despotic; overbearing.

tyranny *n* oppressive government; despotism.

tyrant *n* a despot; an oppressor.

tyre *n* a protective ring, *usu* rubber round the rim of a wheel.

U

ubiquitous *adj* existing everywhere; omnipresent.

udder *n* the milk gland of cows, sheep, etc.

ugly *adj* unattractive; unsightly; repulsive; ill-tempered.

ulcer *n* a festering sore.

ulterior *adj* not evident; on further side; (motives) hidden.

ultimate *adj* utmost; final.

ultimatum *n* a last or final offer.

ultra *pref, adj* beyond; extreme.

ululate *vi* to howl, as with pain.

umbilical *adj* pertaining to the navel.

umbra *n* the dark central part of a shadow.

umbrage *n* resentment; offence.

umbrella *n* a folding frame with handle and covering , etc, as protection from rain; general protection.

umpire *n* a judge or referee.

un- *pref* the addition of this prefix negatives or reverses the original meaning, as **untrue** = not true.

unable *adj* unequal to some task.

unacceptable *adj* unwelcome.

unaccountable *adj* not responsible.

unaccustomed *adj* unusual.

unacknowledged *adj* ignored.

unacquainted *adj* not familiar with.

unadorned *adj* plain; simple.

unaffected *adj* sincere; unmoved.

unaided *adj* without aid.

unalterable *adj* unchangeable.

unappreciated *adj* not duly prized.

unapproachable *adj* inaccessible.

unarmed *adj* defenceless.

unassailable *adj* impregnable.

unassuming *adj* modest.

unattended *adj* solitary; alone.

unattractive *adj* uninteresting.

unauthorised *adj* unwarranted.

unavailing *adj* of no avail.

unbearable *adj* intolerable.

unbend *vi* to make straight.

unbiased *adj* impartial; just.

unbounded *adj* boundless, vast.

unbridled *adj* unrestrained.

unburden *vt* to rid of a load.

uncanny *adj* weird; mysterious.

unceasing *adj* continual.

uncertain *adj* doubtful; variable.

unchallenged *adj* unopposed.

unchanging *adj* constant.

uncharitable *adj* ungenerous.

uncivil *adj* rude; discourteous.

unclean *adj* dirty; impure.

uncomfortable *adj* ill at ease.

uncommunicative *adj* taciturn.

uncompromising *adj* unyielding.

unconditional *adj* unqualified.

unconnected *adj* separate.

unconscionable *adj* inordinate.

unconscious *adj* unaware.

unconstitutional *adj* not according to the principles of the constitution.

uncontrollable *adj* headstrong.

unconventional *adj* free and easy.

uncouple *vt* to set loose.

uncouth *adj* odd in appearance.

uncover *vt* to divest of a cover.

undaunted *adj* intrepid; fearless.

undecided *adj* wavering.

undemonstrative *adj* reserved.

undeniable *adj* indisputable; true.

undisguised *adj* open; candid.

undisturbed *adj* calm; tranquil.

undo *vt* to reverse what's done.

undoing *n* reversal; ruin.

undoubted *adj* unquestionable.

undress *vt, vi* to strip..

undue *adj* unnecessary.

unearned *adj* numerated; (income) not earned by labour or skill.

unearth *vt* to discover; to reveal.

unearthly *adj* weird; ghostly.

uneasy *adj* restless; awkward.

unendurable *adj* intolerable.

unequal *adj* ill-matched.

unequivocal *adj* undoubted; clear.

uneven *adj* unequal; rough; odd.

unexceptionable *adj* irreproachable.

unexpected *adj* sudden.

unfading *adj* ever fresh.

unfailing *adj* sure.

unfair *adj* unjust; biassed.

unfaithful *adj* disloyal; false.

unfamiliar *adj* unaccustomed.

unfasten *vt* to loose.

unfavourable *adj* adverse.

unfeeling *adj* devoid of feeling.

unfit *adj* unsuitable; incompetent.

unflinching *adj* resolute; firm.

unfold *vt, vi* to display.

unforeseen *adj* unexpected; sudden.

unforgiving *adj* implacable.

unfortunate *adj* unlucky; unhappy.

unfounded *adj* false; groundless.

unfrequented *adj* rarely visited.

unfurl *vt* to spread out (sail etc).

unfurnished *adj* without furniture.

ungainly *adj* clumsy; awkward.
ungenerous *adj* stingy; mean.
ungovernable *adj* unruly.
ungraceful *adj* inelegant.
ungrateful *adj* not thankful.
ungrudging *adj* generous; hearty.
unhappily *adv* unfortunately.
unhappy *adj* miserable; sad.
unhealthy *adj* sickly; unwholesome.
unheeded *adj* ignored; disregarded.
unheeding *adj* careless.
unhesitating *adj* instant; prompt.
unhinge *vt* to loosen; to derange.
unholy *adj* profane; wicked.
unimpaired *adj* uninjured.
unimpeachable *adj* irreproachable.
uninhabited *adj* deserted; desolate.
unintelligent *adj* dull; stupid.
unintelligible *adj* incapable of being understood; meaningless.
unintentional *adj* accidental.
uninteresting *adj* wearisome.
uninterrupted *adj* continuous.
uninviting *adj* unattractive.
unjust *adj* unfair; bad; biassed.
unkempt *adj* uncombed; rough.
unknowingly *adv* unwittingly.
unlace *vt* to unfasten.
unlawful *adj* illegal.
unlicensed *adj* without legal permission.
unlike *adj* different; dissimilar.
unlimited *adj* unbounded; limitless.
unlucky *adj* unfortunate; ill-fated.
unmanageable *adj* beyond control.
unmannerly *adj* rude; ill-bred.
unmask *vt* to expose.
unmeasured *adj* boundless.
unmerited *adj* undeserved.
unmitigated *adj* unqualified.
unnatural *adj* inhuman; affected.
unobtrusive *adj* retiring; modest.
unoccupied *adj* empty; at leisure.
unopposed *adj* meeting with no opposition.
unorthodox *adj* unconventional.
unpack *vt* to empty a pack, trunk, etc.
unpalatable *adj* unpleasant to taste.
unparalleled *adj* unequalled; matchless.
unpardonable *adj* inexcusable.
unpleasant *adj* disagreeable.
unpractised *adj* raw; unskilful.

unprecedented *adj* unparalleled.
unpretentious *adj* modest.
unprincipled *adj* immoral; wicked.
unproductive *adj* barren.
unprofessional *adj* contrary to professional etiquette.
unprofitable *adj* fruitless; futile.
unqualified *adj* untrained; incompetent.
unquestionable *adj* indisputable.
unravel *vt* to disentangle; to solve.
unreadable *adj* illegible.
unreal *adj* sham; visionary.
unreasonable *adj* immoderate; absurd.
unrecorded *adj* not placed on record.
unrelenting *adj* hard; pitiless.
unreliable *adj* untrustworthy.
unremitting *adj* ceaseless; constant.
unrequited *adj* unrewarded.
unreserved *adj* frank; full; open.
unrest *n* disquiet; uneasiness.
unrestrained *adj* unbridled; loose.
unripe *adj* immature.
unrivalled *adj* peerless.
unroll *vt, vi* to unfold; to display.
unruffled *adj* calm; composed.
unruly *adj* disorderly.
unsatisfactory *adj* not up to expectation.
unsavoury *adj* insipid; unpleasing.
unscathed *adj* uninjured.
unscrupulous *adj* unprincipled.
unseemly *adj* unbecoming.
unsentimental *adj* matter-of-fact.
unserviceable *adj* useless.
unsettle *vt* to upset; to derange.
unshaken *adj* firm; resolute.
unshapely *adj* ill-formed.
unsightly *adj* ugly; repulsive.
unsociable *adj* reserved; solitary.
unsolicited *adj* unsought.
unsophisticated *adj* artless.
unsound *adj* diseased; faulty.
unspeakable *adj* unutterable.
unstable *adj* unsteady; fickle.
unsteady *adj* changeable; unsafe.
unsubstantial *adj* visionary; flimsy.
unsuitable *adj* unfit; unbecoming.
unsullied *adj* pure; stainless.
unsung *adj* not celebrated.
unsurpassed *adj* unexcelled.

unsuspecting *adj* free from suspicion.

unswerving *adj* steadfast; straight.

untenable *adj* not fit to be occupied.

unthinkable *adj* inconceivable.

unthinking *adj* careless; heedless.

untidy *adj* slovenly; careless.

untie *vt* to loosen; to undo.

untimely *adj* ill-timed; unseasonable.

untiring *adj* unwearied.

untold *adj* countless; vast; unrecorded.

untouched *adj* unscathed; unmoved.

untoward *adj* unseemly; unfavourable.

untried *adj* not attempted; inexperienced.

untroubled *adj* calm; unruffled.

untrue *adj* incorrect; faithless.

untrustworthy *adj* unreliable; false.

unusual *adj* rare; peculiar.

unutterable *adj* unspeakable.

unvarnished *adj* plain; unadorned.

unvarying *adj* uniform.

unveil *vt* to disclose to view.

unwarrantable *adj* unjustifiable; illegal.

unwavering *adj* steady; staunch.

unwearied *adj* tireless; incessant.

unwieldy *n* huge; cumbersome.

unwilling *adj* reluctant; loath.

unwind *vt* to wind off.

unwitting *adj* ignorant; unaware.

unworthy *adj* base; worthless.

unwritten *adj* understood though not expressed; traditional.

unyielding *adj* stubborn; unbending.

unanimous *adj* being of one mind.

uncle *n* the brother of one's father or mother.

unctuous *adj* oily; greasy.

under *prep* below; beneath; subject to; inferior; * *adv* in a lower condition or degree; * *adj* lower; subordinate.

undercurrent *n* a current below another.

undergo *vt* to bear; to suffer.

undergraduate *n* a university student studying for a first degree.

undergrowth *n* shrubs growing among large ones; copsewood.

underhand *adj* sly; dishonest.

underline *vt* to mark with a line underneath for emphasis.

undermine *vt* to sap; to injure by underhand means.

underrate *vt* to undervalue.

understand *vt, vi* to comprehend.

understanding *n* comprehension; discernment; knowledge; agreement.

understudy *n* one who gets up a theatrical part to be ready as substitute.

undertake *vt, vi* to take in hand.

undertaker *n* one who manages funerals.

undertaking *n* a task; project; promise.

undertone *n* an undercurrent of feeling.

undertow *n* the backward suction of a wave breaking on shore; undercurrent.

underwear *n* underclothes.

underworld *n* the world of criminals.

underwrite *vt* to sign one's name as answerable for a certain amount of insurance.

undulation *n* a waving motion; a gentle slope; vibratory motion.

undulatory *adj* wave-like.

unguent *n* an ointment.

uniform *adj* regular; unvarying; * *n* regulation dress of certain persons.

uniformity *n* sameness; agreement; conformity to one type.

unify *vt* to form into one.

union *n* concord; a league; a trade union.

unionist *n* a trade unionist.

unique *adj* being the only one of its kind.

unison *n* harmony; concord.

unit *n* a single thing or person; an individual; a standard quantity.

unite *vt, vi* to combine; to connect.

unity *n* harmony; oneness; the number 1.

universal *adj* all-embracing, total.

universe *n* the whole creation; the world.

university *n* educational institution for higher learning and research.

unless *conj* if it be not that.

until *prep, conj* up to the time that; till.

unto *prep* to.

up *adv* aloft; in or to a higher position; upright; out of bed; * *prep* from below to

upbraid *vt* to reproach; to taunt.

upbringing *n* training; breeding.

upheaval *n* great social or political changes.

uphold *vt* to support; to sustain.

upholster *vt* to furnish (chairs, sofas, etc) with springs, stuffing, etc.

upkeep *n* maintenance.

upon *prep* up and on; on.

upper *adj* higher in place or rank.

upright *adj* erect; trustworthy.

uproar *n* a great tumult.

uproot *vt* to tear up by roots.

upset *vt* to overturn; to discompose; * *n* act of upsetting; * *adj* fixed.

upshot *n* final issue; end.

upstairs *adj, adv* one of the upper stories of building; house, etc.

upstart *n* one who has suddenly risen in position; an arrogant person.

urban *adj* belonging to a city.

urbane *adj* sophisticated; polite.

urge *vt* to press to do something.

urgent *adj* pressing; imperative.

urine *n* fluid excreted from kidneys and bladder.

us *pron* the objective case of we.

usage *n* treatment; customary practice.

use *n* employment practice; need; * *vt* to put to use; to avail one's self of; to employ.

user *n* one who uses

useful *adj* helpful; serviceable.

usual *adj* customary; common.

usurer *n* one who takes exorbitant interest.

usurp *vt* to seize and hold without right.

usury *n* extortionate interest for loan.

utensil *n* a kitchen implement.

utility *n* usefulness; profit.

utilise *vt* make use of.

utmost *adj* the highes degree.

utopia *n* an ideal state or govern-ment.

utopian *adj* ideally perfect; visionary.

utter *adj* complete; total; * *vt* to speak; pronounce; spread abroad.

V

vacancy *n* empty space; an unfilled post.

vacant *adj* empty; unfilled; silly.

vacate *vt* to quit possession of

vacation *n* holiday time.

vaccinate *vt* to inoculate against disease.

vaccine *n* a drug which inoculates.

vacillate *vi* to waver; to be undecided.

vacuous *adj* empty; void; vacant.

vacuum *n* a space void of air; empty space; a vacuum cleaner.

vagrant *adj* wandering; * *n* a tramp.

vague *adj* indefinite; hazy.

vain *adj* empty; fruitless; conceited; in ~ to no purpose.

vale *n* a valley.

valedictory *n* farewell.

valentine *n* a love gift or missive sent on Valentine's day (14th February),

valet *n* a manservant.

valiant *adj* brave; heroic.

valid *adj* well grounded; sound.

valley *n* the low ground between hills.

valour *n* bravery; courage.

valuable *adj* of great worth; * *npl* precious belongings.

valuator *n* an appraiser or valuer.

value *n* worth; importance; price; * *vt* to estimate; to prize; to appraise.

valve *n* a lid or flap for an opening, giving passage in one direction only.

van *n* a covered motor vehicle.

vandal *n* a barbarian; a person who wilfully damages property.

vane *n* a weathercock; blade of a windmill, etc.

vanguard *n* front part of an army; the leading position of any movement.

vanilla *n* a flavouring prepared from tropical orchid.

vanish *vi* to disappear; to pass away.

vanity n idle show; craving for praise; emptiness; conceit.

vanquish vt to conquer; overcome.

vapid adj spiritless; flat; dull.

vaporise vt to convert or pass off into vapour.

vapour n a gas or fume given off by a body when sufficiently heated.

variable adj fickle; changeable.

variant n an alternative form.

variation n change; alteration.

varicose adj (of veins) enlarged.

varied adj diverse; various.

variegated pp diversified in colour.

variety n diversity; change in assortment; a species.

various adj different; several.

varnish n a resinous solution used to give gloss to wood, paper, etc; a gloss.

vary vt, vi to change; to alter; to differ; to disagree.

vascular adj pertaining to vessels, ducts, etc, of organic bodies.

vase n a jar-shaped vessel for ornament or use.

vast adj of great extent; immense.

vat n a huge tub or tank for holding liquors.

vault n an arched roof; cellar; a leap; * vi to leap.

vaunt vi, vt to brag; to exult; to boast.

veal n the flesh of a calf.

veer vi to change direction.

vegetable adj, n a plant grown for food.

vegetarian n a person who consumes a diet that excludes meat and fish.

vegetate vi to live a plant's life; to lead an aimless life.

vegetation n plants in general.

vehement adj ardent; forcible.

vehicle n any kind of land carriage; a medium.

veil n a screen; a face shade; a disguise; * vt to conceal.

vein n a blood vessel which returns blood to heart; sap tube or rib in leaves; a seam of ore; disposition; mood; streak.

velocity n rate and direction of motion.

velvet n a rich soft fabric.

vend vt to sell.

vendetta n a feud.

veneer n a thin facing of fine wood glued on a less valuable sort; a gloss; * vt to overlay with veneer; to gloss.

venerable adj worthy of respect and admiration.

venerate vt to revere; honour.

vengeance n punishment in return for an injury.

venison n the flesh of deer.

venom n poison; spite; malice.

vent n an outlet; a flue; expression; * vt to emit; utter.

ventilate vt to give air to; to discuss freely.

ventral adj abdominal.

ventricle n a small cavity in body, esp one of those in heart or brain.

venture n a risky undertaking; * vi to dare; * vt to risk.

venturesome adj bold; hazardous.

venue n the appointed place of trial (law); meeting place.

veracity n truthfulness.

veranda n a portico or balcony along front of house.

verb n the predicative word in a sentence.

verbal adj spoken; oral.

verbally adv by word of mouth.

verbatim adv word for word.

verbosity n superabundance of words; wordiness.

verdant adj green.

verdict n the finding of a jury; considered opinion.

verge n border; margin; brink; * vi to incline; to border.

verification n a proving true.

verify vt to prove to be true; to confirm.

veritable adj true; real; actual.

vermilion n a beautiful red colour.

vermin n noxious animals or insects as rats, lice, etc.

vernacular adj native; * n mother tongue.

versatile adj readily turning; variable; many-sided.

verse n a line of poetry; metre; poetry; a stanza; a short division of any composition.

versed adj conversant; skilled, with in.

version *n* a translation; rendering.

versus *prep* against.

vertebra *n* (*pl* vertebrae) one of bones of spine; *pl* the spine.

vertebrate *adj* having a backbone.

vertex *n* (*pl* vertexes, vertices) the highest point; apex; zenith.

vertical *adj* upright; plumb.

vertigo *n* giddiness.

verve *n* spirit; energy.

very *adj* true; real; * *adv* truly.

vesicle *n* a small bladder or blister.

vessel *n* a hollow utensil for holding things; a ship.

vest *n* a waistcoat; an undergarment; * *vi* to furnish with (power, property, etc); * *vt* to invest.

vested *adj* robed; established.

vestibule *n* lobby or hall of house.

vestige *n* footprint; mark or trace.

vestment *n* a garment, *esp* priestly garment.

vestry *n* room where clerical vestments are kept.

veteran *adj* long experienced, *esp* in war.

veterinary *adj* pertaining to diseases of domestic animals.

veto *n* the right to reject or forbid; * *vt* to refuse assent to.

vexatious *adj* annoying; troublesome.

vexed *adj* annoyed; much disputed.

via *prep* by way of.

viaduct *n* an arched bridge over a valley.

vial *n* a small glass bottle.

vibrant *adj* vibrating; tremulous.

vibrate *vt*, *vi* to wave to and fro; to swing; to quiver.

vice *n* a blemish; moral failing; profligacy; an instrument for gripping things firmly.

vice- *prefix* denoting depute or one who acts in the place of another, *eg* vice-president.

vicinity *n* neighbourhood.

vicious *adj* malicious; bad-tempered.

victim *n* a person who has suffered injury; a dupe.

victimise *vt* to make a victim of.

victor *n* conqueror; winner.

victory *n* defeat of enemy or rival; triumph.

vie *vi* to contend; to compete.

view *n* a look; inspection; survey; range of vision; scene; intention; * *vt*, *vi* to see; to survey; to consider.

vigil *n* a watching, *esp* by night, *esp* for religious exercises.

vigilance *n* watchfulness.

vigilant *adj* watchful.

vigour *n* energy; force; strength.

vile *adj* base; depraved.

vilify *vt* to slander.

villa *n* a country or suburban house.

village *n* a collection of houses smaller than a town.

villain *n* a criminal; a scoundrel.

vim *n* vigour; energy.

vinaigrette *n* a salad dressing of oil, vinegar and seasoning.

vindicate *vt* to justify; uphold.

vindictive *adj* revengeful.

vine *n* a plant that bears grapes.

vinegar *n* a liquid containing acetic acid, used as a condiment and preserve.

vineyard *n* a plantation of vines.

vintage *n* the yearly produce of vine; wine of particular year.

vintner *n* a wine seller.

viola *n* a large violin; genus of plants including violet, pansy, etc.

violate *vt* to injure; to outrage.

violation *n* infringement.

violence *n* great force; injury.

violent *adj* vehment; furious.

violin *n* a four-stringed musical instrument.

virago *n* a bad tempered woman.

virescent *adj* slightly green.

virgin *n* a person who has never had sexual intercourse; * *adj* untouched; pure.

virginal *adj* of, pertaining to, or like a virgin.

virile *adj* sexually potent; strong.

virtual *adj* in effect, but not in name.

virtue *n* moral goodness; admirable quality.

virtuous *adj* moral; upright.

virulent *adj* poisonous; malignant.

virus *n* a micro-organism capable of causing ill-health; illness caused by a virus.

visa *n* an endorsement on a passport allowing the holder to travel in the country of the government issuing it.

visage n the face or countenance.

viscera npl the entrails.

viscous adj glutinous.

visible adj perceivable by the eye.

vision n sight; object of sight; a dream.

visionary adj imaginary; fanciful; * n an unpractical person.

visit vt to call upon; to afflict; * vi to make calls; * n a call.

visor n the movable faceguard of a helmet.

vista n an extended view.

vital adj mortal; essential.

vitality n vital force; energy.

vitamin n an essential element in diet.

vitreous adj glassy.

vitrify vt to convert into glass.

vitriol n sulphuric acid.

vituperate vt to abuse; to revile.

vivacious adj lively; sprightly.

vivid adj bright; striking.

vivify vt to animate.

vivisection n act of experimenting on a living animal.

vixen n a female fox; a shrew.

vocabulary n a list of words with definitions; an individual's command or use of words.

vocal adj pertaining to the voice.

vocalist n a singer.

vocation n a calling; occupation.

vocative n the vocative case of verbs.

vociferous adj clamorous; noisy.

vogue n temporary fashion.

voice n the sound uttered by the mouth; utterance; speech; sound emitted; vote; a form of verb inflection; * vt to utter or express.

void adj empty; null; * n an empty space; * vt to make vacant; to nullify.

volatile adj readily passing off in vapour; flighty.

volcano n a mountain formed by ejections of lava, ashes, etc through an opening in the earth's crust.

volition n will; power of choice.

volley n a simultaneous discharge of missiles.

volt n the SI unit of electromotive force.

volubility n fluency of speech.

voluble adj over fluent; glib.

volume n an amount of space; mass or bulk; a book.

voluminous adj bulky; copious.

voluntary adj acting of one's own free will; without remuneration; deliberate.

volunteer n a person who undertakes military or other service of his own free will; * vi to offer one's services.

vomit vi, vt to throw up from stomach; to eject; matter ejected from stomach.

voracious adj greedy; ravenous.

vortex n (pl vortices, vortexes) a whirling motion as in whirlpool, whirlwind.

vote n the recording of opinion for or against proposal; suffrage; * vi, vt to give a vote; * vt to grant by vote.

vouch vt to attest; to guarantee.

voucher n a written record of a transaction; a token that can be exchanged for something else.

vouchsafe vt to condescend to grant.

vow n a solemn promise; an oath; * vt to promise solemnly.

vowel n a simple vocal sound; letter denoting it.

voyage n a journey, esp by ship.

vulgar adj coarse in manners.

vulgarity n rudeness of manners.

vulnerable adj liable to injury.

vulture n a large bird of prey; a rapacious person.

W

wad n a fibrous mass; a bundle of paper money.

wadding n any soft material for use in packing, padding, etc.

waddle vi to walk with rolling gait.

wade vi to walk through water; to walk with difficulty.

wafer n a thin crisp cracker or biscuit.

waft vt to sail or bear along gently.

wag vt, vi to shake up and down or to and fro; * n a wit; joker.

wage vt to stake; to carry on, esp war; * n salary; hire; usu in pl.

wager *n* a bet; subject of bet; * *vt* to stake.

wagon *n* a four-wheeled cart; a truck.

waif *n* a homeless, neglected child.

wail *vi* to lament; to cry aloud; * *n* a moaning cry.

waist *n* part of body from ribs to hips.

waistcoat *n* a sleeveless under-coat; a vest.

wait *vi* to stay in expectation; to attend; to serve at table; * *n* period of waiting.

waiter *n* a servant in attendance at table.

waive *vt* to forgo; give up.

wake *vi* to be awake; * *vt* to arouse; * *n* vigil over dead; track left by ship.

waken *vt, vi* to arouse; wake.

walk *vi* to advance step by step; * *n* a ramble; a road, path; sphere of life.

wall *n* a rigid vertical structure for enclosing, dividing or protecting.

wallet *n* a flat pocketbook for paper money, cards, etc.

wallow *vi* to roll in mud, to indulge oneself in emotion.

wand *n* a magician's rod.

wander *vi* to ramble; to roam; to err.

wane *vt* to grow less; to decline.

want *n* need; longing; dearth; poverty; * *vt, vi* to lack; need.

wanton *adj* frisky; lustful; * *n* a lewd person.

war *n* a fight between nations; enmity; a contest.

warble *vt, vi* to sing like a bird; to trill.

ward *vt* to guard; to fend off; * *n* guard; custody; one under a guardian; a division of a town or country; apartment of a hospital.

warden *n* a guardian; head of college or hostel.

warder *n* a guard; a keeper.

wardrobe *n* a cabinet or closet for keeping clothes; one's stock of clothes.

ware *n* merchandise; goods, *usu* in *pl*; * *adj* wary.

warehouse *n* a building for storing wares, goods.

warfare *n* military service; war.

warm *adj* moderately hot; zealous; excited; lively; * *vt, vi* to make or become warm or animated.

warmth *n* gentle heat; cordiality.

warn *vt* to caution; to advise.

warning *n* caution; previous notice.

warp *vt, vi* to twist; to pervert; * *n* lengthways threads in loom; a twist.

warped *adj* twisted by shrinking; perverted.

warrant *vt* to guarantee; to author-ise; to justify; * *n* a guarantee; writ or summons; voucher.

warranty *n* warrant; guarantee.

warrior *n* a gallant soldier.

wart *n* a hard contagious growth on skin.

wary *adj* cautious; prudent.

was *vb* past tense of to be.

wash *vt, vi* to cleanse with water; to colour lightly; * *n* flow or dash of water; a lotion; thin coat of colour.

washer *n* a ring of metal, rubber, etc, for tightening nut on screw.

washing *n* clothes washed; a cleansing.

wasp *n* a stinging winged insect.

waspish *adj* like a wasp; venom-ous; irritable; snappish.

wastage *n* lost by use or waste.

waste *vt, vi* to ravage; to damage; to squander; to grow less; * *adj* unused; devastated; * *n* a wilderness; useless spending; decrease; refuse.

watch *n* a guard; vigilance; sentry; a timepiece; * *vt, vi* to guard; to observe carefully; to await.

watchful *adj* vigilant; cautious.

watchmaker *n* one who makes or repairs watches.

water *n* the commonest of liquids, clear and transparent when pure; * *vt, vi* to supply with water; to irrigate; to dilute; to take in water.

watercolour *n* a pigment ground up with water and gum instead of oil; a picture painted with watercol-ours.

watercourse *n* a channel for water.

waterfall *n* a stream falling over rocks; a cascade.

waterlogged *adj* soaked or filled with water.

waterproof *adj* impervious to water; * *n* cloth so made.

watershed *n* dividing ridge between river systems.

waterspout *n* a column of water sucked up by whirlwind.

watery *adj* like water; tasteless.

wave *vi*, *vt* to move up and down, or to and fro; to brandish; to beckon; * *n* a rising motion on surface of water, etc; a waving of hand as signal.

waved *adj* undulating.

waver *vi* to move to and fro; falter; flicker.

wax *n* secretion by bees; anything like wax; * *vt* to rub with wax; to grow larger.

waxwork *n* modelling in wax; *pl* figures in wax.

way *n* a track, path, or road. distance traversed; direction; condition; method; course.

wayfarer *n* a traveller.

waylay *vt* to lie in wait for; to accost.

wayside *n* the side of a road.

wayward *adj* wilful; perverse.

we *pron* plural of I.

weak *adj* feeble; frail; foolish; vacillating.

weaken *vt*, *vi* to make or become weak.

weakling *n* a weak creature.

weal *n* a raised mark on skin.

wealth *n* riches; abundance.

wean *vt* to break off from any habit; to discontinue giving mother's milk.

weapon *n* any instrument of offence or defence.

wear *vt* to have on, as clothes; to waste by rubbing; to exhibit; * *vi* to last; to exhaust.

wearisome *adj* tiresome; tiring.

weary *adj* tired; jaded; * *vt* to wear out strength or patience; to become weary.

weather *n* the general atmospheric conditions at any particular time; * *vt* to affect by weather, as rocks; to bear up against (storms, etc).

weathercock *n* a vane turning with wind.

weave *vt* to form by interlacing threads; to compose or fabricate.

web *n* woven cloth; tissue or texture; film; membrane between toes of waterfowl.

webbed *adj* having the toes united by a membrane.

webbing *n* a strong narrow band used for girths, etc.

wed *vt*, *vi* to marry; unite together.

wedding *n* marriage; nuptials.

wedge *n* a block sloping to thin edge at one end; * *vt* to cleave, fix, or fasten with wedge.

wedlock *n* marriage.

Wednesday *n* fourth day of week.

weed *n* a useless plant; tobacco; * *vt* to remove weeds.

week *n* seven consecutive days.

weep *vi*, *vt* to shed tears; to mourn.

weigh *vi* to find heaviness of; to reflect on; to raise anchor; * *vi* to have weight; to bear heavily.

weight *n* heaviness; gravity; heavy mass; pressure.

weir *n* a dam across a stream.

weird *n* fate; * *adj* unearthly; queer.

welcome *adj* pleasing; * *n* a kind reception.

weld *vt* to fuse together, *esp* metal; to unite.

welfare *n* well-being; state provision of financial aid to the unemployed, sick, etc.

well *n* a spring; a pit sunk for water; staircase or lift space; * *vi* to bubble up; to issue forth.

well *adv* rightly; smartly; * *adj* hale; hearty.

went past tense of go.

west *n* one of the four compass points; sun's setting place.

western *adj* in or from the west.

wet *adj* covered with water; moist; rainy; * *n* water; rain; * *vt* to make wet.

whale *n* any of the larger marine mammals of the order *Cetacea*.

whaler *n* a ship employed in whale fishery.

wharf *n* (*pl* wharfs, wharves) a loading place for ships; quay.

wheat *n* a cereal from which flour is obtained.

wheel *n* a round spoked frame

turning on axis; anything like a wheel; * *vt*, *vi* to revolve or cause to revolve.

wheelbarrow *n* a hand carriage with one wheel.

wheeze *vi* to breathe hard and audibly.

whelk *n* a shellfish; a periwinkle.

when *adv*, *conj* at what or which time; while; whereas.

whence *adv*, *conj* from what place.

where *adv*, *conj* at or in what place.

whereas *conj* that being so.

whereby *adv*, *conj* by which or what.

wherefore *adv*, *conj* for which reason; why.

whereon *adv*, *conj* on which or on what.

whereupon *adv* upon which.

wherever *adv* at whatever place.

whet *vt* to sharpen; edge; stimulate.

whether *pron* which of two; * *conj*, *adv* which of two or more.

whetstone *n* a stone for sharpening blades.

which *pron* an interrogative pronoun; a relative pronoun, the neuter of who.

whiff *n* a puff of air, smoke, smell.

while *n* short space of time; * *conj* during that time that; * *vt* to pass (time) pleasantly.

whilst *adv* while.

whim *n* a sudden fancy.

whimper *vi* to whine; * *n* a pathetic cry.

whimsical *adj* fantastic; odd.

whine *vi* utter plaintive cry; * *n* a wail.

whip *vt* to lash; flog; beat into froth.

whir *vi* to fly with buzzing sound.

whirl *vt*, *vi* to revolve rapidly.

whirlpool *n* a whirling eddy of water.

whirlwind *n* a whirling eddy of air; a tornado.

whisk *vt* to stir or move rapidly; * *n* a jerking motion; small brush; an egg-beater.

whisker *n* hair on cheeks.

whisky, whiskey *n* spirit distilled from barley, etc.

whisper *vt*, *vi* to speak very softly; * *n* a low voice.

whist *interj* hush; * *n* a game of cards.

whistle *vi* to make a shrill sound

with lips or instrument; * *n* a shrill sound; a small wind instrument.

white *adj* snow-coloured; pure.

whitewash *n* lime and water for whitening walls, etc; to conceal the truth.

whither *adv* to what or which place.

whittle *vt* to pare down.

who *pron*, *rel*, *interr* referring to persons only.

whole *adj* hale and sound; * *n* the total; all.

wholesale *n* sale of goods in large quantities; * *adj* extensive.

wholesome *adj* healthy; salutary.

wholly *adv* entirely.

whoop *n* a loud shout.

whose *pron* the possessive case of who or which.

why *adv*, *conj* for what reason.

wick *n* the thread of a lamp or candle.

wicked *adj* bad; sinful; roguish.

wicket *n* a small gate; the three upright stumps in cricket.

wide *adj* broad; extensive.

widen *vt*, *vi* to make or grow wide.

widow *n* a woman whose husband is deceased.

widower *n* a man whose wife is deceased.

width *n* breadth.

wield *vt* to handle; to exercise.

wife *n* (*pl* wives) a married woman.

wig *n* an artificial head of hair.

wild *adj* in a state of nature; untamed; stormy.

wilderness *n* a desert; waste.

wildfire *n* sheet lightning.

wile *n* fraud; trick; * *vt* to entice.

wilful *adj* stubborn; headstrong.

will *vb*, *aux* expressing futurity or resolve; * *vt*, *vi* to determine by choice; to wish; to bequeath; * *n* wish; choice; determination; purpose; last testament; feeling.

willing *adj* ready; instant; ungrudging.

willow *n* a tree or shrub, valuable for basketmaking, etc; a cricket bat.

wily *adj* cunning; sly.

win *vt* to gain; to allure; * *vi* to gain victory.

wince *vi* to shrink, as from pain.

winch *n* crank of wheel or axle; a windlass.

wind *n* a current of air; breath; flatulence; * *vt* to put out of breath; to rest.

wind *vt* to twist; to coil; * *vi* to twine; to meander.

windfall *n* fruit blown down; an unexpected financial gain.

winding *adj* bending; twisting; * *n* a turn; a bend.

windmill *n* a mill driven by wind.

window *n* a glazed opening in wall for light.

windpipe *n* the air passage to lungs; trachea.

wine *n* the fermented juice of grapes.

winepress *n* an apparatus for pressing juice from grapes.

wing *n* organ of flight; side extension of building, army, etc; side; * *vt* to fly; to wound.

wink *vi* to shut and open eyelids; to give hint by eyelids; to connive; * *n* a winking or hint given by it.

winning *adj* attractive; charming.

winter *n* the cold season of year; * *vi* to pass the winter.

wipe *vt* to clean by gentle rubbing; to efface.

wire *n* a thread of metal; a telegram; * *vt* to bind with wire; * *vi* to telegraph.

wiry *adj* wire-like; sinewy.

wisdom *n* sound judgement and knowledge; prudence.

wise *adj* learned; judging rightly.

wish *vi* to have a desire; to long; * *vt* to express desire; * *n* a desire.

wisp *n* a small bundle of straw, etc; anything slender.

wistful *adj* pensive; yearning.

wit *vt, vi* to know; to be aware; * *n* understanding; humour; a humorist.

witch *n* a woman who practices magic and is considered to have dealings with the devil.

witchcraft *n* the practice of magic.

with *prep* expressing nearness or connection; among; possessing.

withdraw *vt* to draw back; to retract; * *vi* to retire.

wither *vi* to fade or shrivel.

withhold *vt* to hold back; not to grant.

within *prep* inside; * *adv* inwardly.

without *prep, adv* outside.

withstand *vt, vi* to oppose; to resist.

witness *n* testimony; evidence; one who gives sworn evidence; * *vt, vi* to see; to attest; to sign as witness.

witticism *n* a witty remark.

witty *adj* humorous; smart and droll.

wizard *n* a magician; conjuror.

wizened *adj* shrivelled.

wobble *vi* to sway from side to side.

woe *n* grief; misery.

wolf *n* (*pl* wolves) a wild carnivorous mammal, *Canis lupus*.

woman *n* (*pl* women) an adult female; female sex.

womanhood *n* the state or qualities of a woman.

won *past t, pp* of win.

wonder *n* something very strange; a marvel; feeling excited by something strange; * *vi* to be struck with wonder; to marvel.

wood *n* a collection of growing trees; timber.

wooden *adj* made of wood; stiff.

woodwork *n* carpentry.

wool *n* the fleece of sheep, goats, etc.

woollen *adj* made of wool; * *n* cloth made of wool.

word *n* an articulate sound expressing an idea; information; a saying; motto; promise; *pl* wrangle.

wording *n* the mode of expressing in words.

wordy *adj* using many words; verbose.

work *n* effort; employment; a task; achievement; a book or other composition; (in *pl*) a factory; * *vi* to labour; to be employed; * *vt* to bring about; to influence; to fashion.

working class *n* people who work for wages, *esp* manual workers.

workman *n* an artisan; a skilled worker.

workmanship *n* skill of a worker or quality of his work.

workshop *n* a place where some craft is carried on.

world *n* the whole creation; the earth; mankind; the public.

worldly *adj* relating to this world or this life.

worm *n* a small creeping animal; thread of screw; spiral pipe in a condenser; * *vi* to work slowly and secretly; * *vt* to undermine; to extract.

worn *pp* of wear.

worry *vt* to harass; to fret; * *n* anxiety.

worse *adj* bad or ill in greater degree; inferior.

worship *n* religious service; adoration; reverence; title of honour; * *vt* to adore; to perform religious service.

worshipful *adj* honourable.

worst *adj* bad or evil in highest degree; * *vt* to defeat.

worsted *n* woollen yarn used in knitting.

worth *adj* equal in value to; deserving of; * *n* value; price.

worthy *adj* deserving; befitting; * *n* a notable person.

would-be *adj* wishing to be; pretended.

wound *n* a cut or stab, etc; injury; * *vt*, *vi* to inflict a wound; to pain.

wove *pret* of weave.

wrack *n* seaweed generally; wreck; a thin flying cloud.

wrangle *vi* to dispute angrily; * *n* a dispute.

wrap *vt* to fold or roll; to envelop; * *n* a shawl or rug.

wrapper *n* a loose morning gown; cover for postal packets, as books, etc.

wrath *n* violent anger; rage.

wreak *vt* to inflict, execute (vengeance, etc).

wreath *n* a garland.

wreathe *vt* to entwine; to encircle.

wreck *n* ruin; destruction of ship at sea; * *vt* to ruin; destroy.

wreckage *n* remains of wrecked ship.

wrench *n* a violent twist; tool for screwing nuts, etc; * *vt* to pull with a twist.

wrest *vt* to twist; to distort.

wrestle *vi* to contend by grappling and trying to throw down.

wretch *n* a miserable person; base creature.

wretched *adj* unhappy; worthless.

wriggle *vi*, *vt* to twist about.

wring *vt* to twist and squeeze; to extort.

wrinkle *n* a crease in skin; furrow; hint; * *vt*, *vi* to crease.

wrist *n* the joint uniting hand to arm.

writ *n* a written court order.

write *vt*, *vi* to form by a pen, etc; to set down in words; to communicate by letter; to compose.

writer *n* an author; a clerk; a law agent.

writhe *vt*, *vi* to turn and twist, as in pain.

wrong *adj* not right; false; * *n* an injury; * *vt* to treat unjustly.

wrongful *adj* injurious; unjust.

wry *adj* contorted; twisted; ironic.

X

xenophobia *n* fear or dislike of foreigners or strangers.

X-ray, x-ray *n* electro-magnetic radiation of very short wavelengths, capable of penetrating solid bodies; * *vt* to photograph by x-rays.

xylophone *n* a musical instrument of wooden bars freely suspended and vibrating when struck.

Y

yacht *n* a light sailing vessel for pleasure or racing.

yahoo *n* a rude brutish or crude person.

yak *n* a Tibetan ox.

yam *n* any tropical or subtropical climbing plant of the genus *dioscorea*; its tuber.

yap *vi* to talk constantly.

yard *n* a standard measure of three feet; an enclosure; a spar hung across a mast to support a sail.

yarn *n* any spun thread; a spun-out story.

yaw *vi* to swerve suddenly in sailing.

yawl *n* a ship's small boat; a small yacht.

yawn *vi* to open the jaws involuntarily, as from drowsiness; * *n* act of yawning.

year *n* the period of earth's complete revolution round sun; 12 months.

yearling *n* a one-year-old animal.

yearn *vi* to be filled with longing, love, or pity for.

yeast *n* fungus substance for fermenting wine, bread.

yell *vi* to scream; * *n* a shrill cry.

yellow *adj, n* a bright golden colour.

yelp *vi* to utter a sharp bark.

yesterday *n* the day before the present.

yet *adv* in addition; still; * *conj* nevertheless.

yew *n* a large evergreen tree.

yield *vt* to produce in return for labour, etc; to afford; to give up; * *vi* to submit; * *n* product; crop.

yoga *n* a system of exercises for attaining bodily and spiritual control and well-being.

yoke *n* a neckpiece of wood binding oxen together in drawing; a pair of draught oxen; a bond or link; * *vt* to couple.

yokel *n* a country person regarded as unsophisticated.

yolk *n* the yellow part of an egg.

yonder *adv* over there.

you *pron* the 2nd person singular and plural, the person or persons spoken to.

young *adj* not old; youthful; * *n* offspring; young persons.

youngster *n* a boy; young person.

youth *n* period from childhood to manhood; a young man; young people.

yule *n* Christmas.

Z

zany *adj* comical; eccentric.

zeal *n* eagerness; ardour; fanaticism.

zebra *n* any of various African mammals, *esp Equus burchelli*, with a black and white striped coat, related to the horse.

zenith *n* the point of heavens right overhead; highest point.

zephyr *n* the west wind; any soft breeze.

zeppelin *n* a rigid, cigar-shaped airship.

zero *n* a cipher; nothing; point from which marking of a scale begins.

zest *n* relish; keen enjoyment.

zigzag *adj, n* a line with short sharp turns; * *vi* to turn sharply this way and that.

zinc *n* a soft bluish-white metal.

zone *n* a girdle or belt; one of the five great belts of the earth; any well-defined tract.

zoology *n* the science of animal life.

zoroastrian *n* believer in religion of Zoroaster, founder of Parseeism, or fire worship.

zygote *n* a cell formed by the fusion of two gametes, capable of developing into a new individual.